Love Me,
Love Me Not

6

IO SAKISAKA

Contents

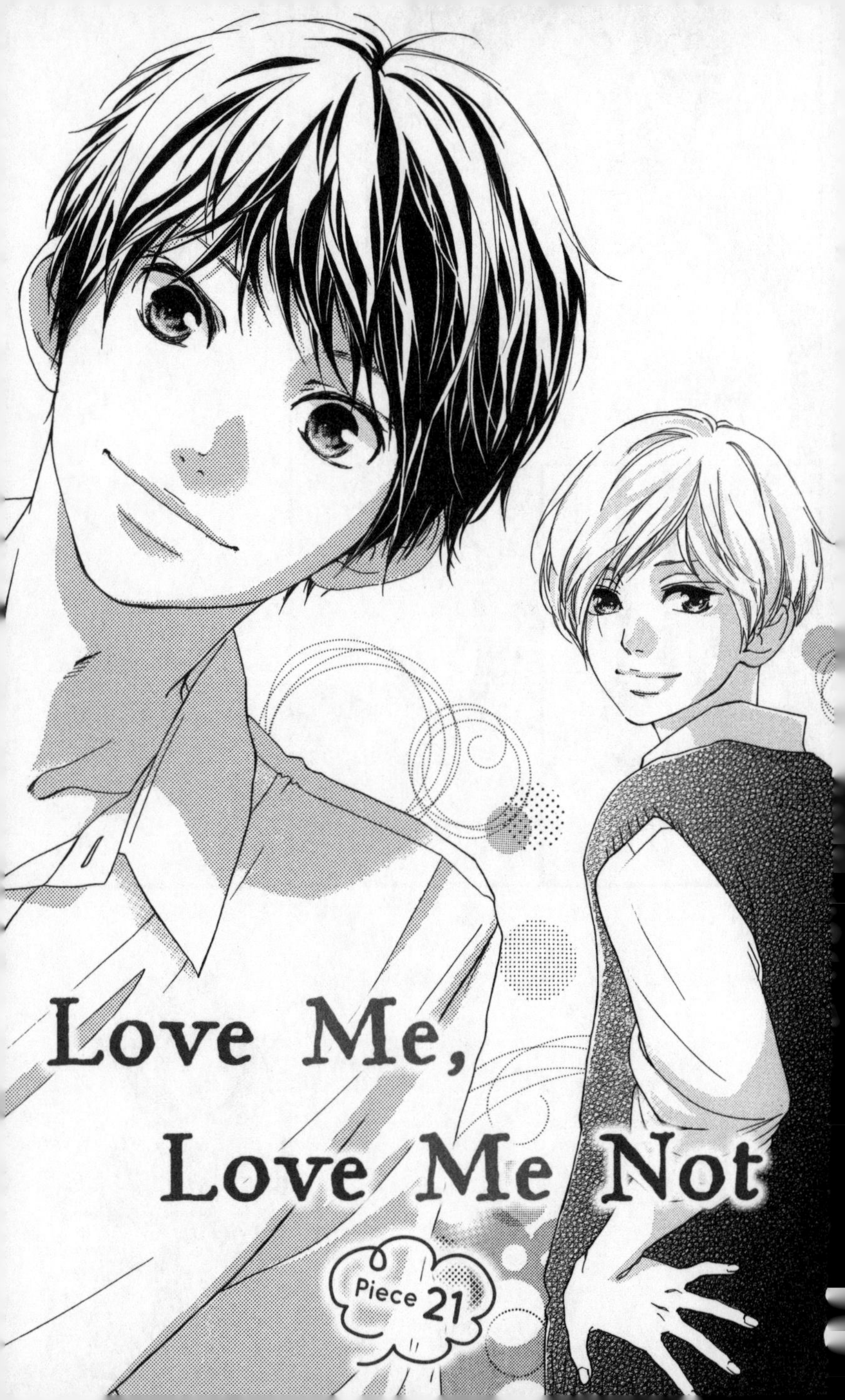
Love Me,
Love Me Not
Piece 21

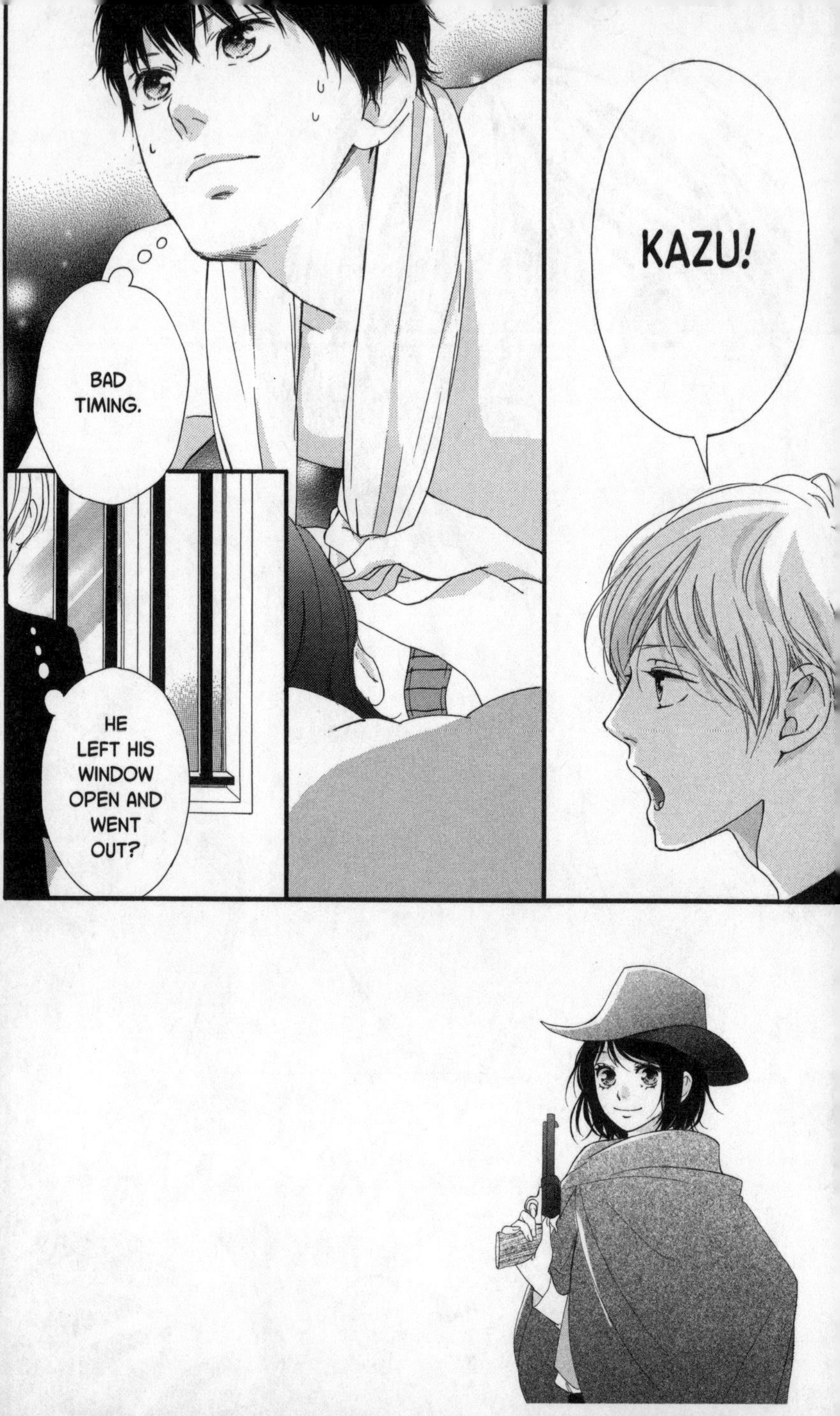
KAZU!
BAD TIMING.
HE LEFT HIS WINDOW OPEN AND WENT OUT?

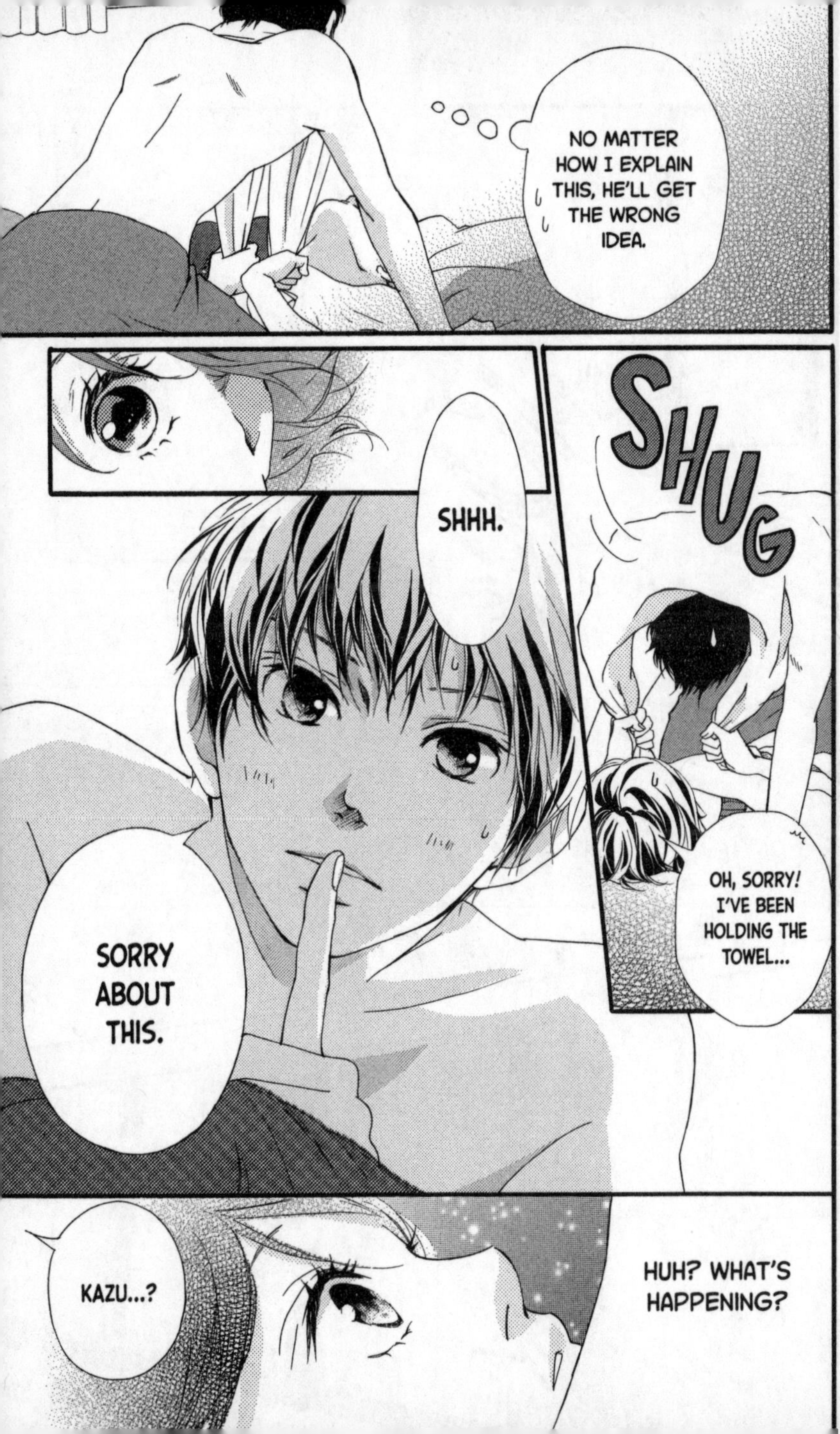
NO MATTER HOW I EXPLAIN THIS, HE'LL GET THE WRONG IDEA.
SHUG
OH, SORRY! I'VE BEEN HOLDING THE TOWEL...
SHHH.
SORRY ABOUT THIS.
HUH? WHAT'S HAPPENING?
KAZU...?

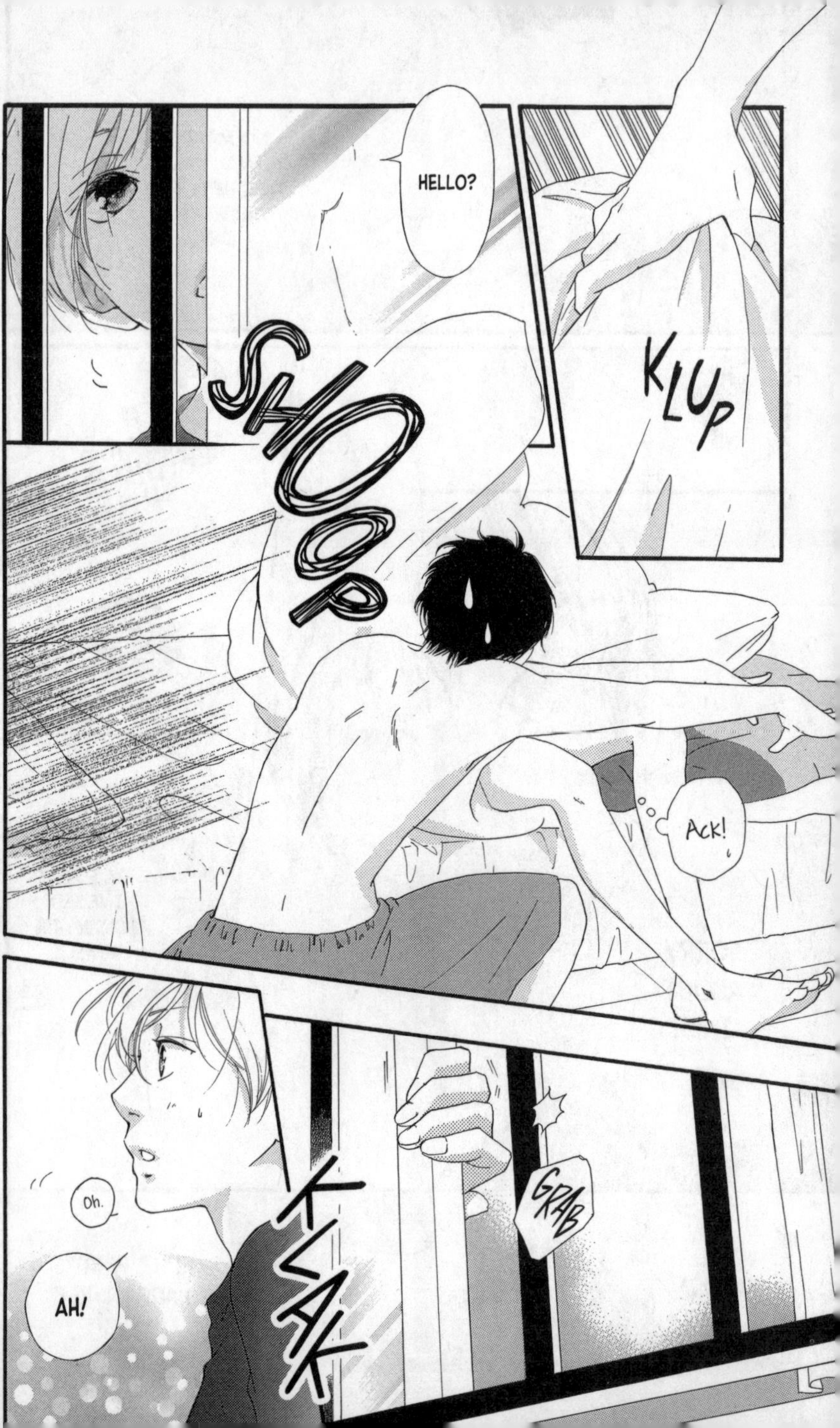
KLUP
HELLO?
SHOOP
ACK!
GRAB
KLAK
Oh.
AH!

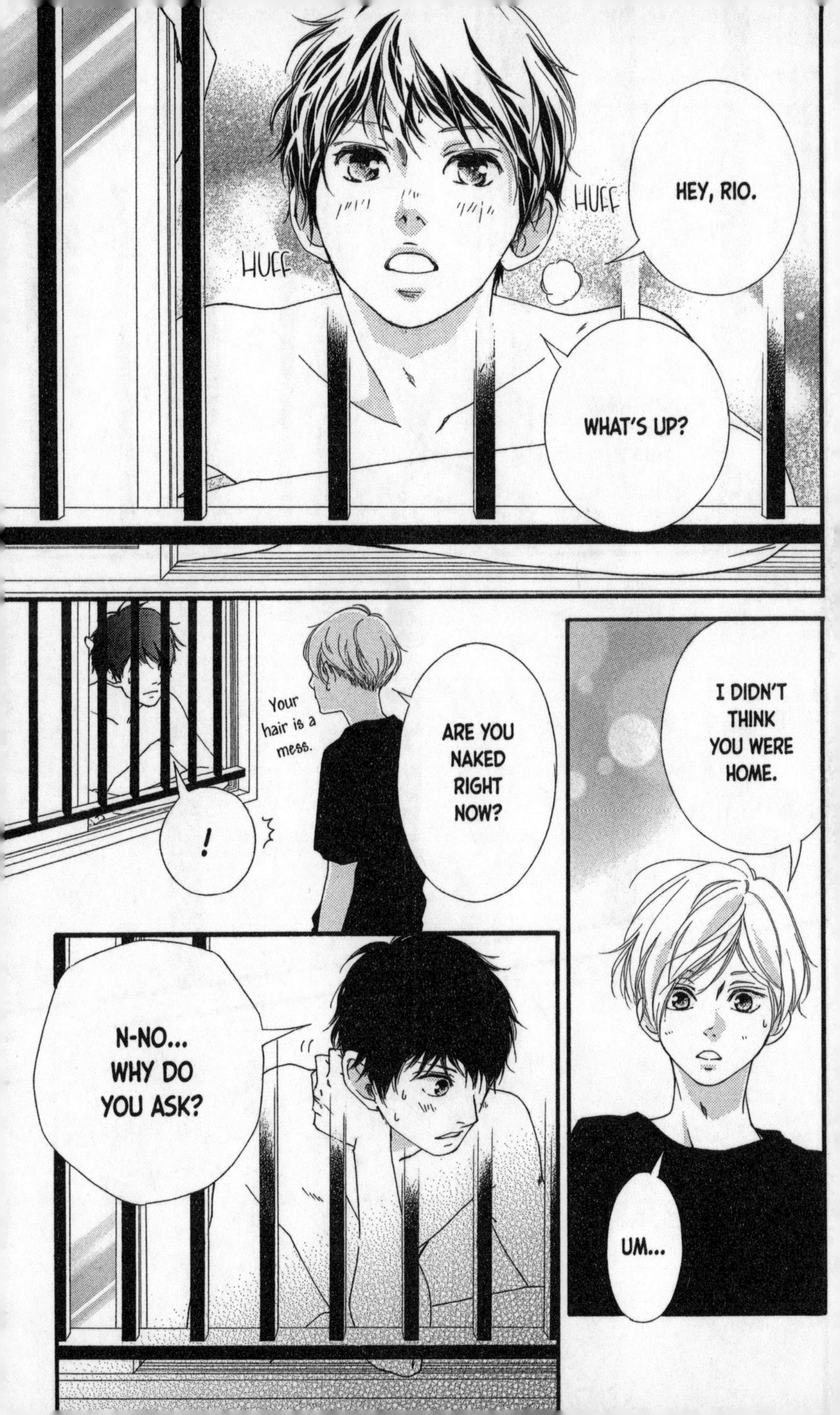
HEY, RIO.
HUFF
WHAT'S UP?
HUFF
I DIDN'T THINK YOU WERE HOME.
UM...
ARE YOU NAKED RIGHT NOW?
Your hair is a mess.
!
N-NO... WHY DO YOU ASK?

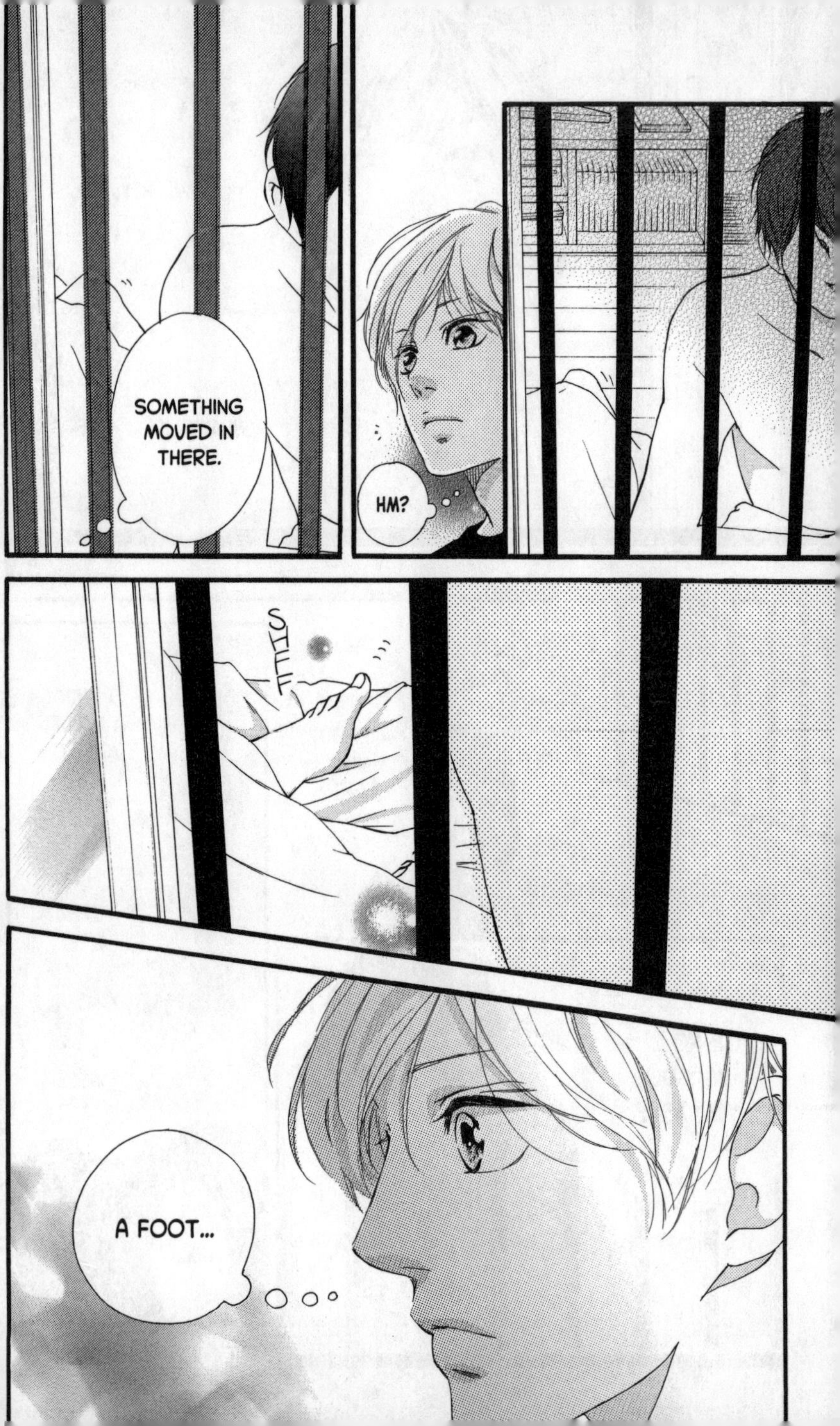
HM?
SOMETHING MOVED IN THERE.
SHFF
A FOOT...

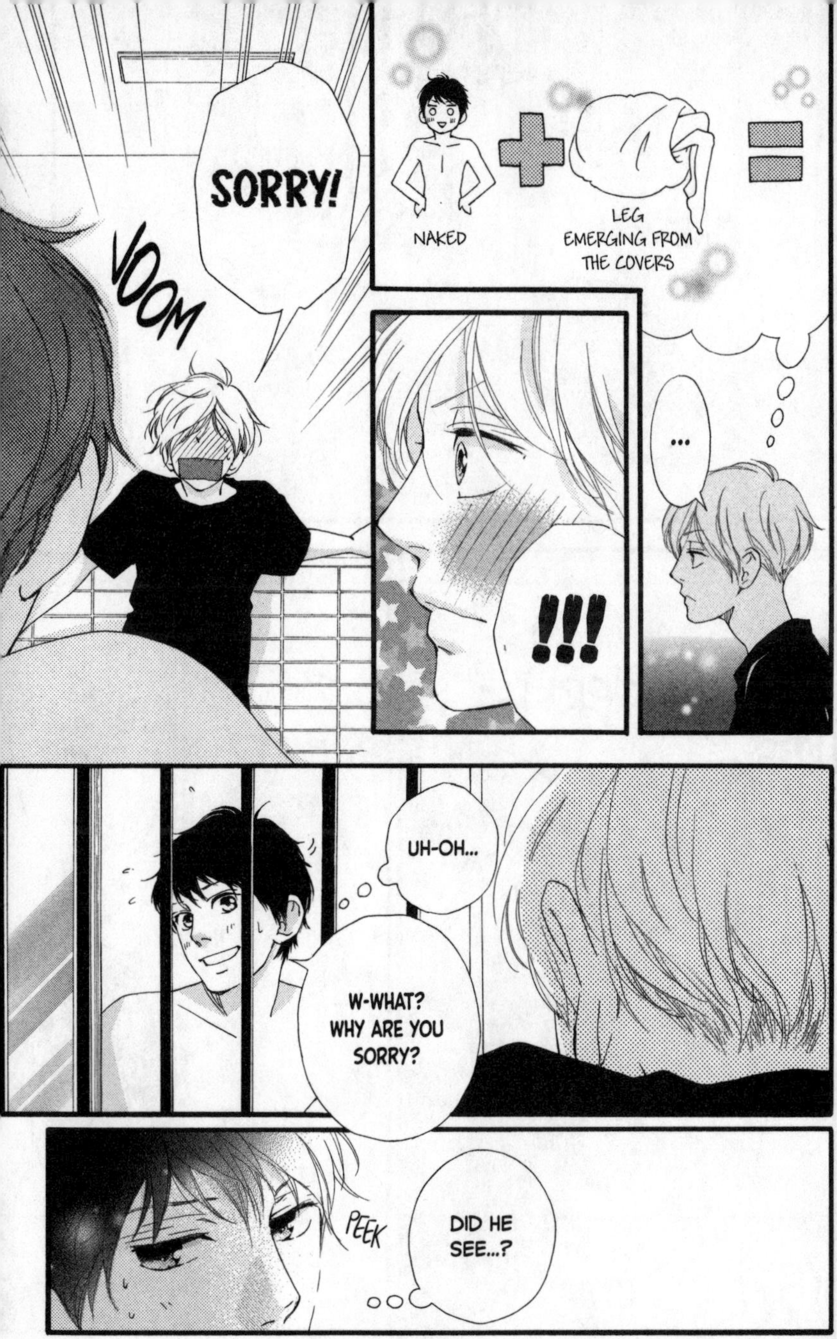
NAKED
LEG EMERGING FROM THE COVERS
...
!!!
SORRY!
VOOM
UH-OH...
W-WHAT? WHY ARE YOU SORRY?
DID HE SEE...?
PEEK

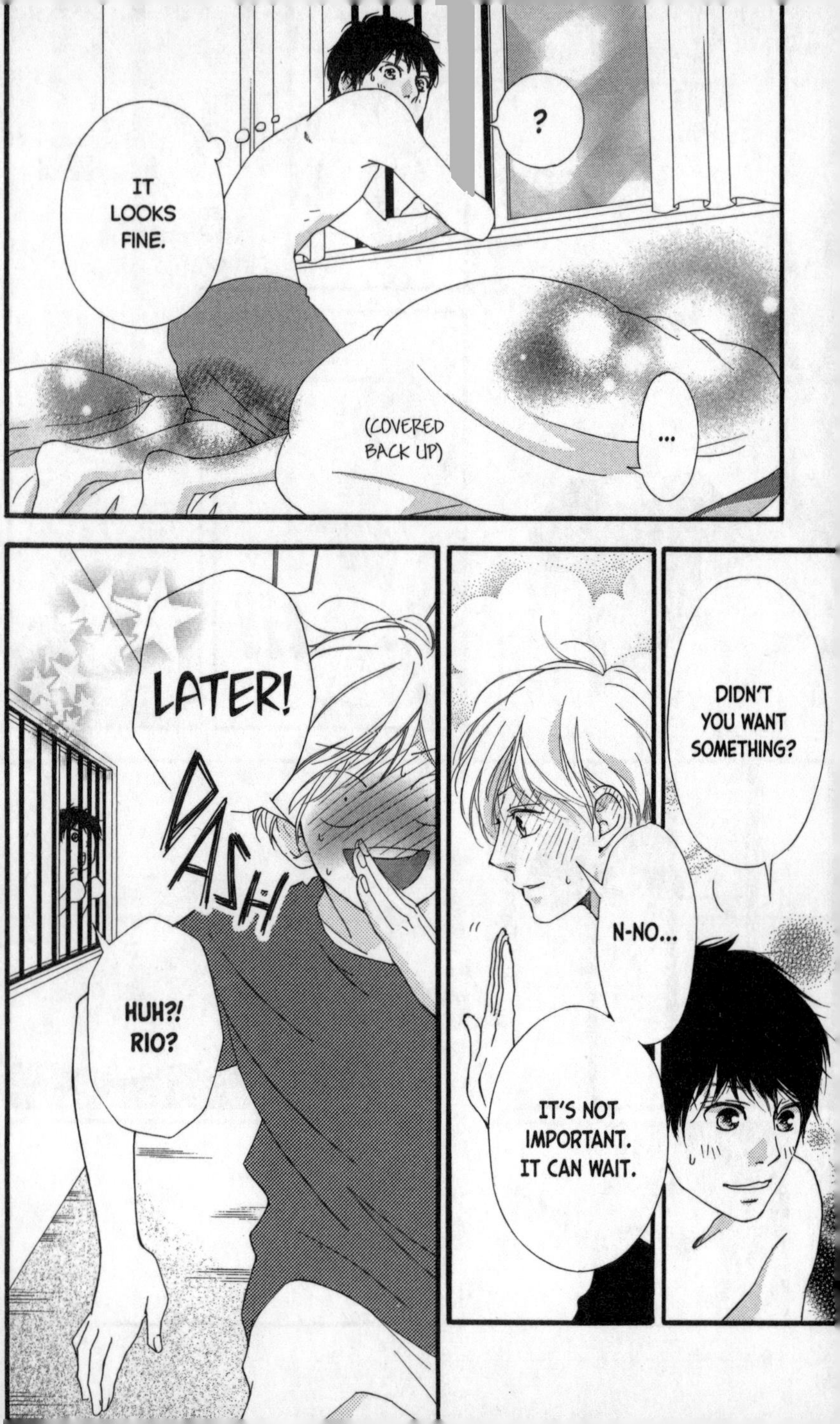
?
IT LOOKS FINE.
...
(COVERED BACK UP)
DIDN'T YOU WANT SOMETHING?
N-NO...
IT'S NOT IMPORTANT. IT CAN WAIT.
LATER!
DASH
HUH?! RIO?

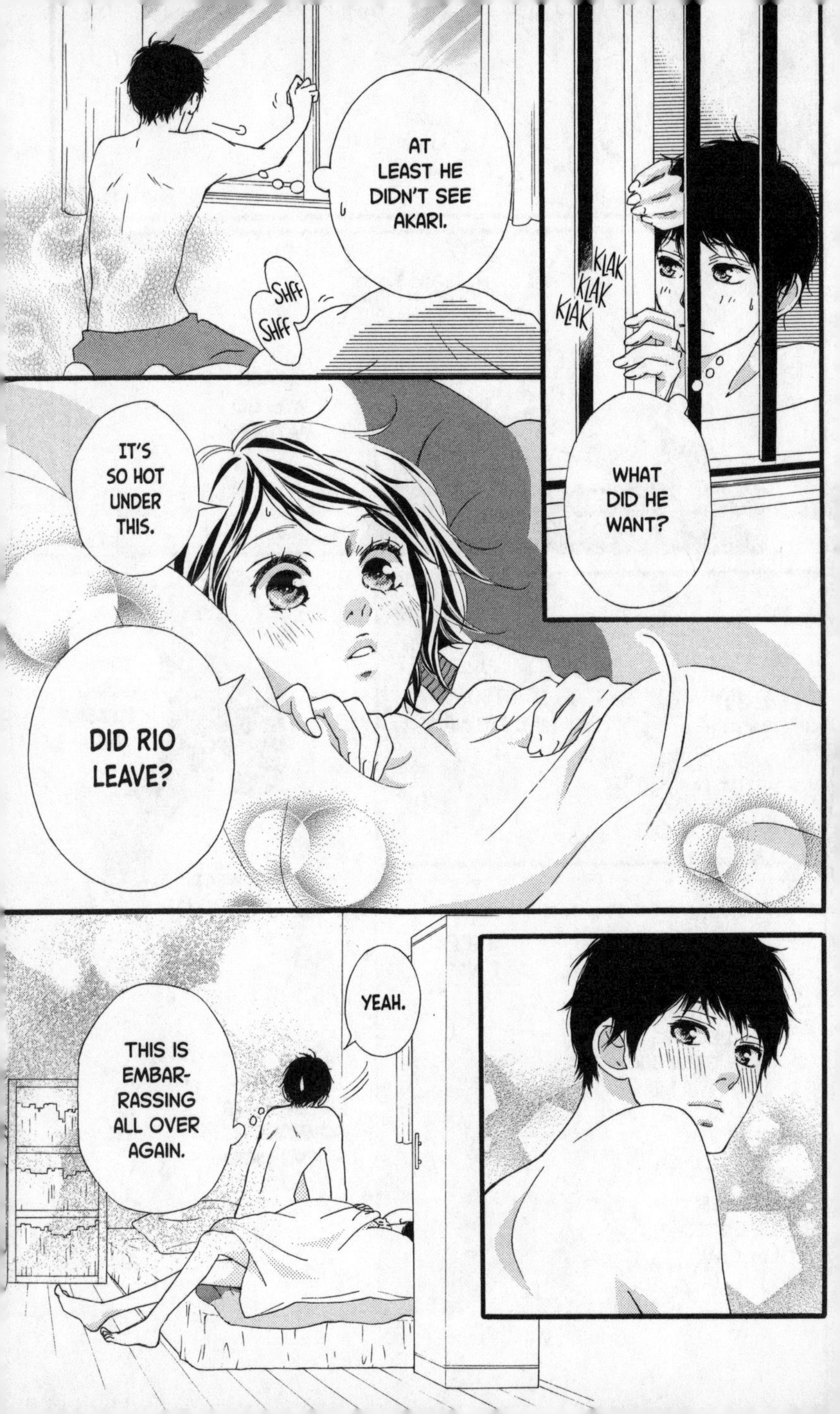
KLAK KLAK KLAK
WHAT DID HE WANT?
AT LEAST HE DIDN'T SEE AKARI.
SHFF SHFF
IT'S SO HOT UNDER THIS.
DID RIO LEAVE?
YEAH.
THIS IS EMBARRASSING ALL OVER AGAIN.

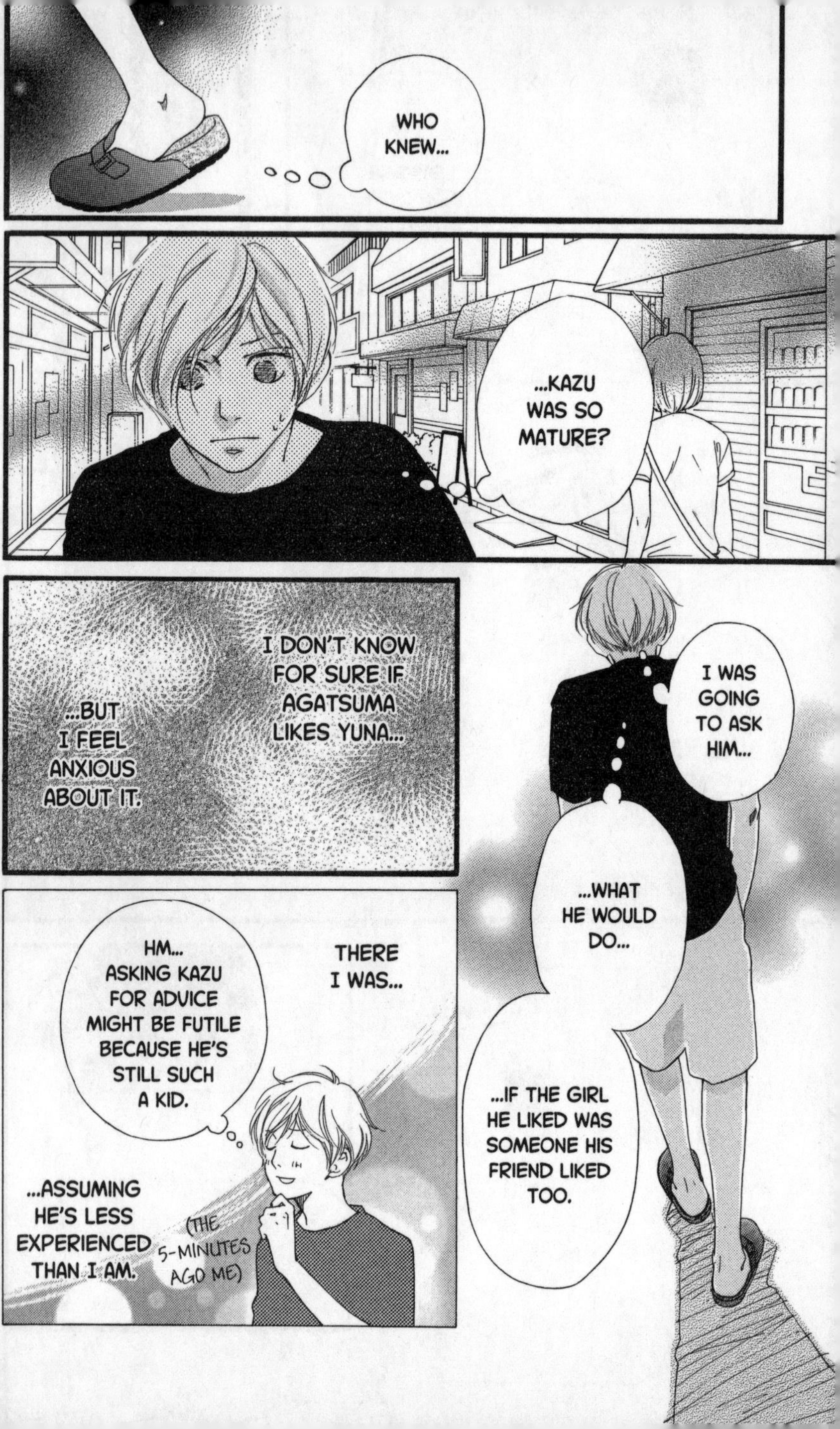
WHO KNEW...
...KAZU WAS SO MATURE?
I WAS GOING TO ASK HIM...
...WHAT HE WOULD DO...
...IF THE GIRL HE LIKED WAS SOMEONE HIS FRIEND LIKED TOO.
I DON'T KNOW FOR SURE IF AGATSUMA LIKES YUNA...
...BUT I FEEL ANXIOUS ABOUT IT.
THERE I WAS...
HM... ASKING KAZU FOR ADVICE MIGHT BE FUTILE BECAUSE HE'S STILL SUCH A KID.
...ASSUMING HE'S LESS EXPERIENCED THAN I AM.
(THE 5-MINUTES AGO ME)

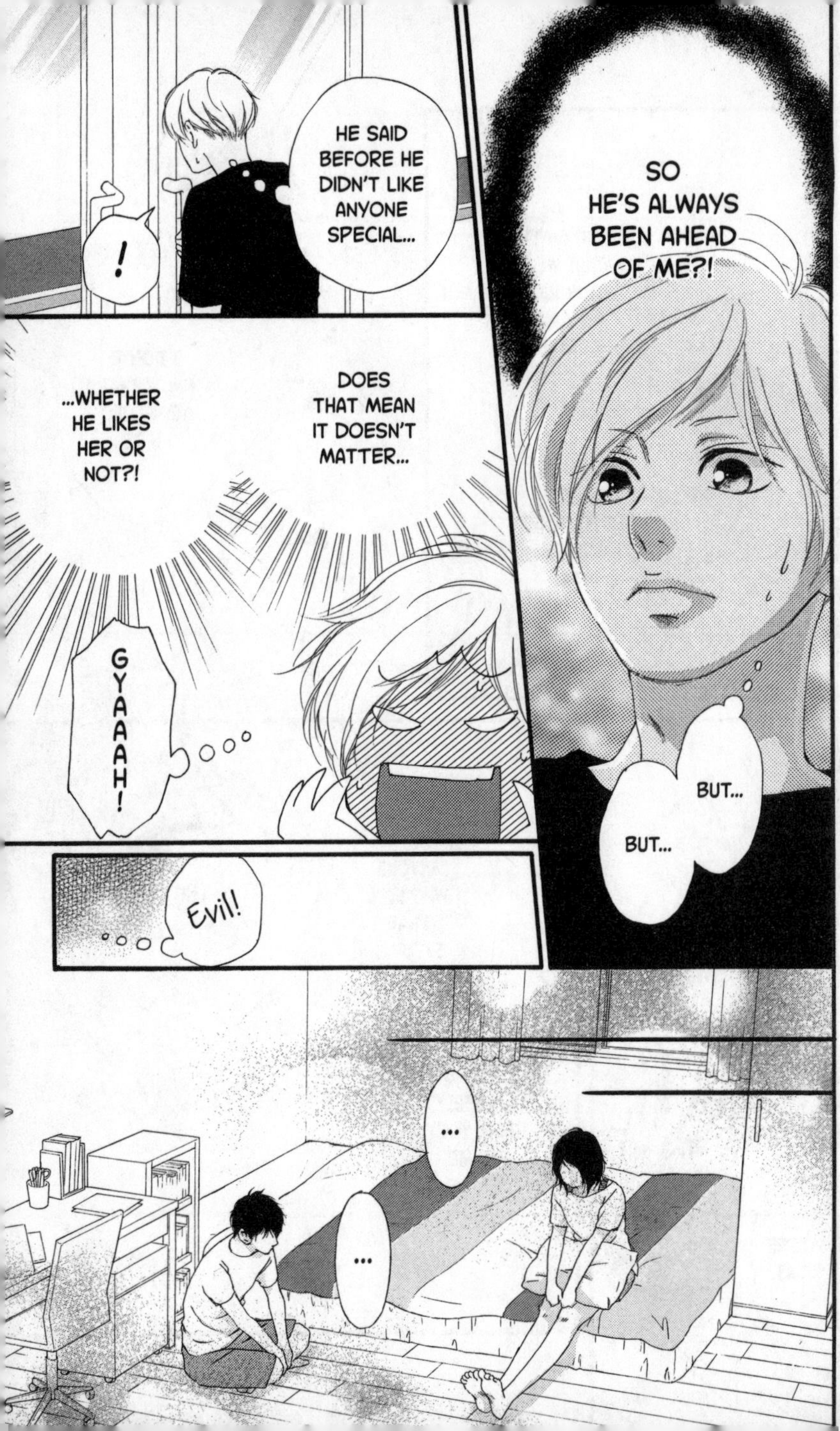
SO HE'S ALWAYS BEEN AHEAD OF ME?!
BUT...
BUT...
HE SAID BEFORE HE DIDN'T LIKE ANYONE SPECIAL...
!
DOES THAT MEAN IT DOESN'T MATTER...
...WHETHER HE LIKES HER OR NOT?!
GYAAAAH!
Evil!
...
...

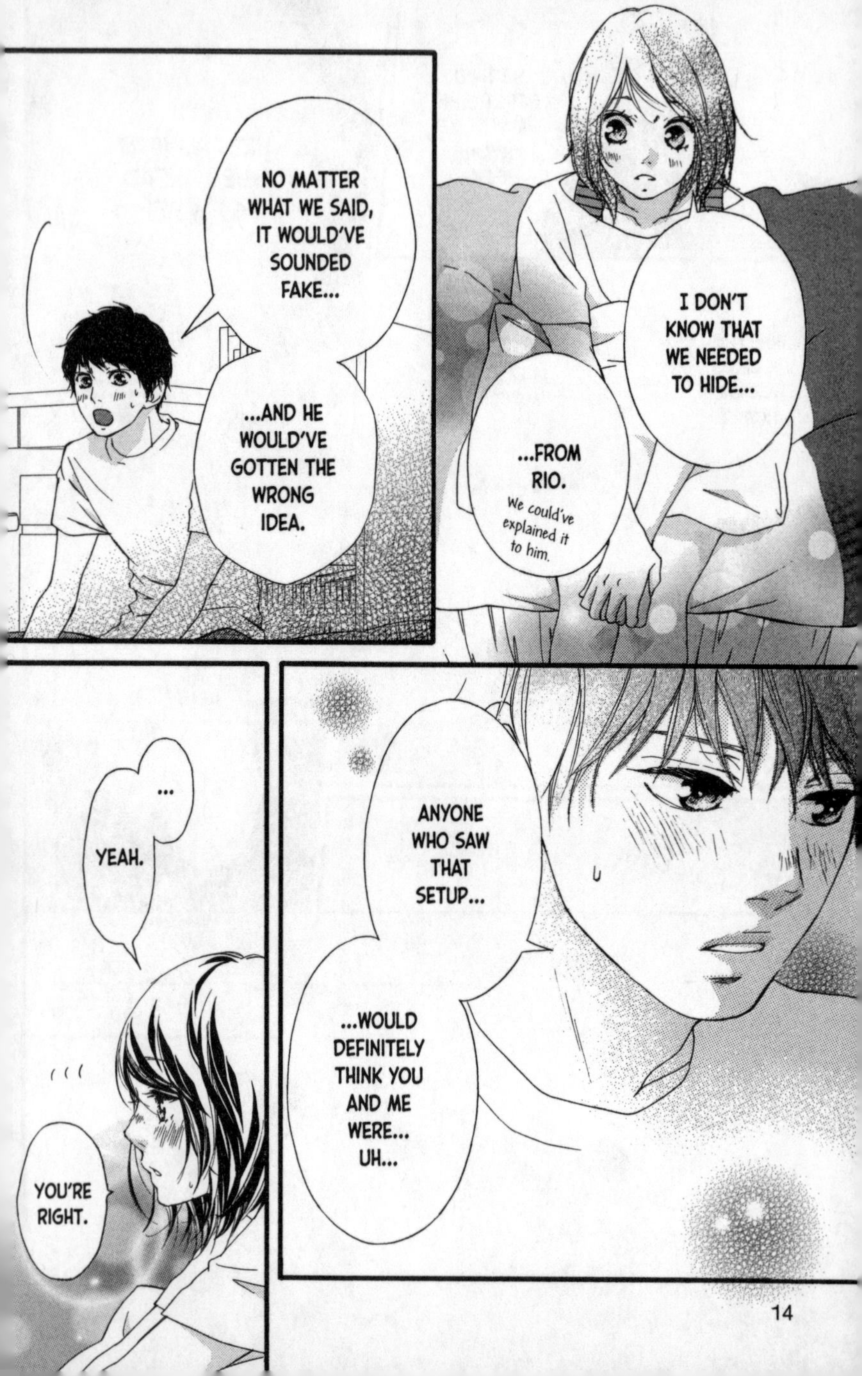
I DON'T KNOW THAT WE NEEDED TO HIDE...
...FROM RIO.
We could've explained it to him.
NO MATTER WHAT WE SAID, IT WOULD'VE SOUNDED FAKE...
...AND HE WOULD'VE GOTTEN THE WRONG IDEA.
ANYONE WHO SAW THAT SETUP...
...WOULD DEFINITELY THINK YOU AND ME WERE... UH...
... YEAH.
YOU'RE RIGHT.

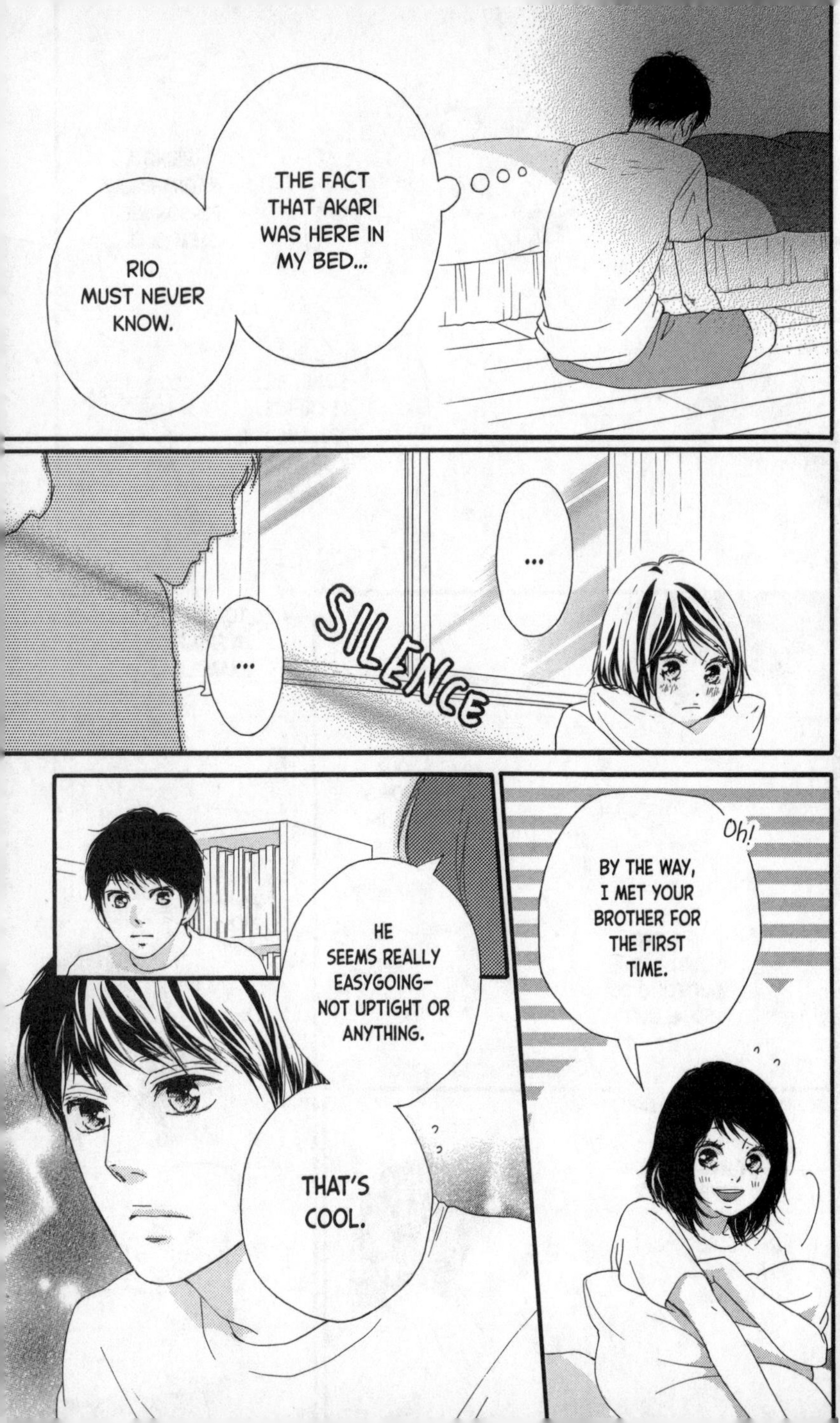
THE FACT THAT AKARI WAS HERE IN MY BED...
RIO MUST NEVER KNOW.
...
SILENCE
...
Oh!
BY THE WAY, I MET YOUR BROTHER FOR THE FIRST TIME.
HE SEEMS REALLY EASYGOING—NOT UPTIGHT OR ANYTHING.
THAT'S COOL.

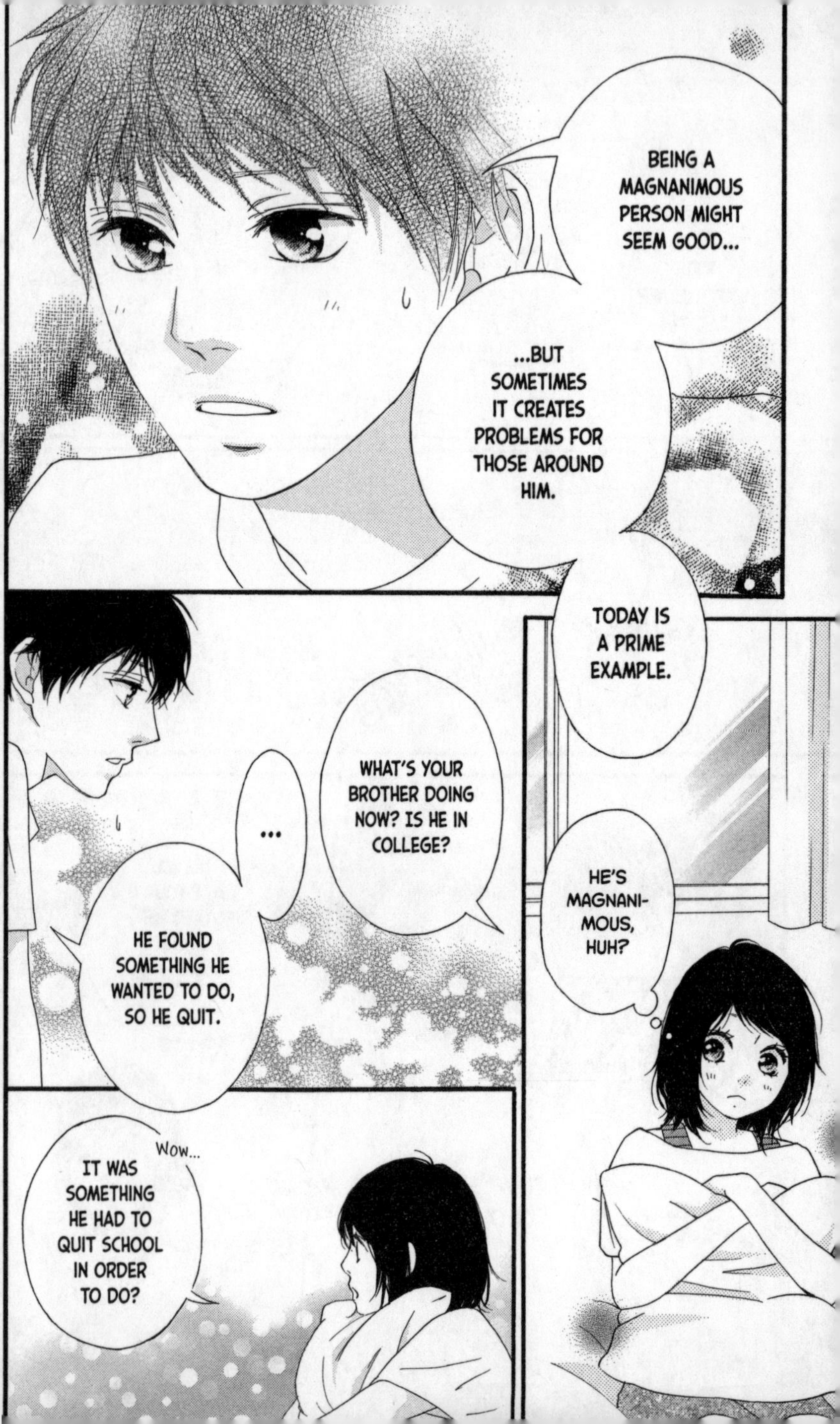
BEING A MAGNANIMOUS PERSON MIGHT SEEM GOOD...
...BUT SOMETIMES IT CREATES PROBLEMS FOR THOSE AROUND HIM.
TODAY IS A PRIME EXAMPLE.
HE'S MAGNANI-MOUS, HUH?
WHAT'S YOUR BROTHER DOING NOW? IS HE IN COLLEGE?
...
HE FOUND SOMETHING HE WANTED TO DO, SO HE QUIT.
WOW...
IT WAS SOMETHING HE HAD TO QUIT SCHOOL IN ORDER TO DO?

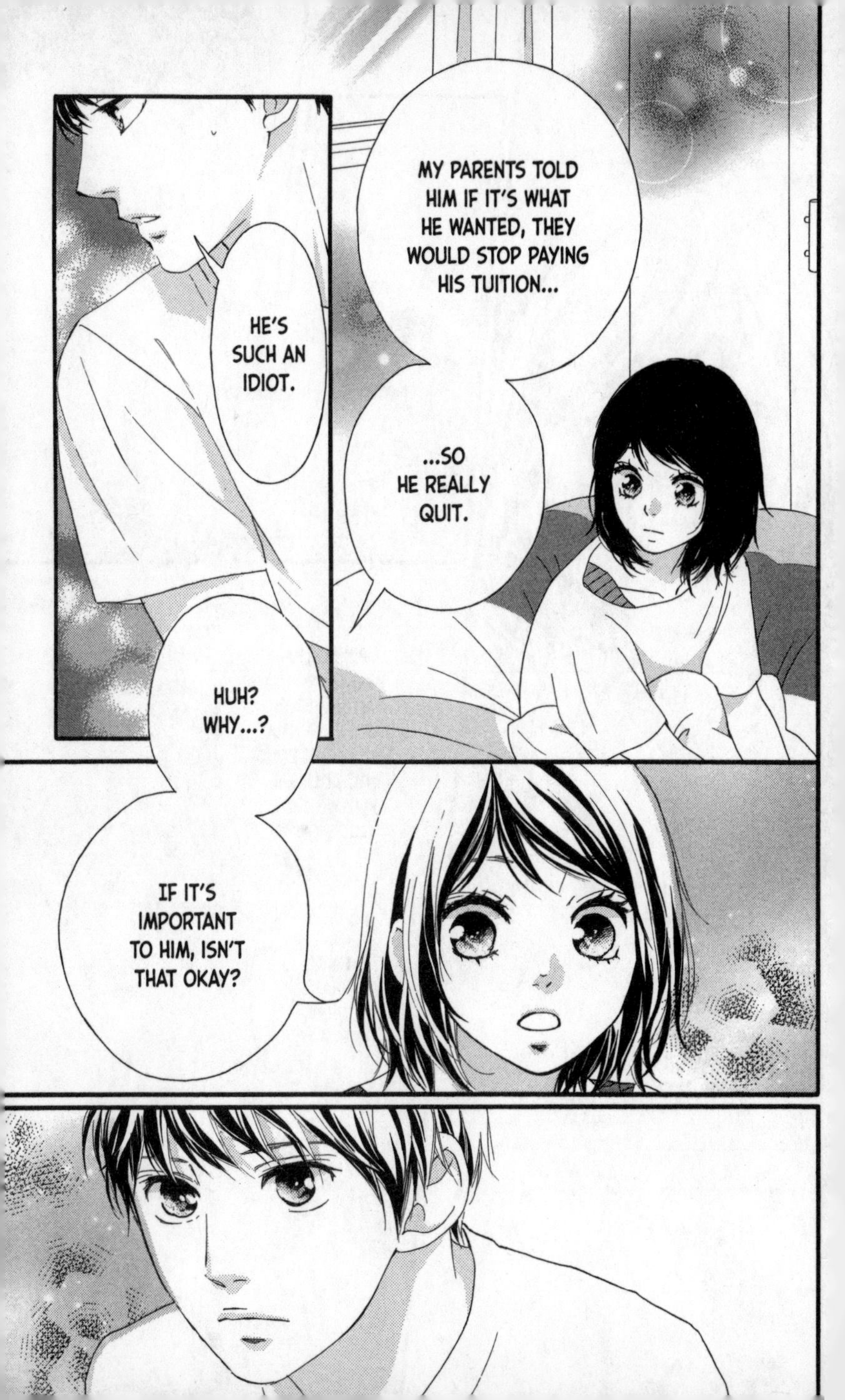
MY PARENTS TOLD HIM IF IT'S WHAT HE WANTED, THEY WOULD STOP PAYING HIS TUITION...
...SO HE REALLY QUIT.
HE'S SUCH AN IDIOT.
HUH? WHY...?
IF IT'S IMPORTANT TO HIM, ISN'T THAT OKAY?

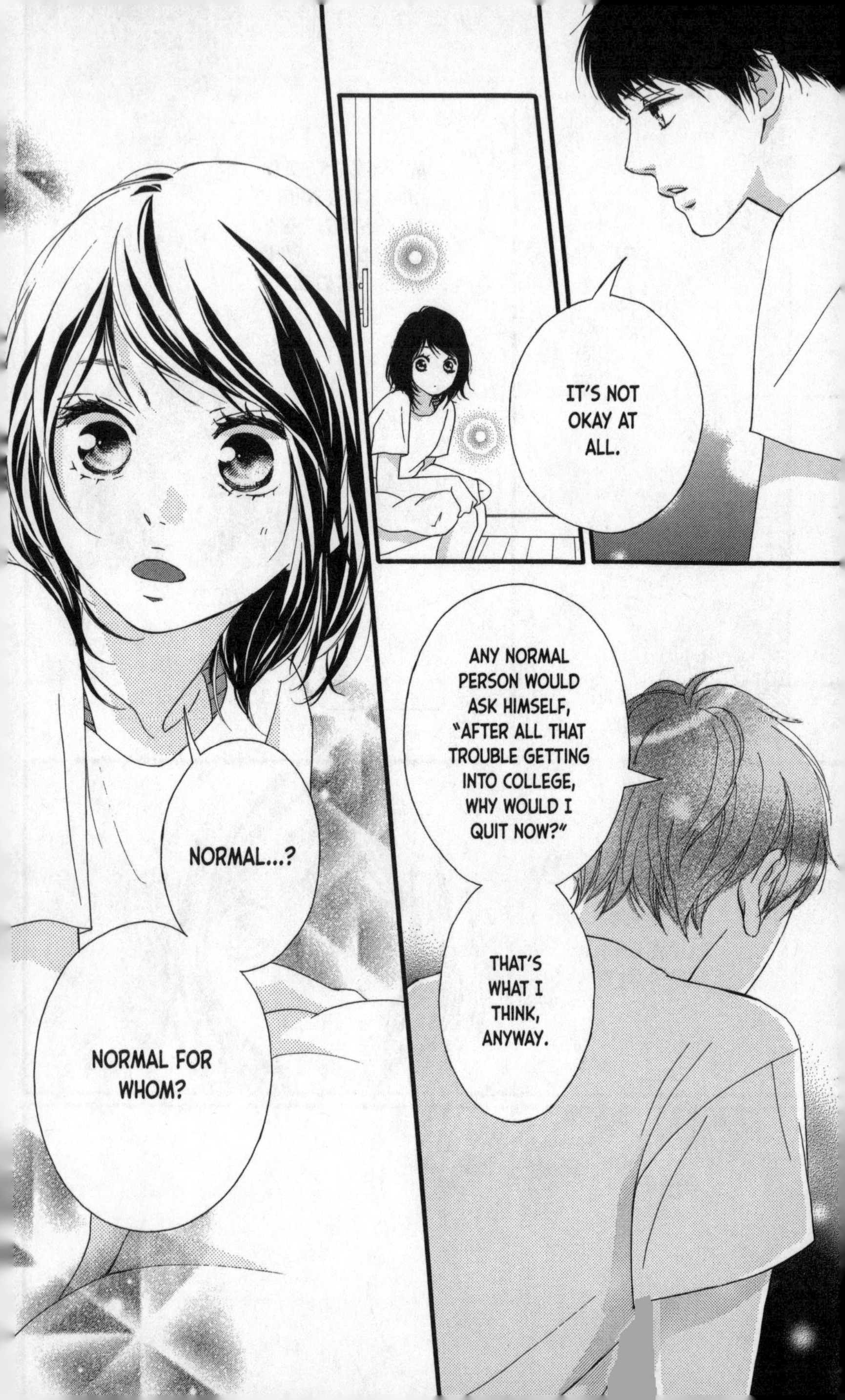
IT'S NOT OKAY AT ALL.
ANY NORMAL PERSON WOULD ASK HIMSELF, "AFTER ALL THAT TROUBLE GETTING INTO COLLEGE, WHY WOULD I QUIT NOW?"
THAT'S WHAT I THINK, ANYWAY.
NORMAL...?
NORMAL FOR WHOM?

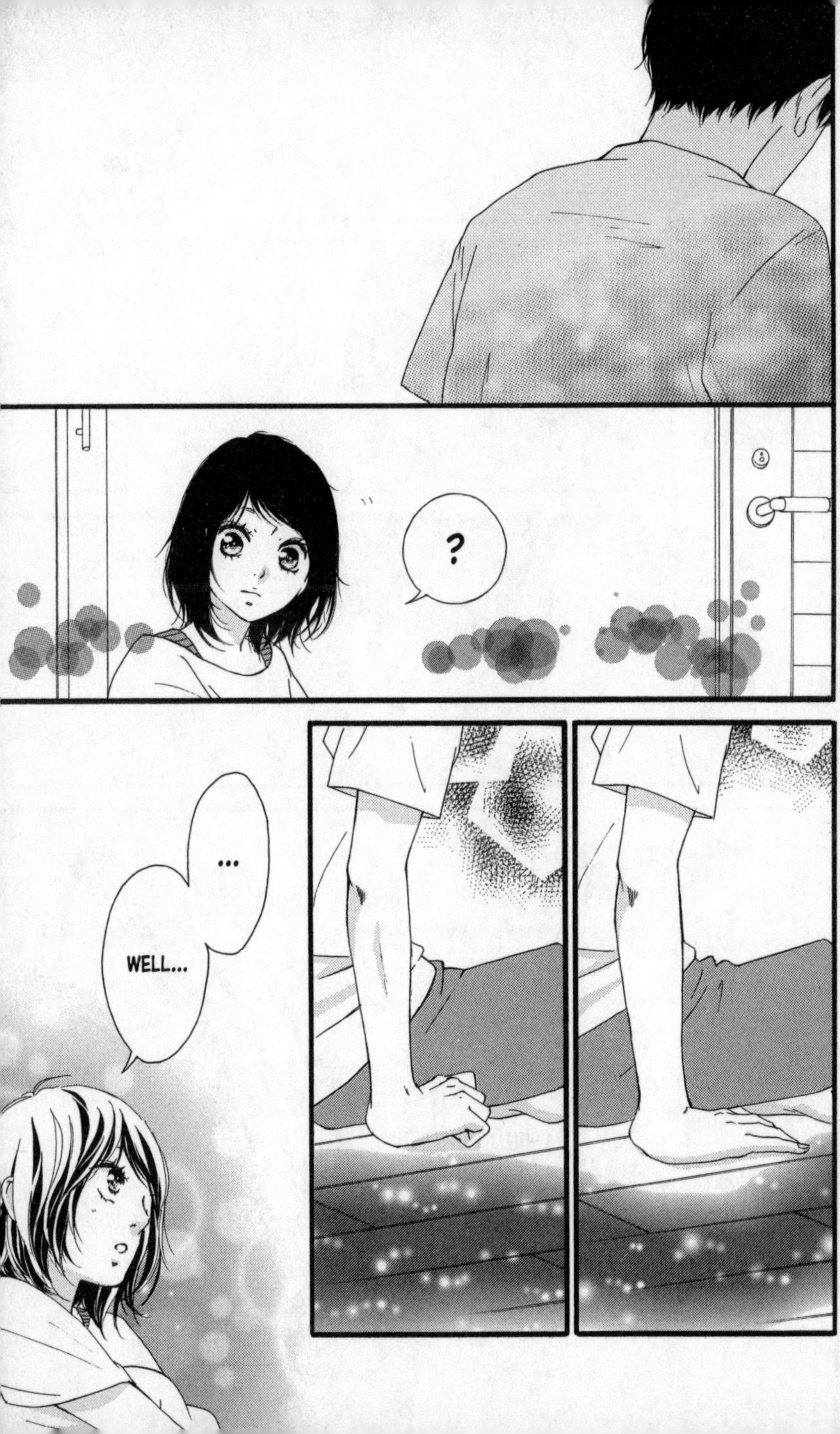
?
...
WELL...

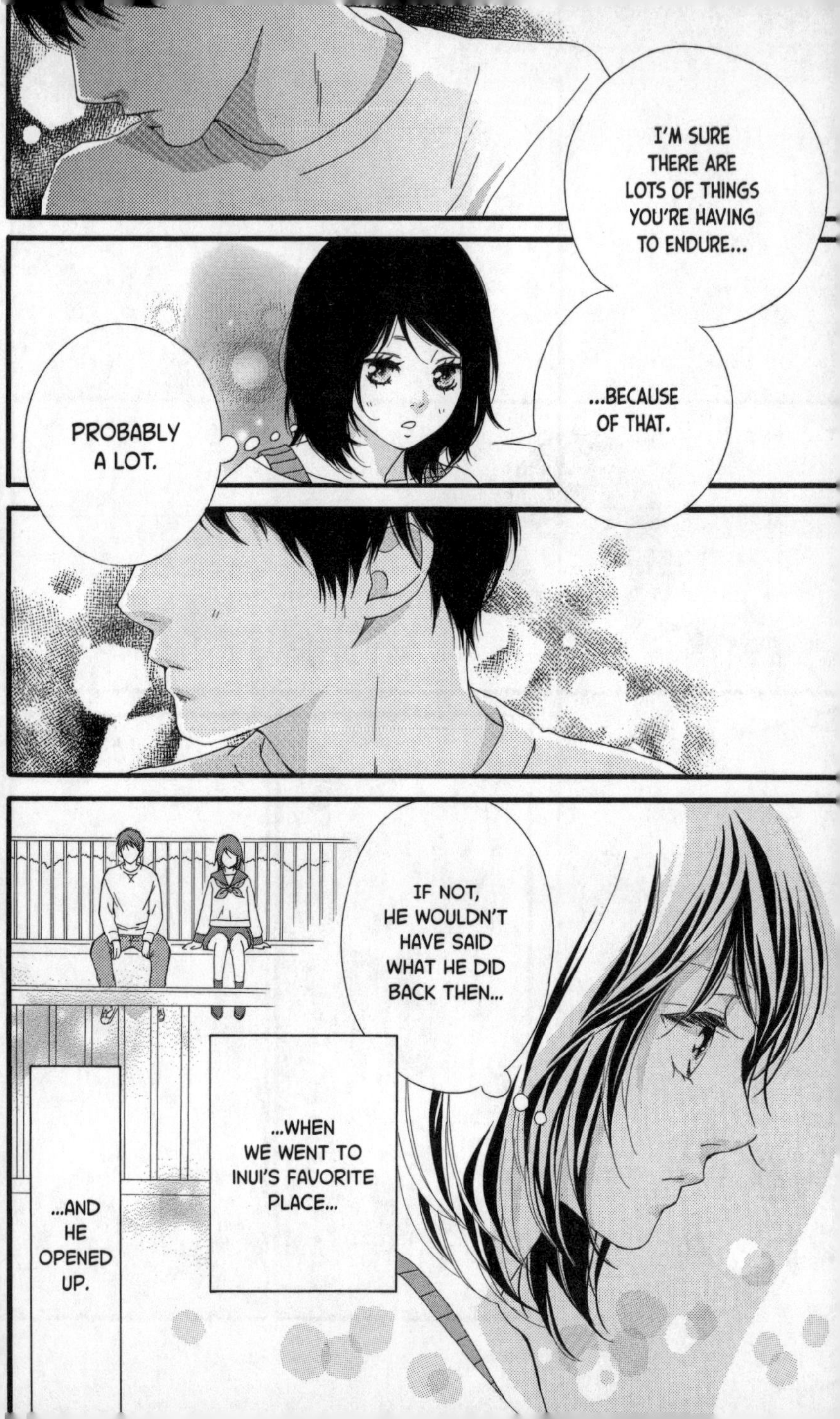
I'M SURE THERE ARE LOTS OF THINGS YOU'RE HAVING TO ENDURE...
...BECAUSE OF THAT.
PROBABLY A LOT.
IF NOT, HE WOULDN'T HAVE SAID WHAT HE DID BACK THEN...
...WHEN WE WENT TO INUI'S FAVORITE PLACE...
...AND HE OPENED UP.

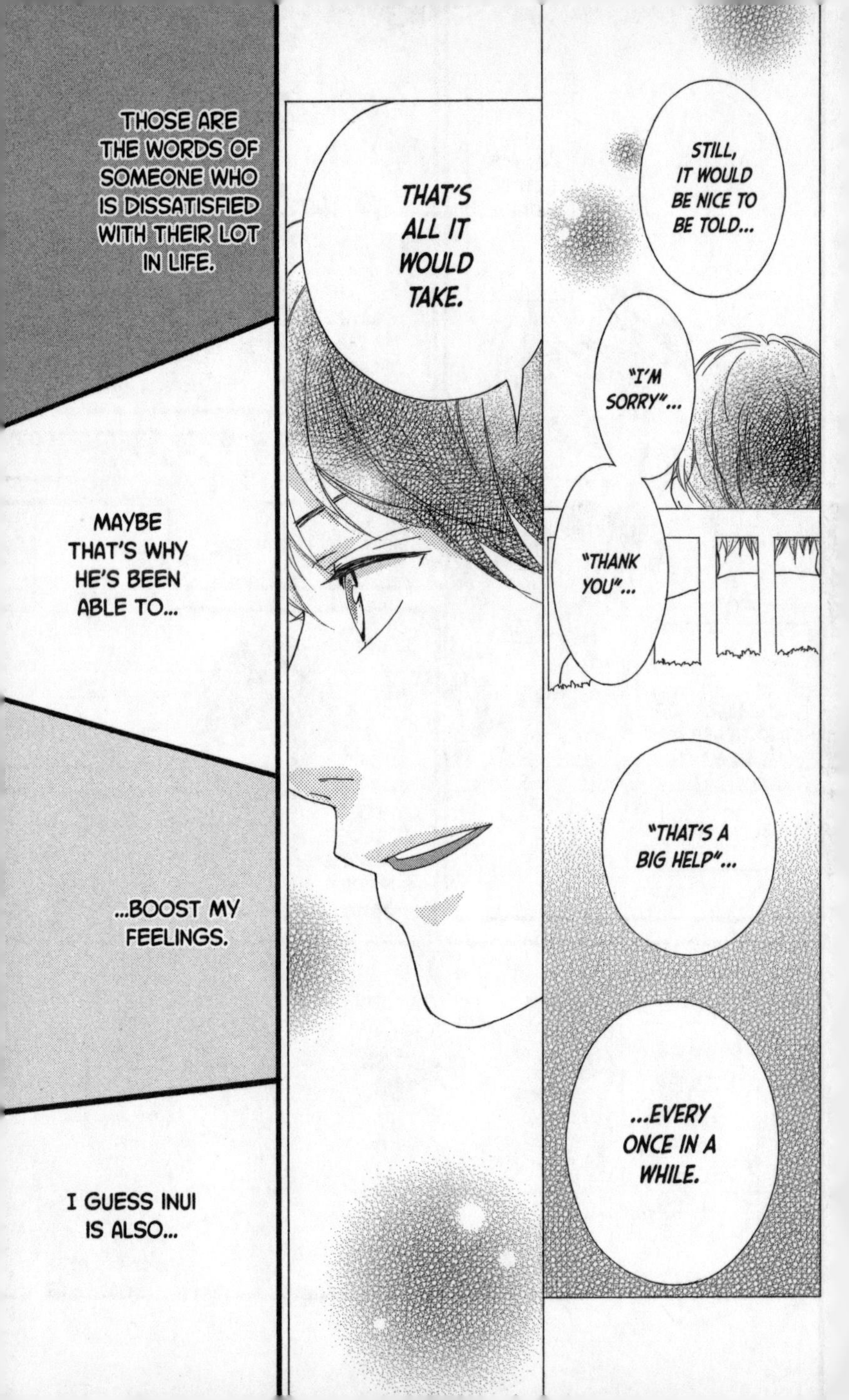
STILL, IT WOULD BE NICE TO BE TOLD...
"I'M SORRY"...
"THANK YOU"...
"THAT'S A BIG HELP"...
...EVERY ONCE IN A WHILE.
THAT'S ALL IT WOULD TAKE.
THOSE ARE THE WORDS OF SOMEONE WHO IS DISSATISFIED WITH THEIR LOT IN LIFE.
MAYBE THAT'S WHY HE'S BEEN ABLE TO...
...BOOST MY FEELINGS.
I GUESS INUI IS ALSO...

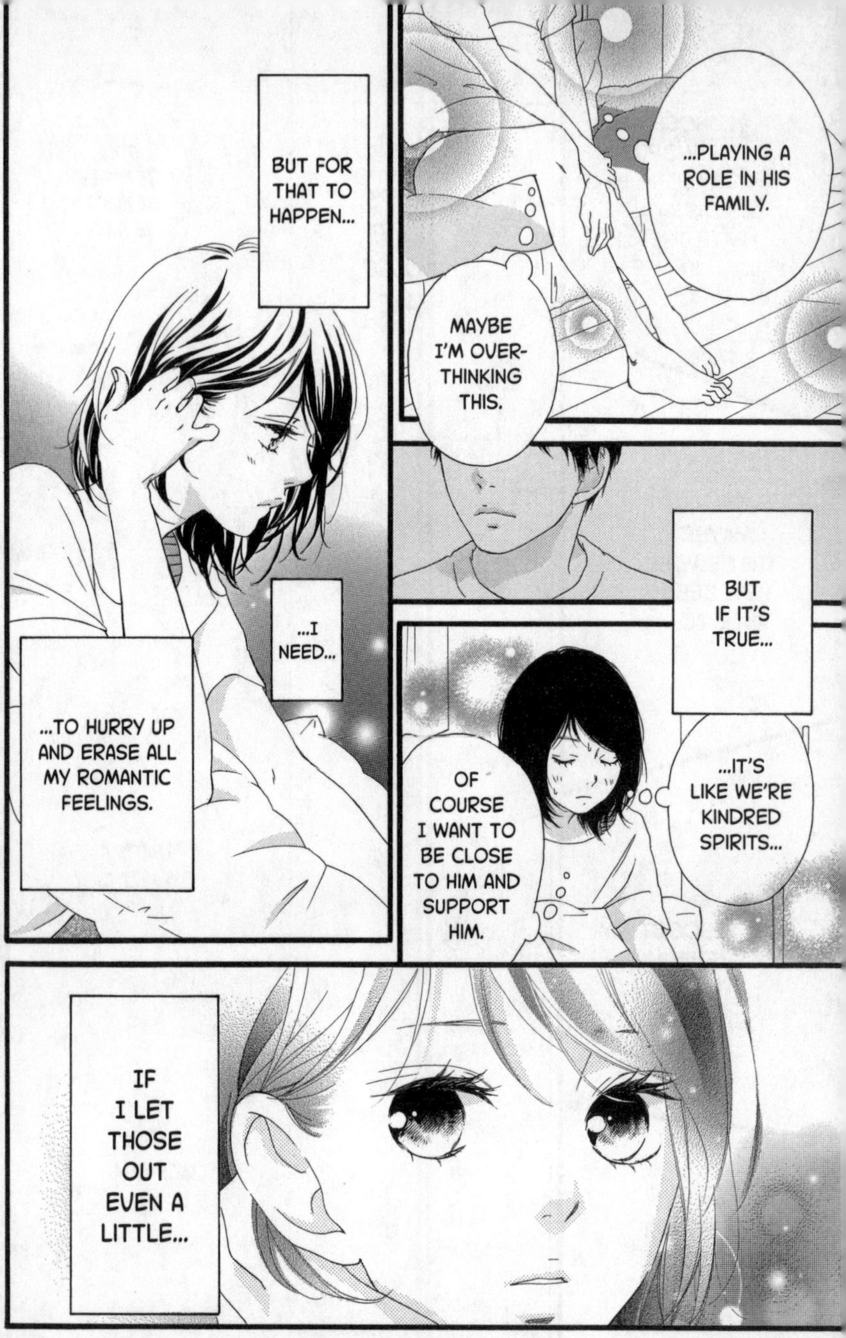
...PLAYING A ROLE IN HIS FAMILY.
MAYBE I'M OVER-THINKING THIS.
BUT IF IT'S TRUE...
...IT'S LIKE WE'RE KINDRED SPIRITS...
OF COURSE I WANT TO BE CLOSE TO HIM AND SUPPORT HIM.
BUT FOR THAT TO HAPPEN...
...I NEED...
...TO HURRY UP AND ERASE ALL MY ROMANTIC FEELINGS.
IF I LET THOSE OUT EVEN A LITTLE...

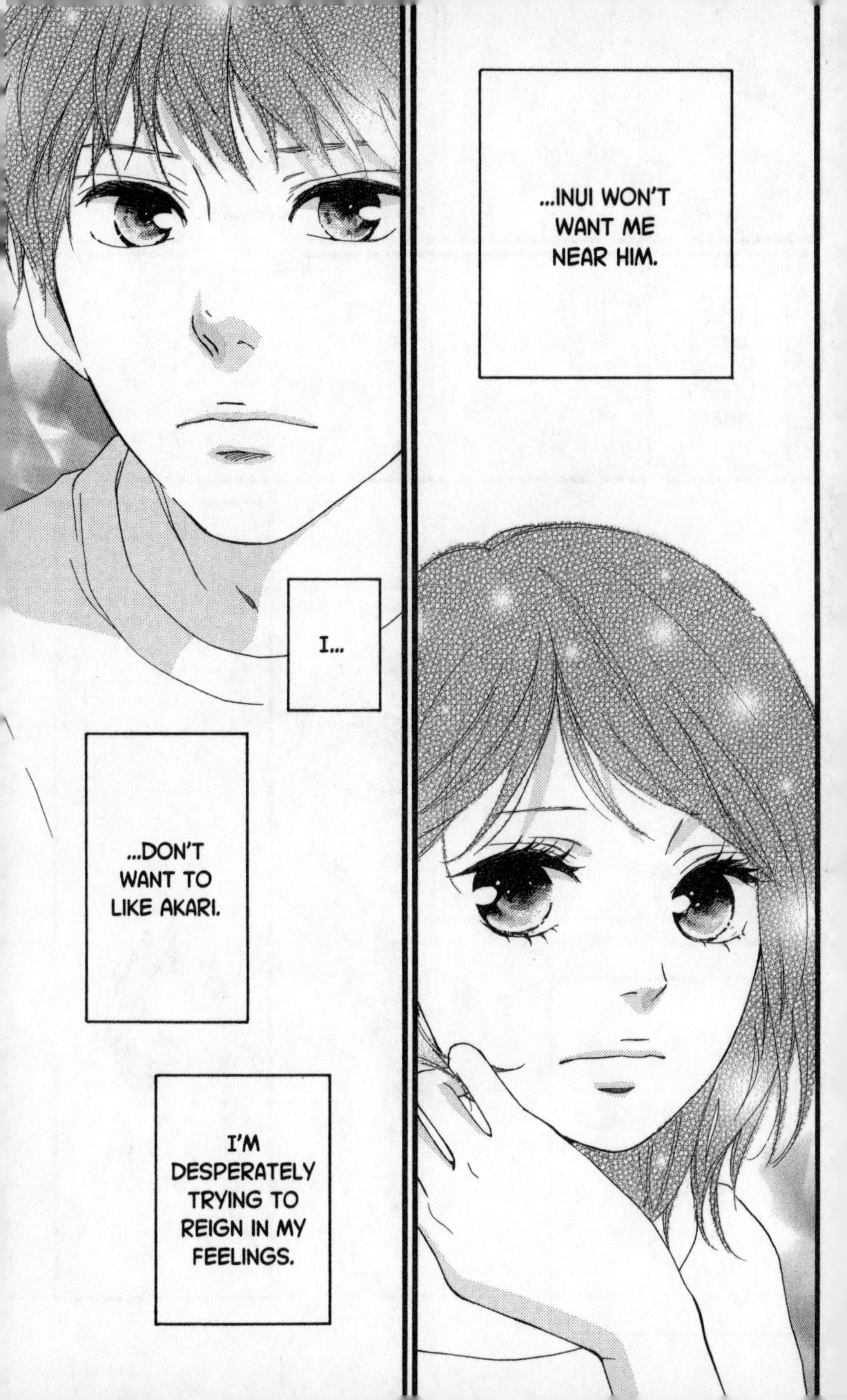
...INUI WON'T WANT ME NEAR HIM.
I...
...DON'T WANT TO LIKE AKARI.
I'M DESPERATELY TRYING TO REIGN IN MY FEELINGS.

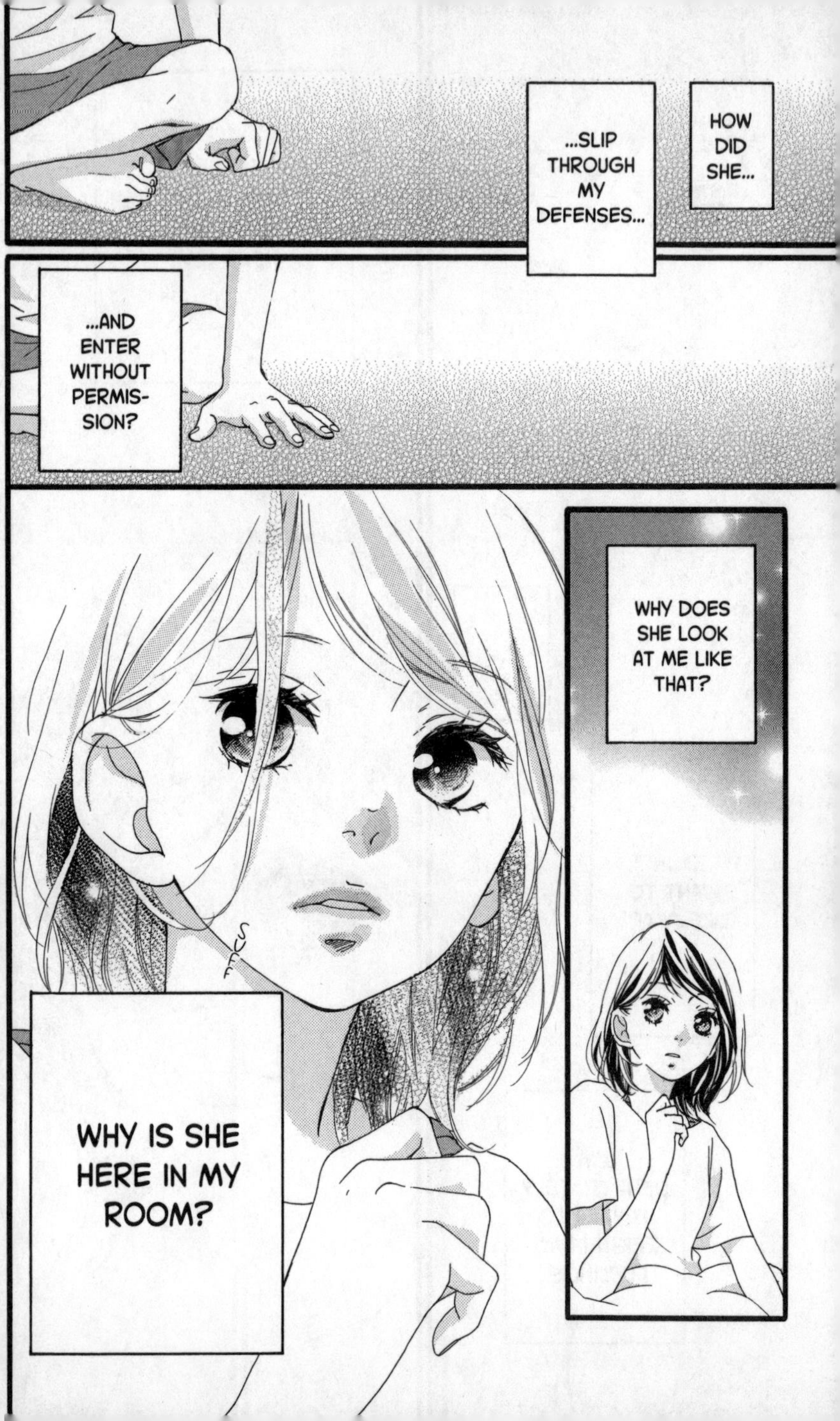
HOW DID SHE...
...SLIP THROUGH MY DEFENSES...
...AND ENTER WITHOUT PERMIS-SION?
WHY DOES SHE LOOK AT ME LIKE THAT?
SUFF
WHY IS SHE HERE IN MY ROOM?

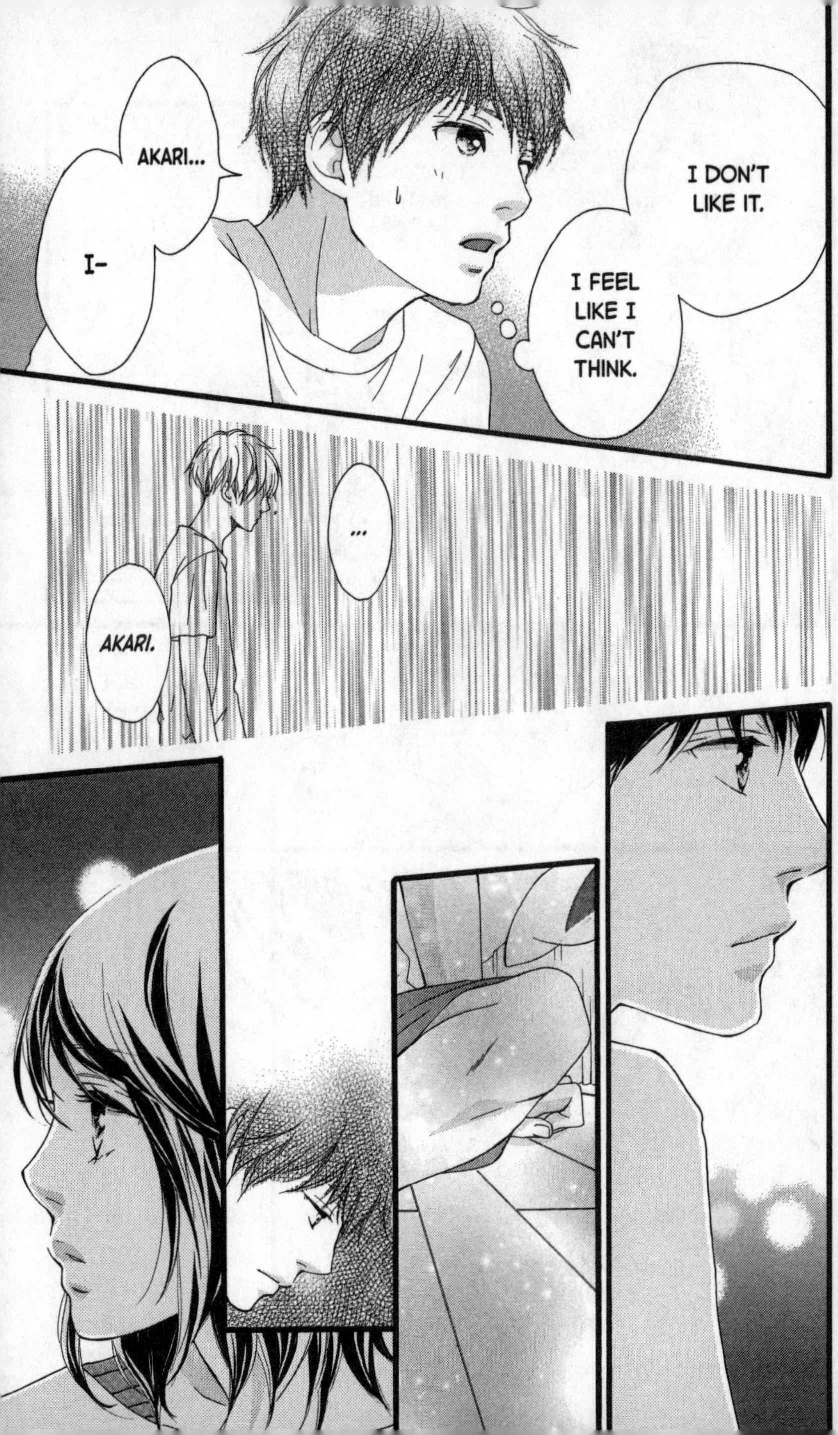
I DON'T LIKE IT.
I FEEL LIKE I CAN'T THINK.
AKARI...
I-
...
AKARI.

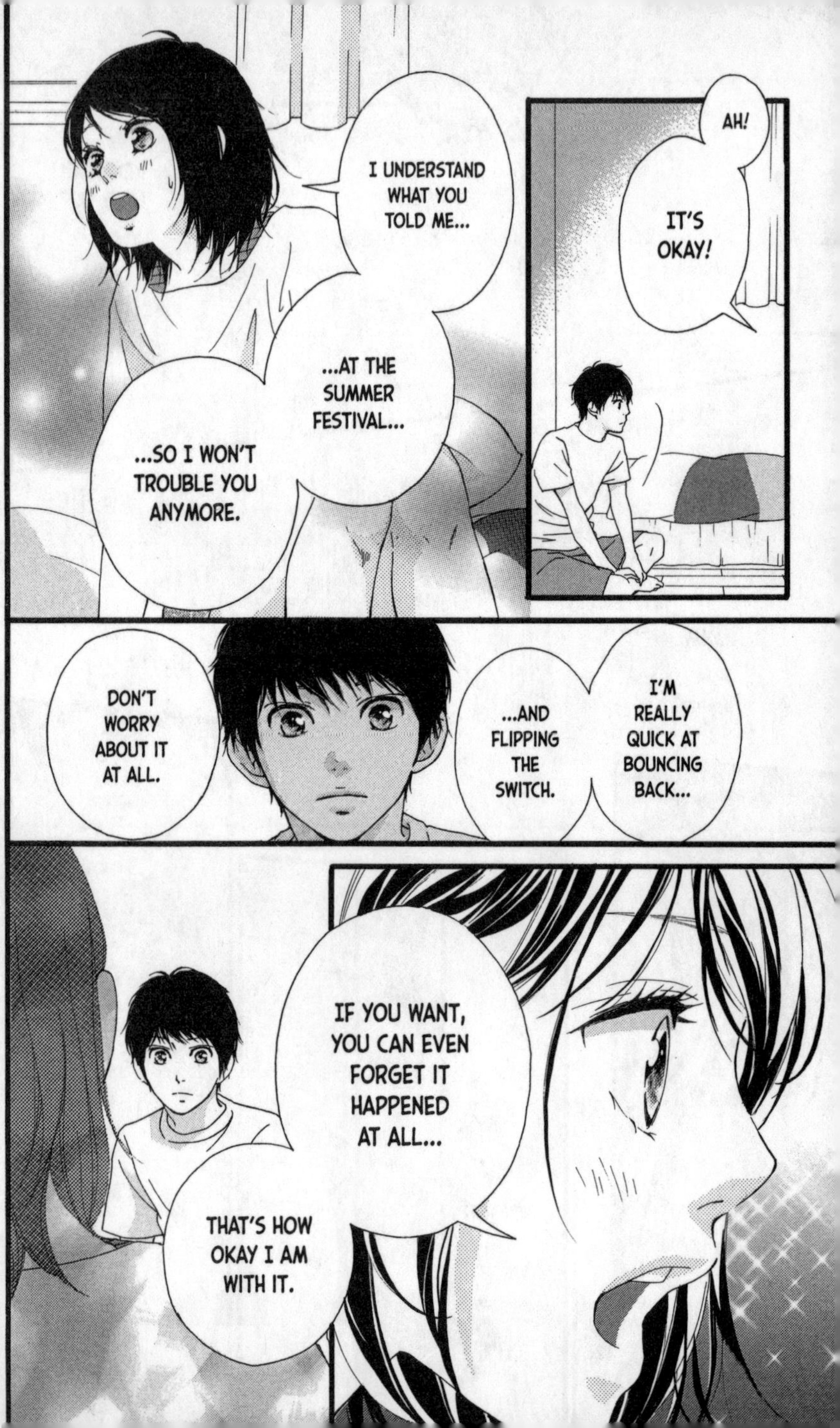
AH!
IT'S OKAY!
I UNDERSTAND WHAT YOU TOLD ME...
...AT THE SUMMER FESTIVAL...
...SO I WON'T TROUBLE YOU ANYMORE.
I'M REALLY QUICK AT BOUNCING BACK...
...AND FLIPPING THE SWITCH.
DON'T WORRY ABOUT IT AT ALL.
IF YOU WANT, YOU CAN EVEN FORGET IT HAPPENED AT ALL...
THAT'S HOW OKAY I AM WITH IT.

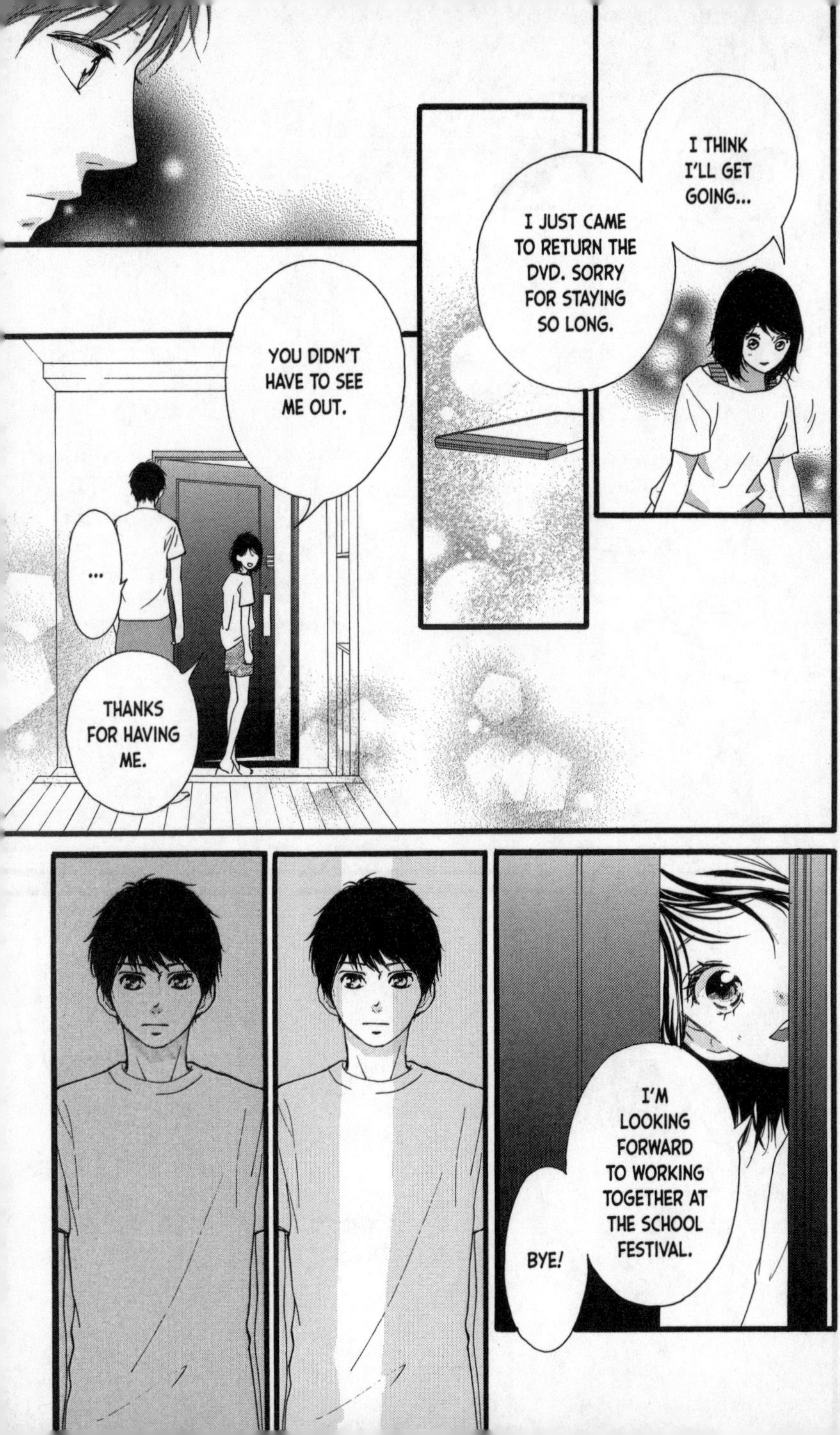
I THINK I'LL GET GOING...
I JUST CAME TO RETURN THE DVD. SORRY FOR STAYING SO LONG.
YOU DIDN'T HAVE TO SEE ME OUT.
...
THANKS FOR HAVING ME.
I'M LOOKING FORWARD TO WORKING TOGETHER AT THE SCHOOL FESTIVAL.
BYE!

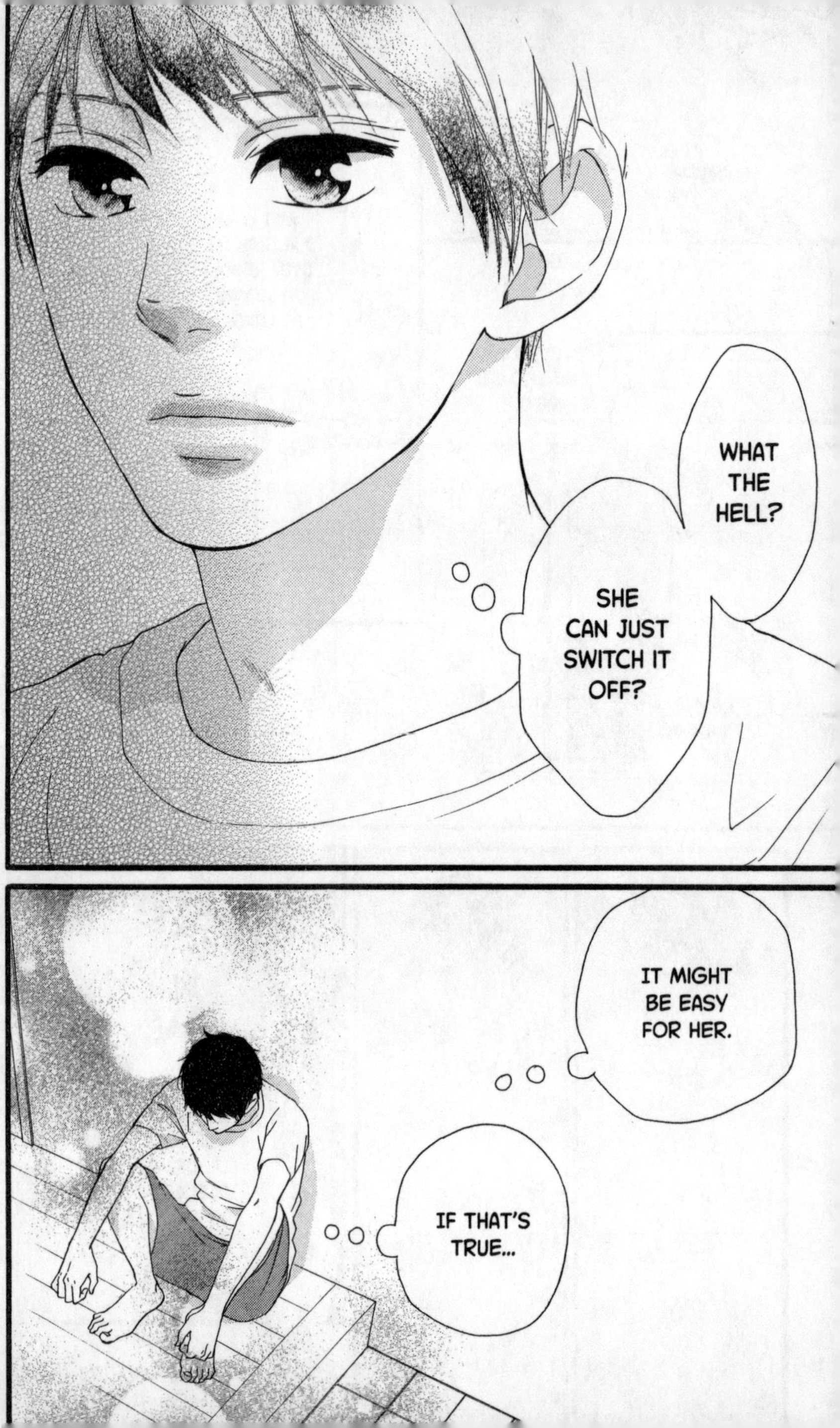
WHAT THE HELL?
SHE CAN JUST SWITCH IT OFF?
IT MIGHT BE EASY FOR HER.
IF THAT'S TRUE...

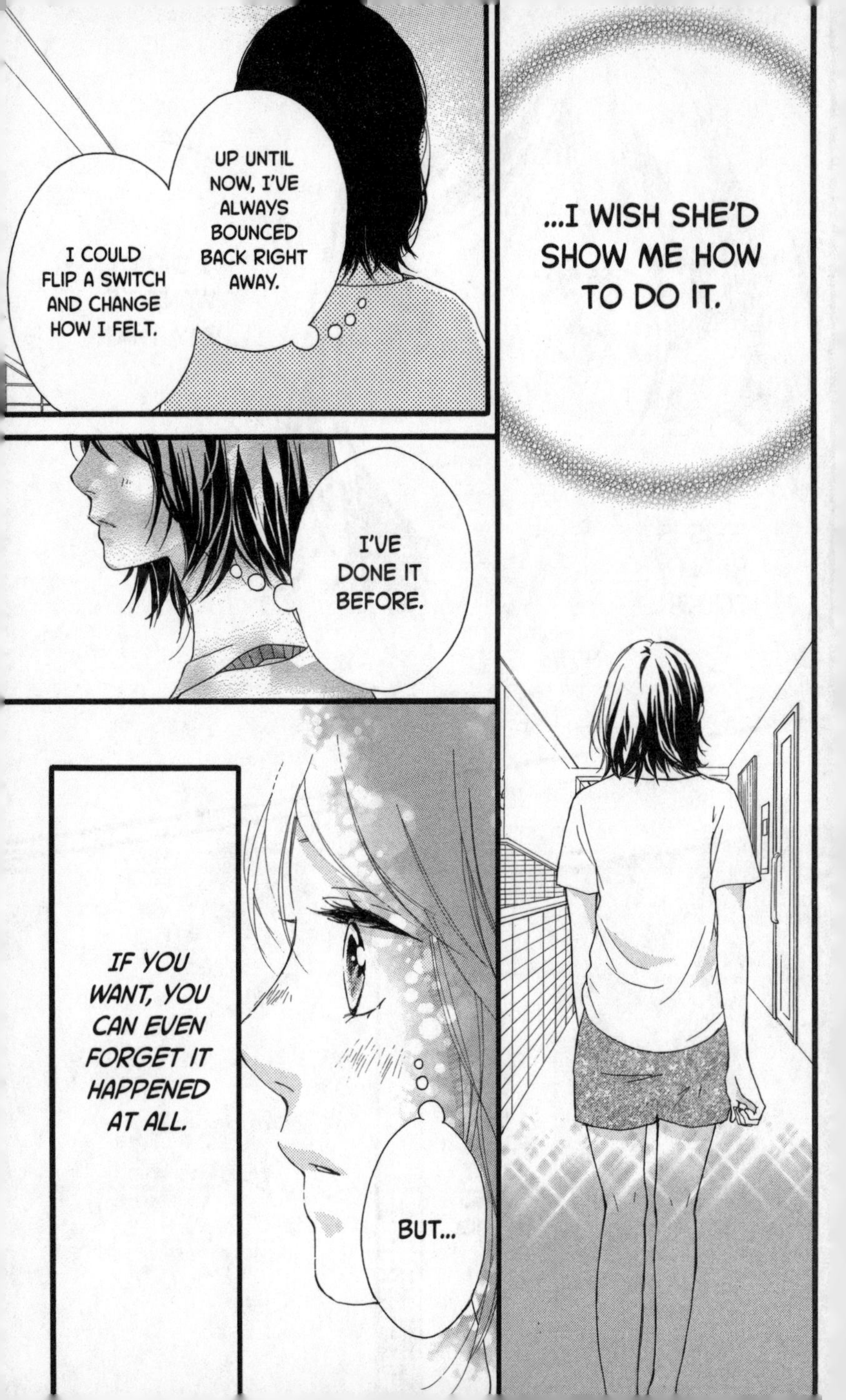
UP UNTIL NOW, I'VE ALWAYS BOUNCED BACK RIGHT AWAY.
I COULD FLIP A SWITCH AND CHANGE HOW I FELT.
I'VE DONE IT BEFORE.
IF YOU WANT, YOU CAN EVEN FORGET IT HAPPENED AT ALL.
BUT...
...I WISH SHE'D SHOW ME HOW TO DO IT.

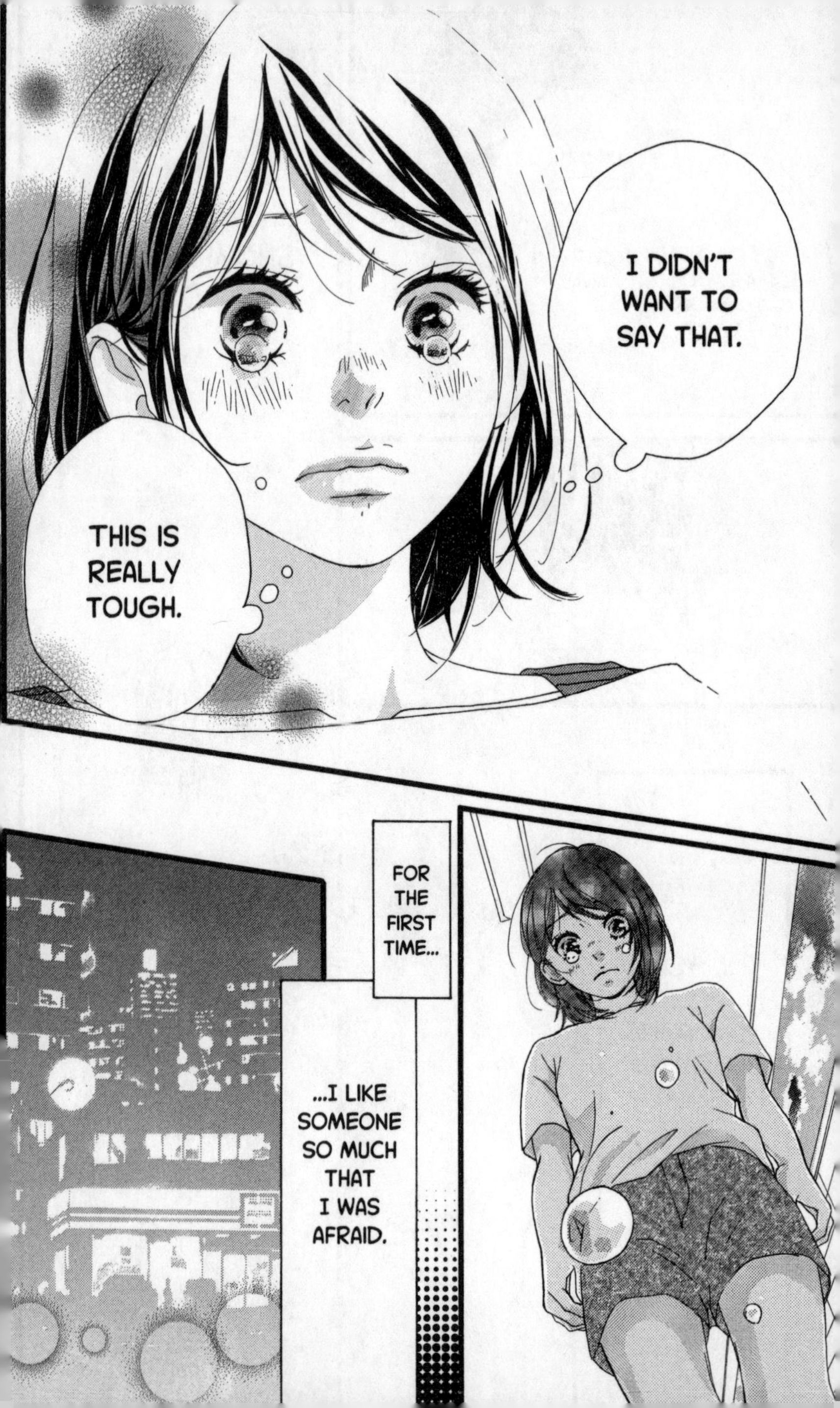
I DIDN'T WANT TO SAY THAT.
THIS IS REALLY TOUGH.
FOR THE FIRST TIME...
...I LIKE SOMEONE SO MUCH THAT I WAS AFRAID.

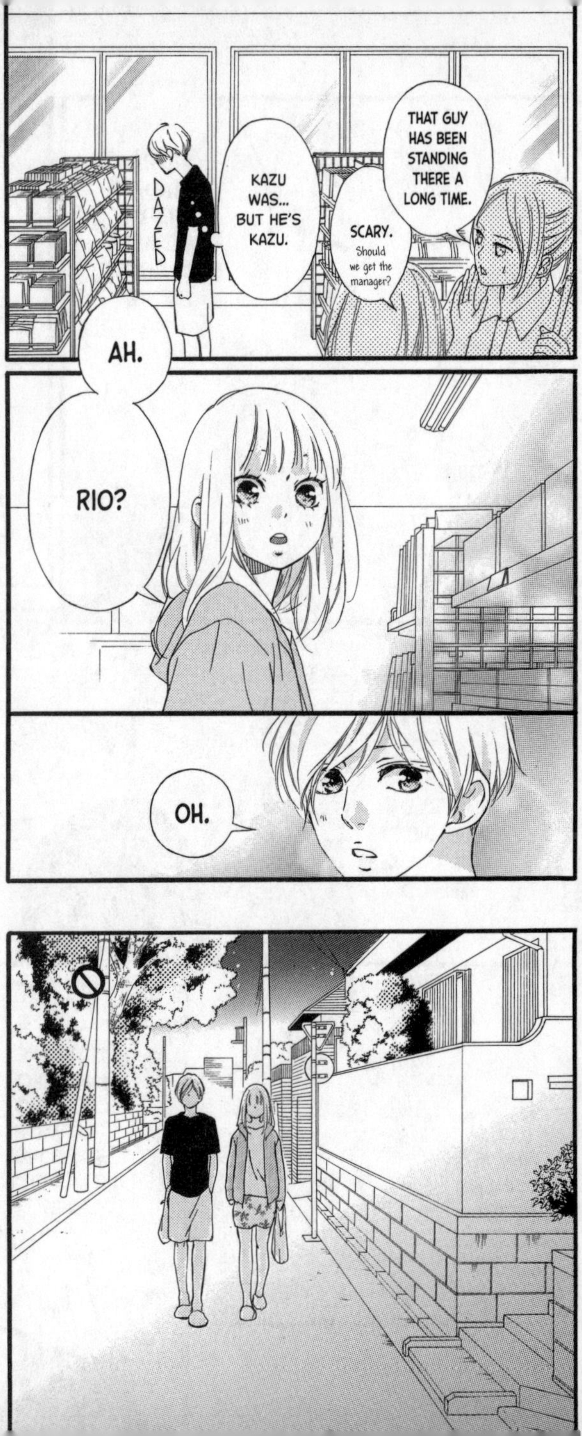
THAT GUY HAS BEEN STANDING THERE A LONG TIME.
SCARY.
Should we get the manager?
KAZU WAS... BUT HE'S KAZU.
DAZED
AH.
RIO?
OH.

From the time I was little, I have always loved the smell of subway platforms. They have their own peculiar smell, don't you think? I just breathe in deeply, and I am in bliss. A long time ago my mother asked, "Isn't that the smell of dust?" But it's not. I don't feel anything at other dusty places. Only on the subway platform do I feel a stirring in my heart. Call it a giddy feeling—like my solar plexus is being tickled—and I personally love it. But it's a little lonely when I try to explain this to people and no one gets it. There's nothing I can do. I don't care if it's dust or whatnot when it makes me feel this blissful. I love it. Yeah. Will my soul mate who's some-where out there feel this same way?

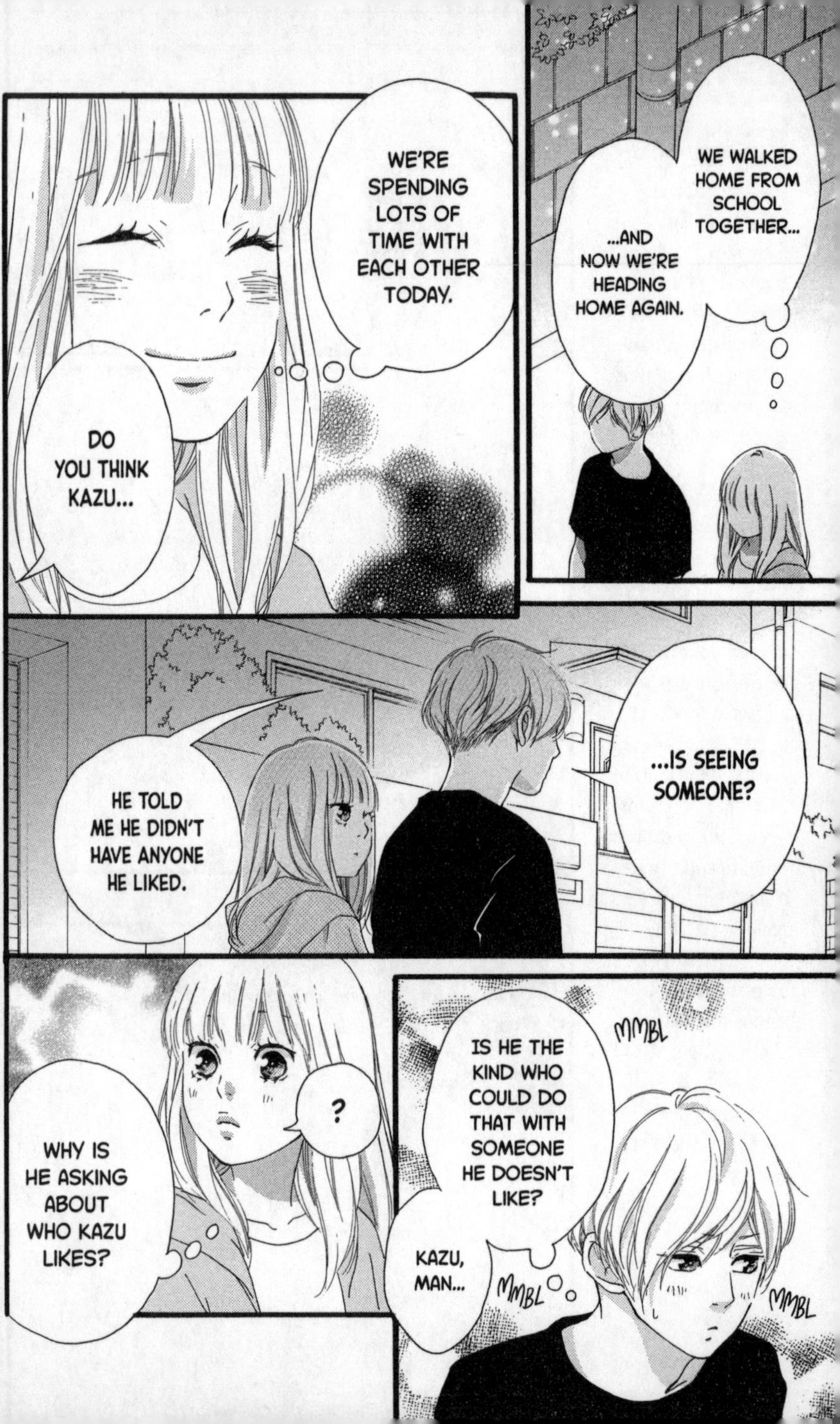

WE WALKED HOME FROM SCHOOL TOGETHER...
...AND NOW WE'RE HEADING HOME AGAIN.
WE'RE SPENDING LOTS OF TIME WITH EACH OTHER TODAY.
DO YOU THINK KAZU...
...IS SEEING SOMEONE?
HE TOLD ME HE DIDN'T HAVE ANYONE HE LIKED.
MMBL
IS HE THE KIND WHO COULD DO THAT WITH SOMEONE HE DOESN'T LIKE?
KAZU, MAN...
MMBL
MMBL
?
WHY IS HE ASKING ABOUT WHO KAZU LIKES?

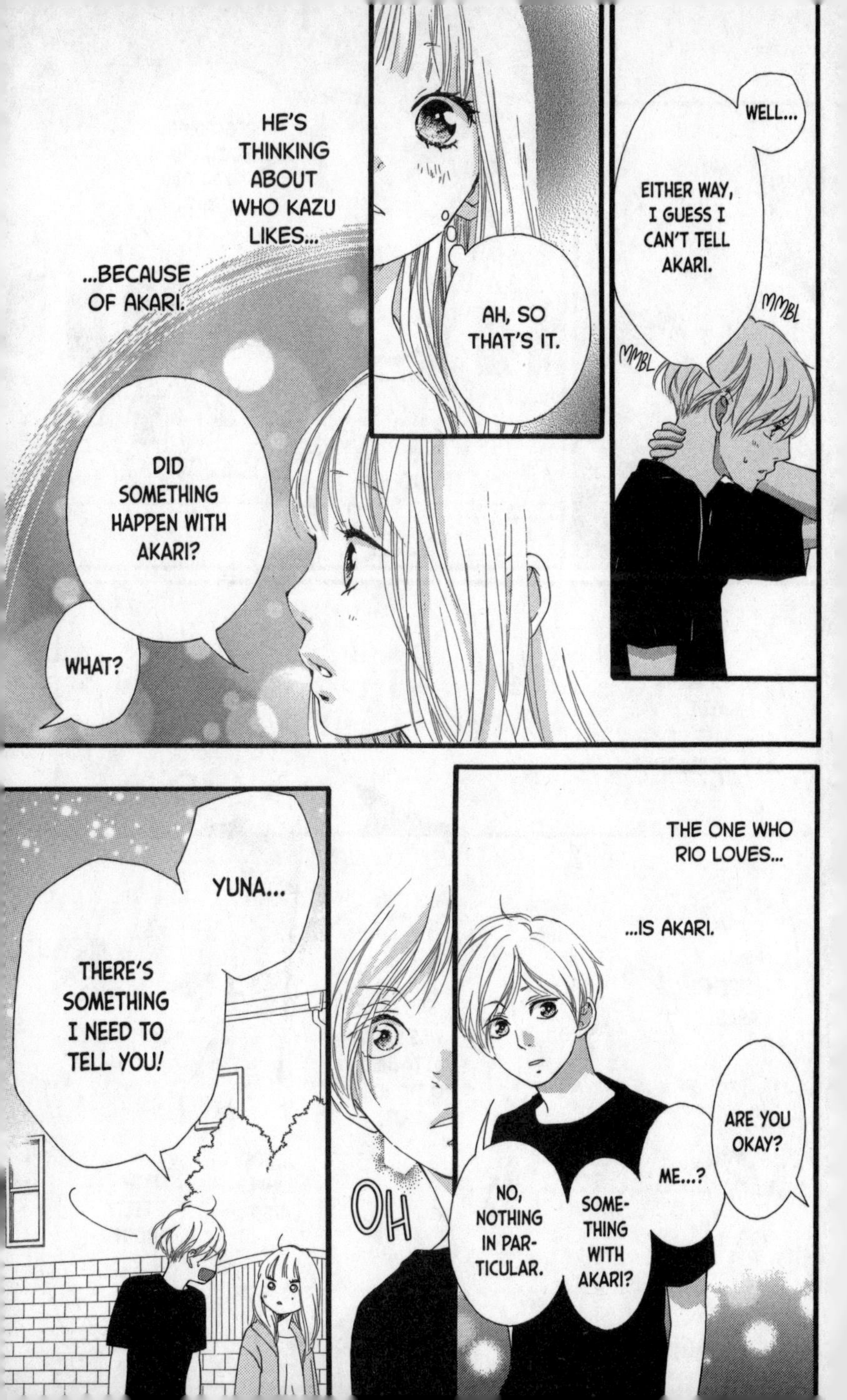
WELL...
EITHER WAY, I GUESS I CAN'T TELL AKARI.
MMBL
MMBL
AH, SO THAT'S IT.
HE'S THINKING ABOUT WHO KAZU LIKES...
...BECAUSE OF AKARI.
DID SOMETHING HAPPEN WITH AKARI?
WHAT?
THE ONE WHO RIO LOVES...
...IS AKARI.
ARE YOU OKAY?
ME...?
SOMETHING WITH AKARI?
NO, NOTHING IN PARTICULAR.
OH
YUNA...
THERE'S SOMETHING I NEED TO TELL YOU!

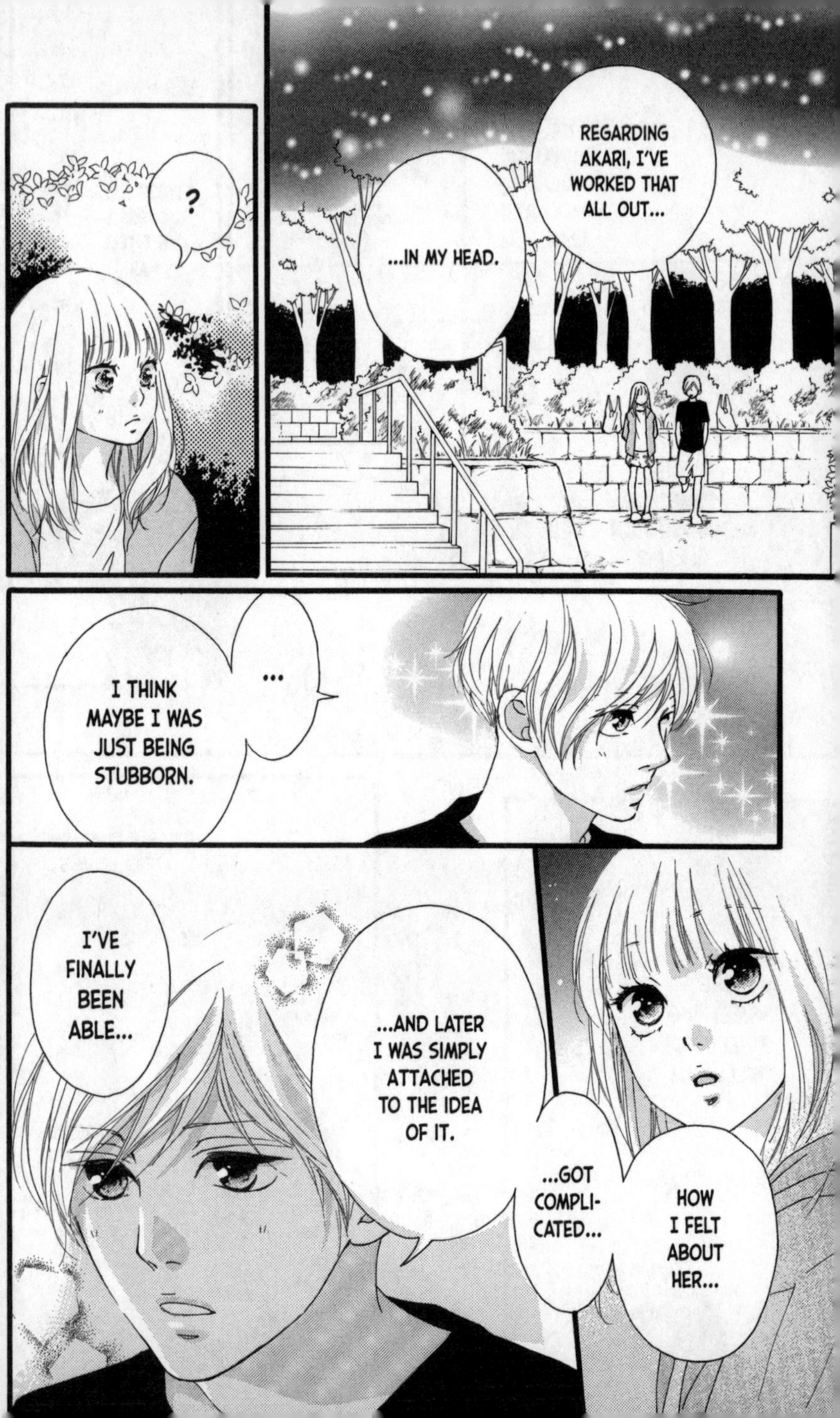
REGARDING AKARI, I'VE WORKED THAT ALL OUT...
...IN MY HEAD.
?
...
I THINK MAYBE I WAS JUST BEING STUBBORN.
HOW I FELT ABOUT HER...
...GOT COMPLICATED...
...AND LATER I WAS SIMPLY ATTACHED TO THE IDEA OF IT.
I'VE FINALLY BEEN ABLE...

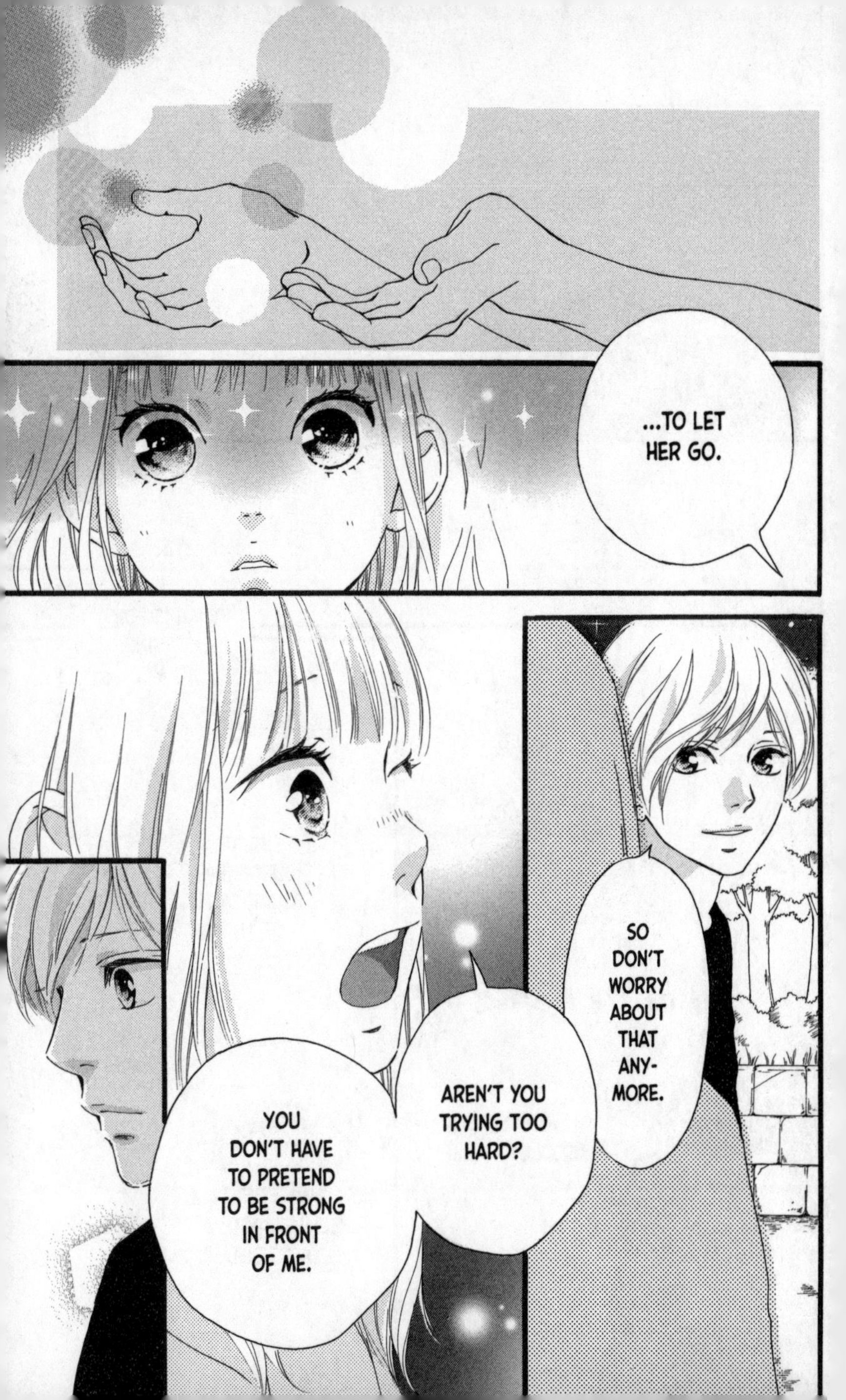
...TO LET HER GO.
SO DON'T WORRY ABOUT THAT ANY-MORE.
AREN'T YOU TRYING TOO HARD?
YOU DON'T HAVE TO PRETEND TO BE STRONG IN FRONT OF ME.

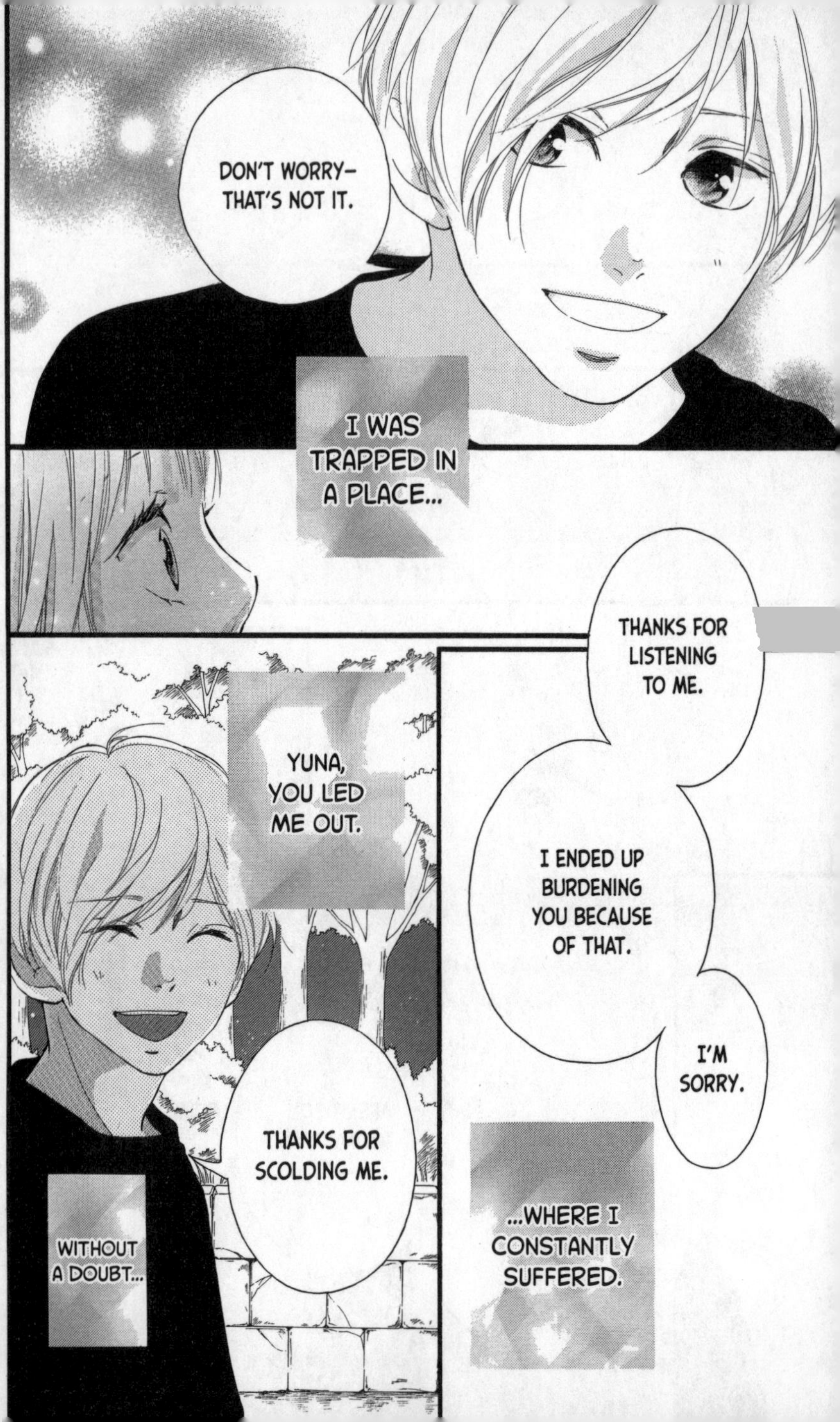
DON'T WORRY— THAT'S NOT IT.
I WAS TRAPPED IN A PLACE...
THANKS FOR LISTENING TO ME.
I ENDED UP BURDENING YOU BECAUSE OF THAT.
I'M SORRY.
...WHERE I CONSTANTLY SUFFERED.
YUNA, YOU LED ME OUT.
THANKS FOR SCOLDING ME.
WITHOUT A DOUBT...

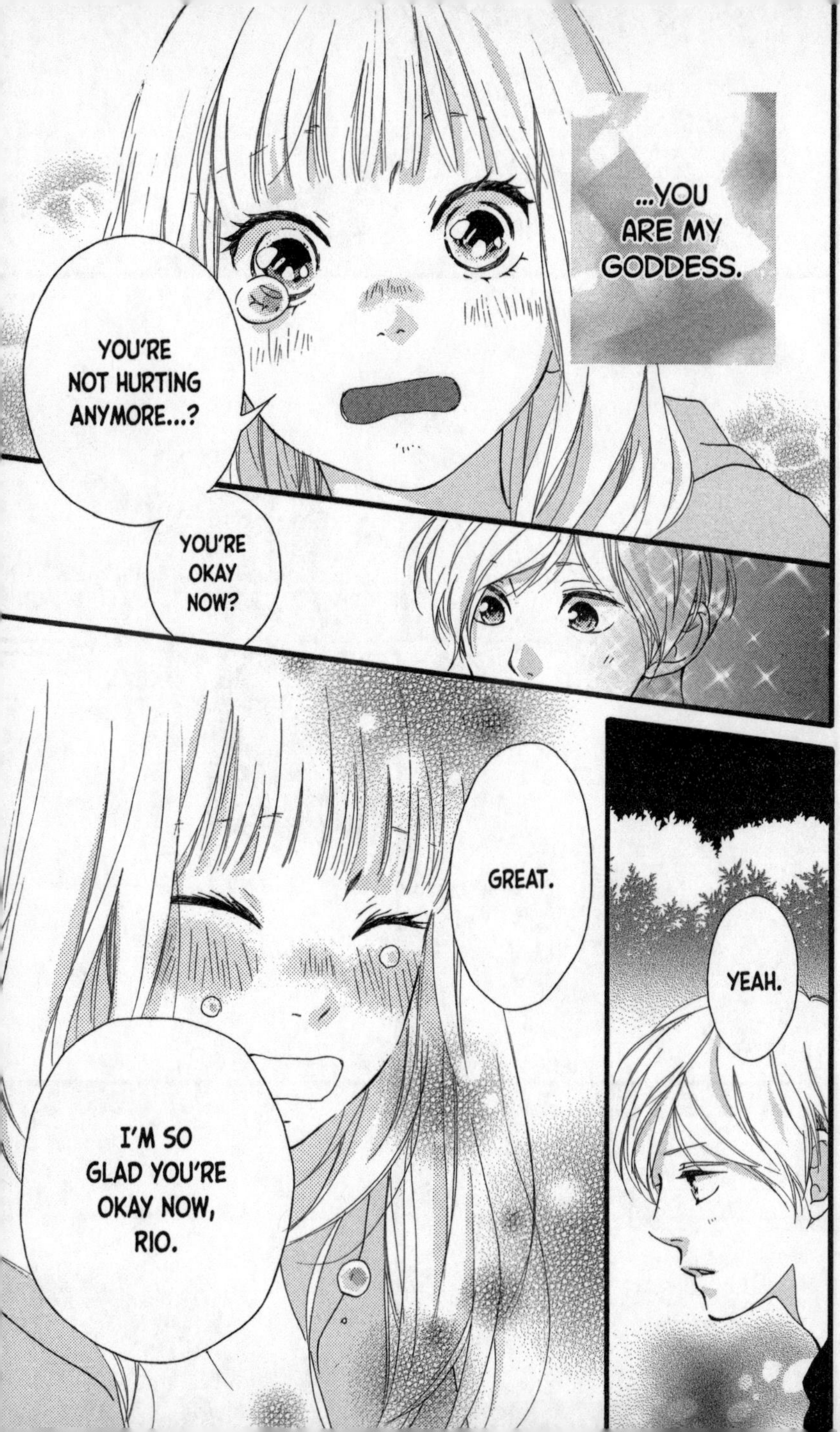
...YOU ARE MY GODDESS.
YOU'RE NOT HURTING ANYMORE...?
YOU'RE OKAY NOW?
YEAH.
GREAT.
I'M SO GLAD YOU'RE OKAY NOW, RIO.

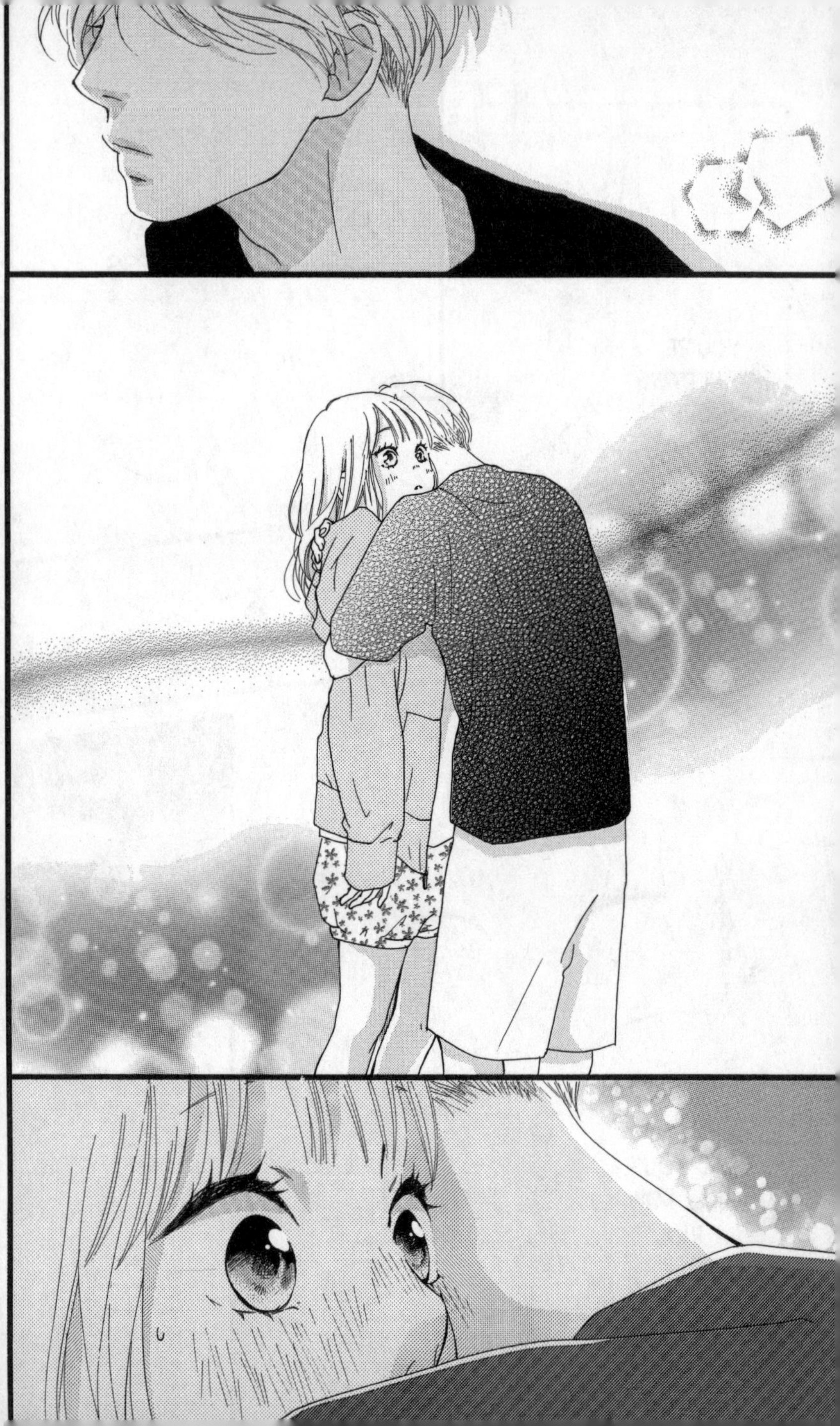

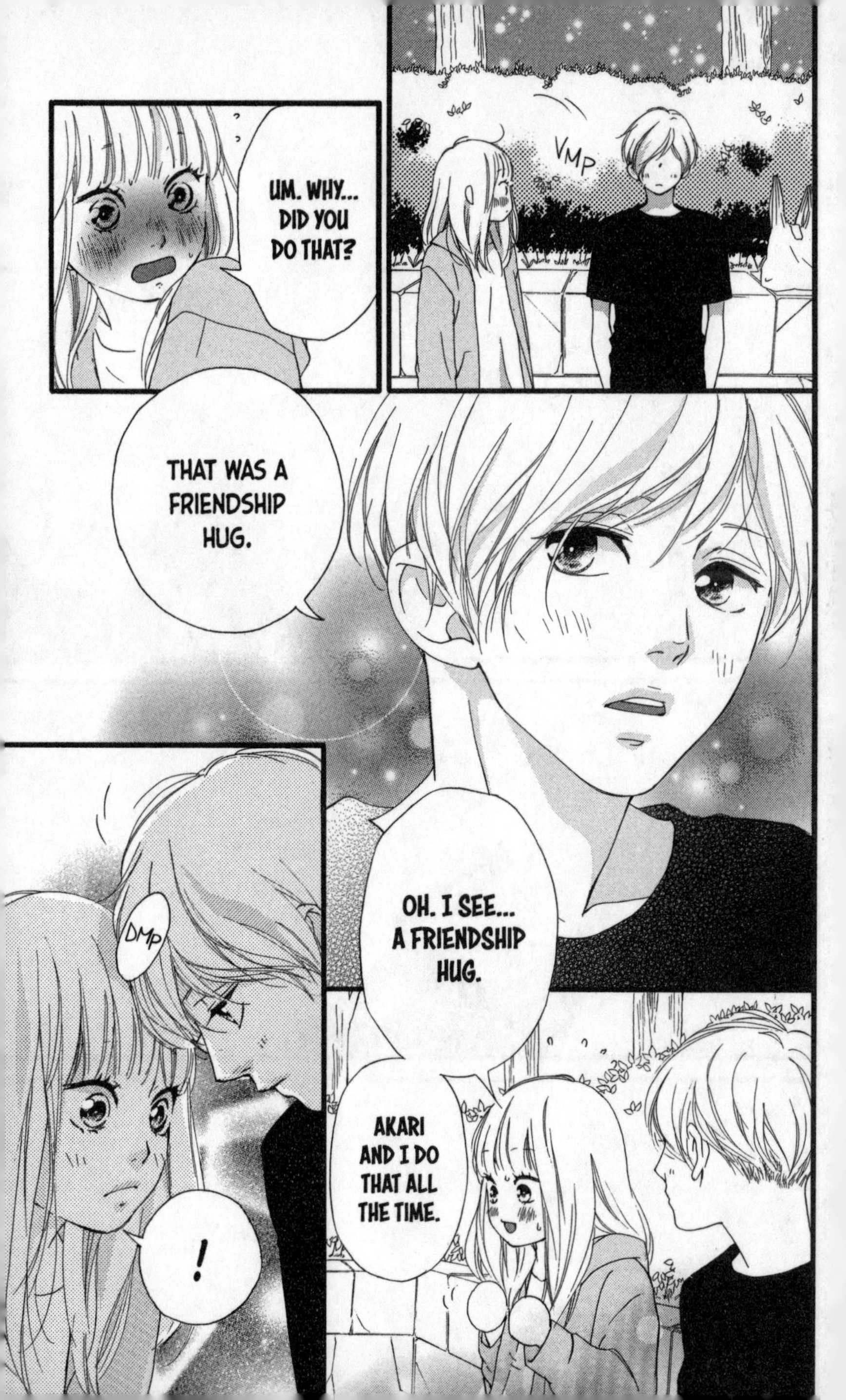
VMP
UM. WHY... DID YOU DO THAT?
THAT WAS A FRIENDSHIP HUG.
OH. I SEE... A FRIENDSHIP HUG.
AKARI AND I DO THAT ALL THE TIME.
DMP
!

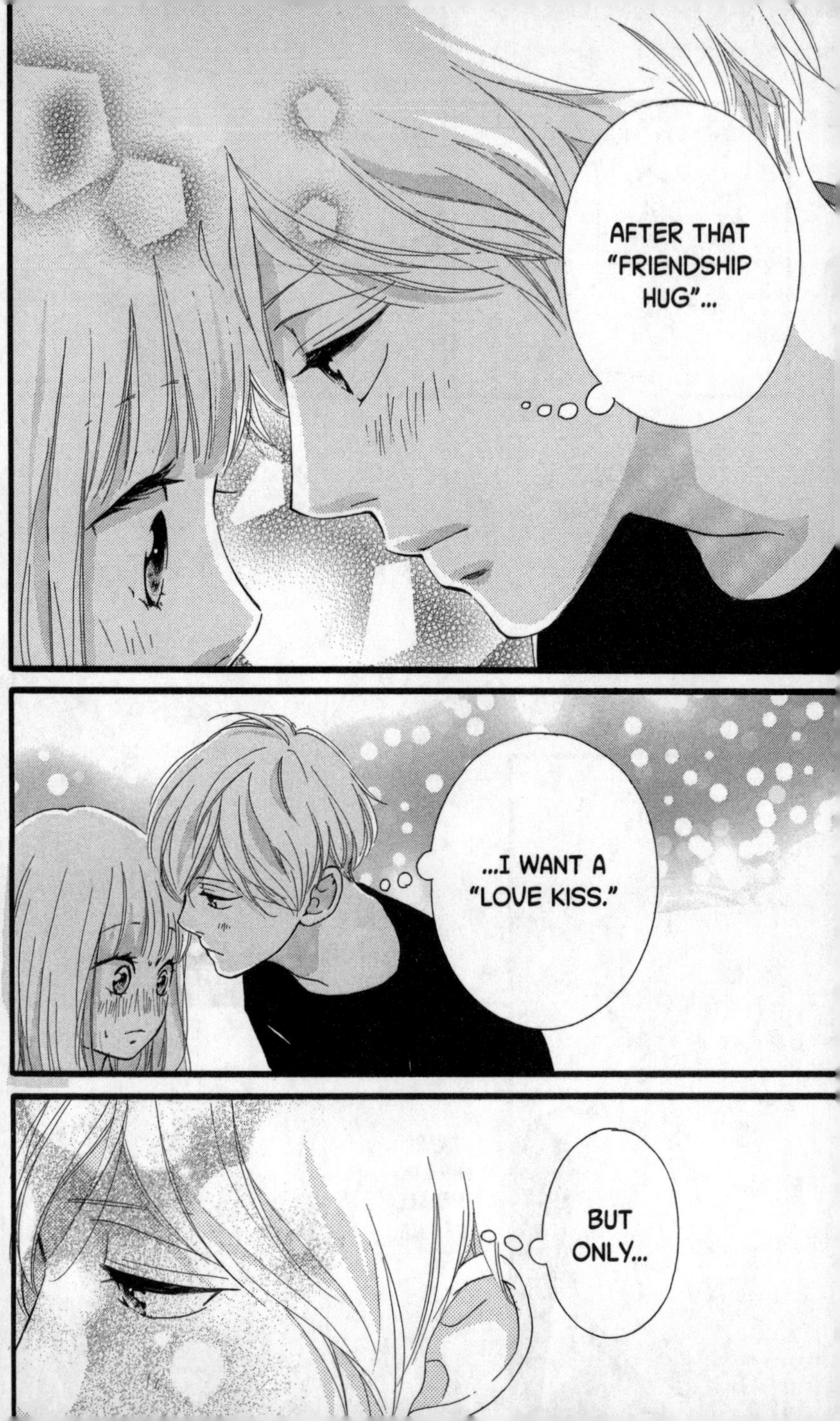
AFTER THAT "FRIENDSHIP HUG"...
...I WANT A "LOVE KISS."
BUT ONLY...

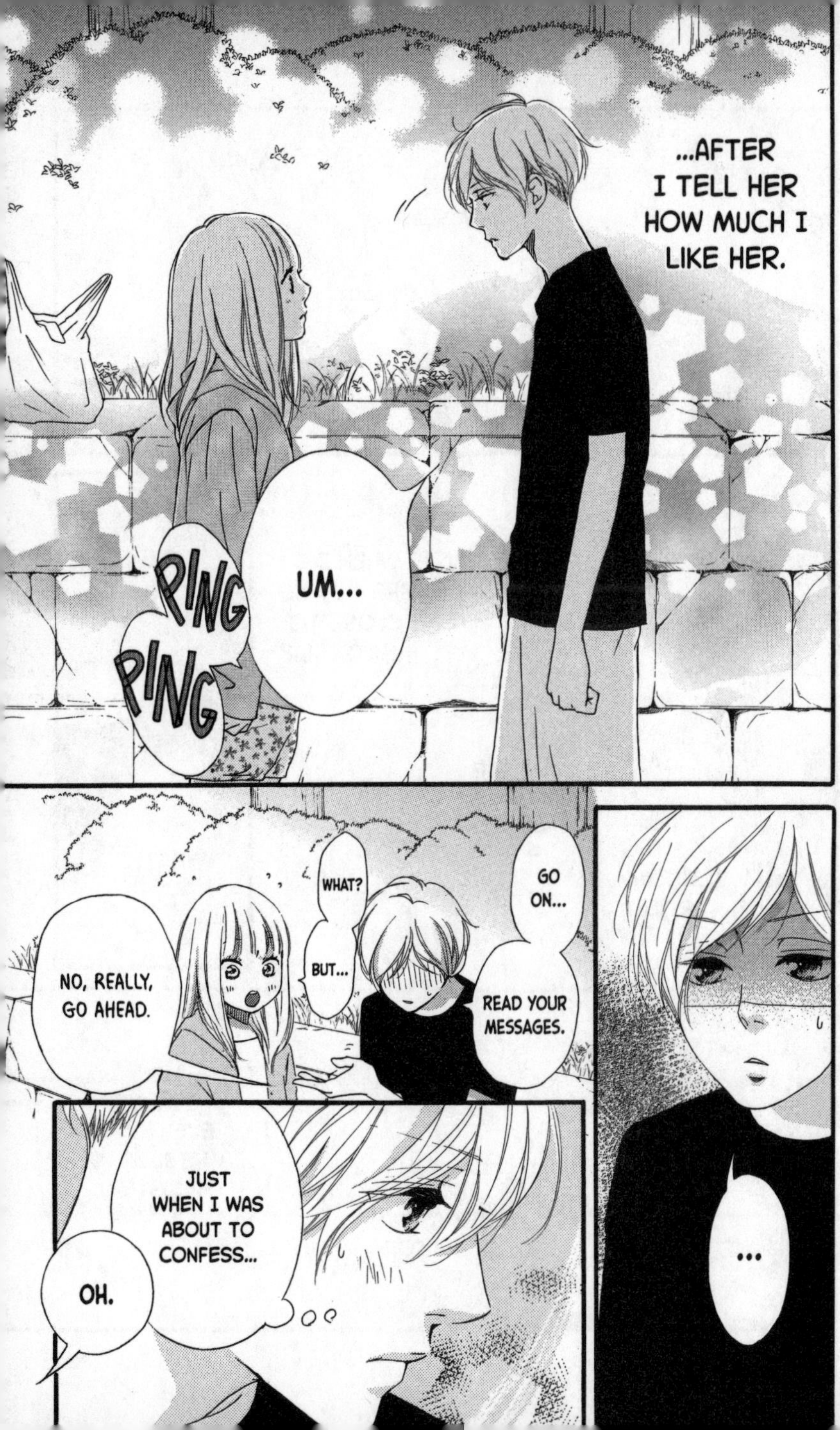
...AFTER I TELL HER HOW MUCH I LIKE HER.
UM...
PING PING
...
GO ON...
READ YOUR MESSAGES.
WHAT?
BUT...
NO, REALLY, GO AHEAD.
JUST WHEN I WAS ABOUT TO CONFESS...
OH.

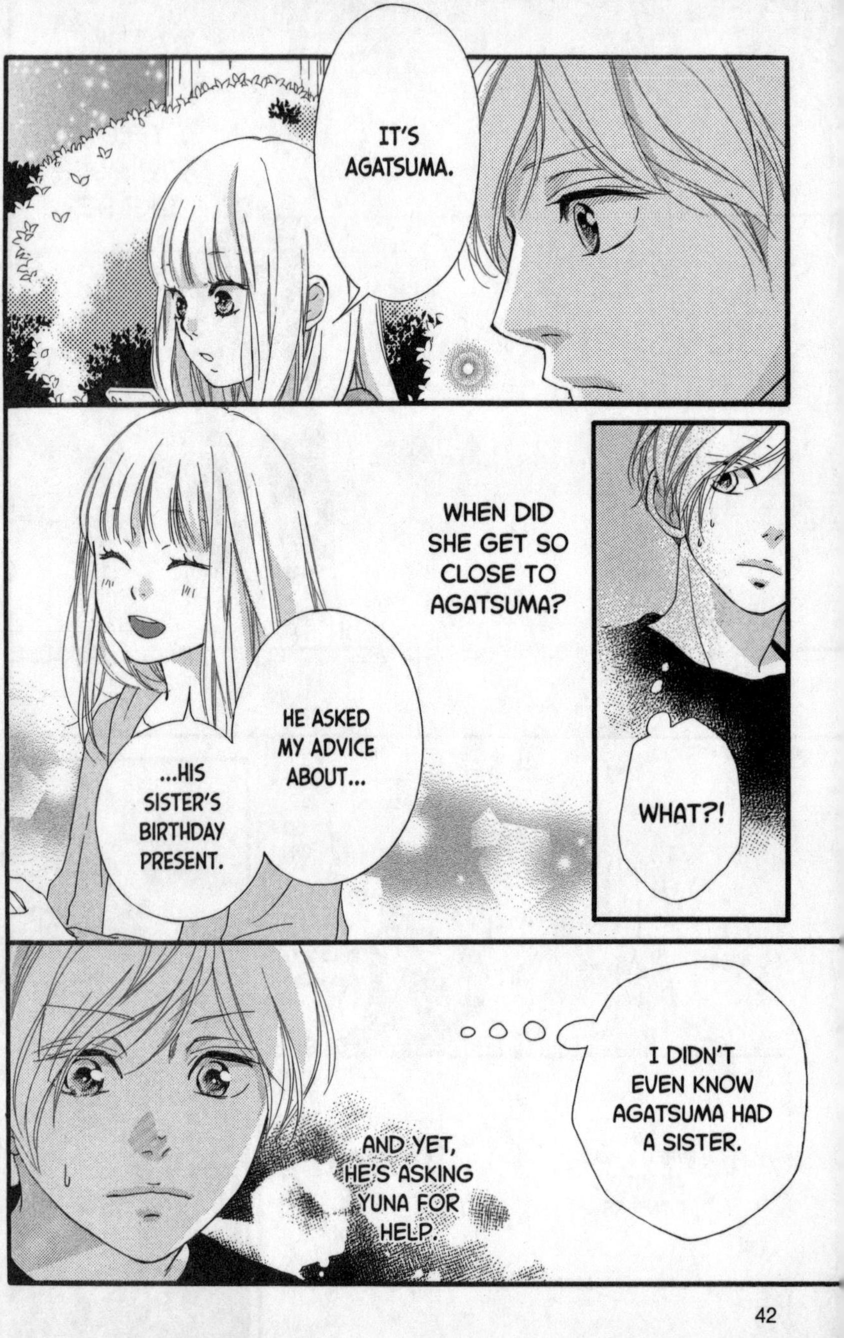
IT'S AGATSUMA.
WHAT?!
WHEN DID SHE GET SO CLOSE TO AGATSUMA?
HE ASKED MY ADVICE ABOUT...
...HIS SISTER'S BIRTHDAY PRESENT.
I DIDN'T EVEN KNOW AGATSUMA HAD A SISTER.
AND YET, HE'S ASKING YUNA FOR HELP.

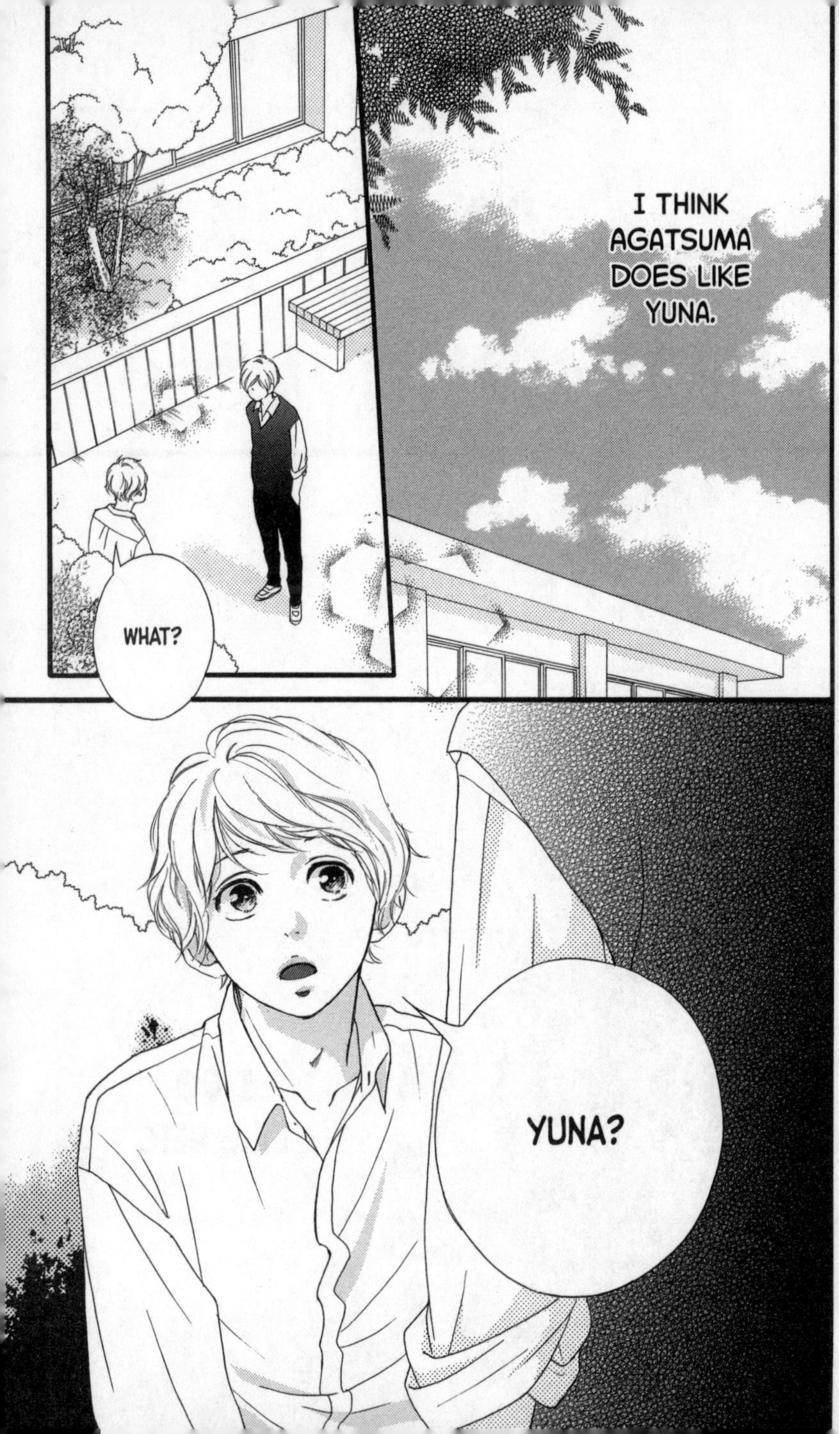
I THINK AGATSUMA DOES LIKE YUNA.
WHAT?
YUNA?

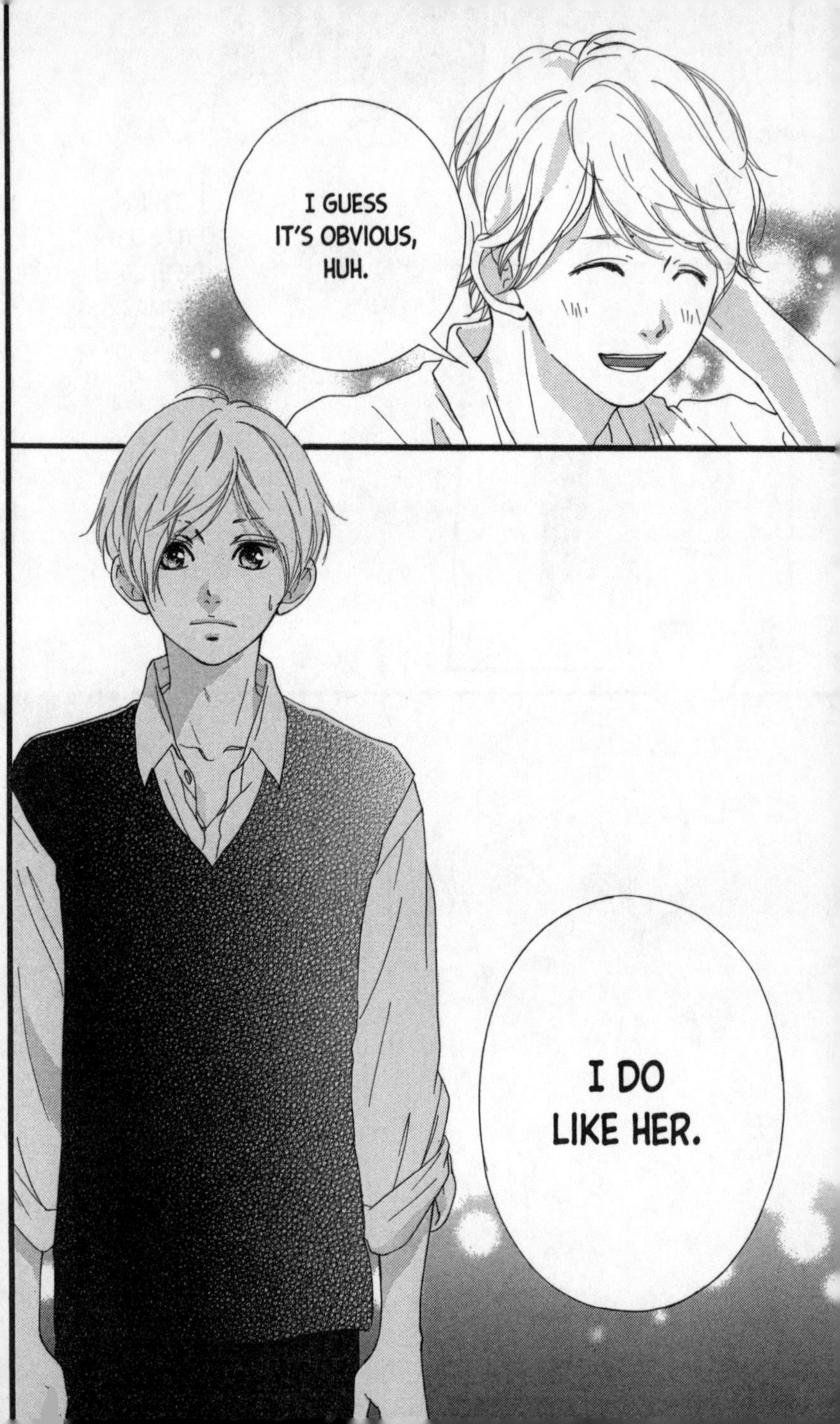
I GUESS IT'S OBVIOUS, HUH.
I DO LIKE HER.

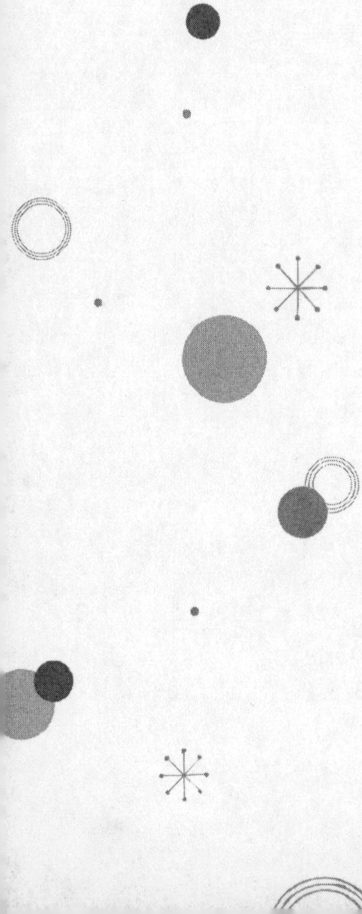

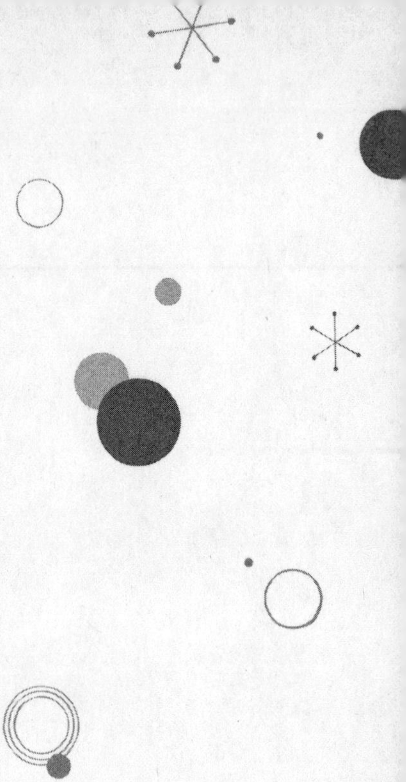

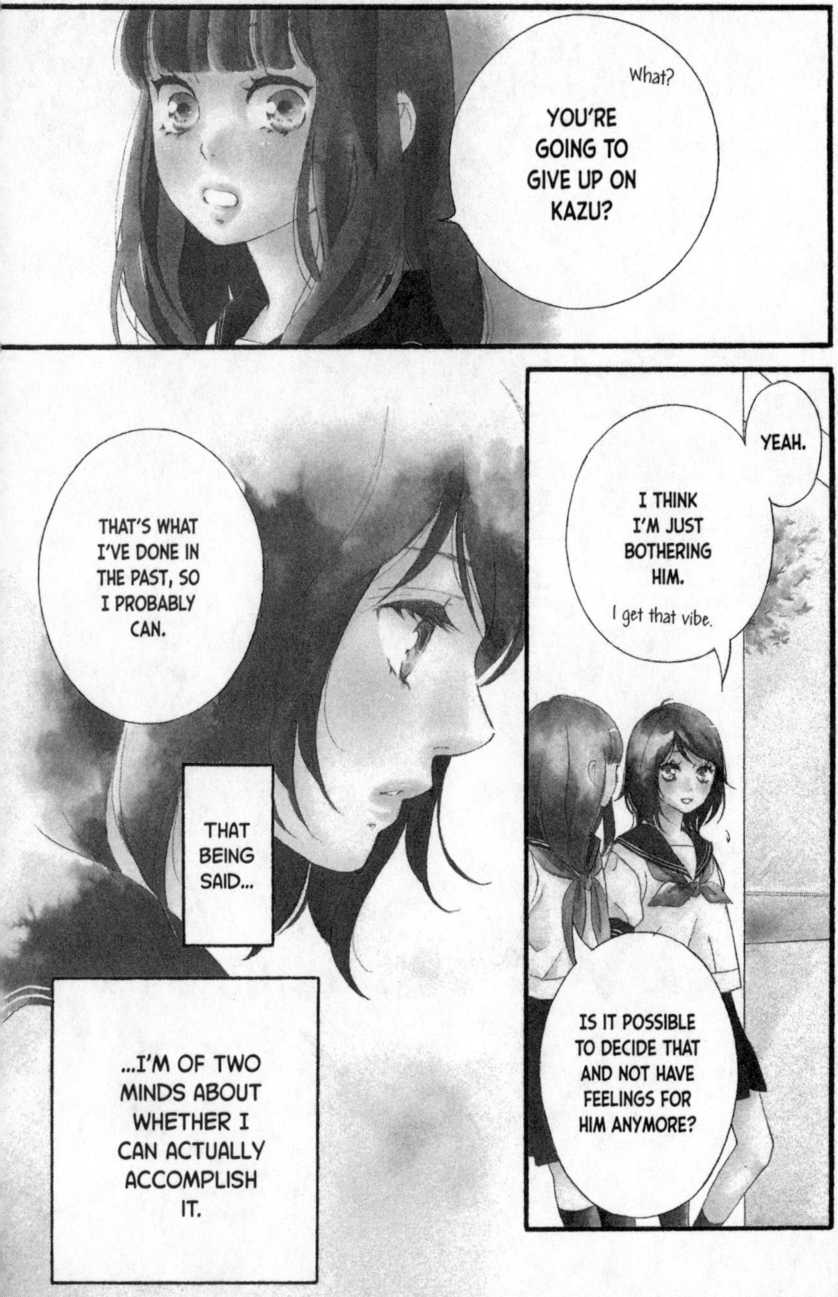
What?
YOU'RE GOING TO GIVE UP ON KAZU?
YEAH.
I THINK I'M JUST BOTHERING HIM.
I get that vibe.
IS IT POSSIBLE TO DECIDE THAT AND NOT HAVE FEELINGS FOR HIM ANYMORE?
THAT'S WHAT I'VE DONE IN THE PAST, SO I PROBABLY CAN.
THAT BEING SAID...
...I'M OF TWO MINDS ABOUT WHETHER I CAN ACTUALLY ACCOMPLISH IT.

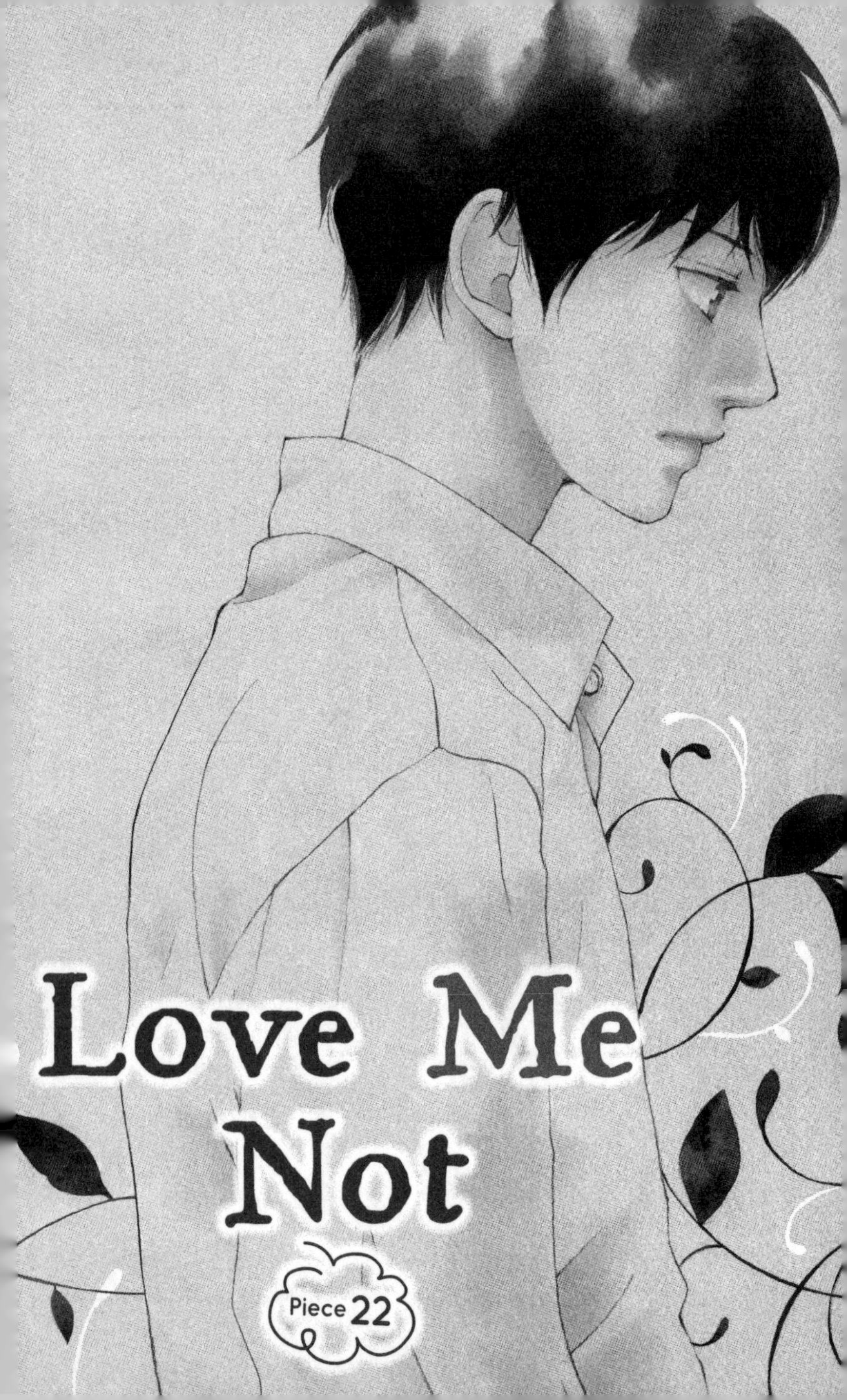
Love Me Not
Piece 22

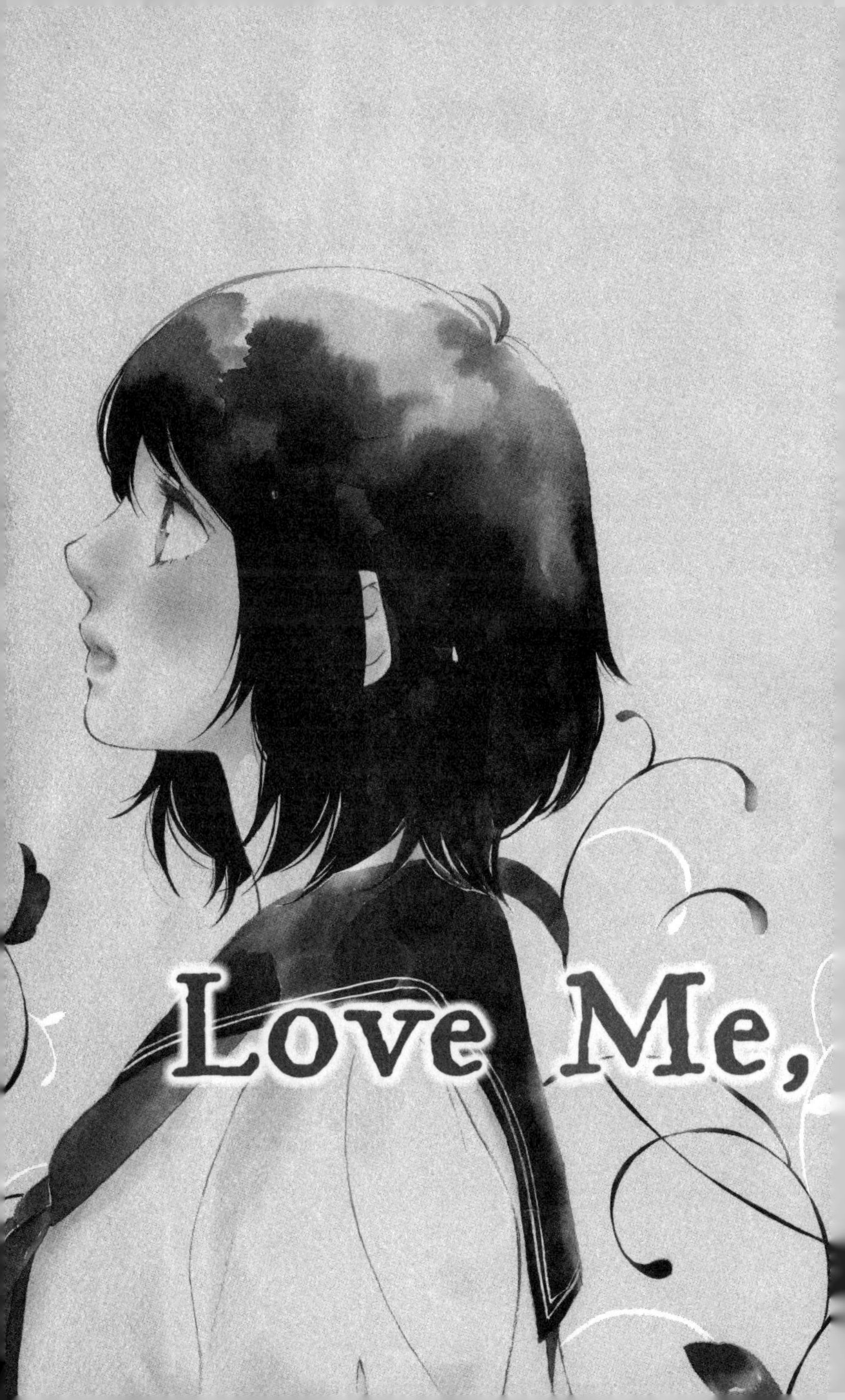
Love Me,

GREETINGS

Hello. I'm Io Sakisaka. Thank you very much for picking up volume 6 of *Love Me, Love Me Not*.

In this volume, the school festival is finally here. I do enjoy drawing school events. That doesn't mean ideas come bubbling up, but it's fun to be able to show the characters in a different way than usual. For the various things at the festival, I asked my assistants what kinds of events they had in the past. Then I had fun trying to work those things into the story. While creating the different parts, I thought, "I want to sneak into a festival at a random high school!" It looks like so much fun. So I may turn up one day at some high school somewhere (or maybe not). I'm not particularly sure what it is I'm declaring, but for the time being, volume 6 serves as a welcome to the school festival for *Love Me, Love Me Not*. Please stay with me through the end.

 Io Sakisaka

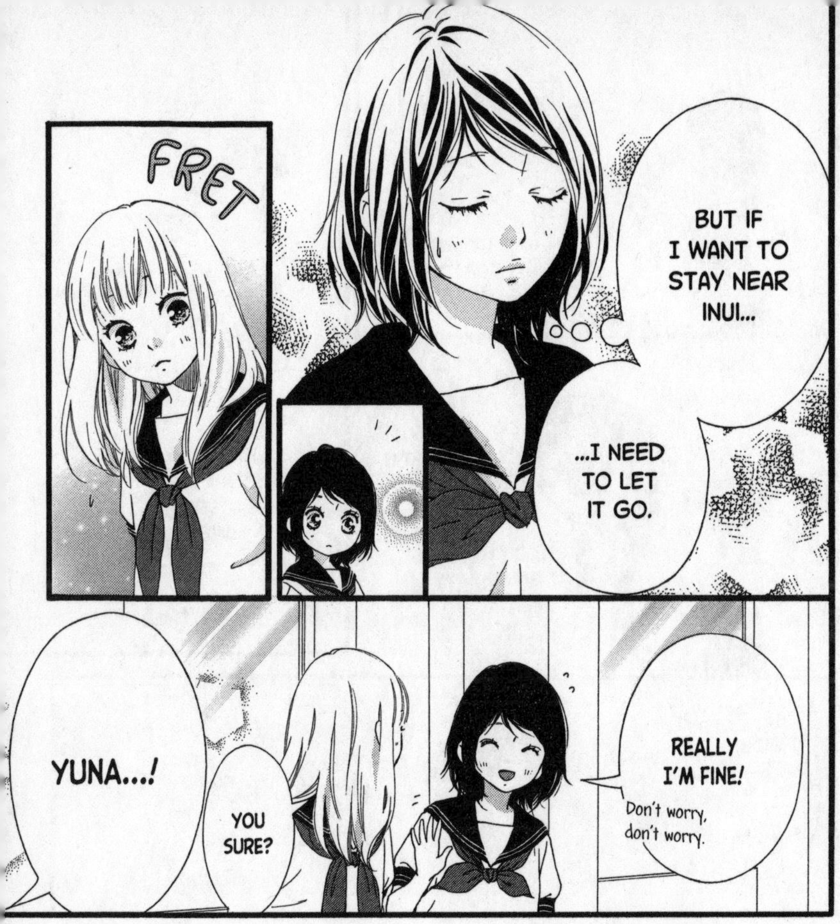
BUT IF I WANT TO STAY NEAR INUI...
...I NEED TO LET IT GO.
FRET
REALLY I'M FINE!
Don't worry, don't worry.
YOU SURE?
YUNA...!

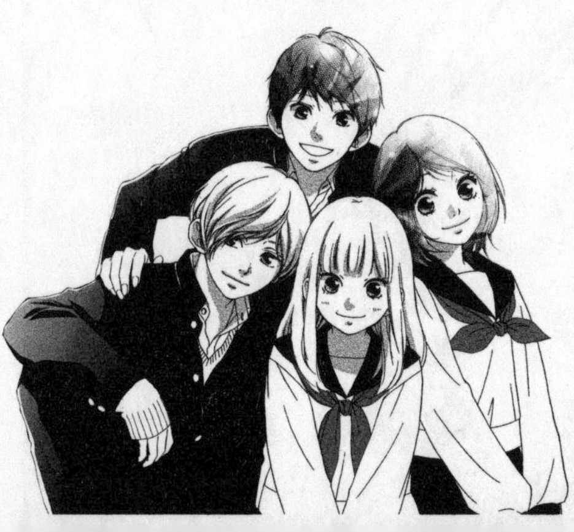

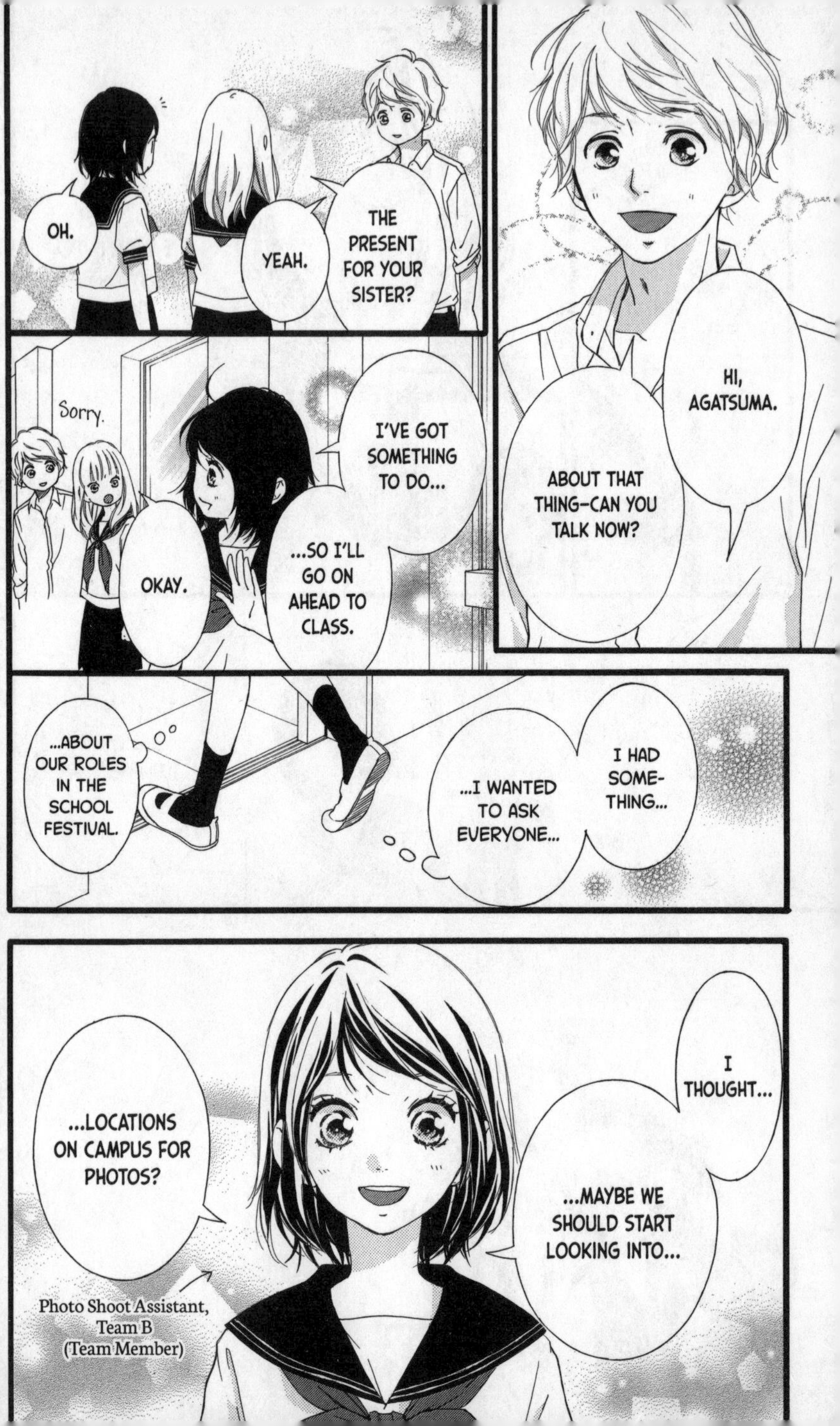
HI, AGATSUMA.
ABOUT THAT THING—CAN YOU TALK NOW?
THE PRESENT FOR YOUR SISTER?
YEAH.
OH.
I'VE GOT SOMETHING TO DO...
...SO I'LL GO ON AHEAD TO CLASS.
Sorry.
OKAY.
I HAD SOME-THING...
...I WANTED TO ASK EVERYONE...
...ABOUT OUR ROLES IN THE SCHOOL FESTIVAL.
I THOUGHT...
...MAYBE WE SHOULD START LOOKING INTO...
...LOCATIONS ON CAMPUS FOR PHOTOS?
Photo Shoot Assistant, Team B (Team Member)

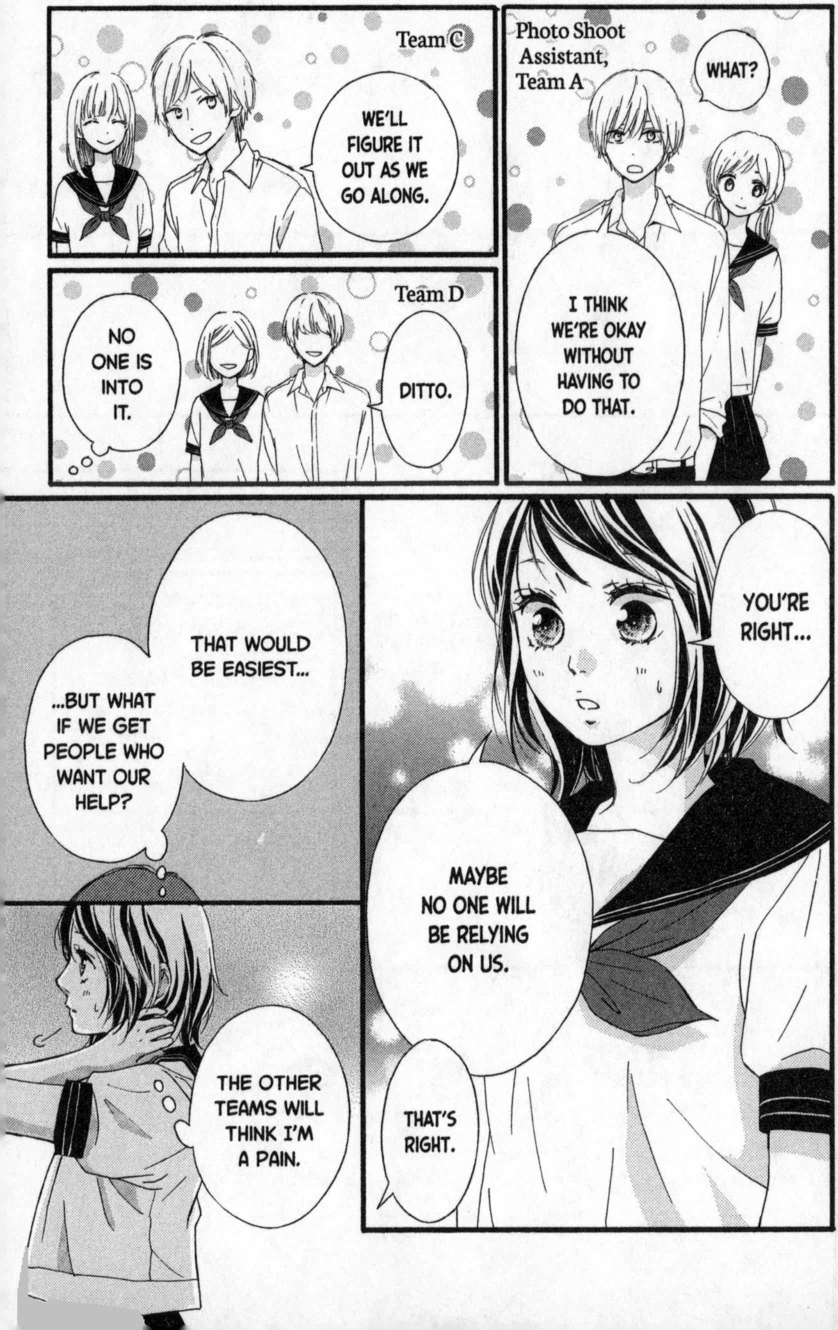
Photo Shoot Assistant, Team A
WHAT?
I THINK WE'RE OKAY WITHOUT HAVING TO DO THAT.
Team C
WE'LL FIGURE IT OUT AS WE GO ALONG.
Team D
DITTO.
NO ONE IS INTO IT.
YOU'RE RIGHT...
MAYBE NO ONE WILL BE RELYING ON US.
THAT'S RIGHT.
THAT WOULD BE EASIEST...
...BUT WHAT IF WE GET PEOPLE WHO WANT OUR HELP?
THE OTHER TEAMS WILL THINK I'M A PAIN.

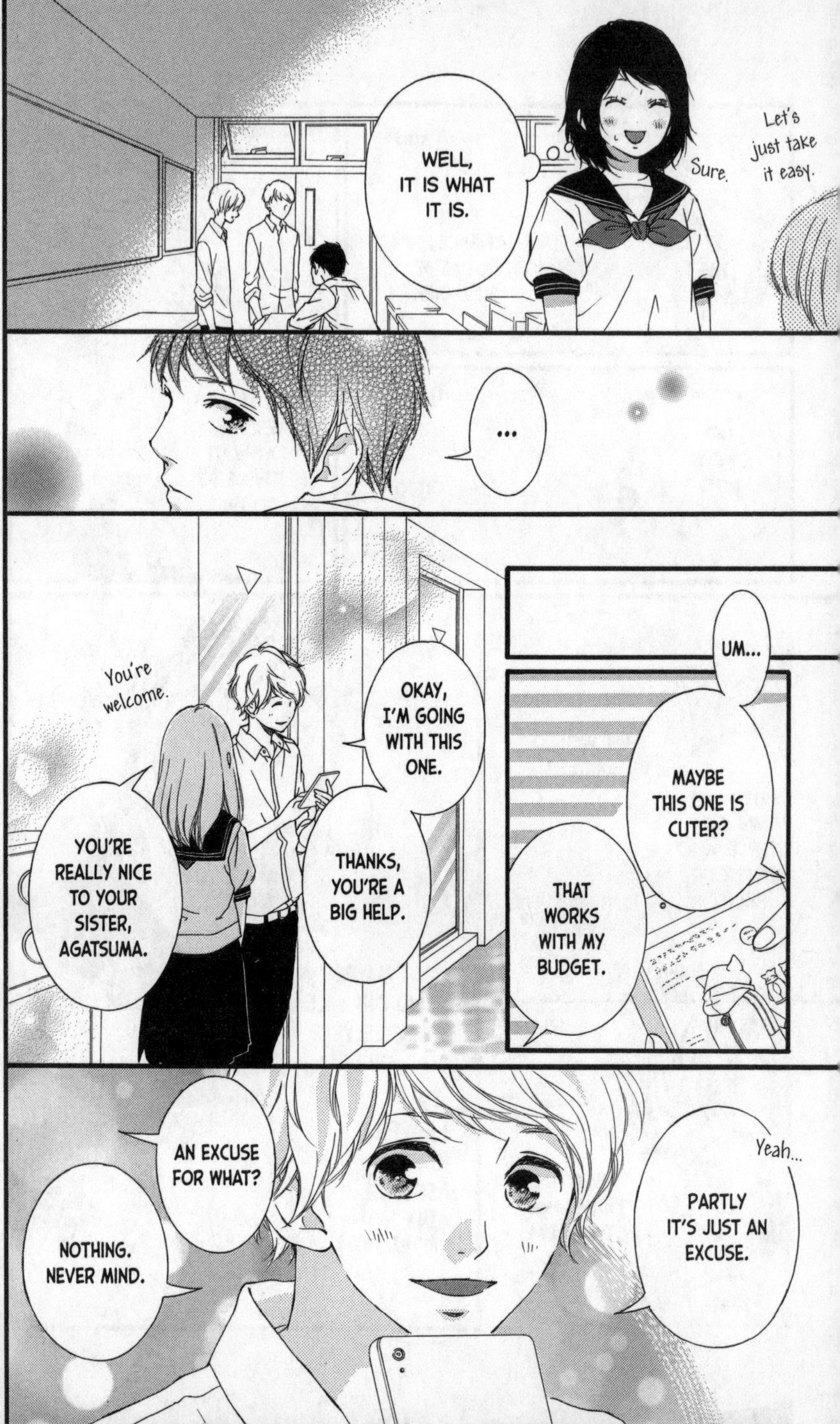
Let's just take it easy.
Sure.
WELL, IT IS WHAT IT IS.
...
UM...
MAYBE THIS ONE IS CUTER?
THAT WORKS WITH MY BUDGET.
OKAY, I'M GOING WITH THIS ONE.
THANKS, YOU'RE A BIG HELP.
You're welcome.
YOU'RE REALLY NICE TO YOUR SISTER, AGATSUMA.
Yeah...
PARTLY IT'S JUST AN EXCUSE.
AN EXCUSE FOR WHAT?
NOTHING. NEVER MIND.

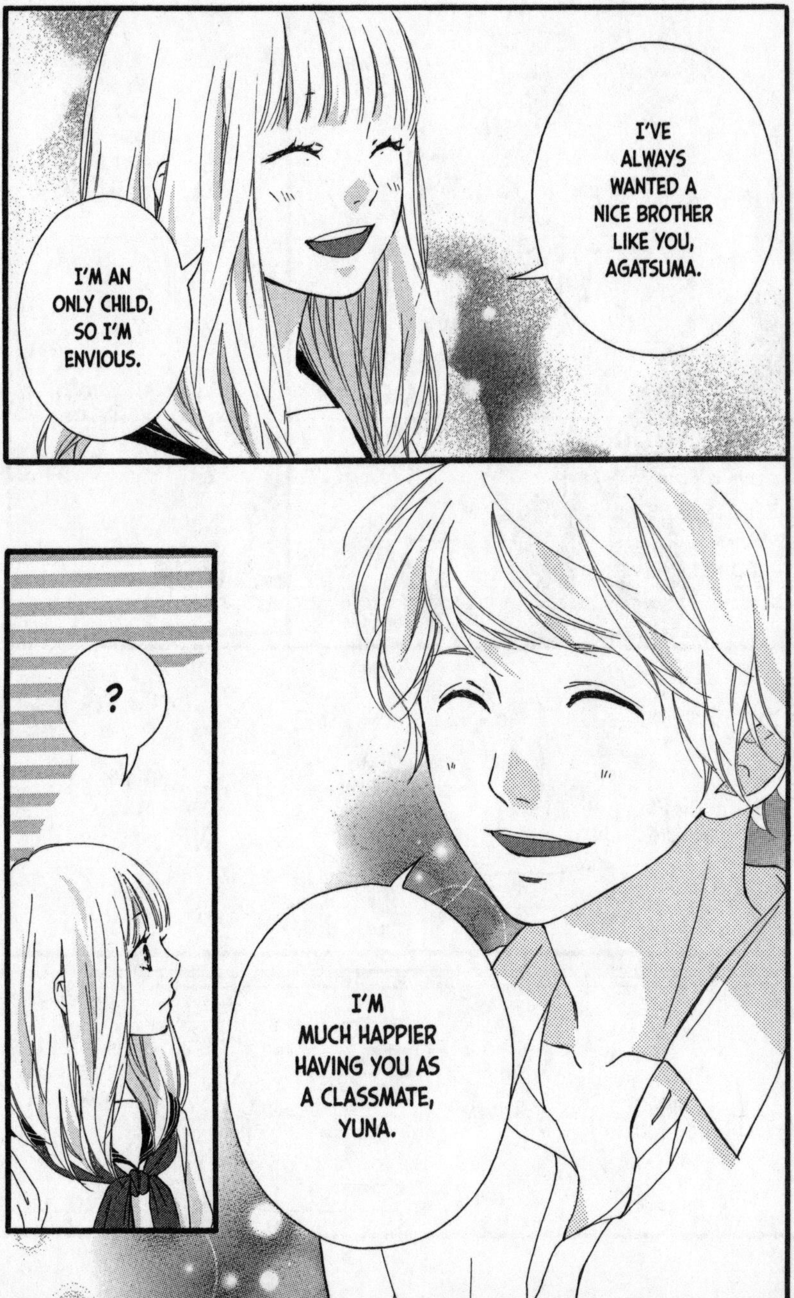
I'VE ALWAYS WANTED A NICE BROTHER LIKE YOU, AGATSUMA.
I'M AN ONLY CHILD, SO I'M ENVIOUS.
I'M MUCH HAPPIER HAVING YOU AS A CLASSMATE, YUNA.
?

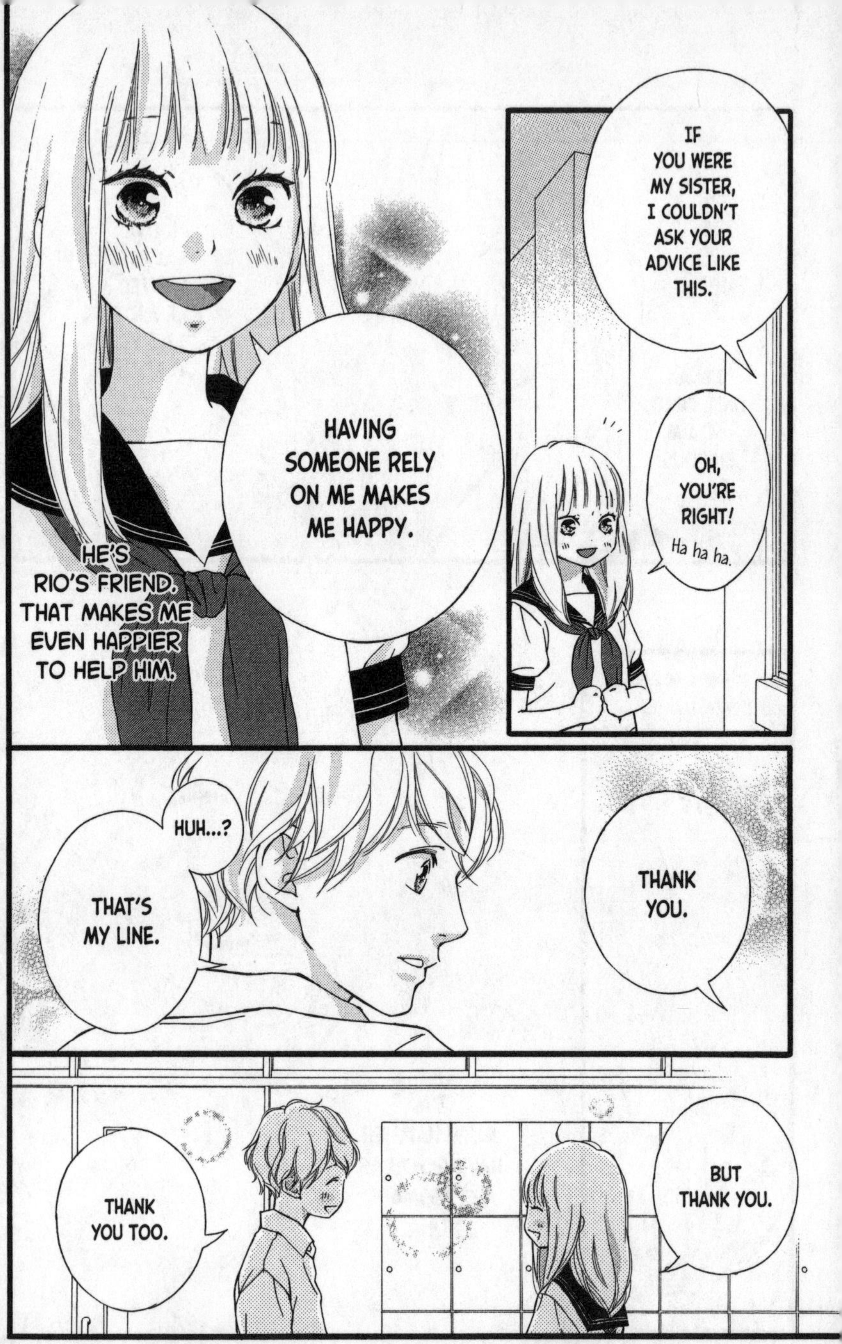
IF YOU WERE MY SISTER, I COULDN'T ASK YOUR ADVICE LIKE THIS.
OH, YOU'RE RIGHT!
Ha ha ha.
HAVING SOMEONE RELY ON ME MAKES ME HAPPY.
HE'S RIO'S FRIEND. THAT MAKES ME EVEN HAPPIER TO HELP HIM.
THANK YOU.
HUH...?
THAT'S MY LINE.
BUT THANK YOU.
THANK YOU TOO.

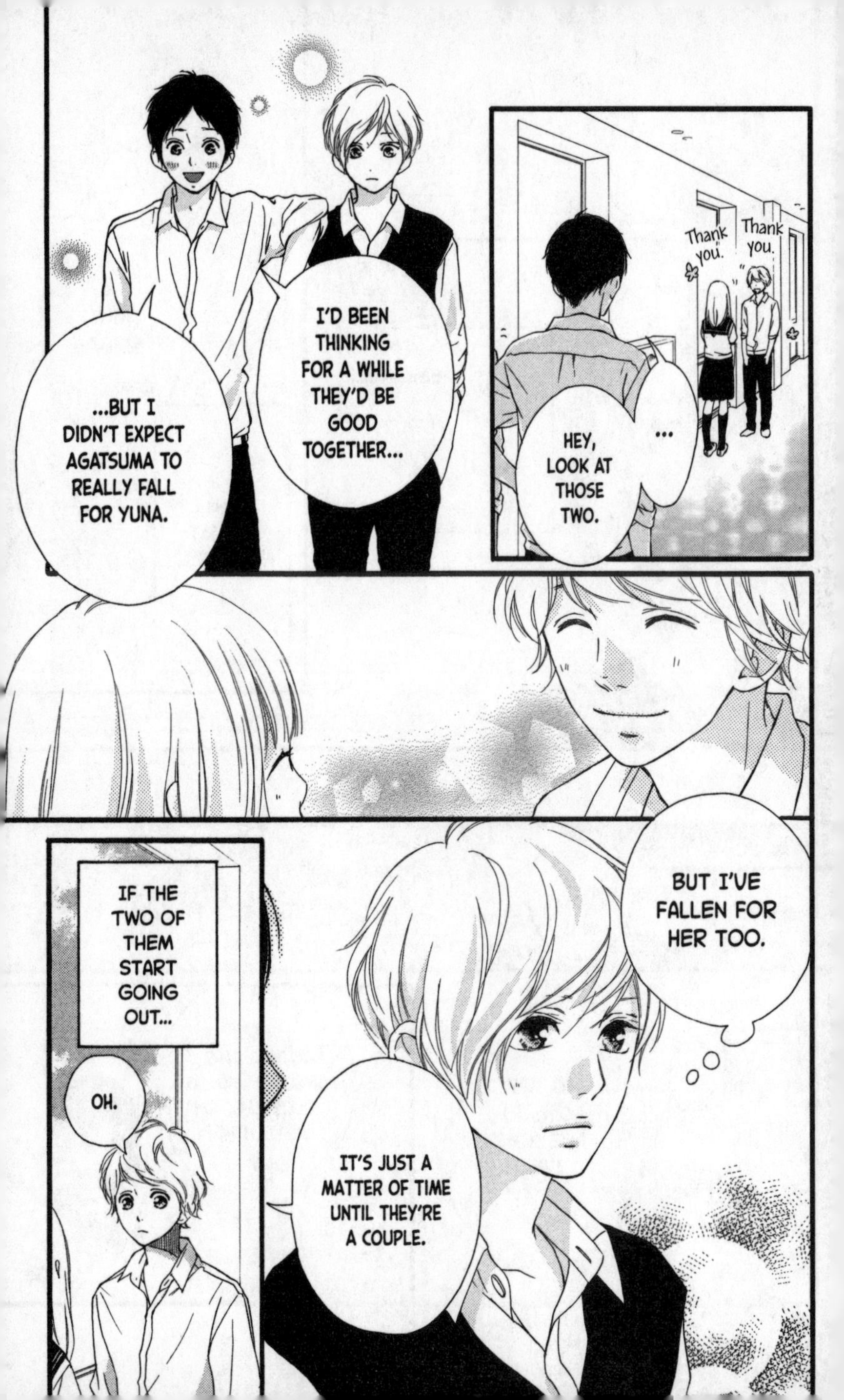
Thank you.
Thank you.
...
HEY, LOOK AT THOSE TWO.
I'D BEEN THINKING FOR A WHILE THEY'D BE GOOD TOGETHER...
...BUT I DIDN'T EXPECT AGATSUMA TO REALLY FALL FOR YUNA.
BUT I'VE FALLEN FOR HER TOO.
IT'S JUST A MATTER OF TIME UNTIL THEY'RE A COUPLE.
IF THE TWO OF THEM START GOING OUT...
OH.

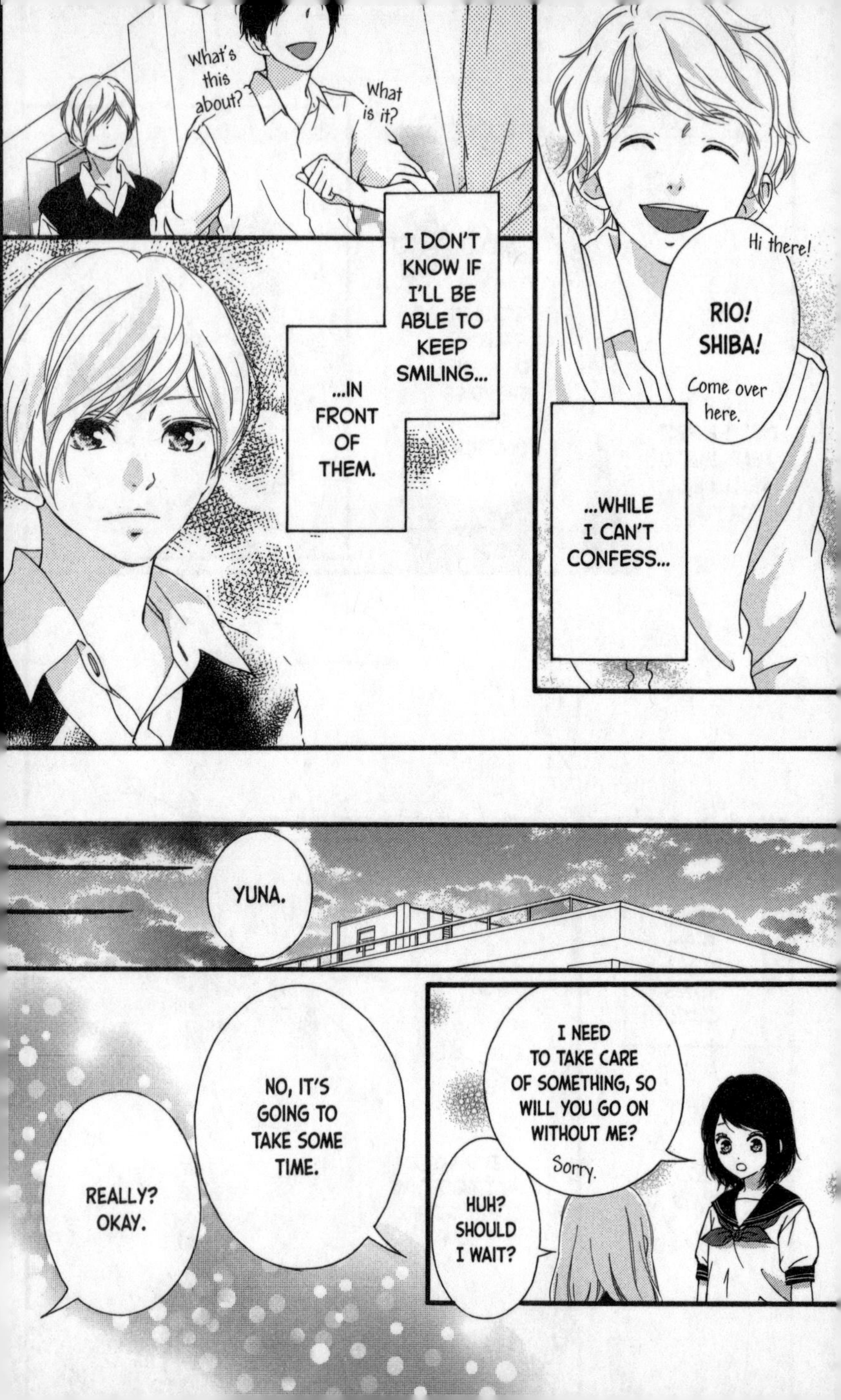
Hi there!
RIO! SHIBA!
Come over here.
...WHILE I CAN'T CONFESS...
What is it?
What's this about?
I DON'T KNOW IF I'LL BE ABLE TO KEEP SMILING...
...IN FRONT OF THEM.
YUNA.
I NEED TO TAKE CARE OF SOMETHING, SO WILL YOU GO ON WITHOUT ME?
Sorry.
HUH? SHOULD I WAIT?
NO, IT'S GOING TO TAKE SOME TIME.
REALLY? OKAY.

Our chinchilla Andrew (14 years old) began losing his appetite one day. We tried changing his food, but he still wouldn't eat any (except his favorite—apples—which he still devoured). I thought it might be malocclusion and took him to the hospital, but they couldn't find anything wrong. They told me, "Well, he's at the age where anything could happen, so just be prepared." I brought him home, but I couldn't give up, so I took him to a different hospital. When they finished examining him, they thought one of his molars might be growing slightly inward. While they weren't sure it would be a fix (all other tests came back negative), they cut his tooth just a tiny bit. Since then he's made a great recovery. Thank goodness! Teeth are so important for both animals and people.

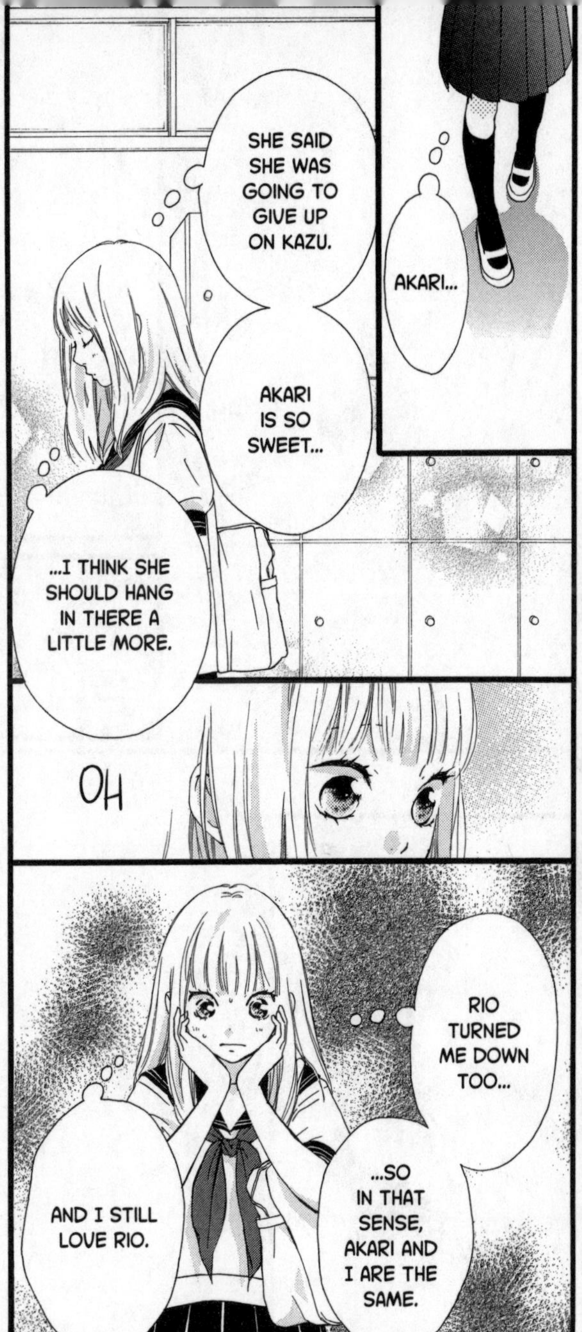
AKARI...
SHE SAID SHE WAS GOING TO GIVE UP ON KAZU.
AKARI IS SO SWEET...
...I THINK SHE SHOULD HANG IN THERE A LITTLE MORE.
OH
RIO TURNED ME DOWN TOO...
...SO IN THAT SENSE, AKARI AND I ARE THE SAME.
AND I STILL LOVE RIO.

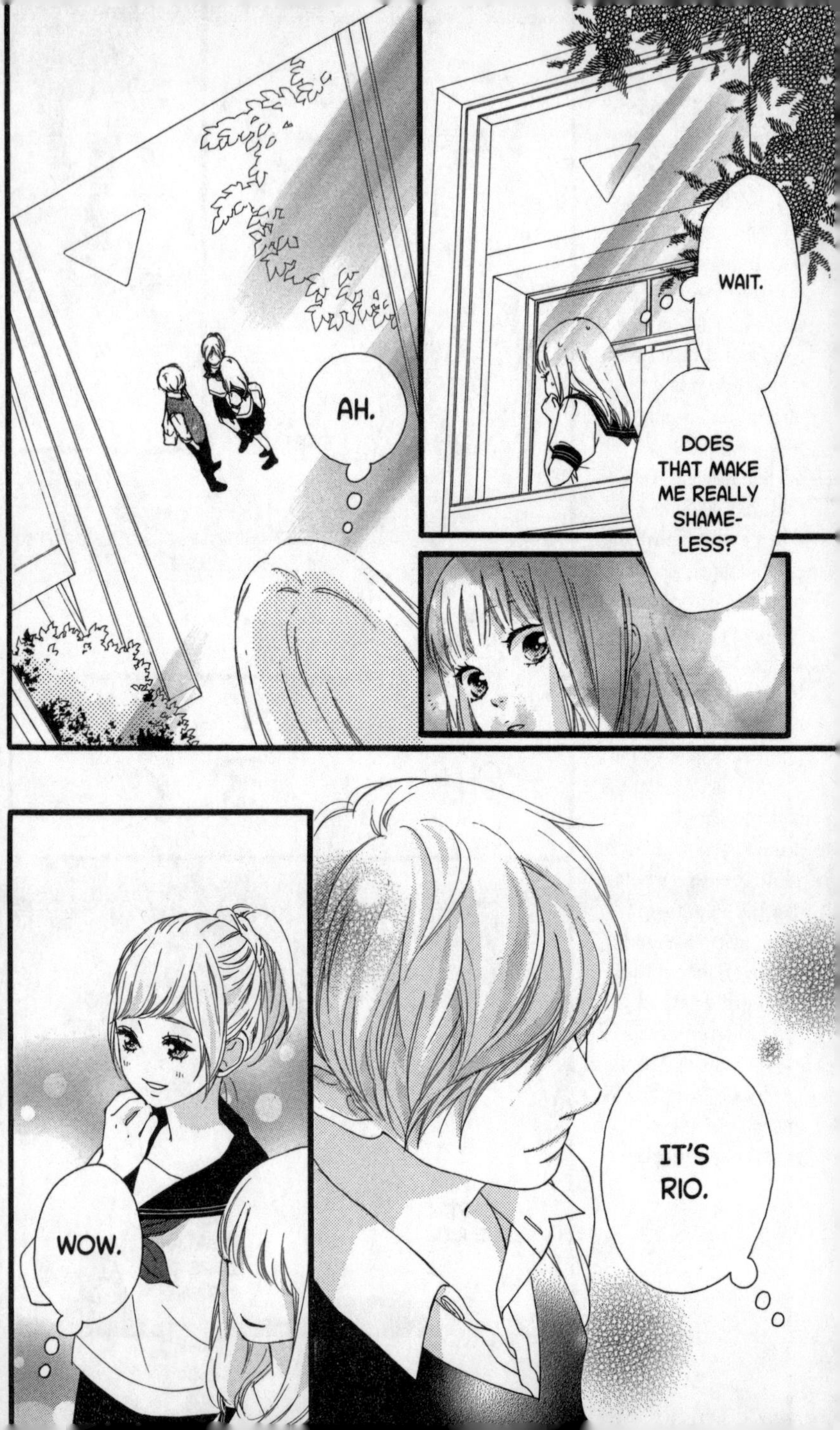
WAIT.
DOES THAT MAKE ME REALLY SHAME-LESS?
AH.
IT'S RIO.
WOW.

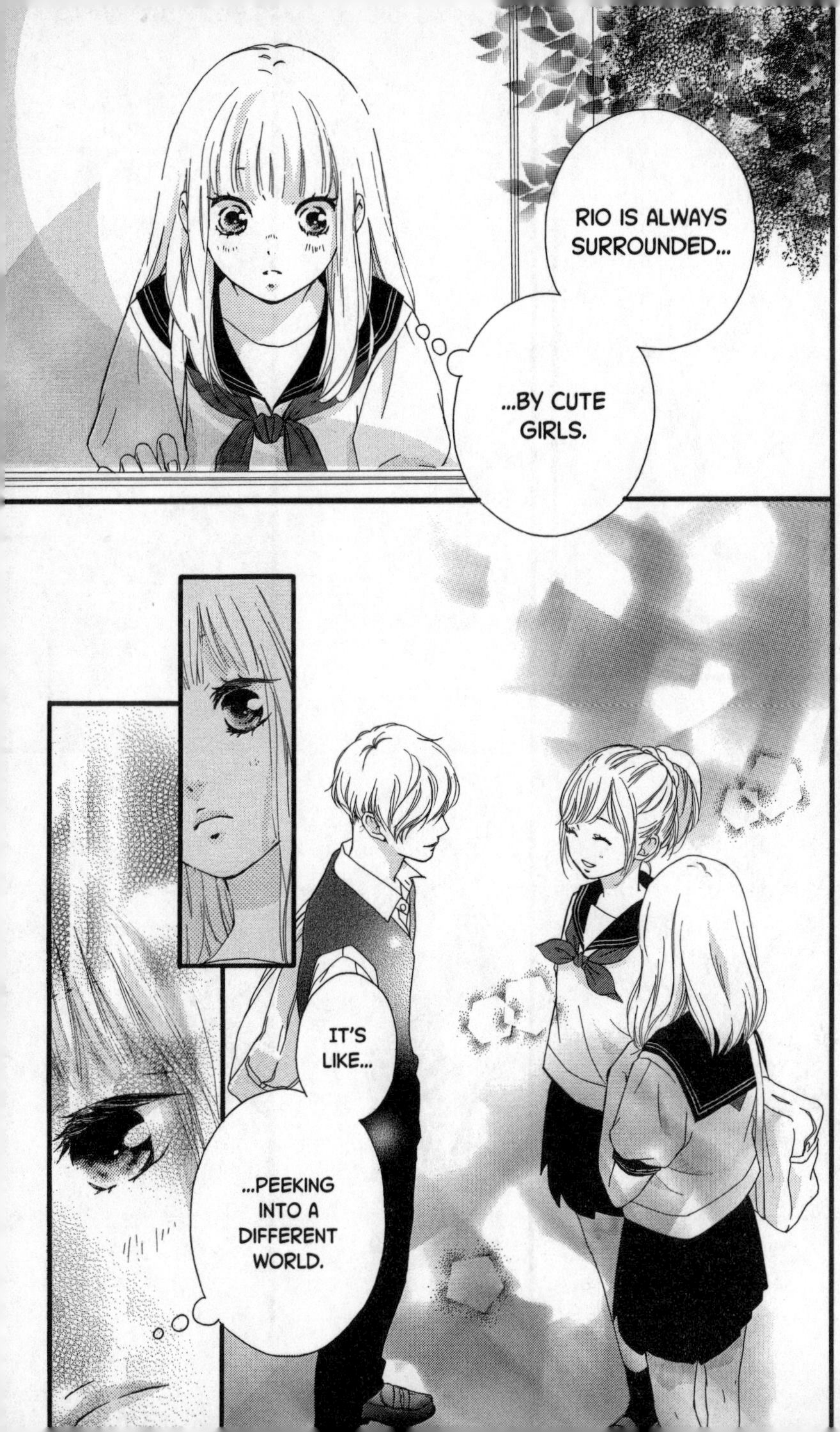
RIO IS ALWAYS SURROUNDED...
...BY CUTE GIRLS.
IT'S LIKE...
...PEEKING INTO A DIFFERENT WORLD.

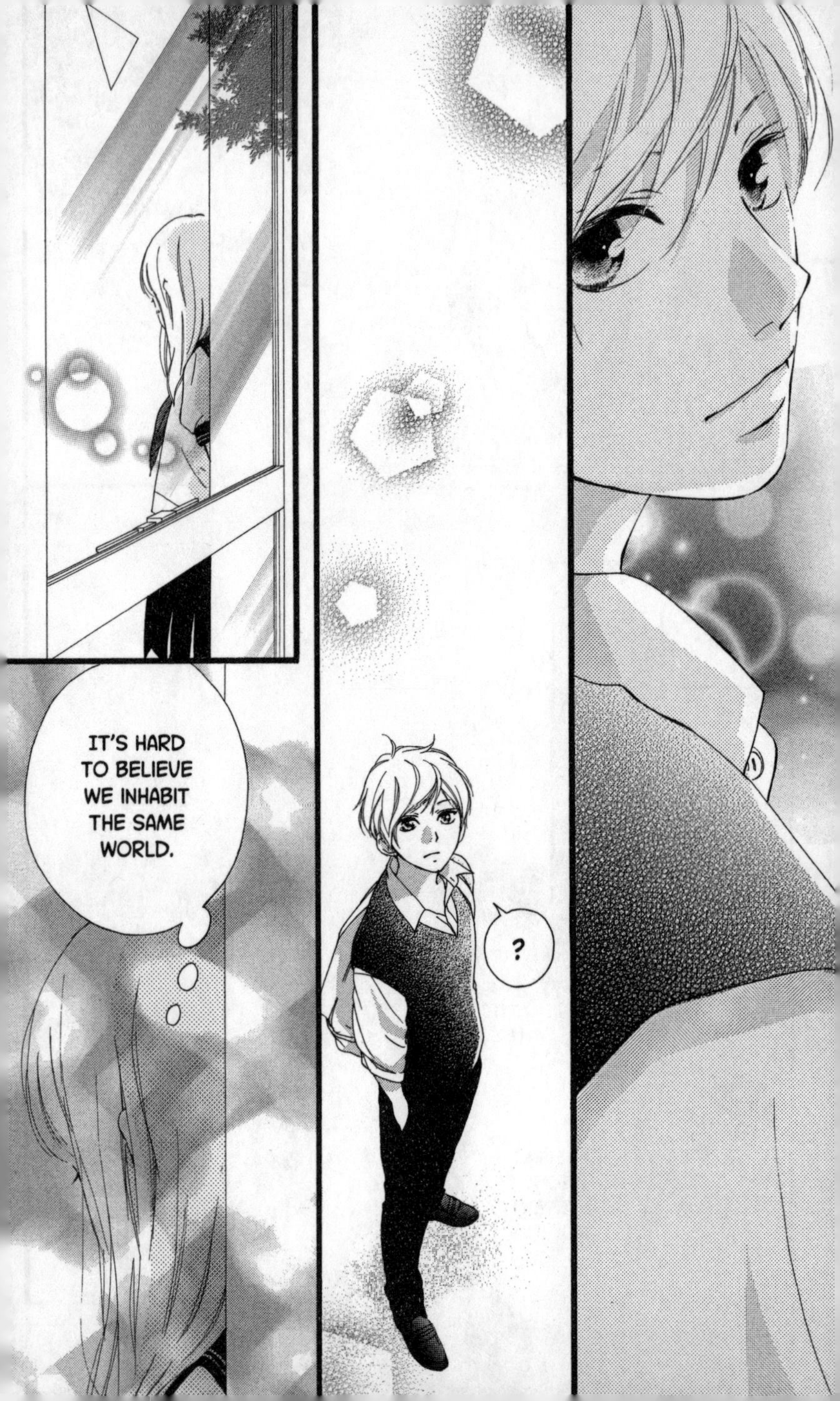
?
IT'S HARD TO BELIEVE WE INHABIT THE SAME WORLD.

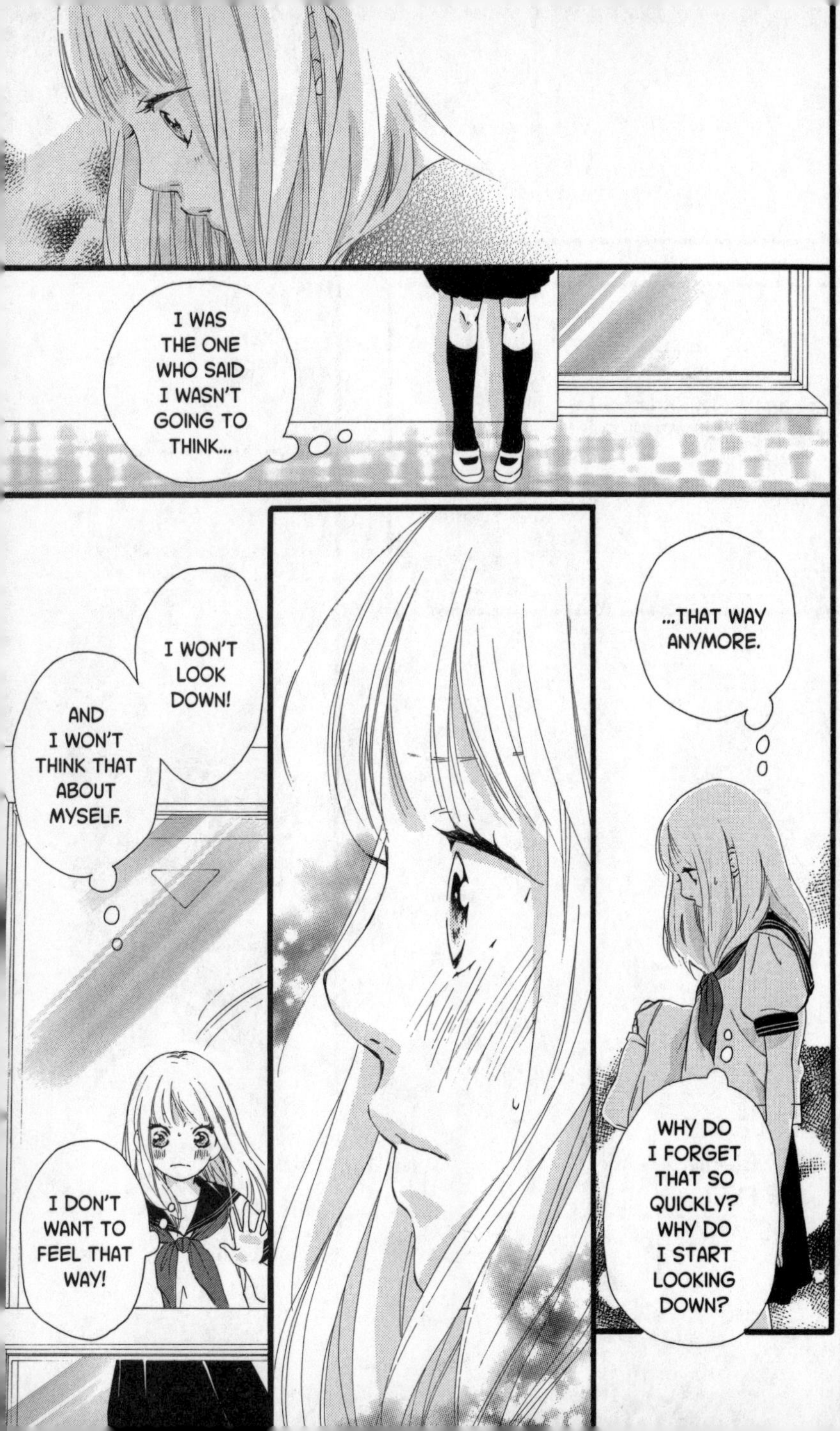
I WAS THE ONE WHO SAID I WASN'T GOING TO THINK...
...THAT WAY ANYMORE.
WHY DO I FORGET THAT SO QUICKLY? WHY DO I START LOOKING DOWN?
I WON'T LOOK DOWN!
AND I WON'T THINK THAT ABOUT MYSELF.
I DON'T WANT TO FEEL THAT WAY!

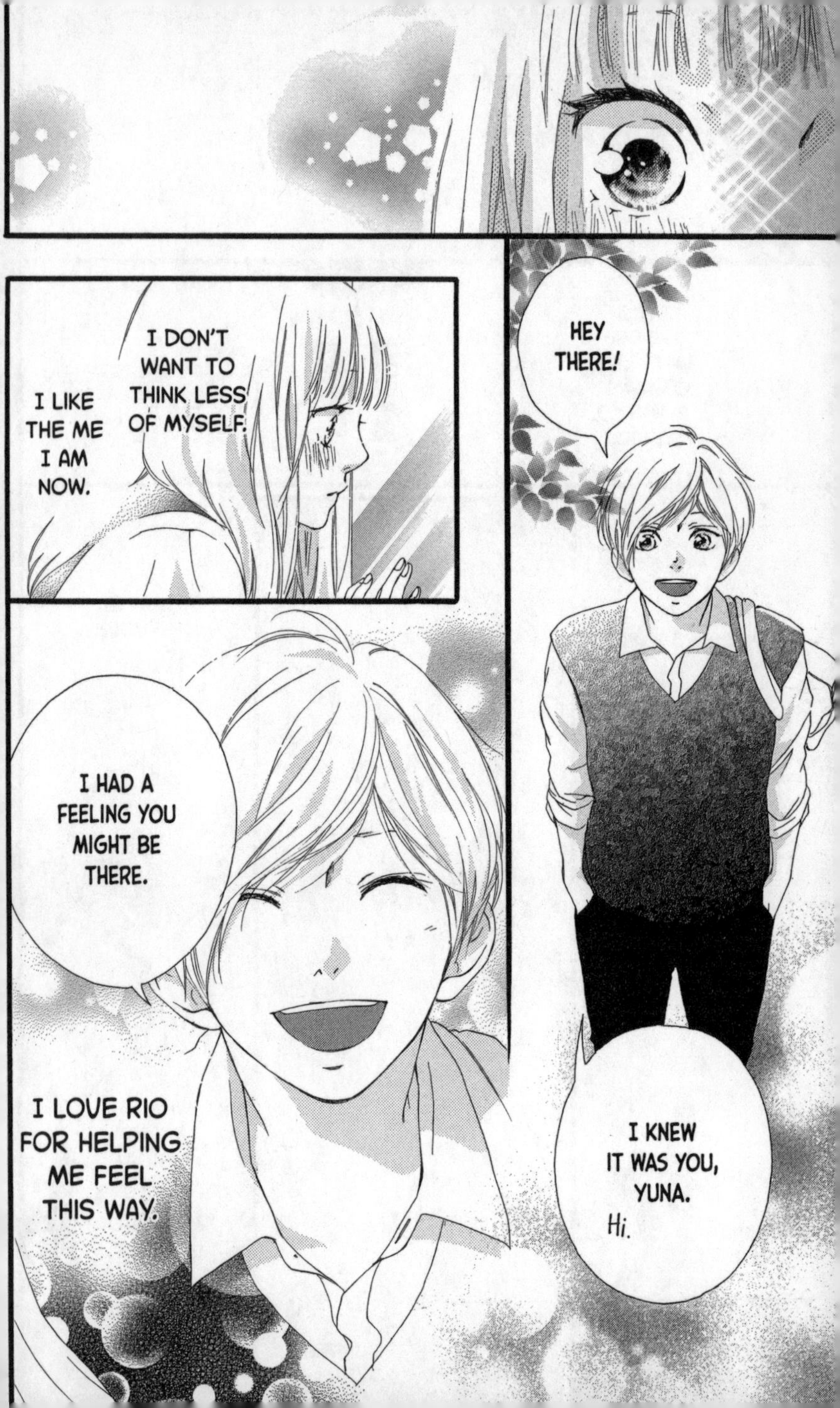
HEY THERE!
I KNEW IT WAS YOU, YUNA.
Hi.
I DON'T WANT TO THINK LESS OF MYSELF.
I LIKE THE ME I AM NOW.
I HAD A FEELING YOU MIGHT BE THERE.
I LOVE RIO FOR HELPING ME FEEL THIS WAY.

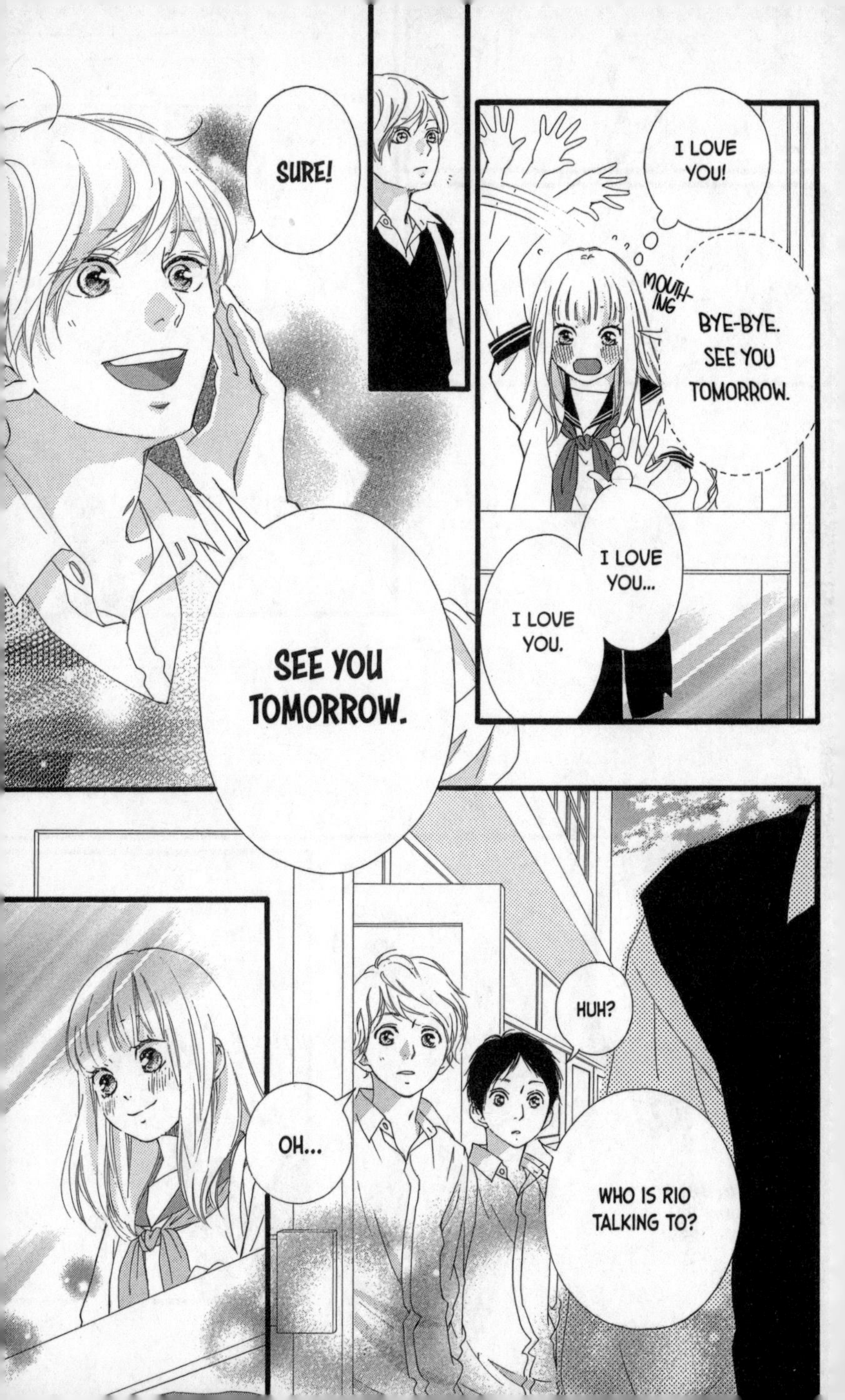
I LOVE YOU!
MOUTHING
BYE-BYE. SEE YOU TOMORROW.
I LOVE YOU...
I LOVE YOU.
SURE!
SEE YOU TOMORROW.
HUH?
WHO IS RIO TALKING TO?
OH...

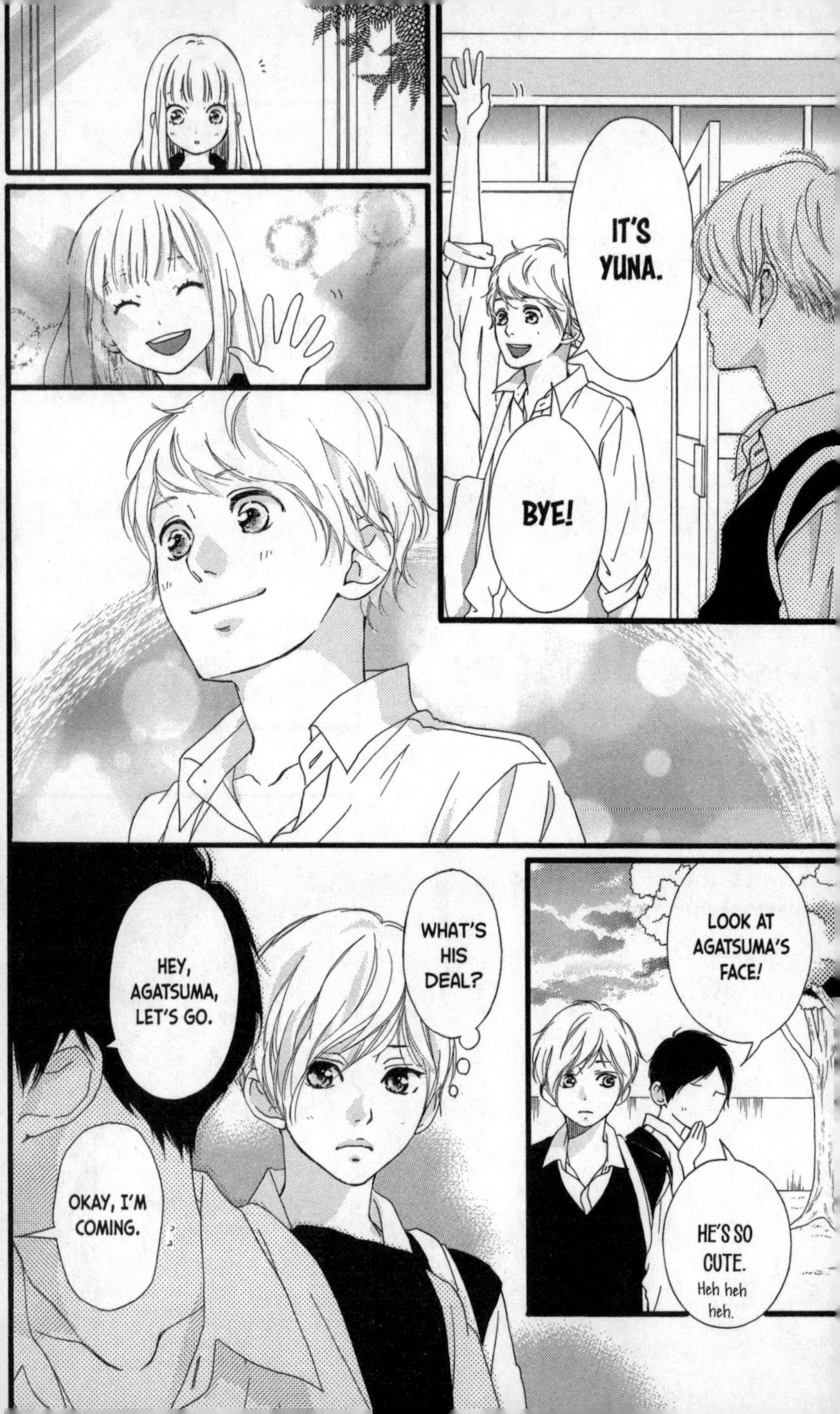
IT'S YUNA.
BYE!
LOOK AT AGATSUMA'S FACE!
HE'S SO CUTE. Heh heh heh.
WHAT'S HIS DEAL?
HEY, AGATSUMA, LET'S GO.
OKAY, I'M COMING.

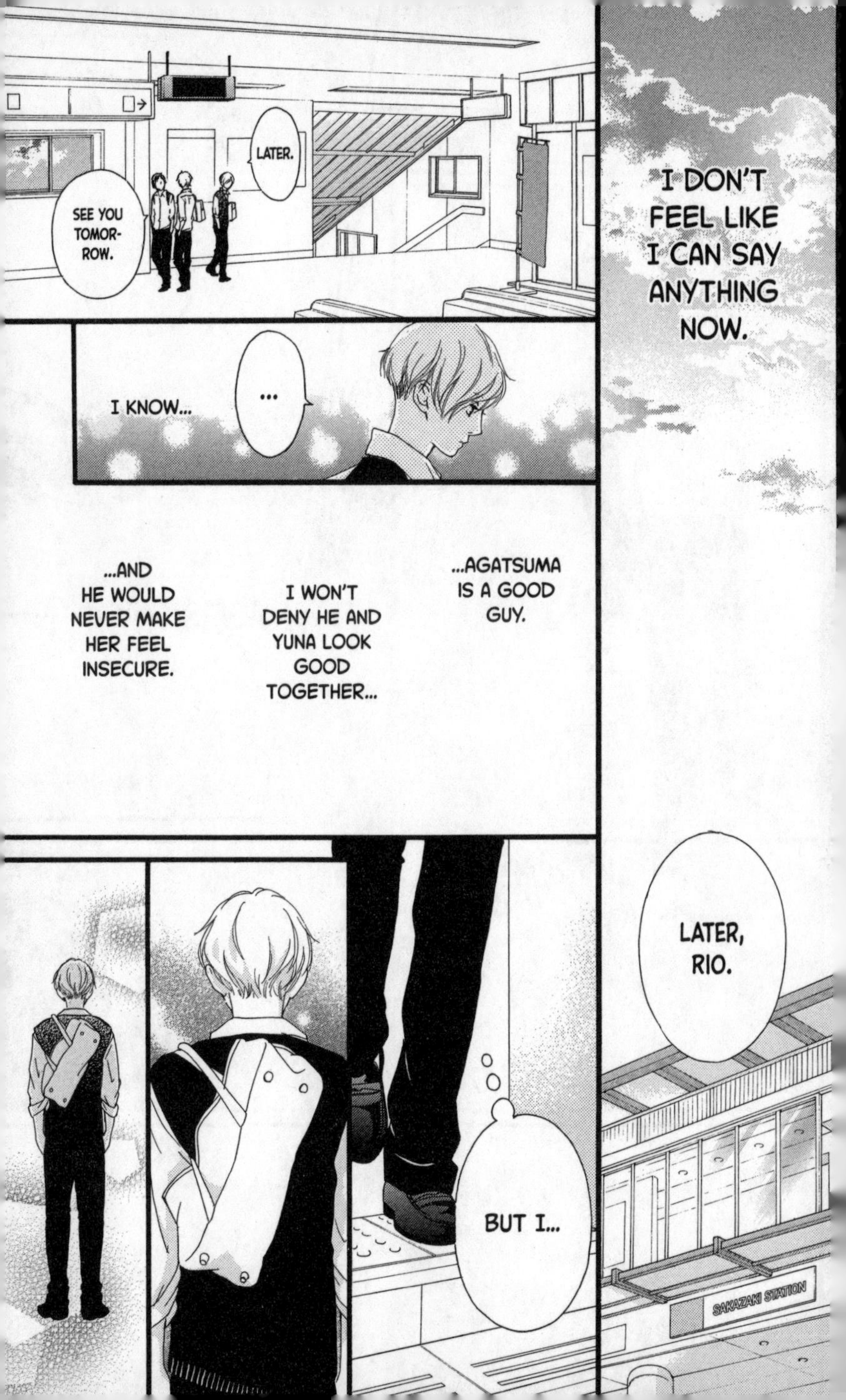

I DON'T FEEL LIKE I CAN SAY ANYTHING NOW.
LATER.
SEE YOU TOMORROW.
...
I KNOW...
...AGATSUMA IS A GOOD GUY.
I WON'T DENY HE AND YUNA LOOK GOOD TOGETHER...
...AND HE WOULD NEVER MAKE HER FEEL INSECURE.
LATER, RIO.
SAKAZAKI STATION
BUT I...

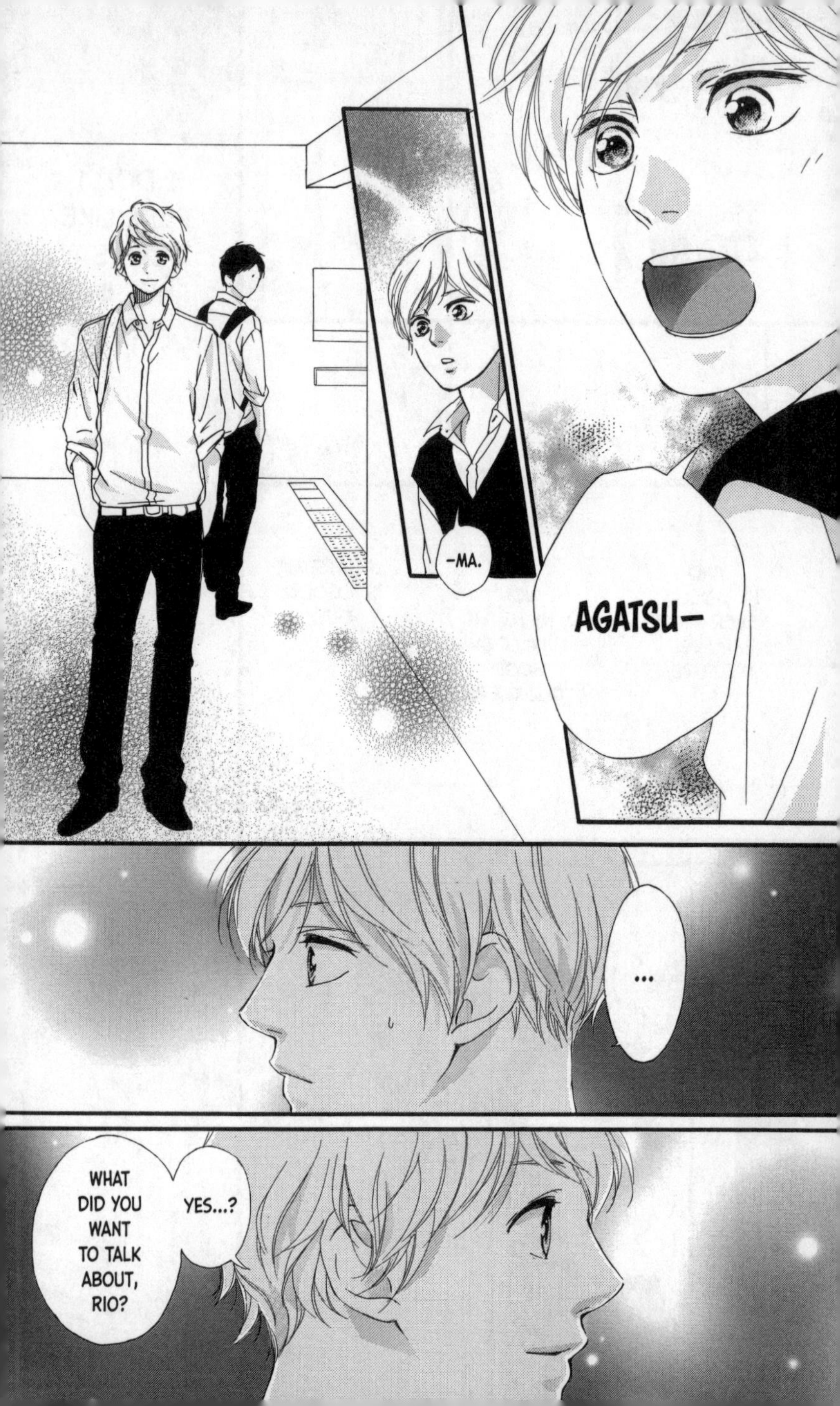
AGATSU-
-MA.
...
YES...?
WHAT DID YOU WANT TO TALK ABOUT, RIO?

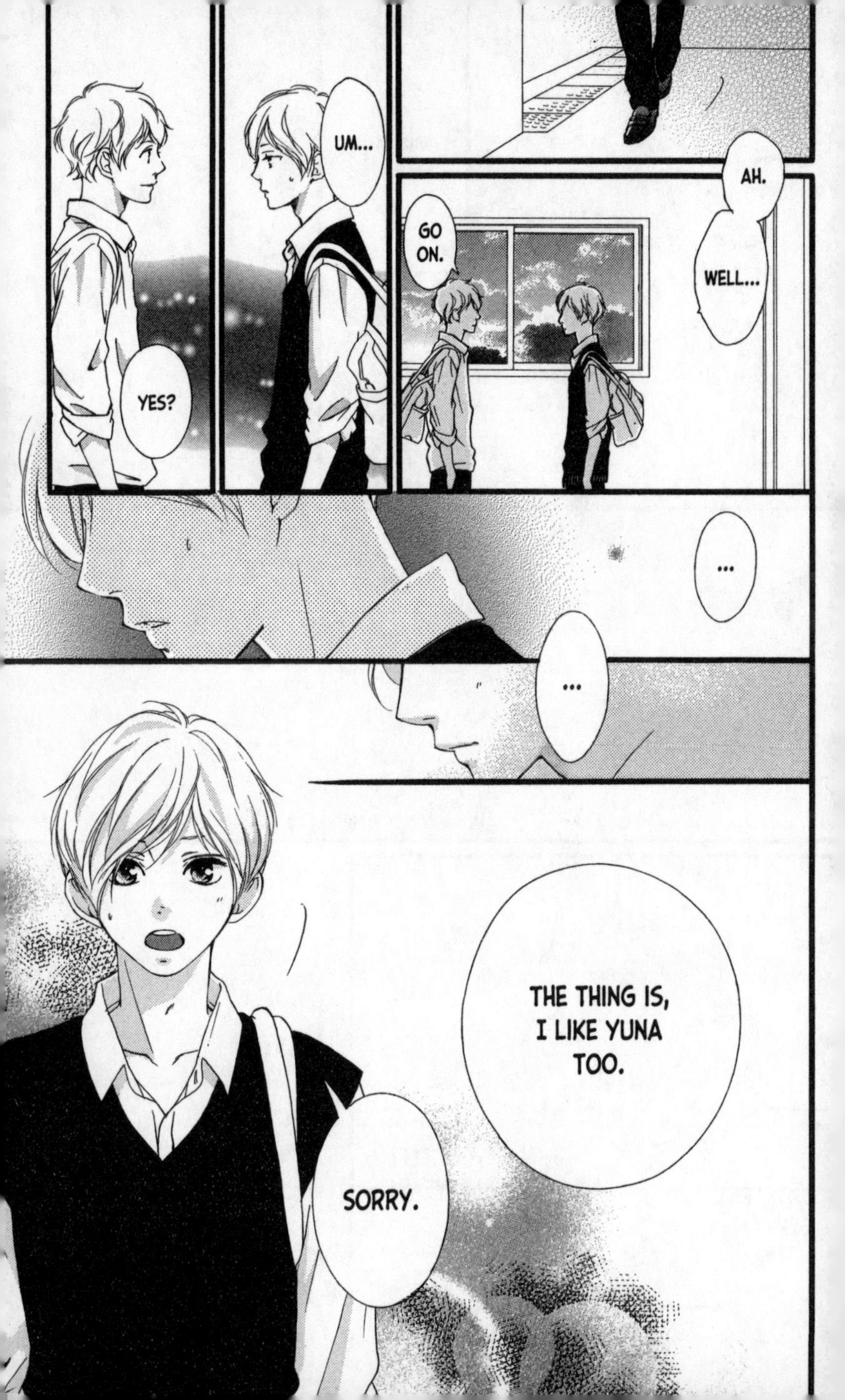
AH.
WELL...
GO ON.
UM...
YES?
...
...
THE THING IS, I LIKE YUNA TOO.
SORRY.

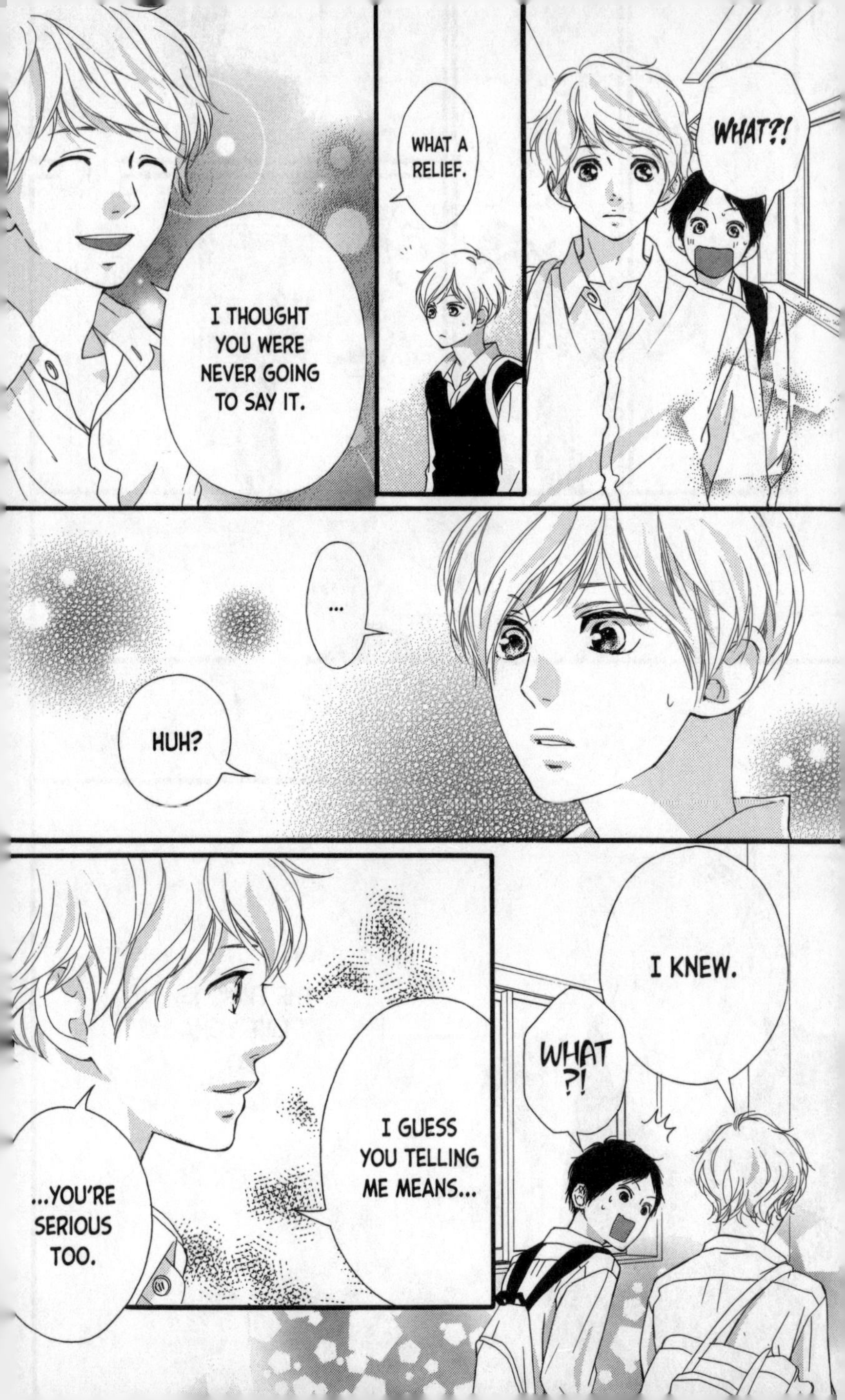
WHAT?!
WHAT A RELIEF.
I THOUGHT YOU WERE NEVER GOING TO SAY IT.
...
HUH?
I KNEW.
WHAT ?!
I GUESS YOU TELLING ME MEANS...
...YOU'RE SERIOUS TOO.

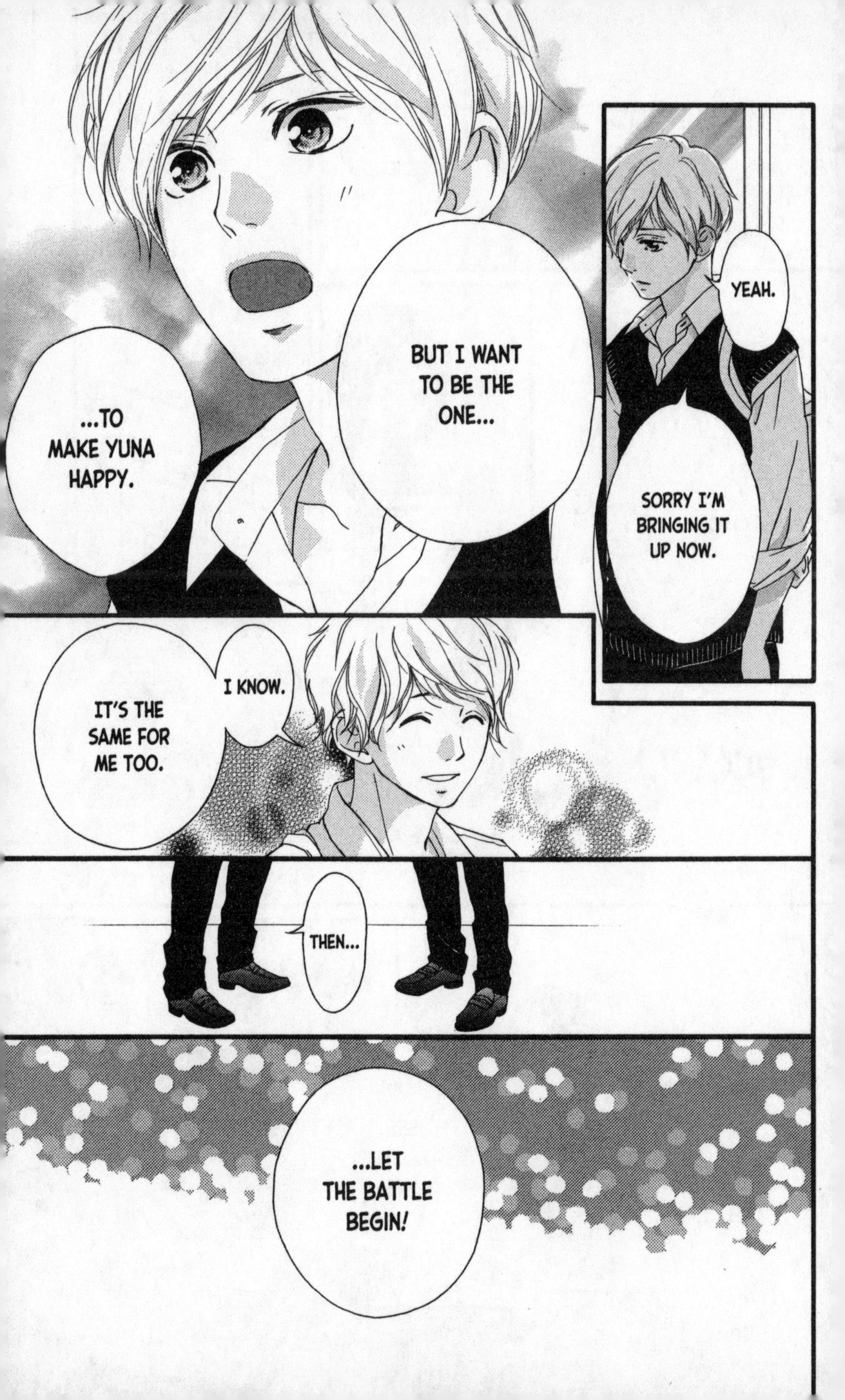
YEAH.
SORRY I'M BRINGING IT UP NOW.
BUT I WANT TO BE THE ONE...
...TO MAKE YUNA HAPPY.
I KNOW.
IT'S THE SAME FOR ME TOO.
THEN...
...LET THE BATTLE BEGIN!

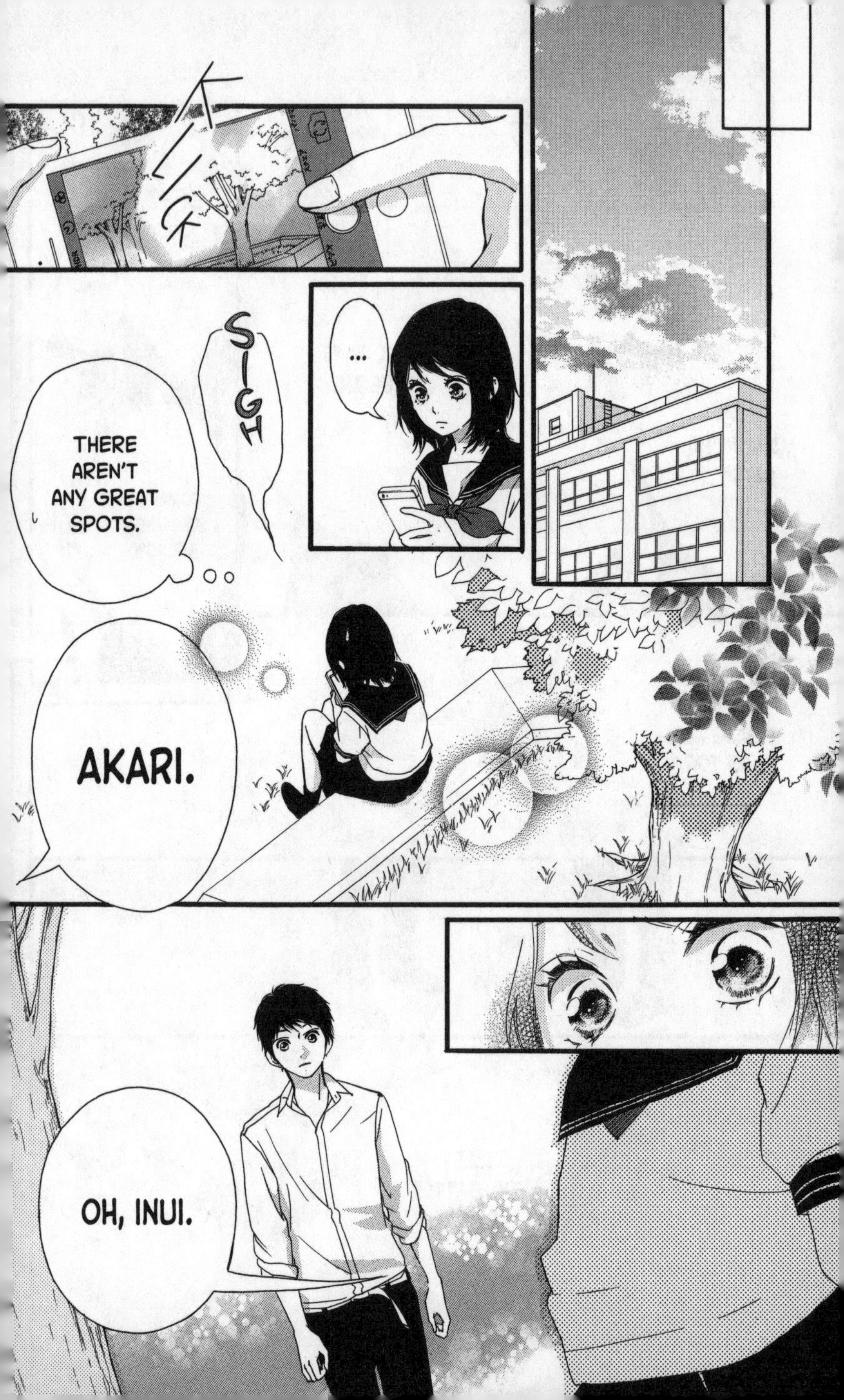
KLICK
...
SIGH
THERE AREN'T ANY GREAT SPOTS.
AKARI.
OH, INUI.

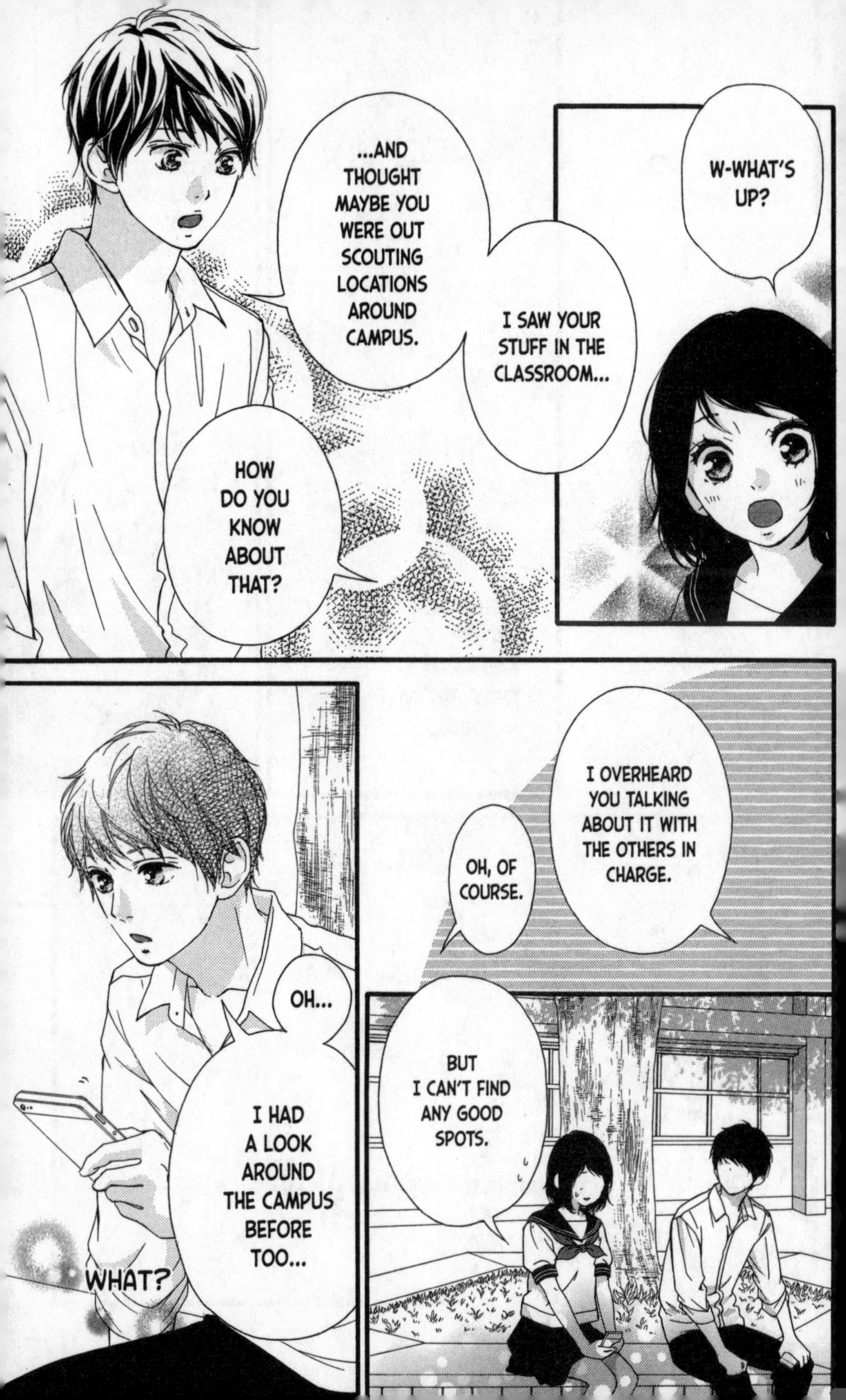
W-WHAT'S UP?
I SAW YOUR STUFF IN THE CLASSROOM...
...AND THOUGHT MAYBE YOU WERE OUT SCOUTING LOCATIONS AROUND CAMPUS.
HOW DO YOU KNOW ABOUT THAT?
I OVERHEARD YOU TALKING ABOUT IT WITH THE OTHERS IN CHARGE.
OH, OF COURSE.
BUT I CAN'T FIND ANY GOOD SPOTS.
OH...
I HAD A LOOK AROUND THE CAMPUS BEFORE TOO...
WHAT?

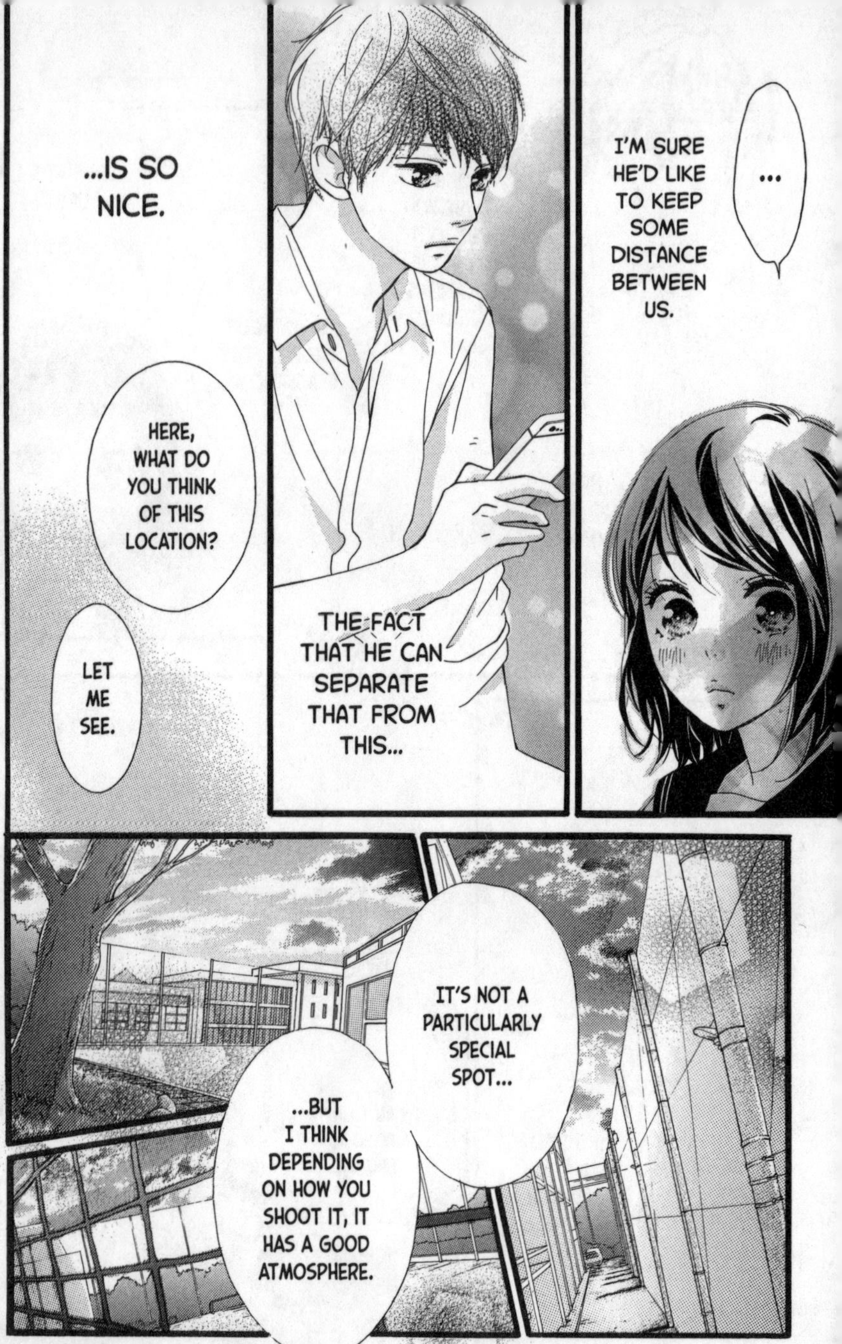
...
I'M SURE HE'D LIKE TO KEEP SOME DISTANCE BETWEEN US.
THE FACT THAT HE CAN SEPARATE THAT FROM THIS...
...IS SO NICE.
HERE, WHAT DO YOU THINK OF THIS LOCATION?
LET ME SEE.
IT'S NOT A PARTICULARLY SPECIAL SPOT...
...BUT I THINK DEPENDING ON HOW YOU SHOOT IT, IT HAS A GOOD ATMOSPHERE.

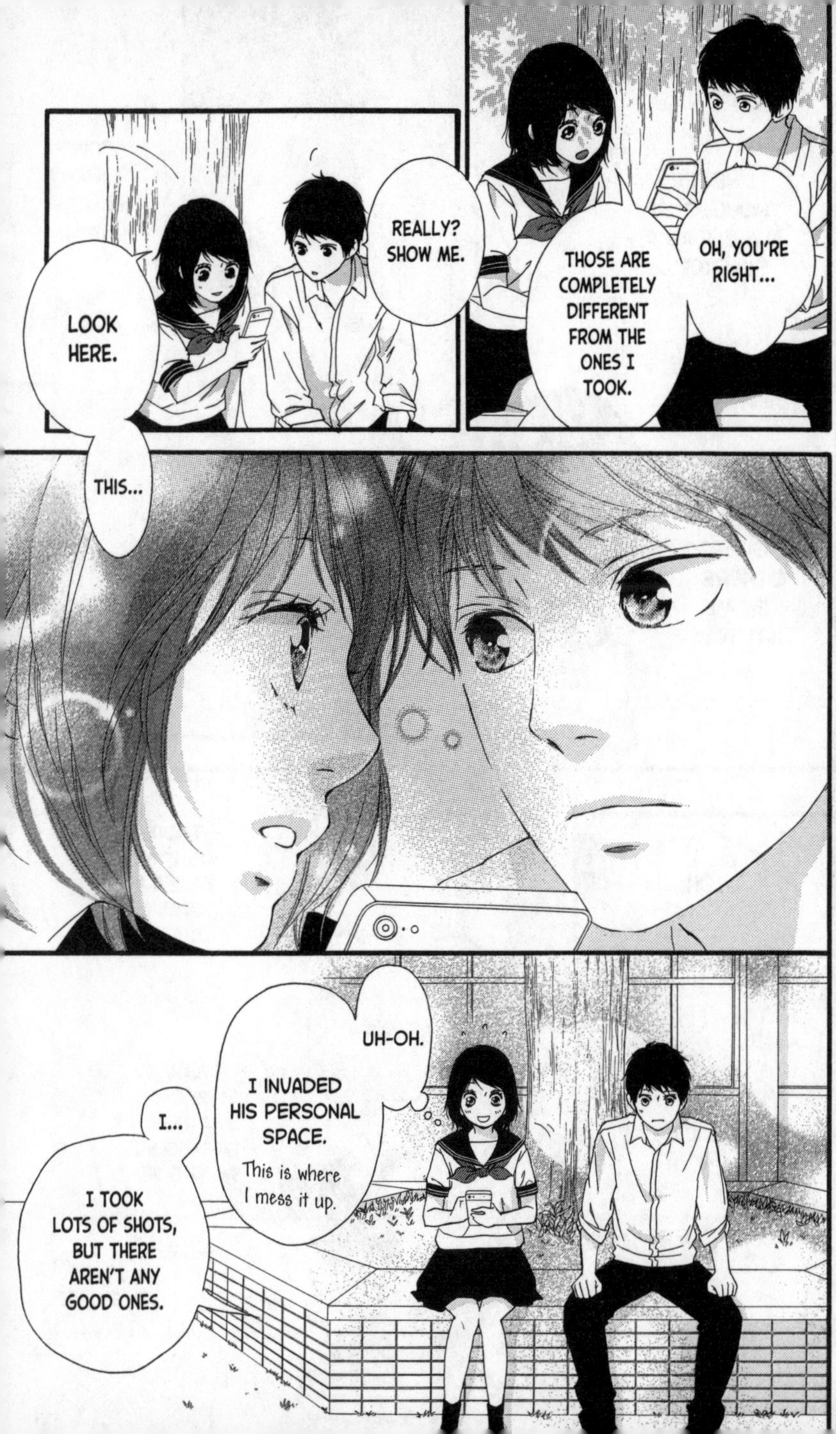
OH, YOU'RE RIGHT...
THOSE ARE COMPLETELY DIFFERENT FROM THE ONES I TOOK.
REALLY? SHOW ME.
LOOK HERE.
THIS...
UH-OH.
I INVADED HIS PERSONAL SPACE.
This is where I mess it up.
I...
I TOOK LOTS OF SHOTS, BUT THERE AREN'T ANY GOOD ONES.

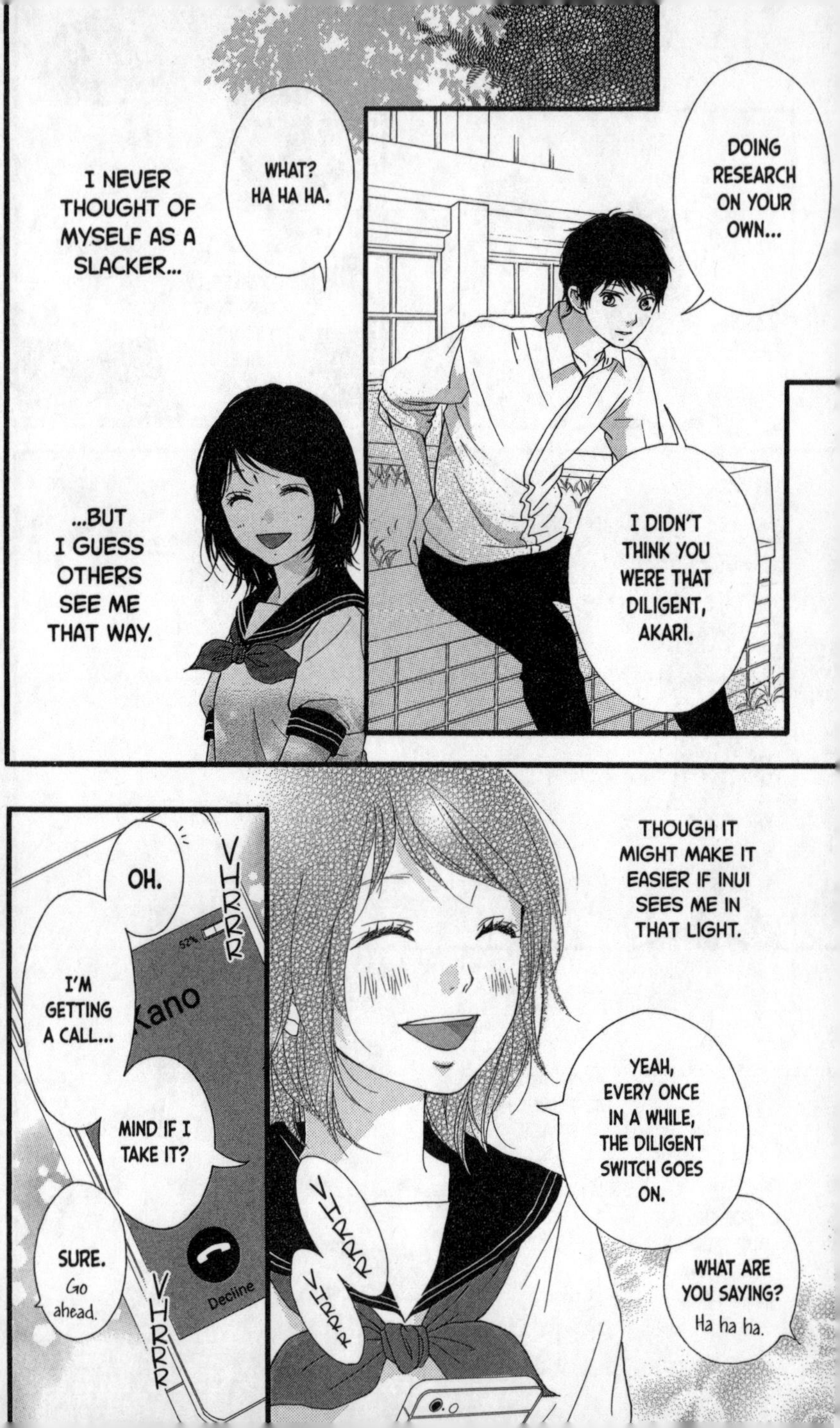
DOING RESEARCH ON YOUR OWN...
I DIDN'T THINK YOU WERE THAT DILIGENT, AKARI.
WHAT? HA HA HA.
I NEVER THOUGHT OF MYSELF AS A SLACKER...
...BUT I GUESS OTHERS SEE ME THAT WAY.
THOUGH IT MIGHT MAKE IT EASIER IF INUI SEES ME IN THAT LIGHT.
YEAH, EVERY ONCE IN A WHILE, THE DILIGENT SWITCH GOES ON.
WHAT ARE YOU SAYING? Ha ha ha.
VIRRR
VIRRR
VHRRR
OH.
52%
Kano
I'M GETTING A CALL...
MIND IF I TAKE IT?
SURE. Go ahead.
Decline
VHRRR

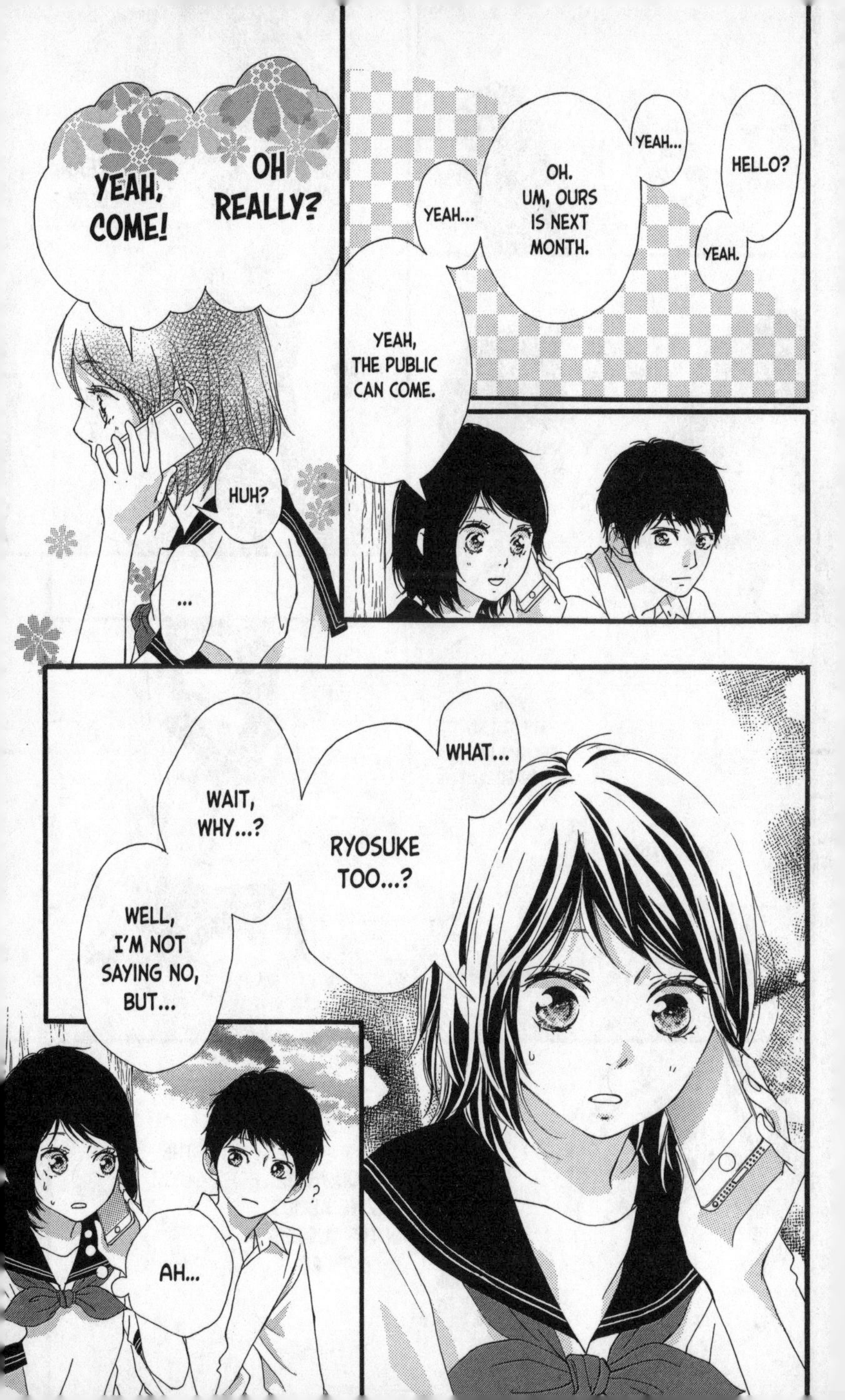
HELLO?
YEAH.
YEAH...
OH. UM, OURS IS NEXT MONTH.
YEAH...
YEAH, THE PUBLIC CAN COME.
OH REALLY?
YEAH, COME!
HUH?
...
WHAT...
RYOSUKE TOO...?
WAIT, WHY...?
WELL, I'M NOT SAYING NO, BUT...
AH...

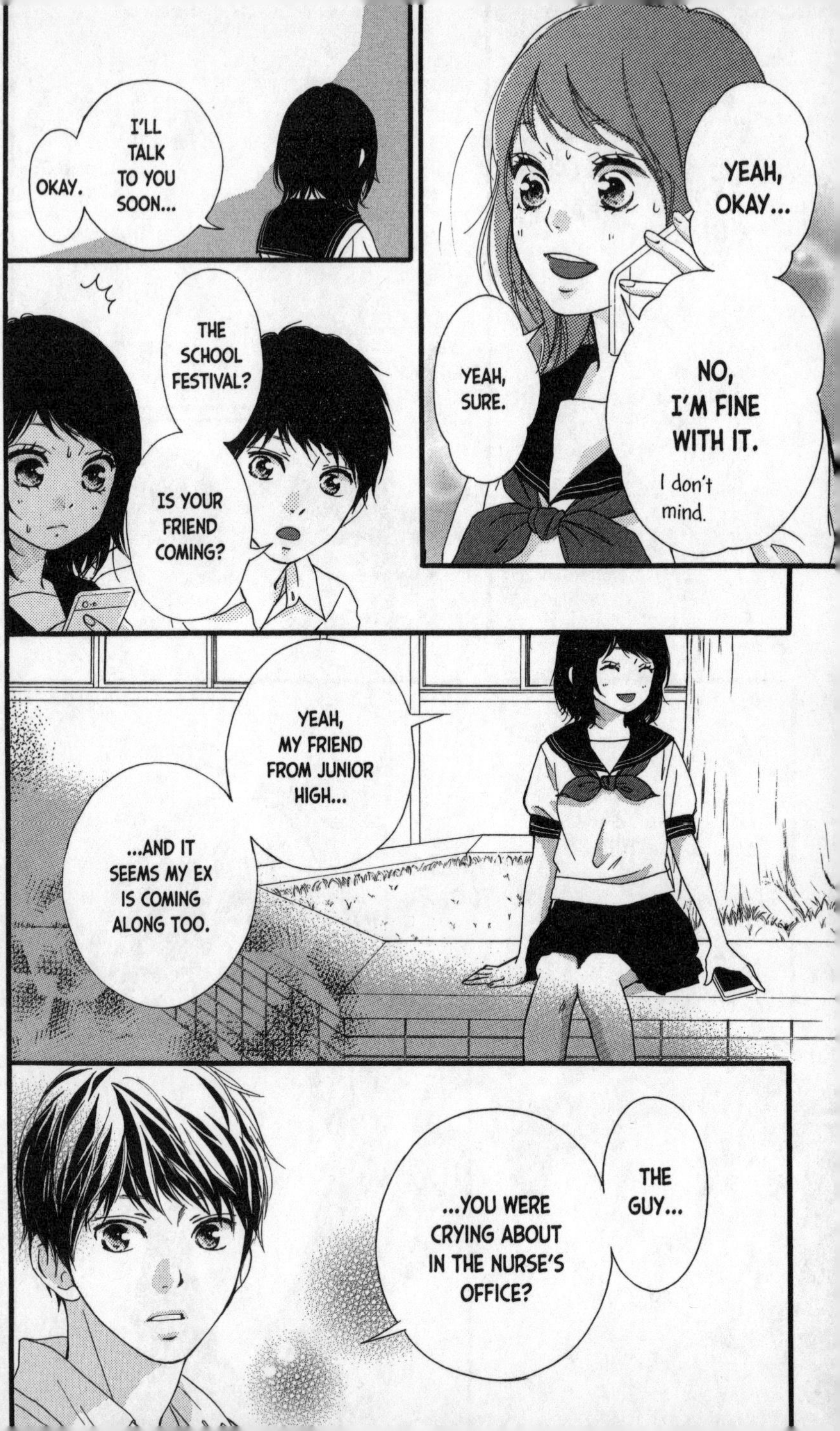
YEAH, OKAY...
NO, I'M FINE WITH IT. I don't mind.
YEAH, SURE.
I'LL TALK TO YOU SOON...
OKAY.
THE SCHOOL FESTIVAL?
IS YOUR FRIEND COMING?
YEAH, MY FRIEND FROM JUNIOR HIGH...
...AND IT SEEMS MY EX IS COMING ALONG TOO.
THE GUY...
...YOU WERE CRYING ABOUT IN THE NURSE'S OFFICE?

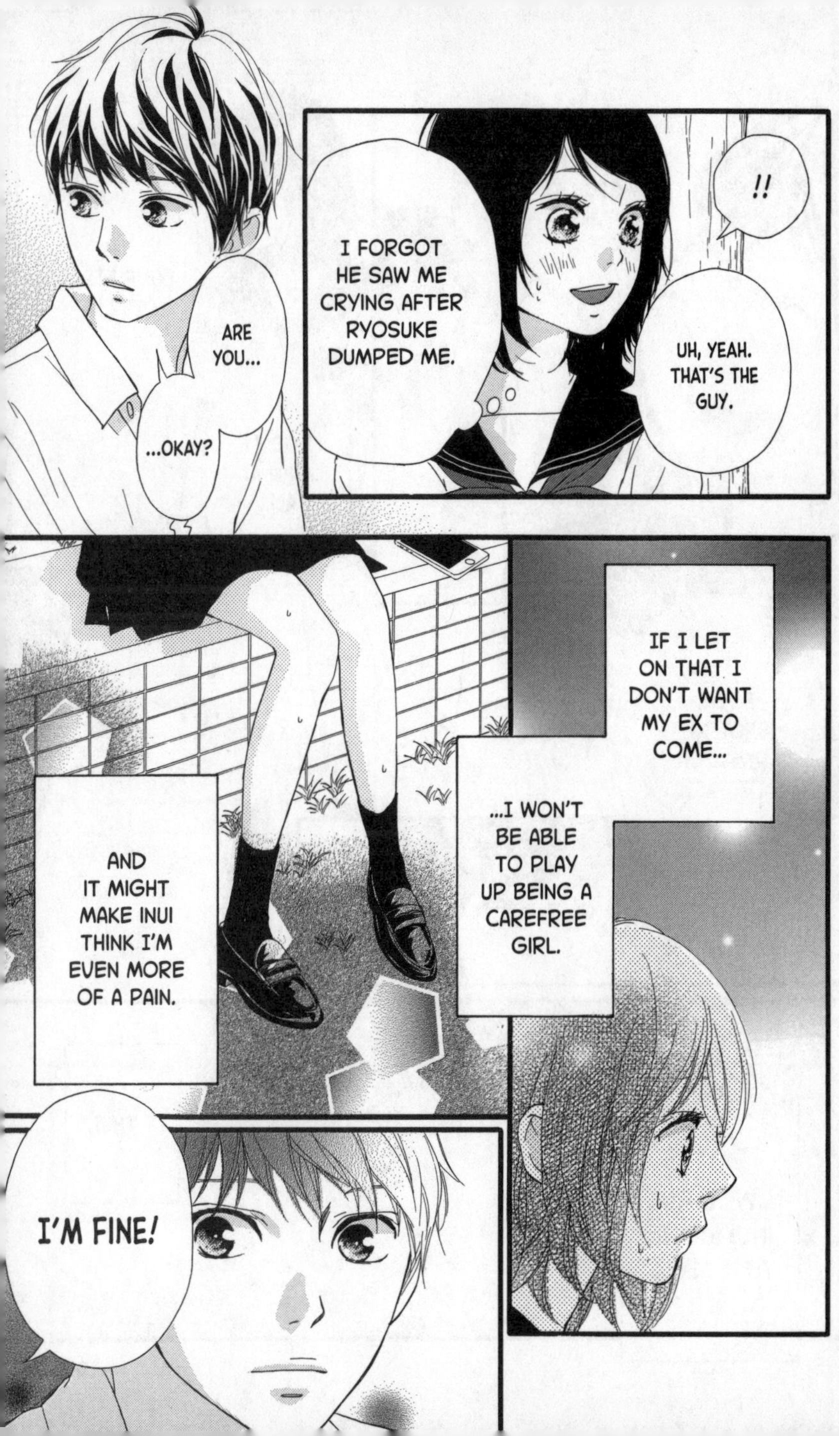
!!
UH, YEAH. THAT'S THE GUY.
I FORGOT HE SAW ME CRYING AFTER RYOSUKE DUMPED ME.
ARE YOU...
...OKAY?
IF I LET ON THAT I DON'T WANT MY EX TO COME...
...I WON'T BE ABLE TO PLAY UP BEING A CAREFREE GIRL.
AND IT MIGHT MAKE INUI THINK I'M EVEN MORE OF A PAIN.
I'M FINE!

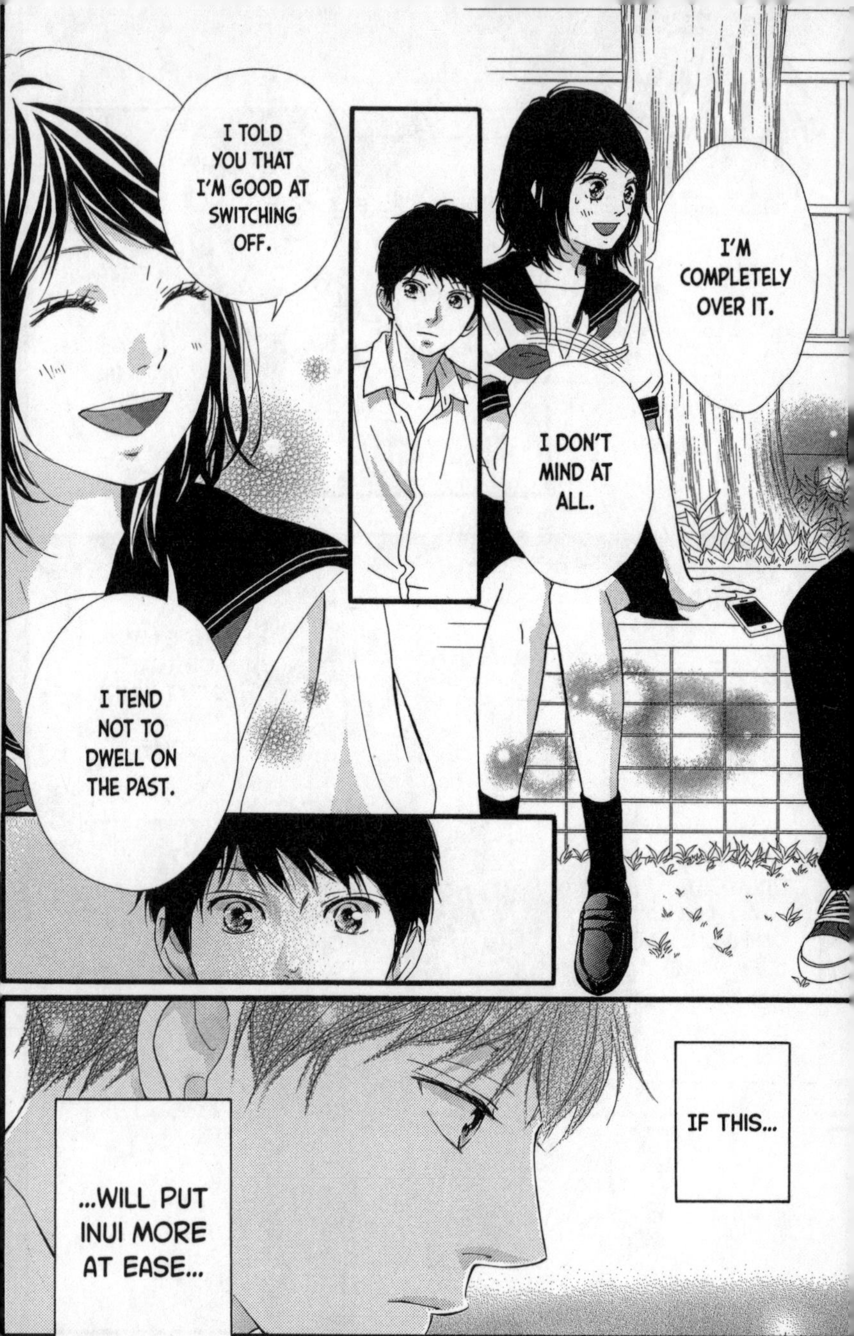
I'M COMPLETELY OVER IT.
I DON'T MIND AT ALL.
I TOLD YOU THAT I'M GOOD AT SWITCHING OFF.
I TEND NOT TO DWELL ON THE PAST.
IF THIS...
...WILL PUT INUI MORE AT EASE...

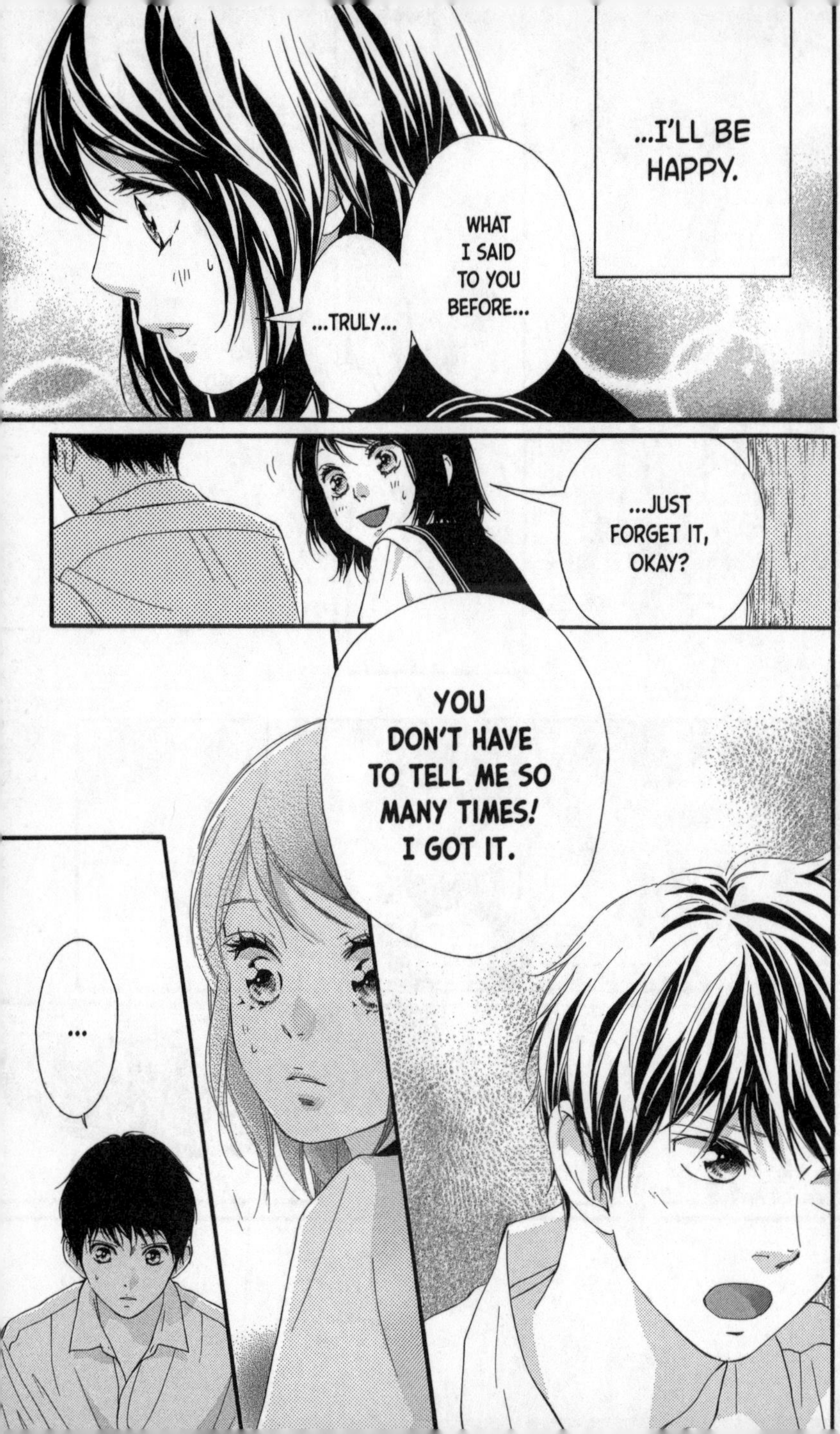
...I'LL BE HAPPY.
WHAT I SAID TO YOU BEFORE...
...TRULY...
...JUST FORGET IT, OKAY?
YOU DON'T HAVE TO TELL ME SO MANY TIMES! I GOT IT.
...

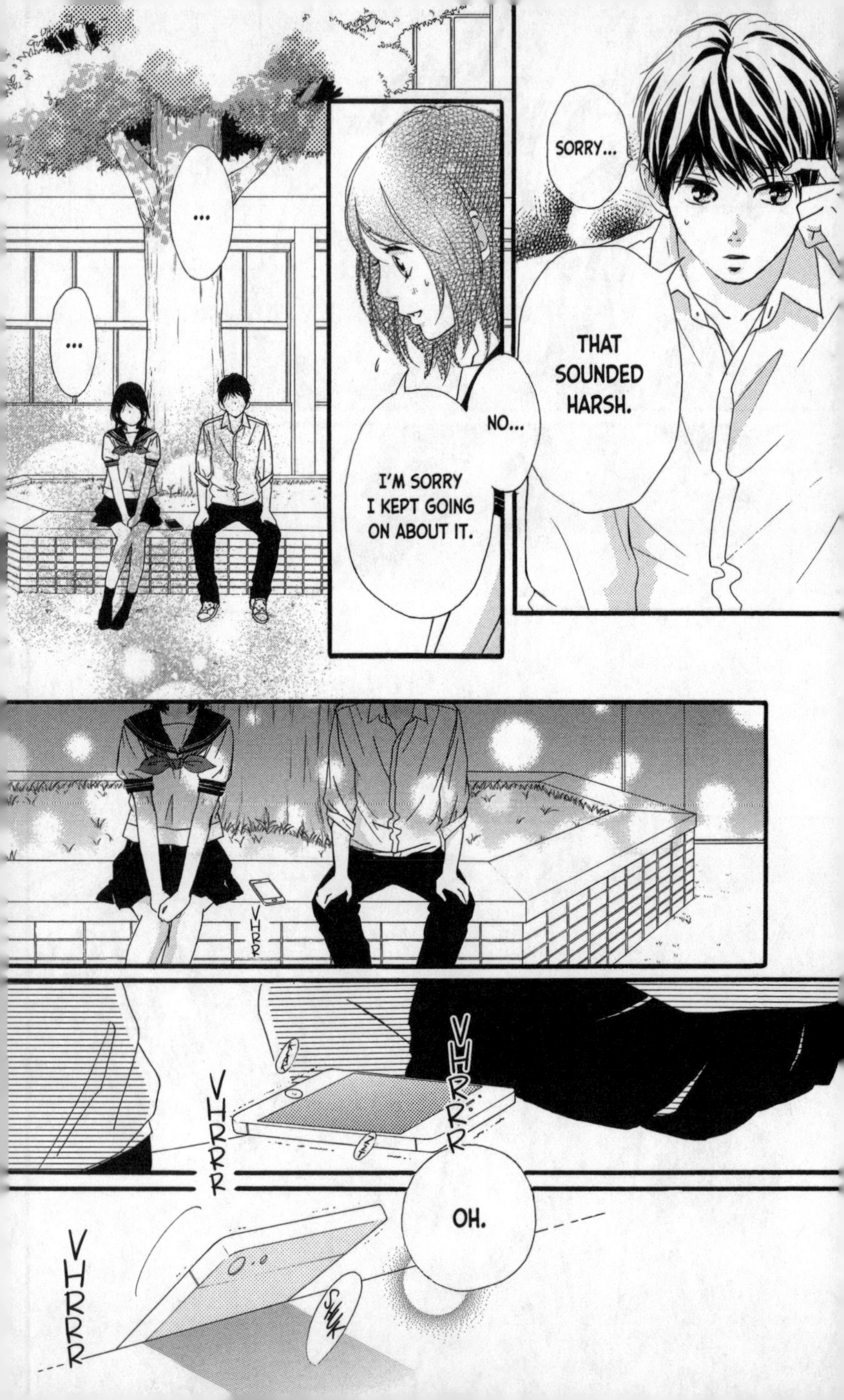
SORRY...
THAT SOUNDED HARSH.
NO...
I'M SORRY I KEPT GOING ON ABOUT IT.
...
...
VHRR
VHRRR
VHRRR
OH.
VHRRR
SHUK

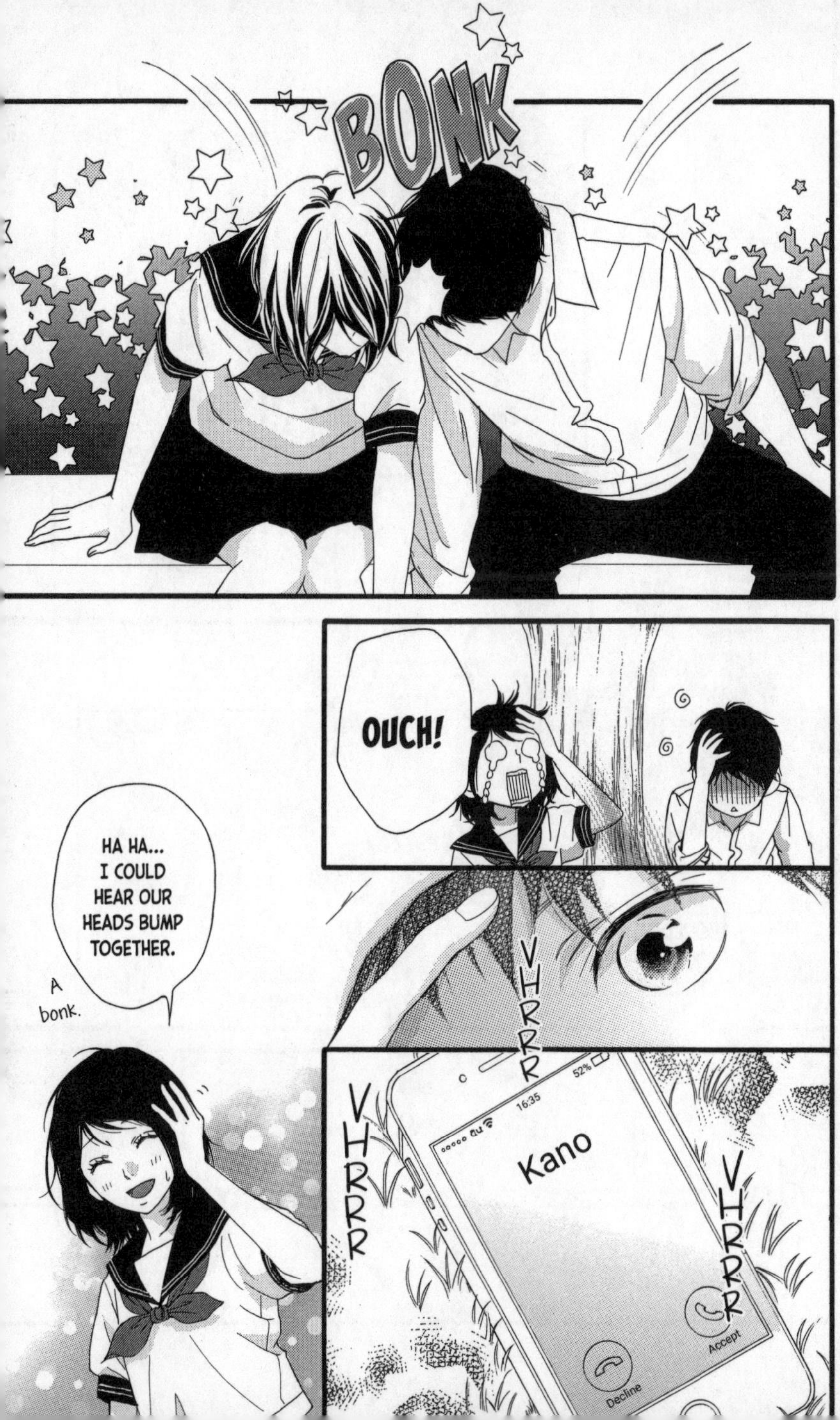
BONK
OUCH!
VHRRR
16:35
52%
Kano
Accept
Decline
VHRRR
VHRRR
HA HA... I COULD HEAR OUR HEADS BUMP TOGETHER.
A bonk.

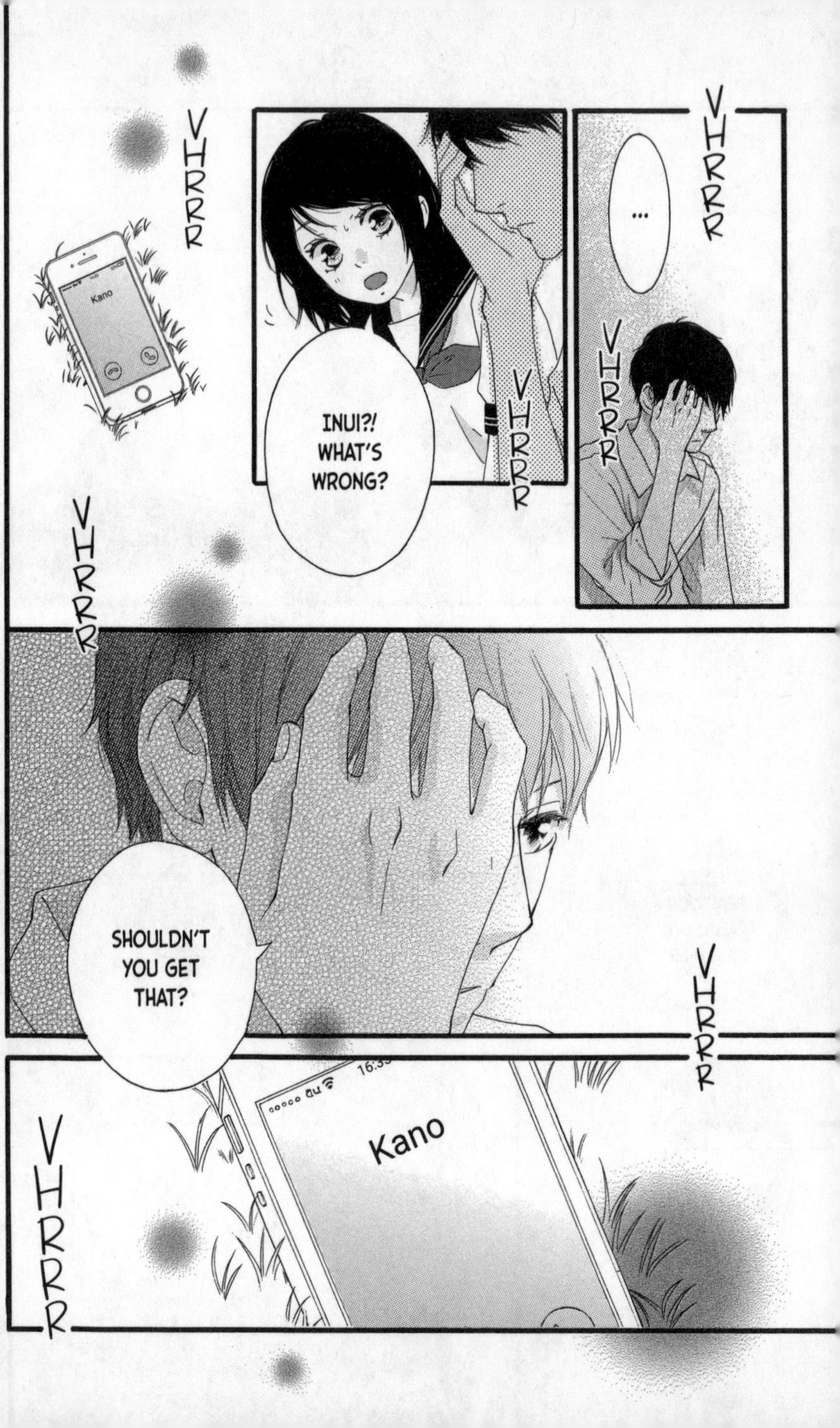
VHRRR
...
VHRRR
INUI?! WHAT'S WRONG?
VHRRR
VHRRR
Kano
VHRRR
SHOULDN'T YOU GET THAT?
VHRRR
Kano
VHRRR

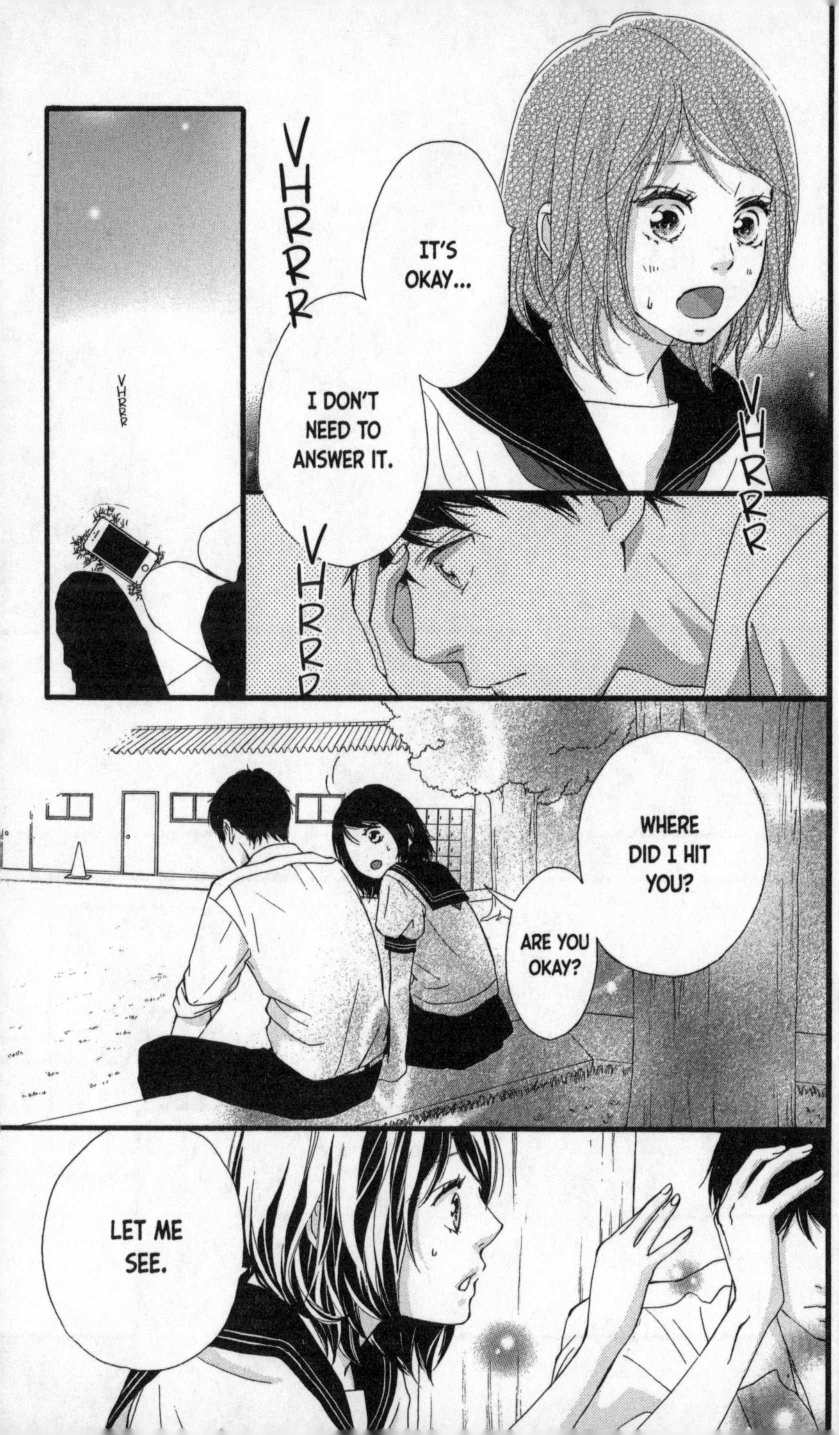
VHRRR
IT'S OKAY...
I DON'T NEED TO ANSWER IT.
VHRRR
VHRRR
VHRRR
WHERE DID I HIT YOU?
ARE YOU OKAY?
LET ME SEE.

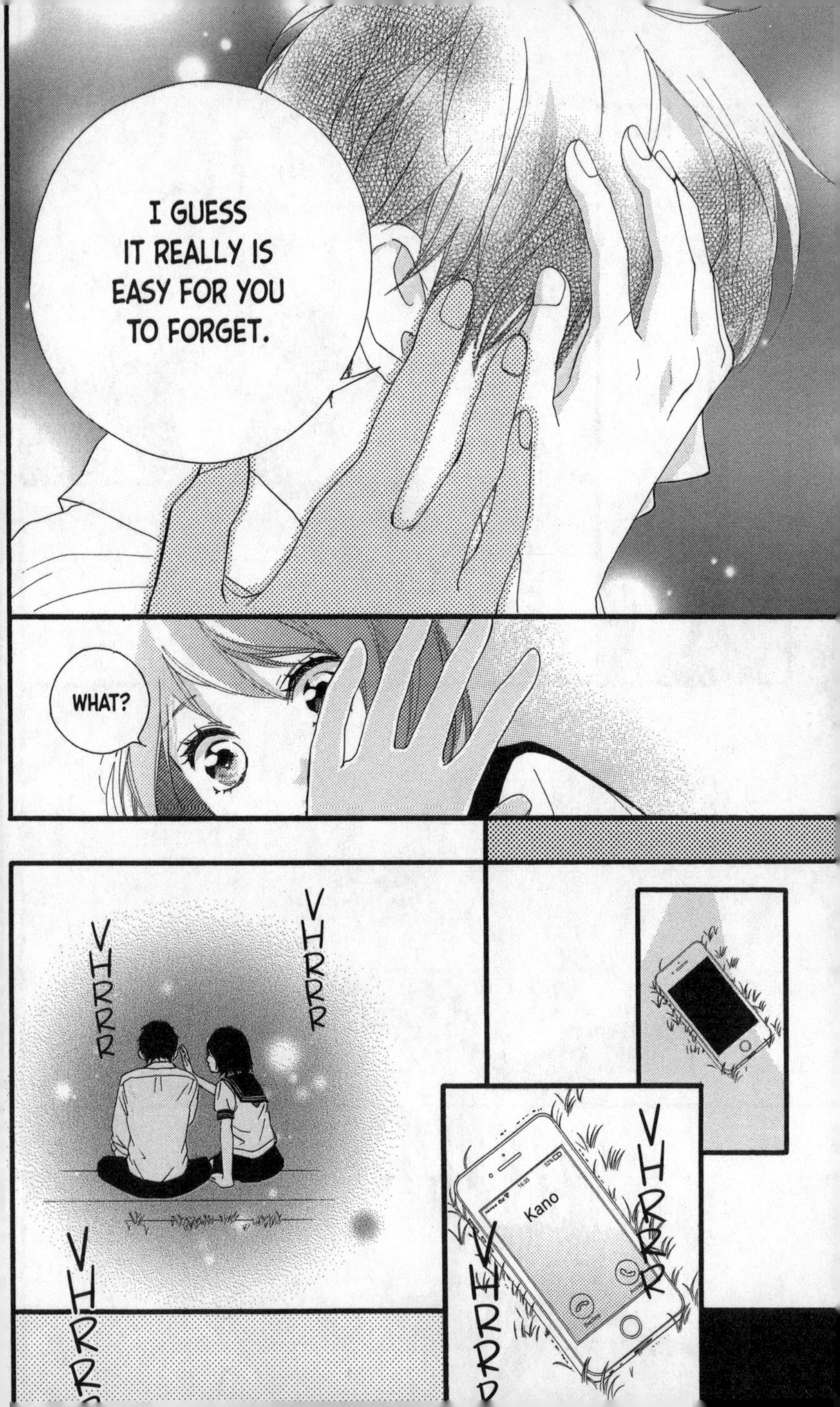
I GUESS IT REALLY IS EASY FOR YOU TO FORGET.
WHAT?
Kano
VHRRR
VHRRR
VHRRR
VHRRR
VHRRR

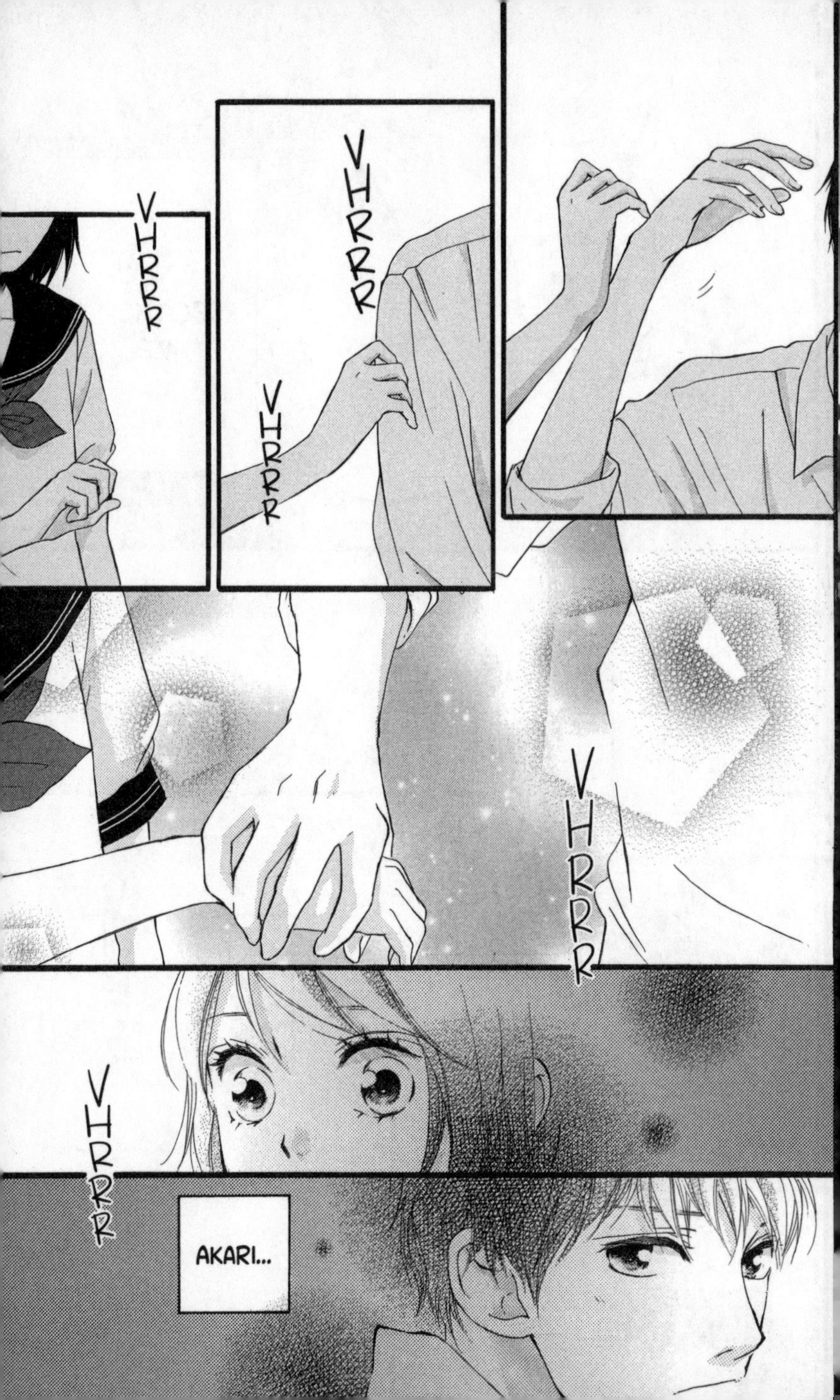
VHRRR
VHRRR
VHRRR
VHRRR
VHRRR
AKARI...

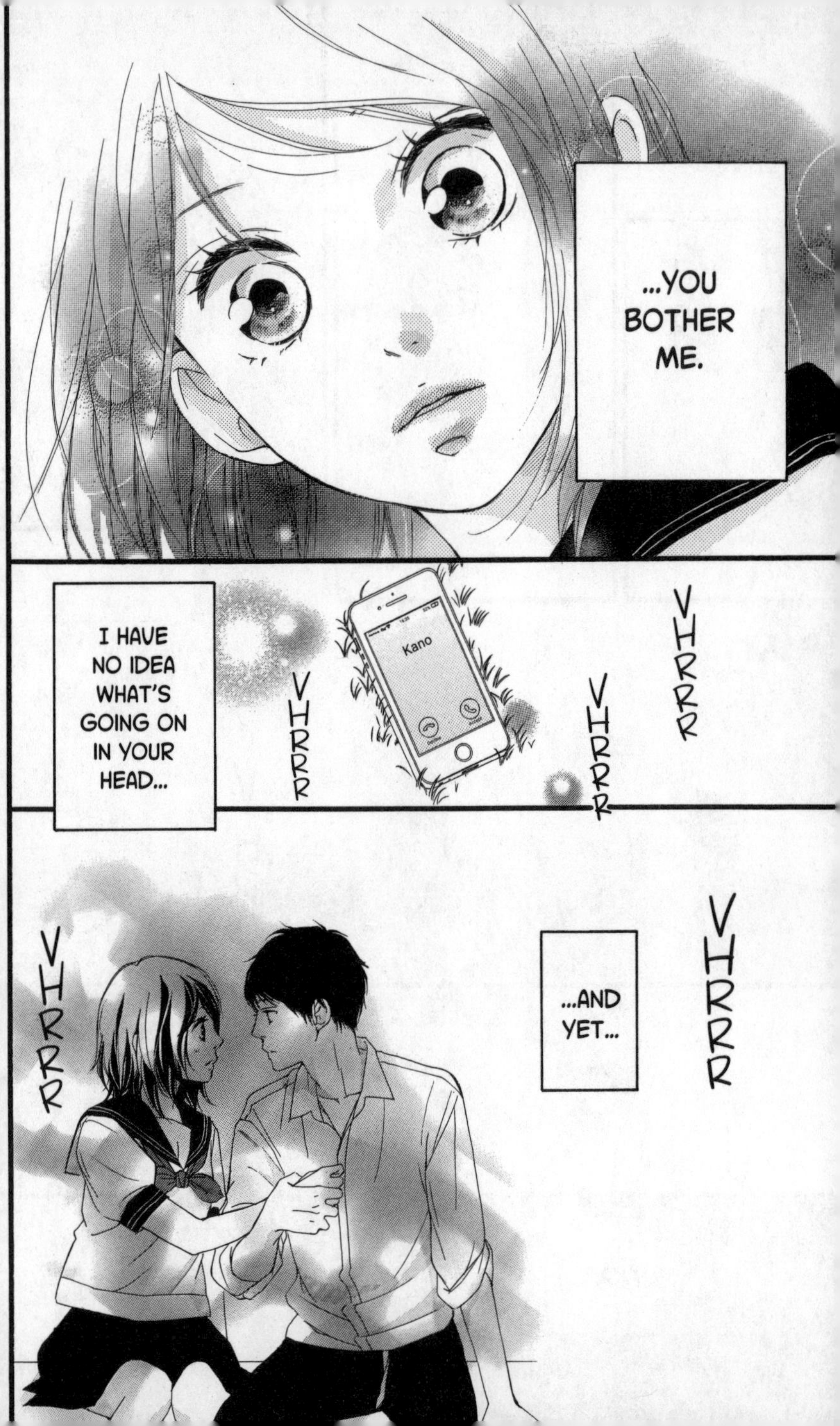
...YOU BOTHER ME.
VHRRR
VHRRR
Kano
VHRRR
I HAVE NO IDEA WHAT'S GOING ON IN YOUR HEAD...
VHRRR
...AND YET...
VHRRR

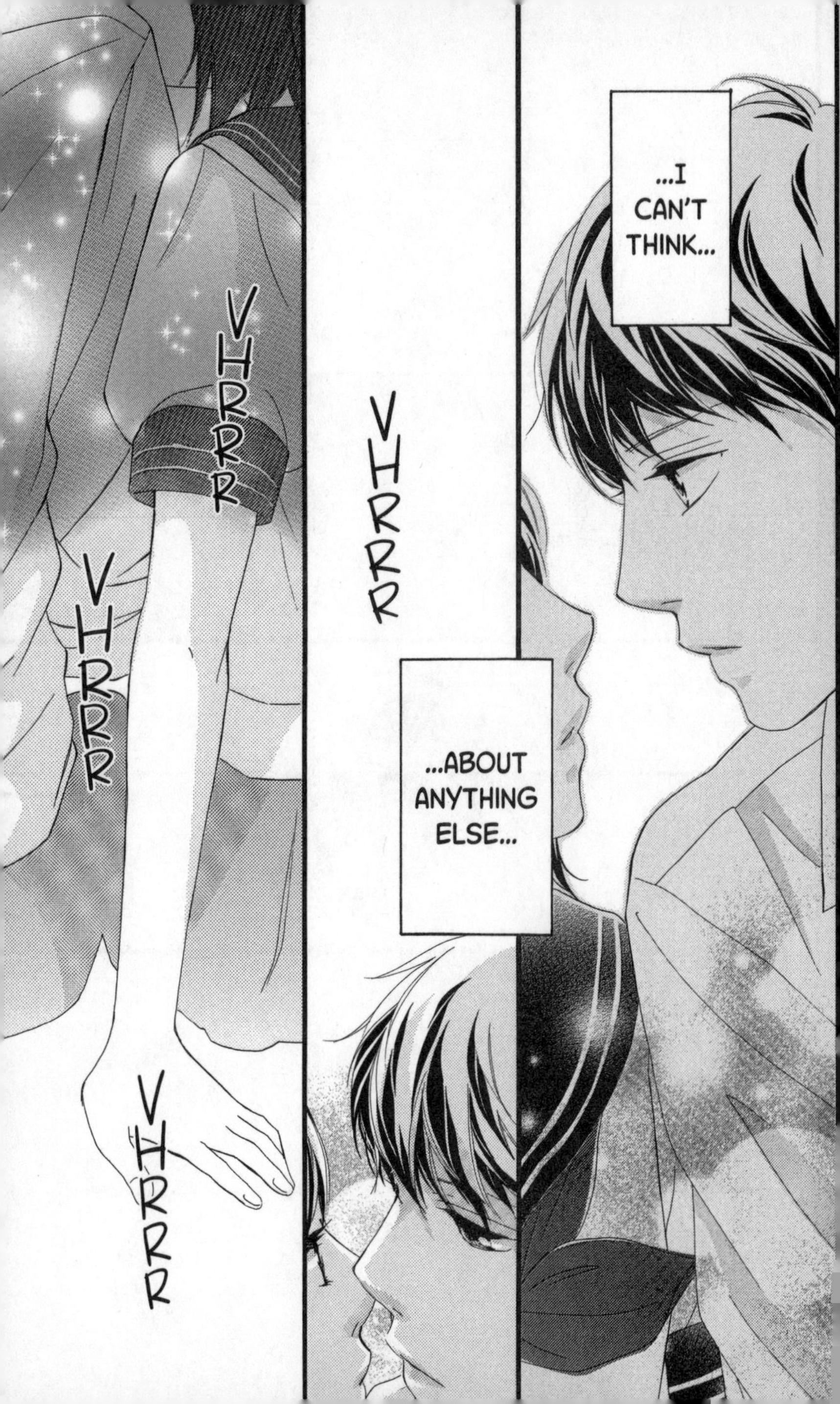
...I CAN'T THINK...
VHRRR
...ABOUT ANYTHING ELSE...
VHRRR
VHRRR
VHRRR

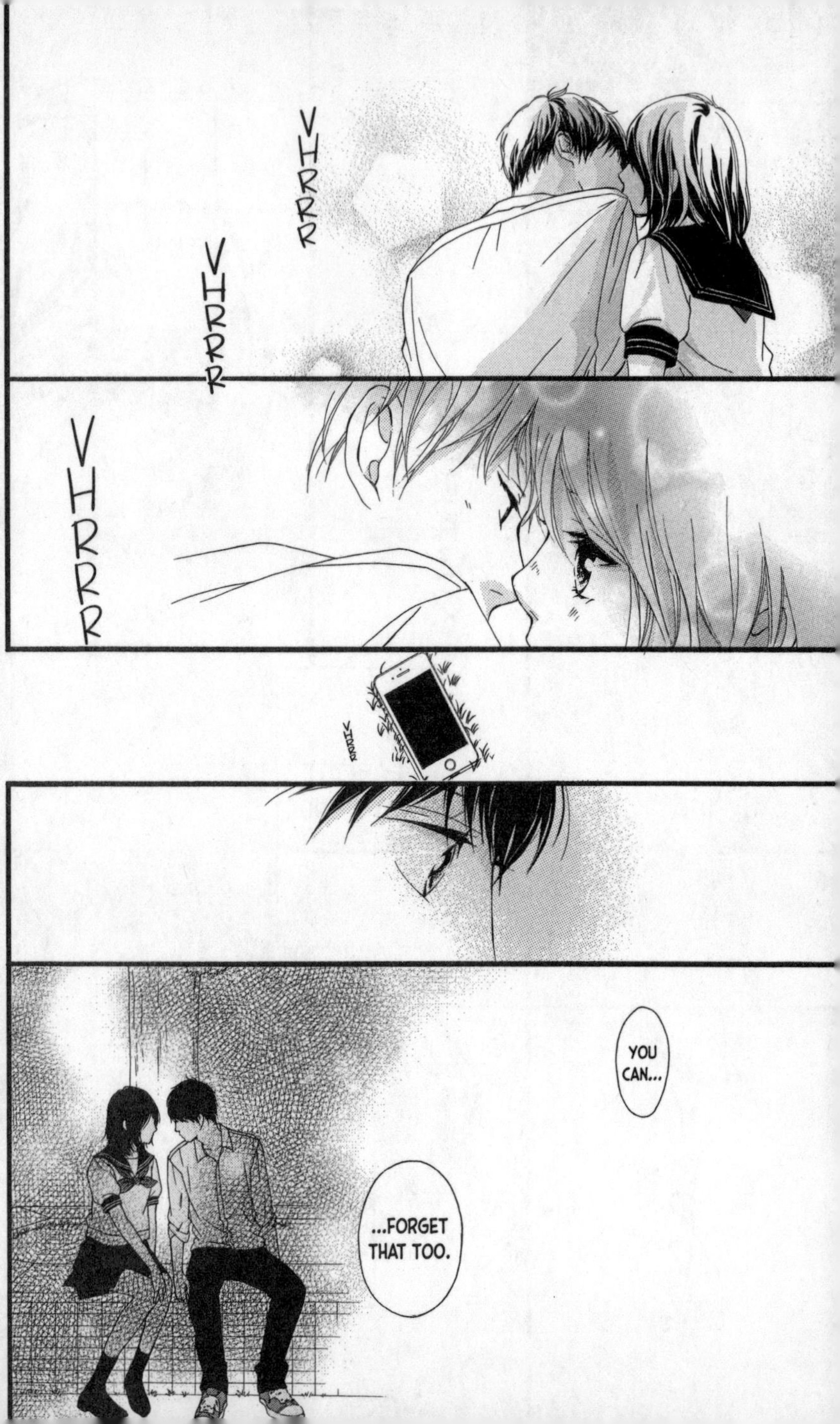
VHRRR
VHRRR
VHRRR
VHRRR
YOU CAN...
...FORGET THAT TOO.

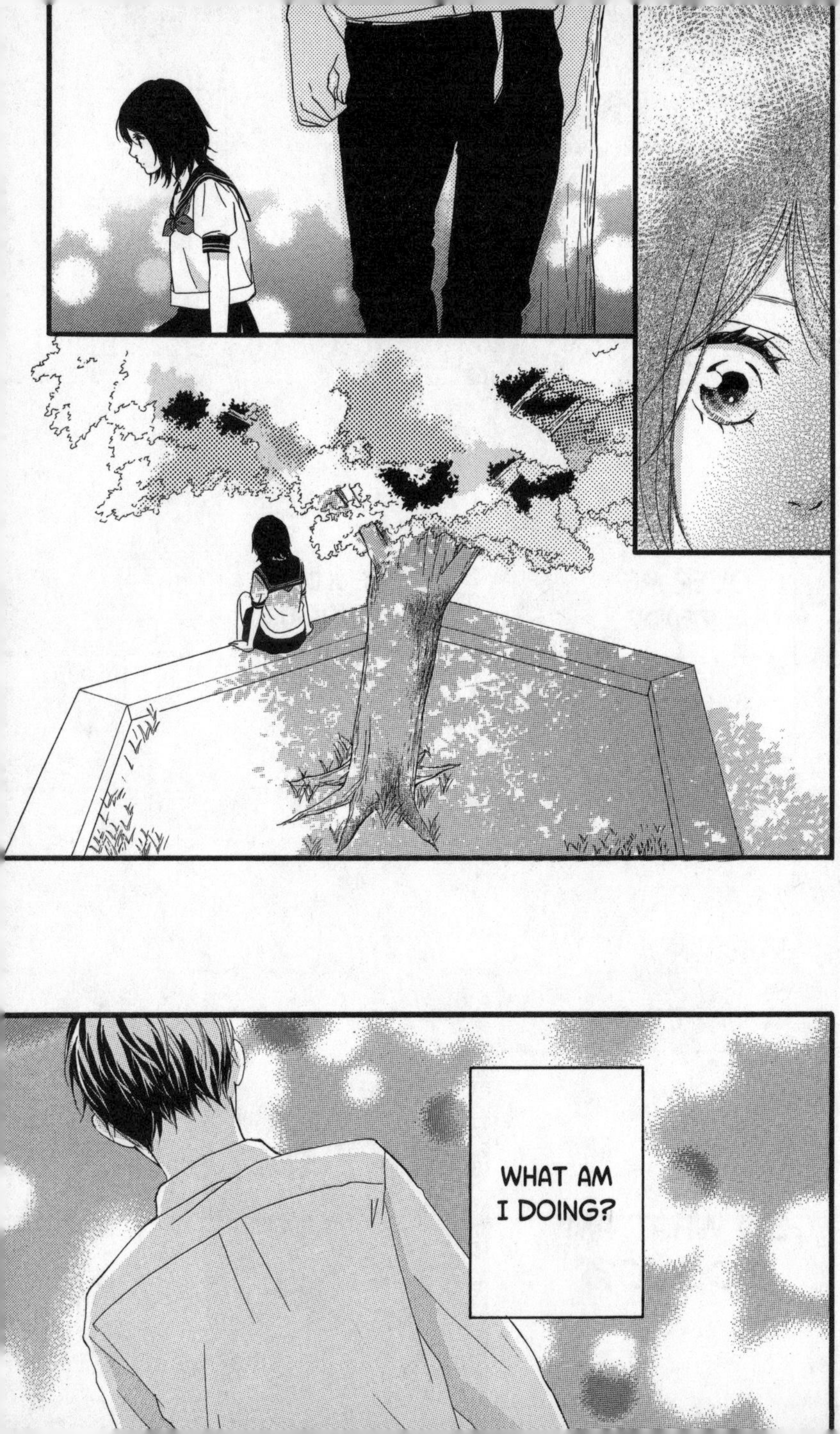
WHAT AM
I DOING?

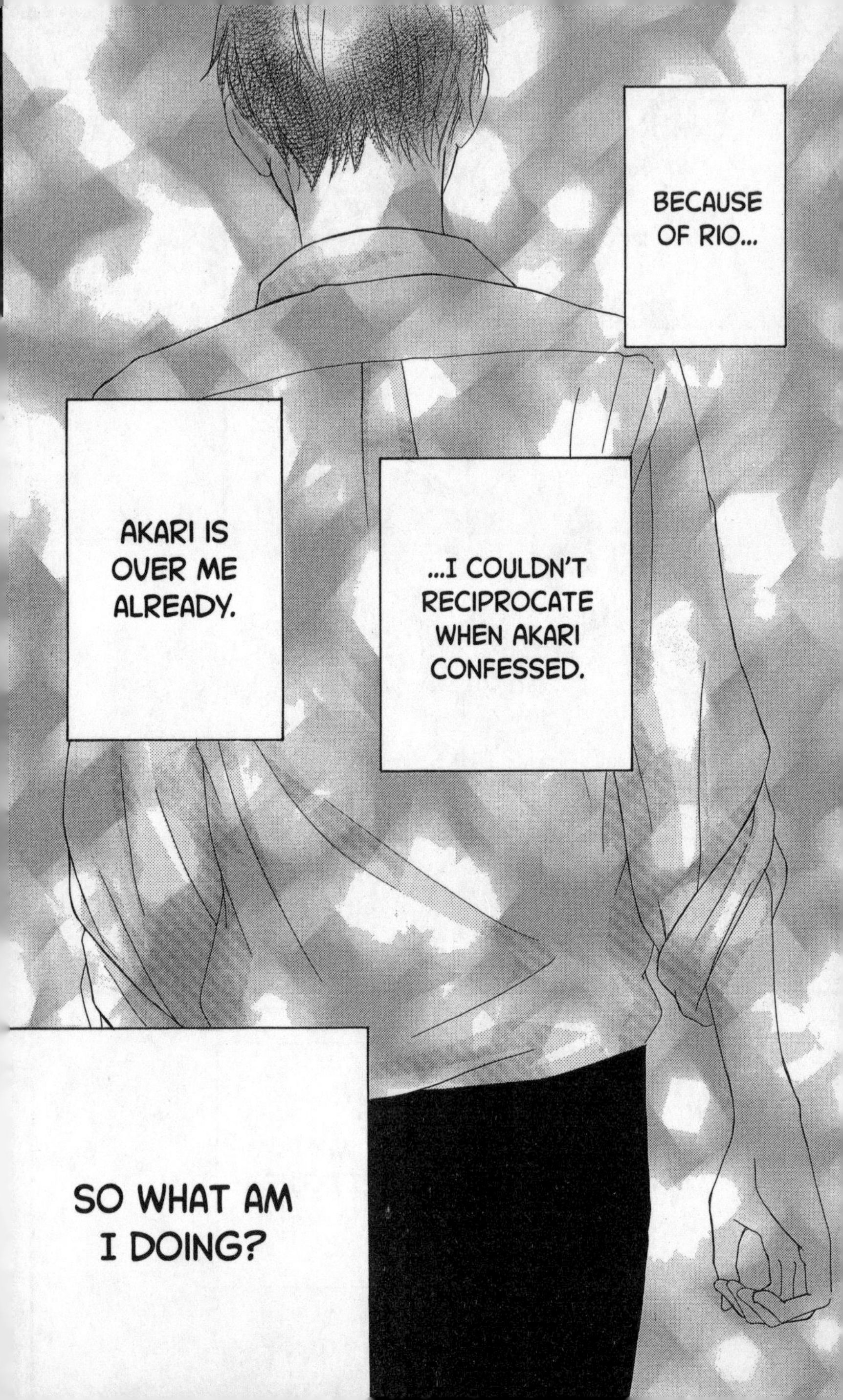
BECAUSE OF RIO...
...I COULDN'T RECIPROCATE WHEN AKARI CONFESSED.
AKARI IS OVER ME ALREADY.
SO WHAT AM I DOING?

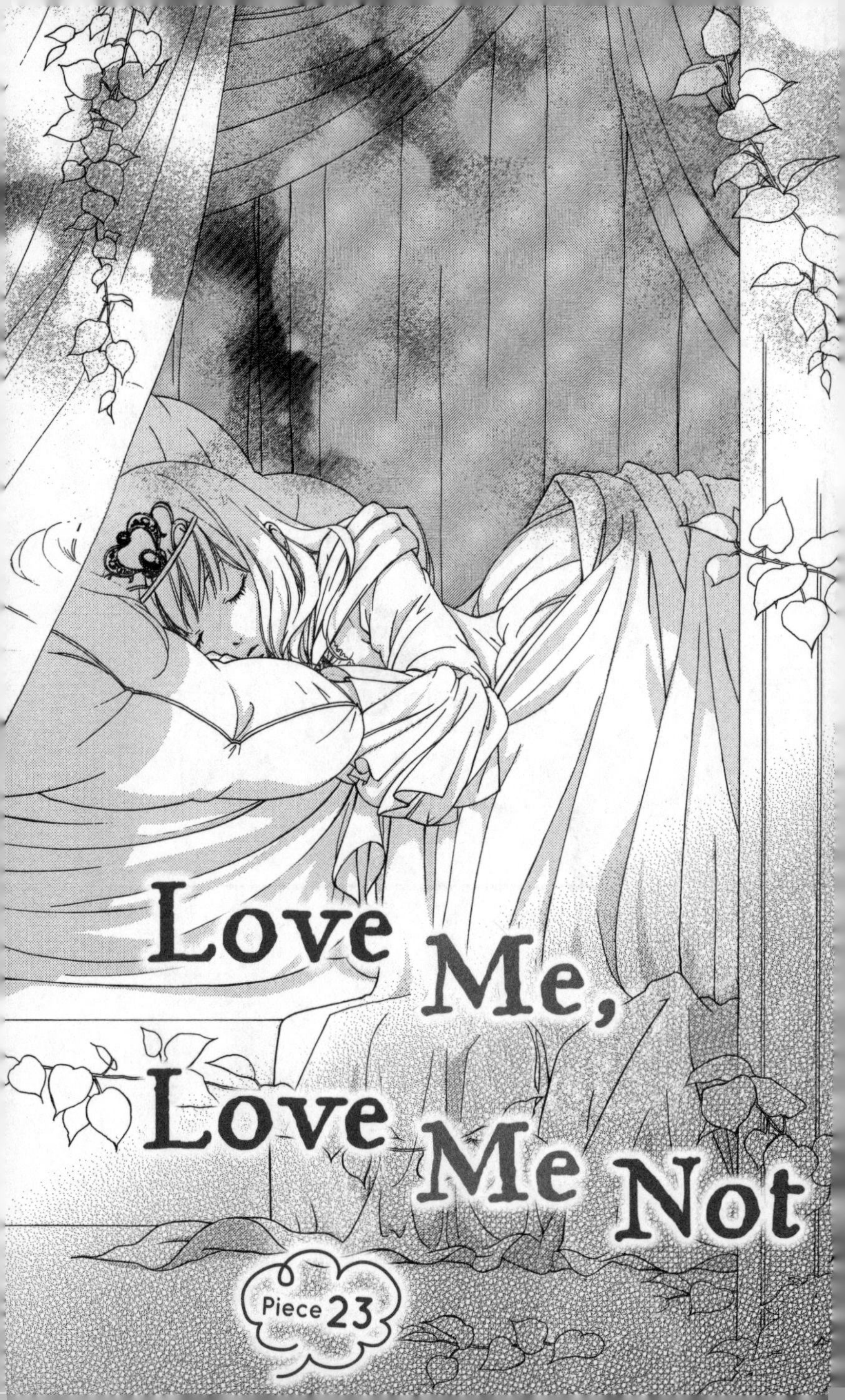
Love Me, Love Me Not
Piece 23

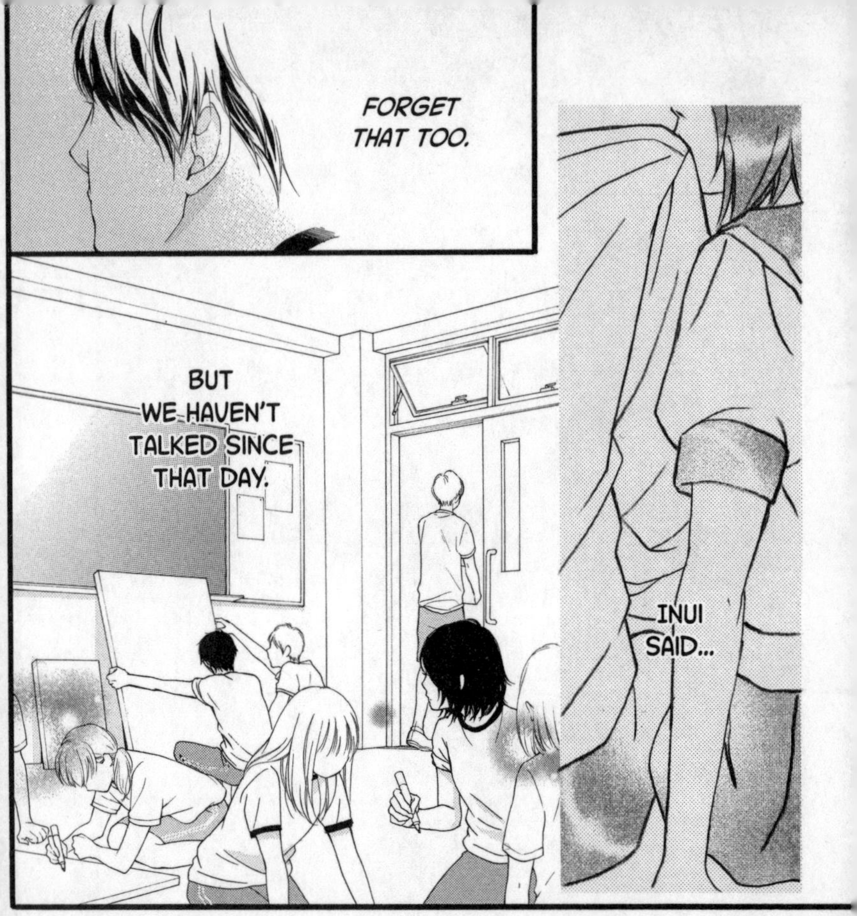
INUI SAID...
FORGET THAT TOO.
BUT WE HAVEN'T TALKED SINCE THAT DAY.

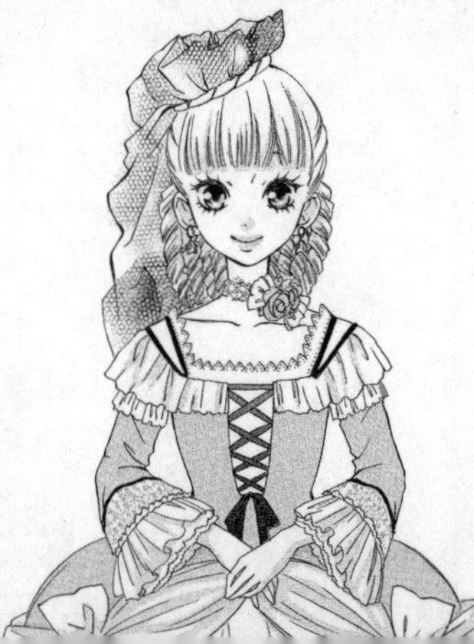

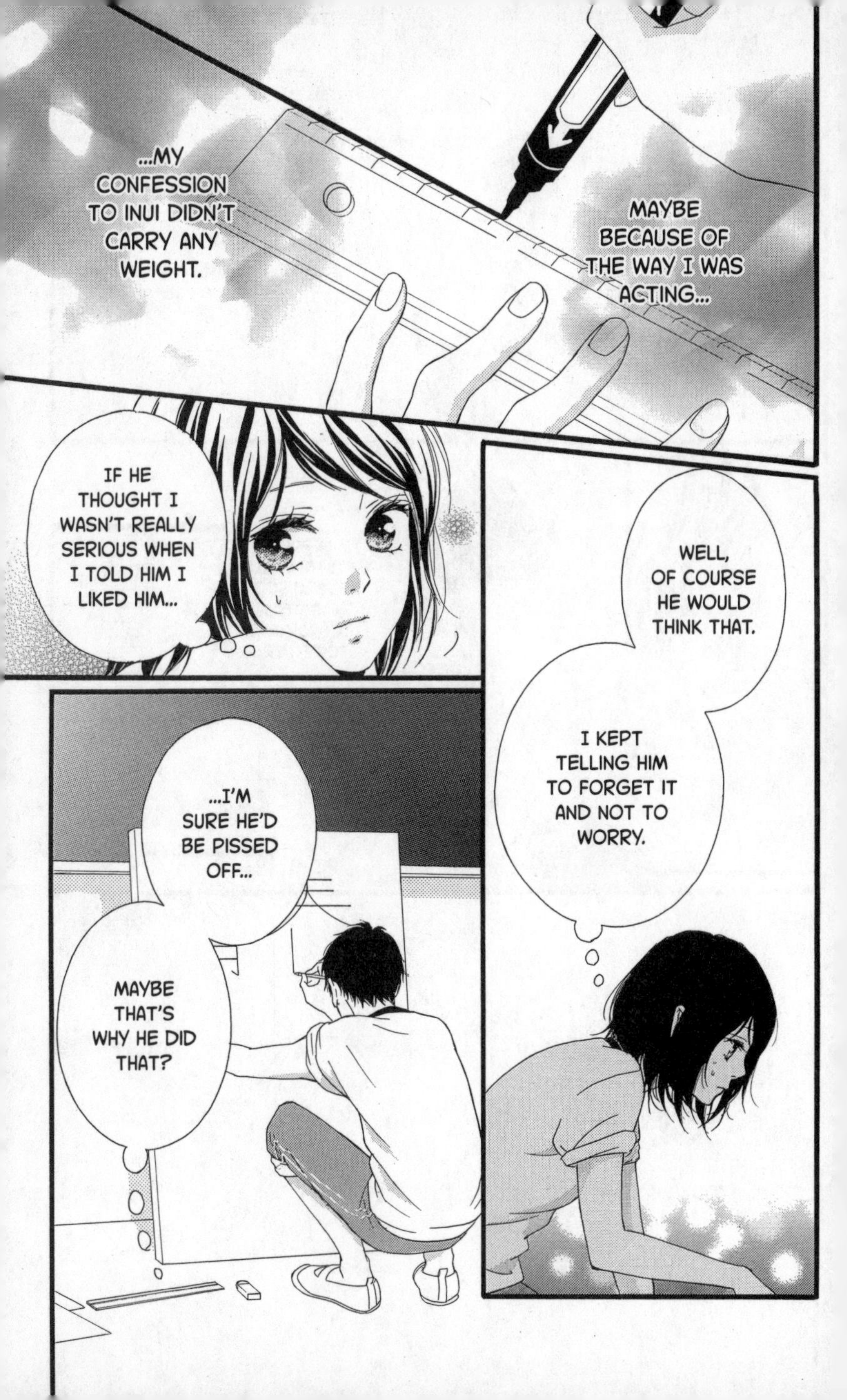
MAYBE BECAUSE OF THE WAY I WAS ACTING...
...MY CONFESSION TO INUI DIDN'T CARRY ANY WEIGHT.
IF HE THOUGHT I WASN'T REALLY SERIOUS WHEN I TOLD HIM I LIKED HIM...
WELL, OF COURSE HE WOULD THINK THAT.
I KEPT TELLING HIM TO FORGET IT AND NOT TO WORRY.
...I'M SURE HE'D BE PISSED OFF...
MAYBE THAT'S WHY HE DID THAT?

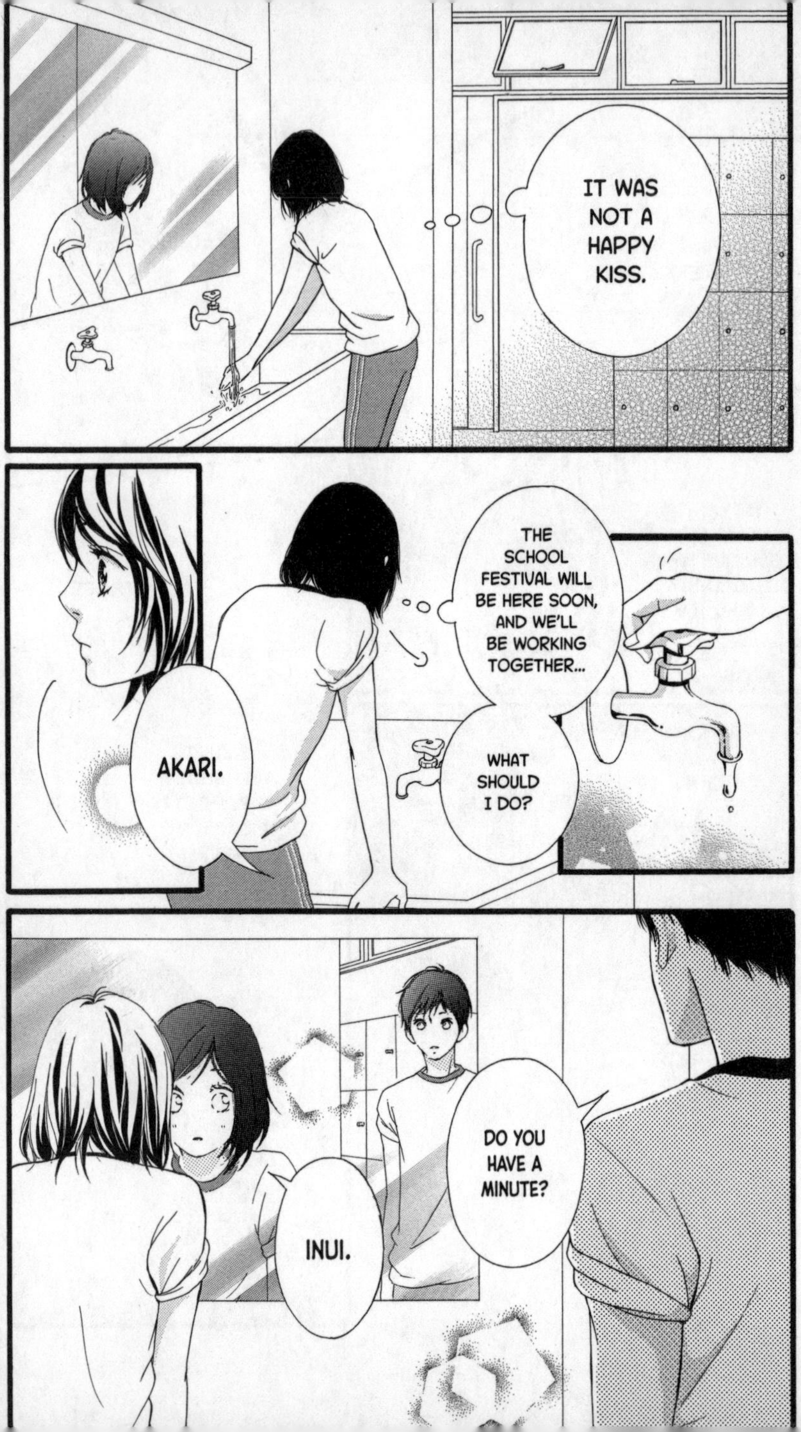
IT WAS NOT A HAPPY KISS.
THE SCHOOL FESTIVAL WILL BE HERE SOON, AND WE'LL BE WORKING TOGETHER...
WHAT SHOULD I DO?
AKARI.
DO YOU HAVE A MINUTE?
INUI.

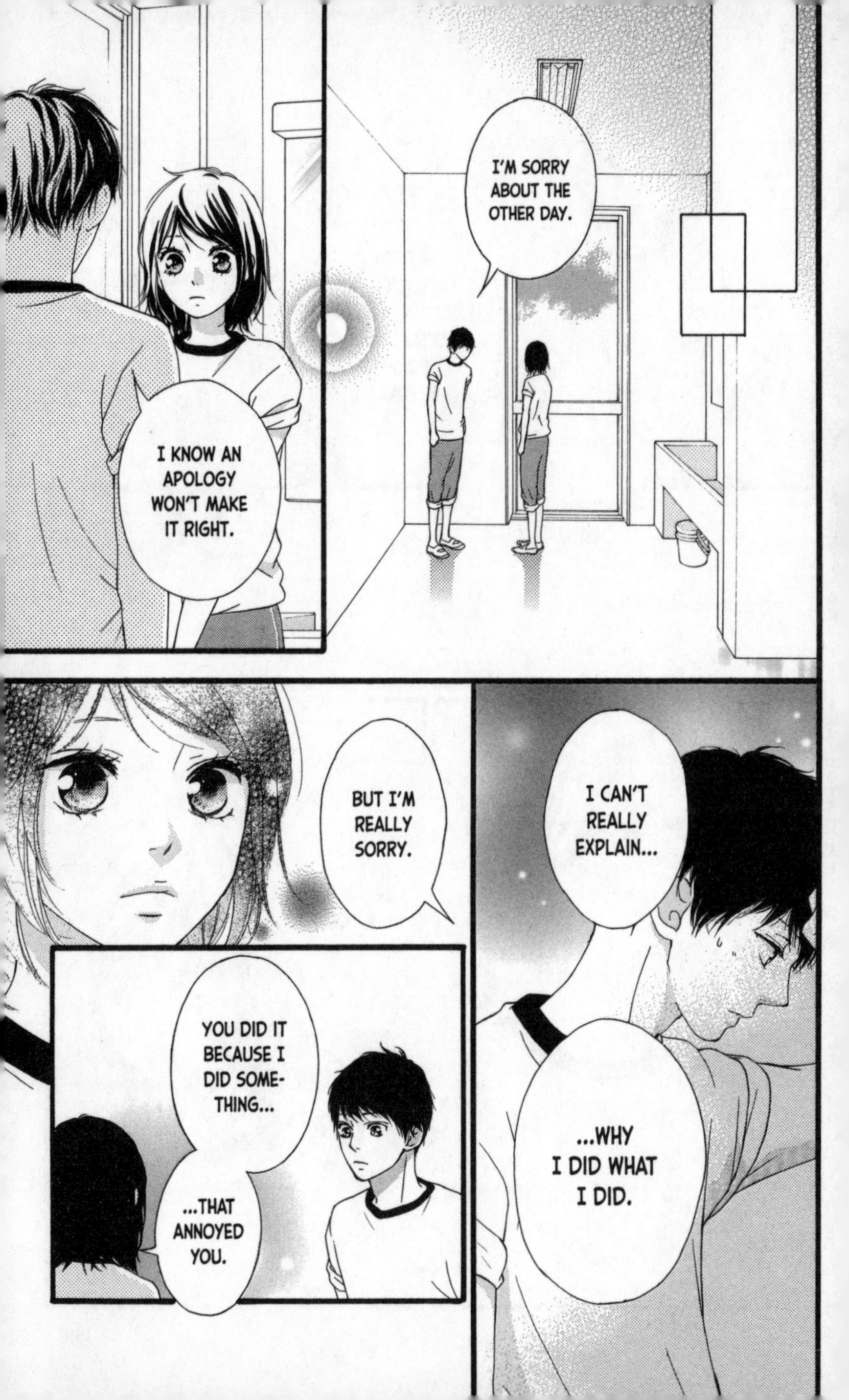
I'M SORRY ABOUT THE OTHER DAY.
I KNOW AN APOLOGY WON'T MAKE IT RIGHT.
I CAN'T REALLY EXPLAIN...
...WHY I DID WHAT I DID.
BUT I'M REALLY SORRY.
YOU DID IT BECAUSE I DID SOME-THING...
...THAT ANNOYED YOU.

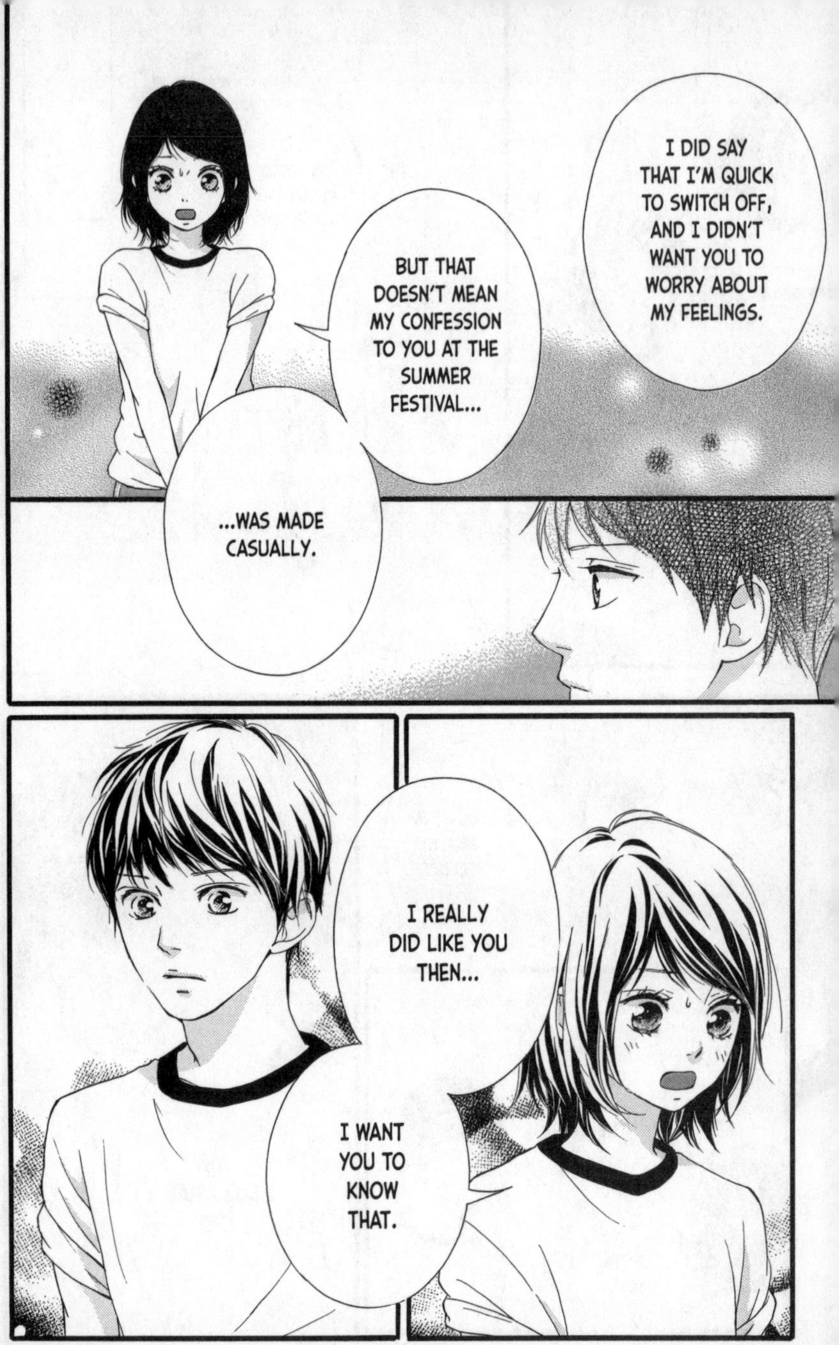
I DID SAY THAT I'M QUICK TO SWITCH OFF, AND I DIDN'T WANT YOU TO WORRY ABOUT MY FEELINGS.
BUT THAT DOESN'T MEAN MY CONFESSION TO YOU AT THE SUMMER FESTIVAL...
...WAS MADE CASUALLY.
I REALLY DID LIKE YOU THEN...
I WANT YOU TO KNOW THAT.

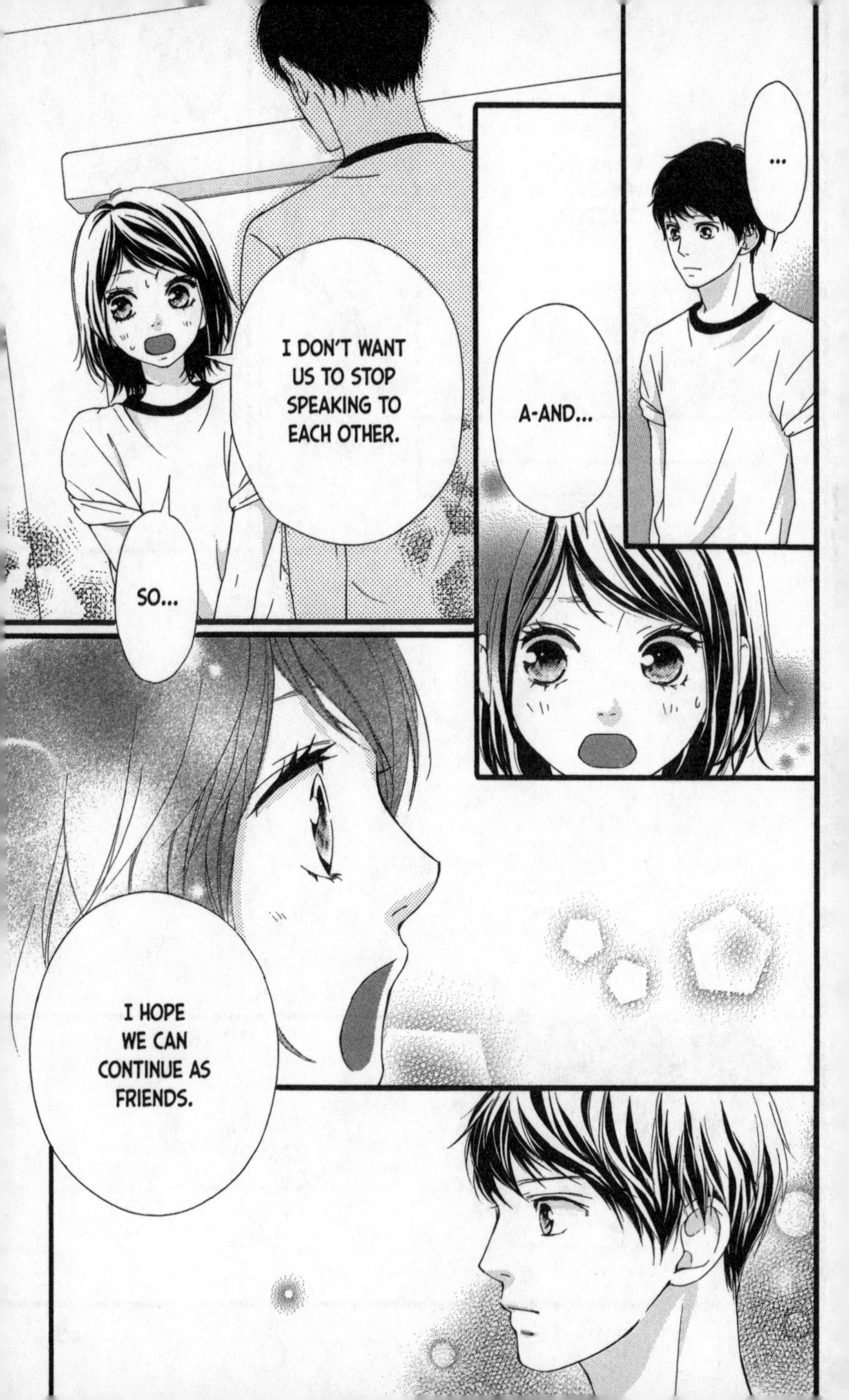
...
A-AND...
I DON'T WANT US TO STOP SPEAKING TO EACH OTHER.
SO...
I HOPE WE CAN CONTINUE AS FRIENDS.

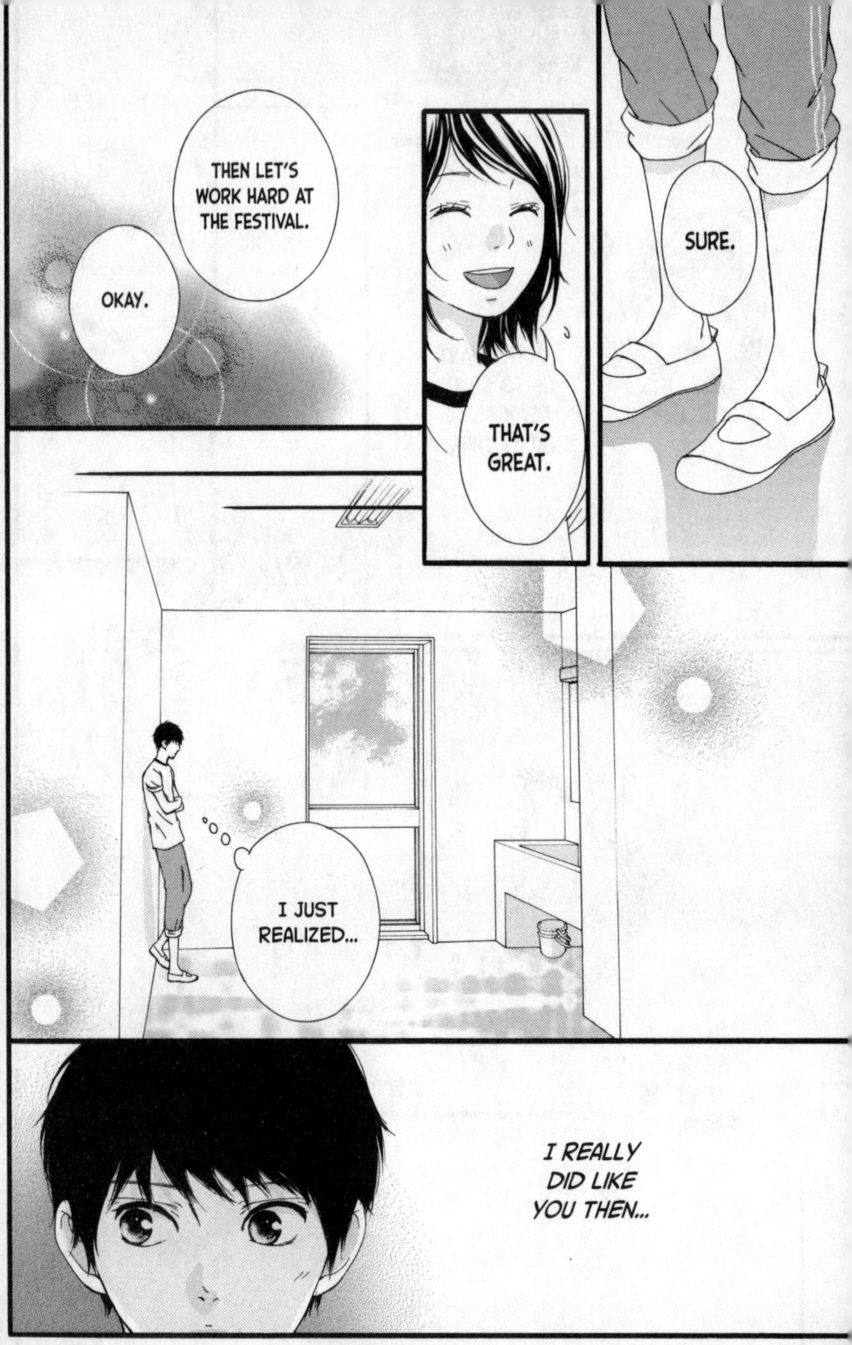
SURE.
THAT'S GREAT.
THEN LET'S WORK HARD AT THE FESTIVAL.
OKAY.
I JUST REALIZED...
I REALLY DID LIKE YOU THEN...

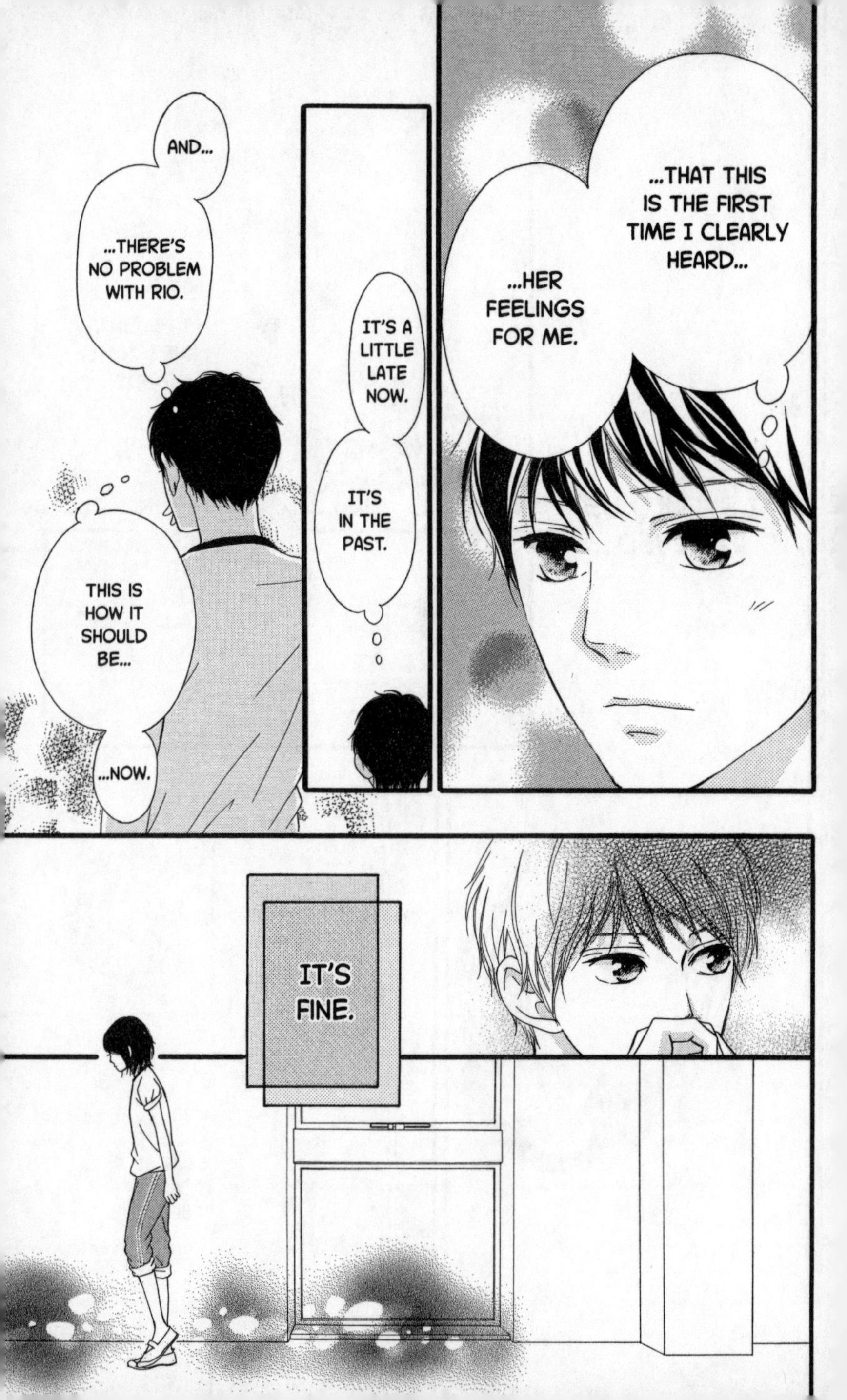
...THAT THIS IS THE FIRST TIME I CLEARLY HEARD...
...HER FEELINGS FOR ME.
IT'S A LITTLE LATE NOW.
IT'S IN THE PAST.
AND...
...THERE'S NO PROBLEM WITH RIO.
THIS IS HOW IT SHOULD BE...
...NOW.
IT'S FINE.

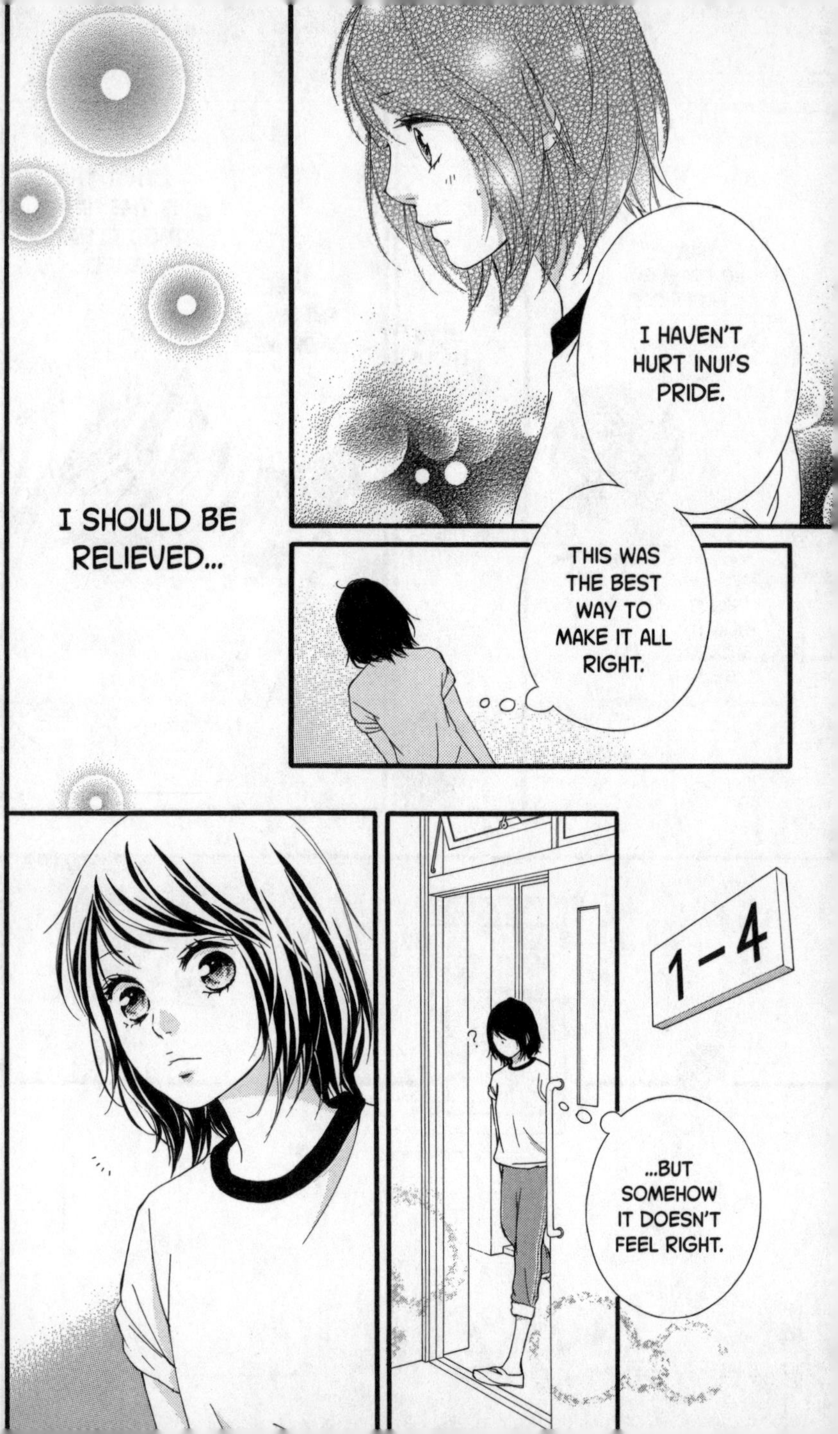
I HAVEN'T HURT INUI'S PRIDE.
THIS WAS THE BEST WAY TO MAKE IT ALL RIGHT.
I SHOULD BE RELIEVED...
1-4
...BUT SOMEHOW IT DOESN'T FEEL RIGHT.

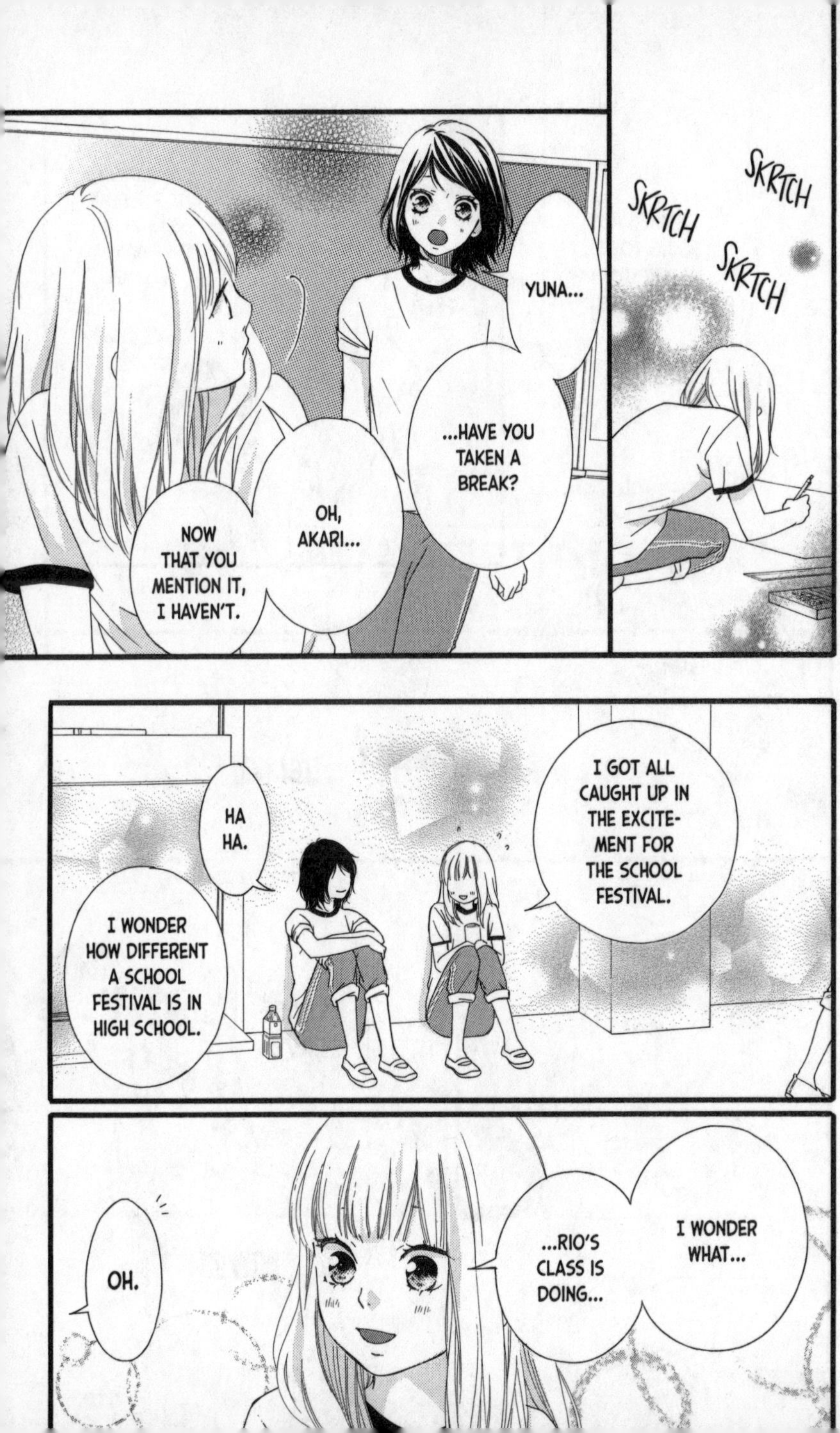
SKRTCH
SKRTCH
SKRTCH
YUNA...
...HAVE YOU TAKEN A BREAK?
OH, AKARI...
NOW THAT YOU MENTION IT, I HAVEN'T.
I GOT ALL CAUGHT UP IN THE EXCITE-MENT FOR THE SCHOOL FESTIVAL.
HA HA.
I WONDER HOW DIFFERENT A SCHOOL FESTIVAL IS IN HIGH SCHOOL.
I WONDER WHAT...
...RIO'S CLASS IS DOING...
OH.

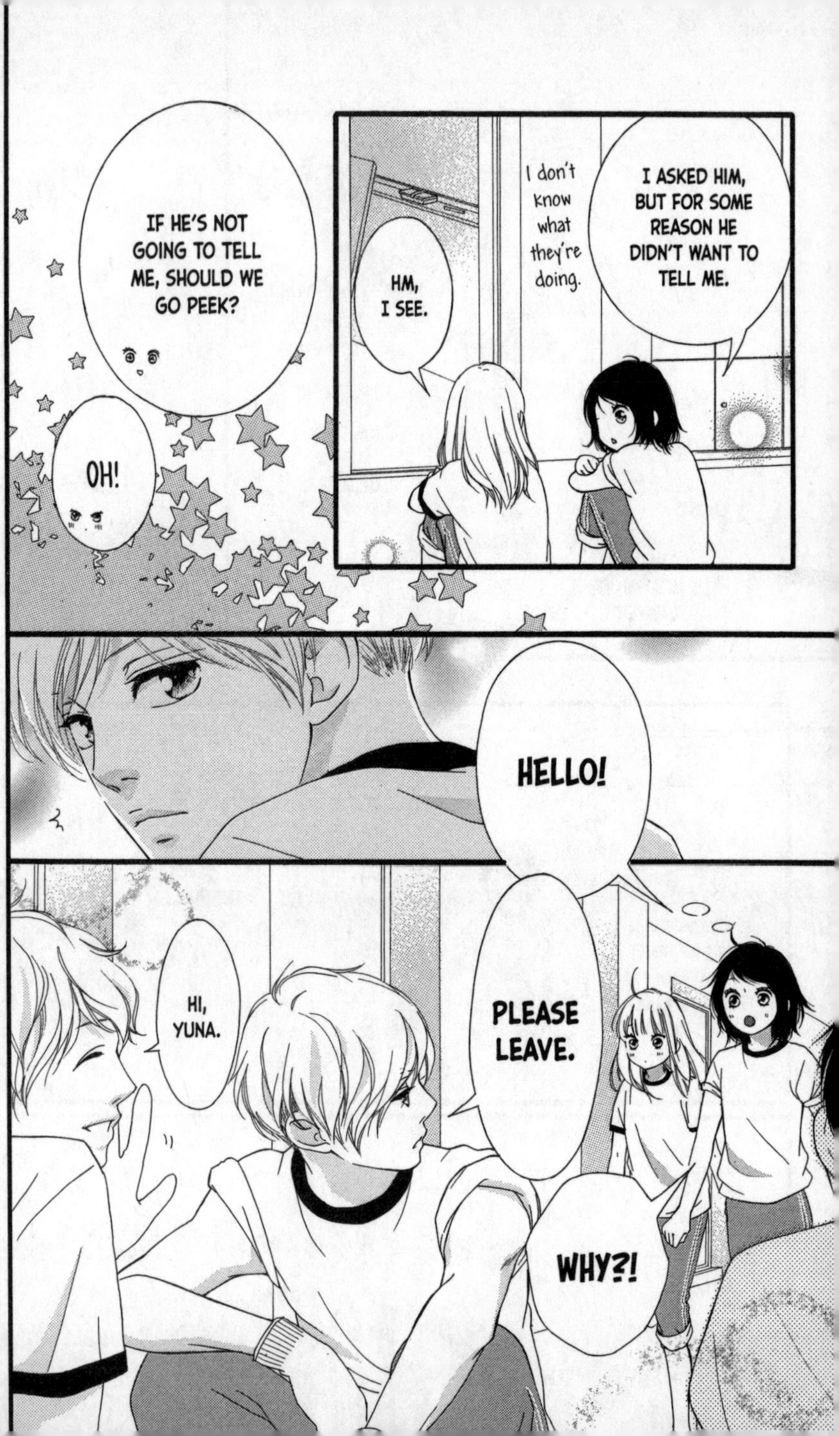

I ASKED HIM, BUT FOR SOME REASON HE DIDN'T WANT TO TELL ME.
I don't know what they're doing.
HM, I SEE.
IF HE'S NOT GOING TO TELL ME, SHOULD WE GO PEEK?
OH!
HELLO!
PLEASE LEAVE.
WHY?!
HI, YUNA.

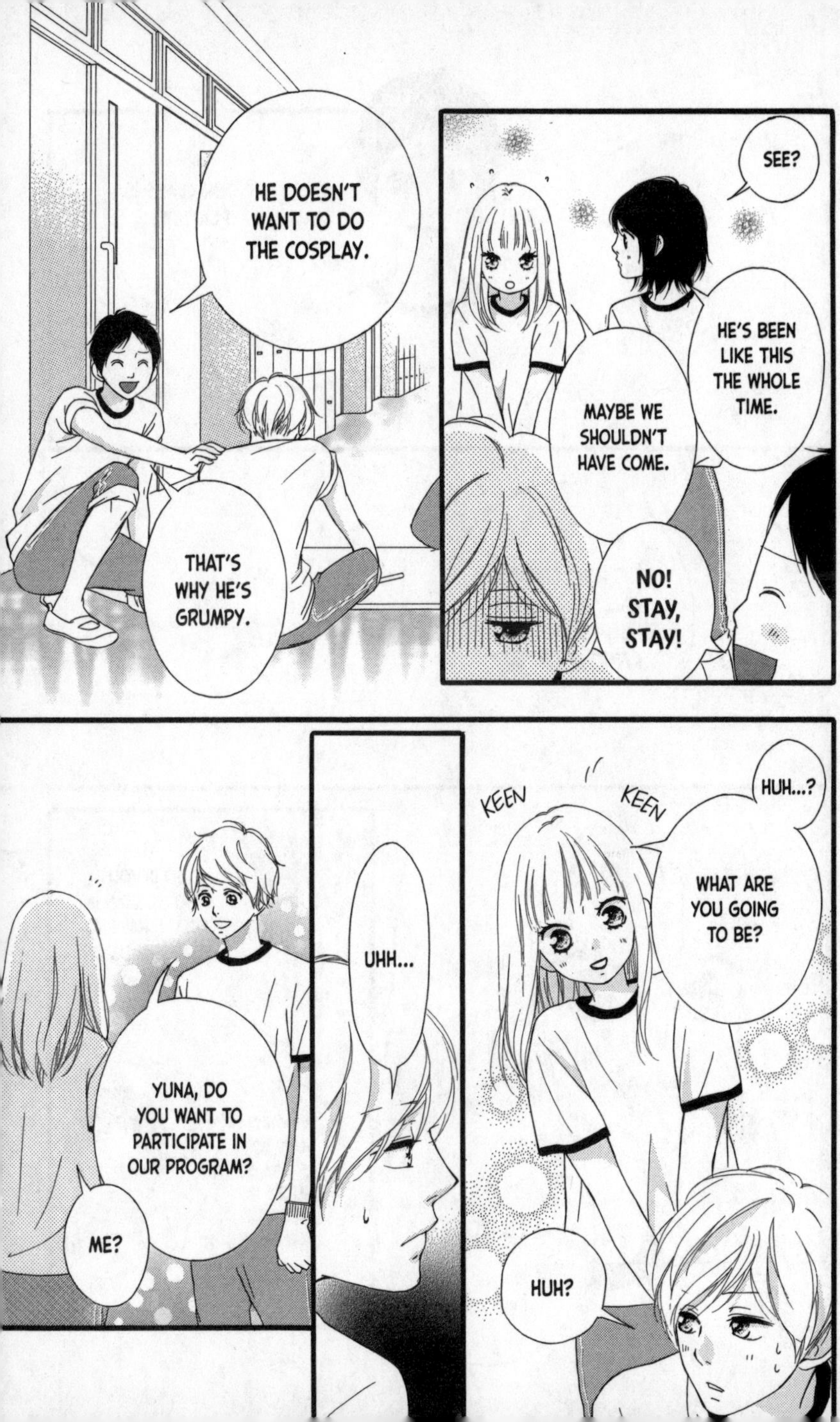
SEE?
HE'S BEEN LIKE THIS THE WHOLE TIME.
MAYBE WE SHOULDN'T HAVE COME.
NO! STAY, STAY!
HE DOESN'T WANT TO DO THE COSPLAY.
THAT'S WHY HE'S GRUMPY.
KEEN
KEEN
HUH...?
WHAT ARE YOU GOING TO BE?
HUH?
UHH...
YUNA, DO YOU WANT TO PARTICIPATE IN OUR PROGRAM?
ME?

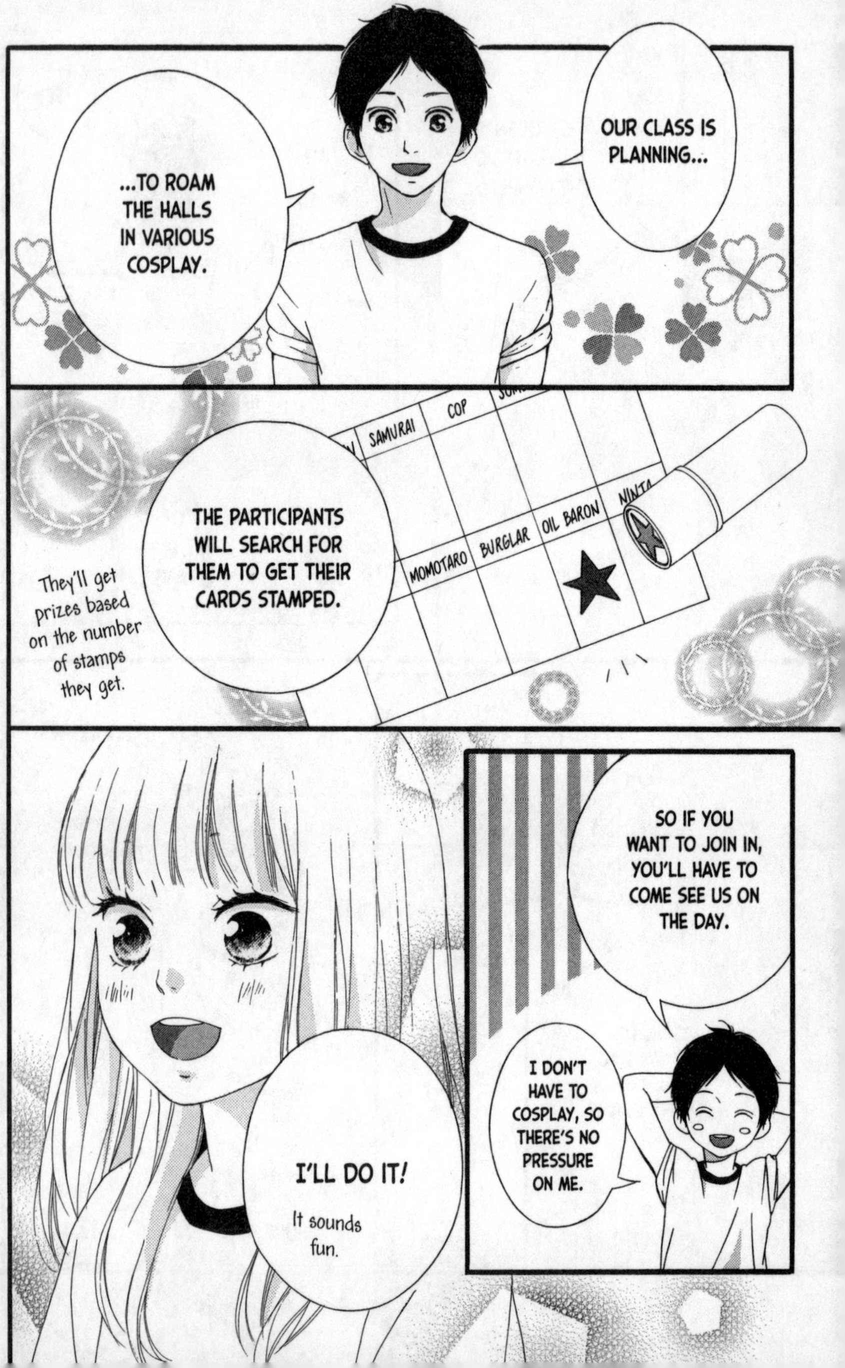
OUR CLASS IS PLANNING...
...TO ROAM THE HALLS IN VARIOUS COSPLAY.
SAMURAI
COP
OIL BARON
MOMOTARO
BURGLAR
THE PARTICIPANTS WILL SEARCH FOR THEM TO GET THEIR CARDS STAMPED.
They'll get prizes based on the number of stamps they get.
SO IF YOU WANT TO JOIN IN, YOU'LL HAVE TO COME SEE US ON THE DAY.
I DON'T HAVE TO COSPLAY, SO THERE'S NO PRESSURE ON ME.
I'LL DO IT!
It sounds fun.

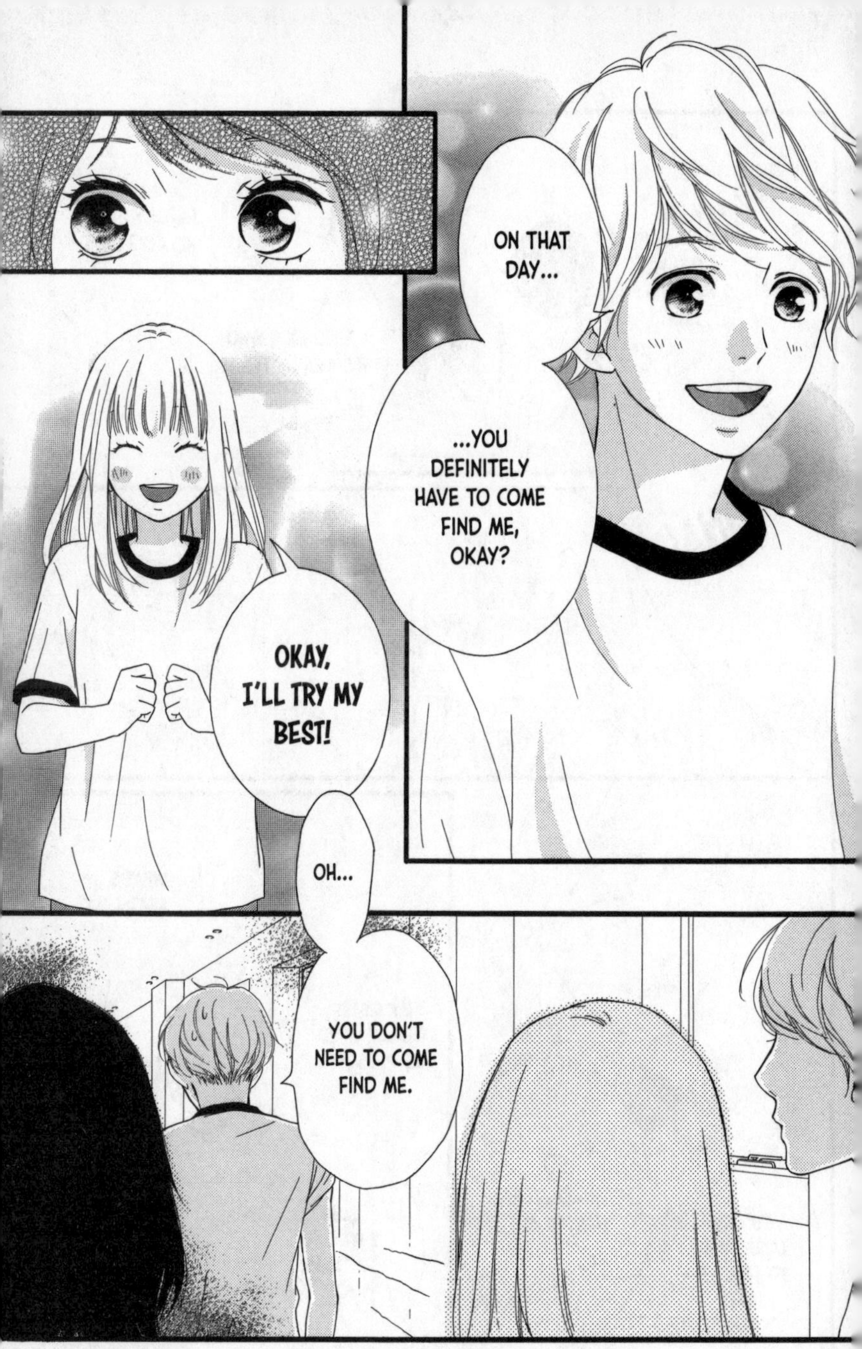
ON THAT DAY...
...YOU DEFINITELY HAVE TO COME FIND ME, OKAY?
OKAY, I'LL TRY MY BEST!
OH...
YOU DON'T NEED TO COME FIND ME.

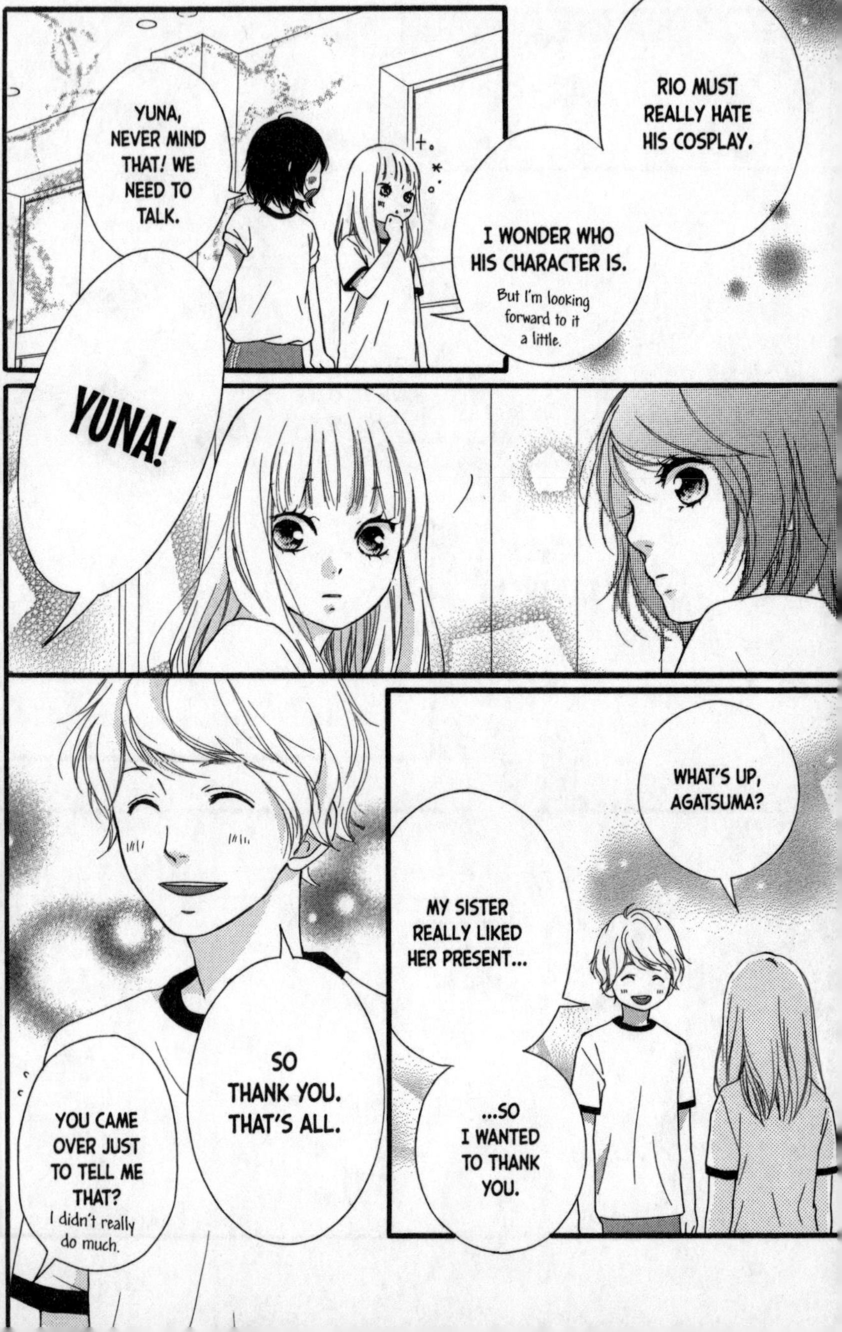
RIO MUST REALLY HATE HIS COSPLAY.
I WONDER WHO HIS CHARACTER IS.
But I'm looking forward to it a little.
YUNA, NEVER MIND THAT! WE NEED TO TALK.
YUNA!
WHAT'S UP, AGATSUMA?
MY SISTER REALLY LIKED HER PRESENT...
...SO I WANTED TO THANK YOU.
SO THANK YOU. THAT'S ALL.
YOU CAME OVER JUST TO TELL ME THAT?
I didn't really do much.

When I heard that T., who always helps me with my manuscripts, goes to a croquis drawing class, I thought, "I want to go too." So the other day, I went along. I'd never done croquis drawing before, so it was a completely unknown world for me. I was pretty excited even before I went. I found that croquis is such a busy activity for your hands. There's a time limit, so I was in a panic the whole time. I kept worrying about the timer and felt frantic. Toward the end, the time limit was only two minutes. The model struck a pretty aggressive pose, and I kept thinking, "Two minutes for this form? Are you serious?!" while furiously concentrating. The exhaustion I felt when it ended was unreal.

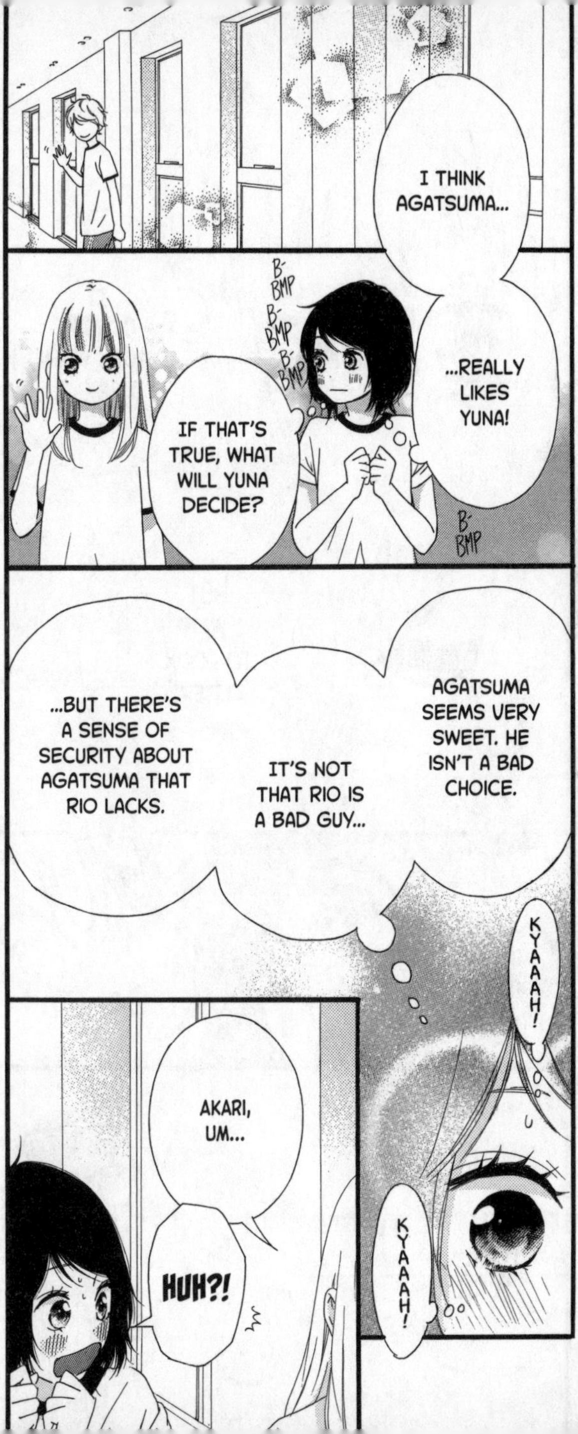
I THINK AGATSUMA...
...REALLY LIKES YUNA!
B-BMP B-BMP B-BMP
B-BMP
IF THAT'S TRUE, WHAT WILL YUNA DECIDE?
AGATSUMA SEEMS VERY SWEET. HE ISN'T A BAD CHOICE.
IT'S NOT THAT RIO IS A BAD GUY...
...BUT THERE'S A SENSE OF SECURITY ABOUT AGATSUMA THAT RIO LACKS.
KYAAAH!
KYAAAH!
AKARI, UM...
HUH?!

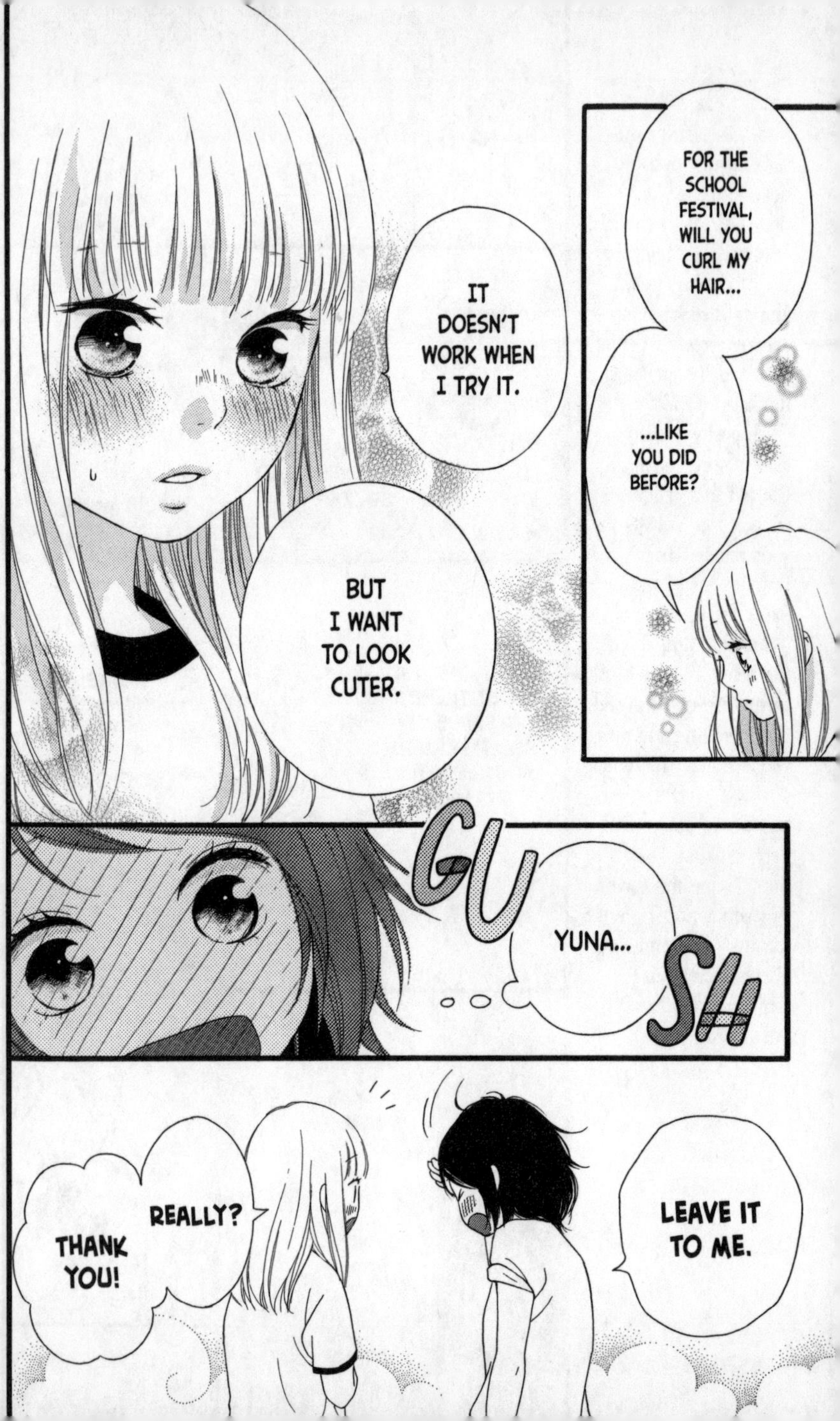
FOR THE SCHOOL FESTIVAL, WILL YOU CURL MY HAIR...
...LIKE YOU DID BEFORE?
IT DOESN'T WORK WHEN I TRY IT.
BUT I WANT TO LOOK CUTER.
GUSH
YUNA...
LEAVE IT TO ME.
REALLY?
THANK YOU!

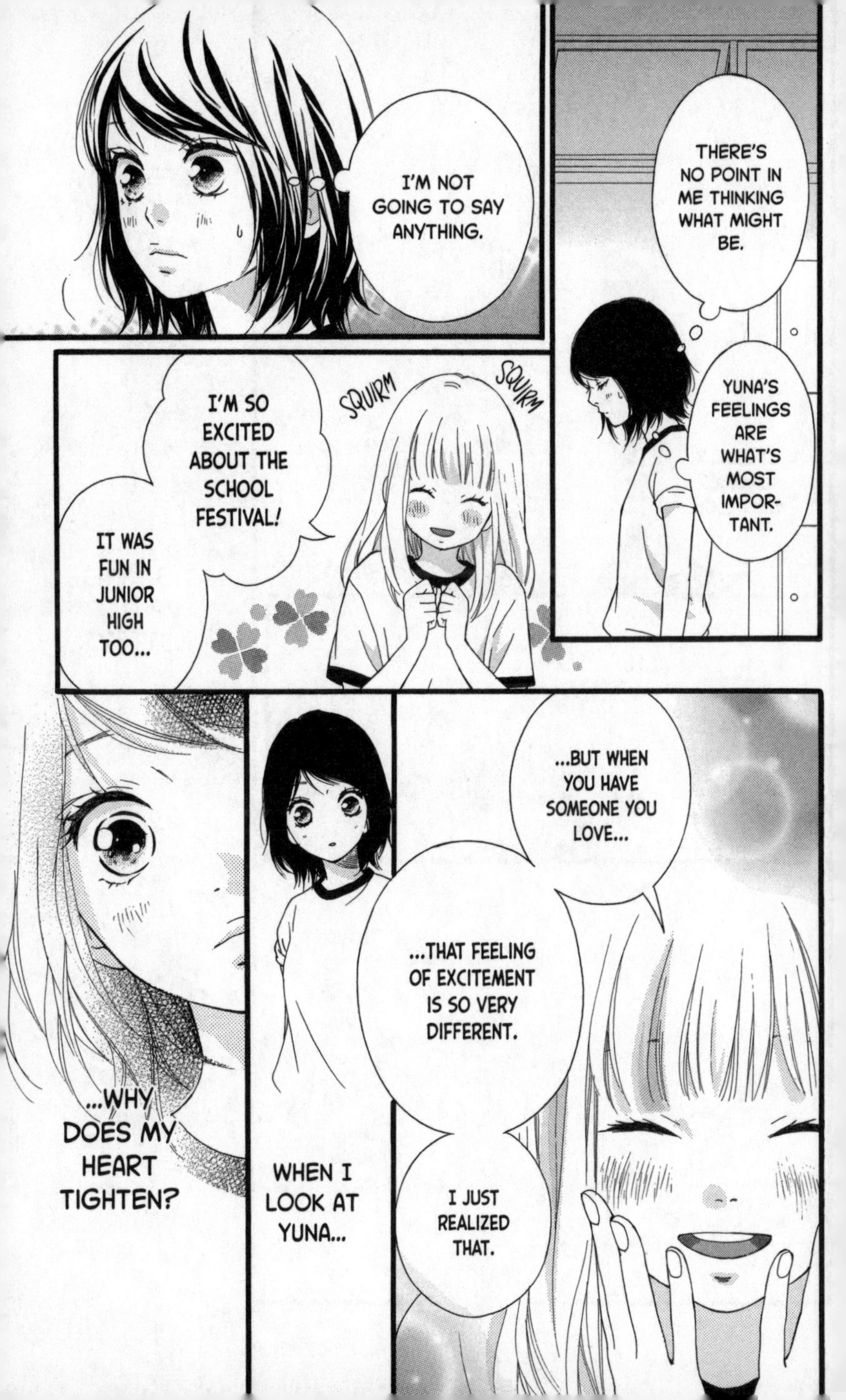
THERE'S NO POINT IN ME THINKING WHAT MIGHT BE.
YUNA'S FEELINGS ARE WHAT'S MOST IMPOR-TANT.
I'M NOT GOING TO SAY ANYTHING.
SQUIRM
SQUIRM
I'M SO EXCITED ABOUT THE SCHOOL FESTIVAL!
IT WAS FUN IN JUNIOR HIGH TOO...
...BUT WHEN YOU HAVE SOMEONE YOU LOVE...
...THAT FEELING OF EXCITEMENT IS SO VERY DIFFERENT.
I JUST REALIZED THAT.
WHEN I LOOK AT YUNA...
...WHY DOES MY HEART TIGHTEN?

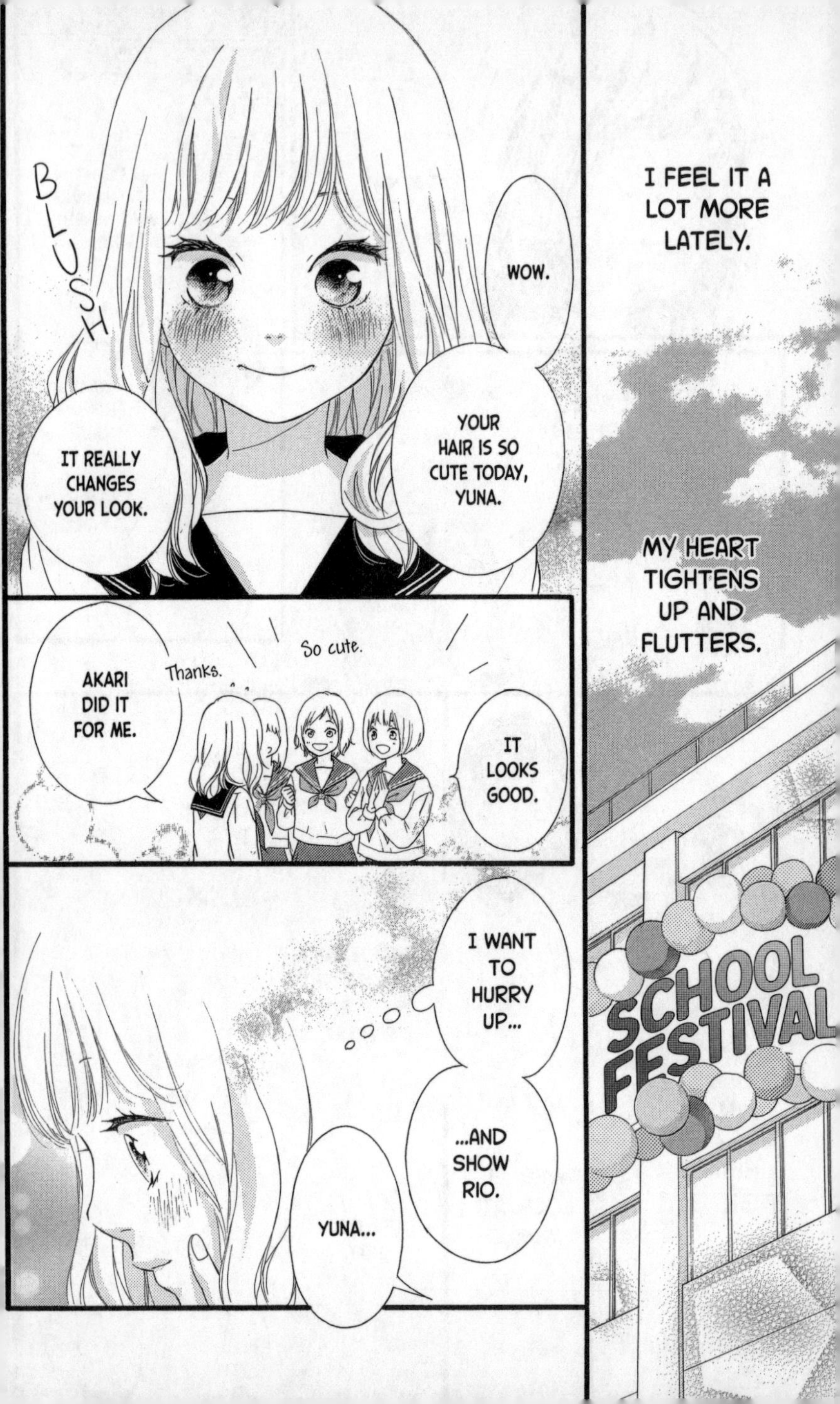
I FEEL IT A LOT MORE LATELY.
MY HEART TIGHTENS UP AND FLUTTERS.
SCHOOL FESTIVAL
WOW.
YOUR HAIR IS SO CUTE TODAY, YUNA.
IT REALLY CHANGES YOUR LOOK.
BLUSH
So cute.
IT LOOKS GOOD.
Thanks.
AKARI DID IT FOR ME.
I WANT TO HURRY UP...
...AND SHOW RIO.
YUNA...

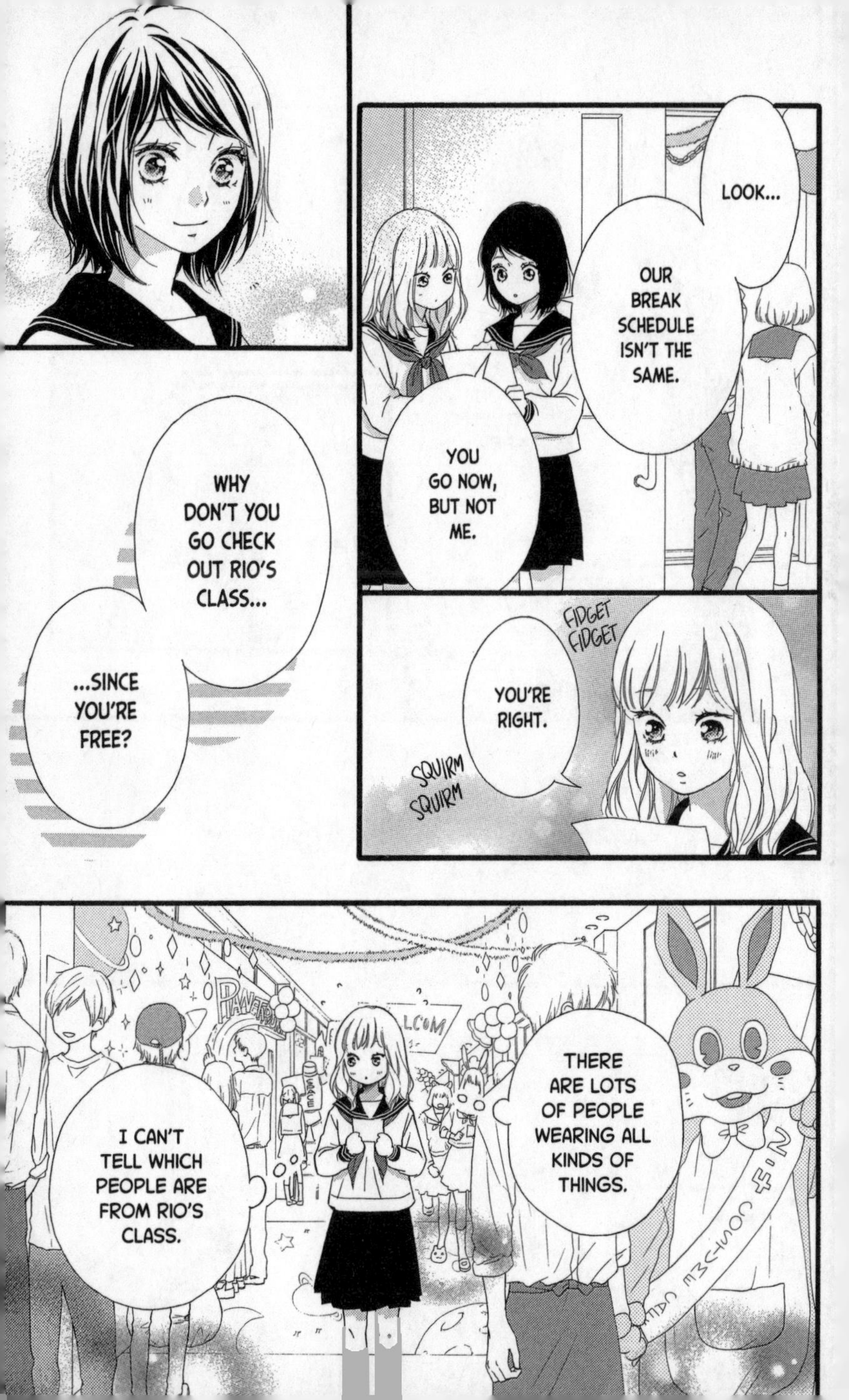
LOOK...
OUR BREAK SCHEDULE ISN'T THE SAME.
YOU GO NOW, BUT NOT ME.
WHY DON'T YOU GO CHECK OUT RIO'S CLASS...
...SINCE YOU'RE FREE?
FIDGET FIDGET
YOU'RE RIGHT.
SQUIRM SQUIRM
THERE ARE LOTS OF PEOPLE WEARING ALL KINDS OF THINGS.
I CAN'T TELL WHICH PEOPLE ARE FROM RIO'S CLASS.

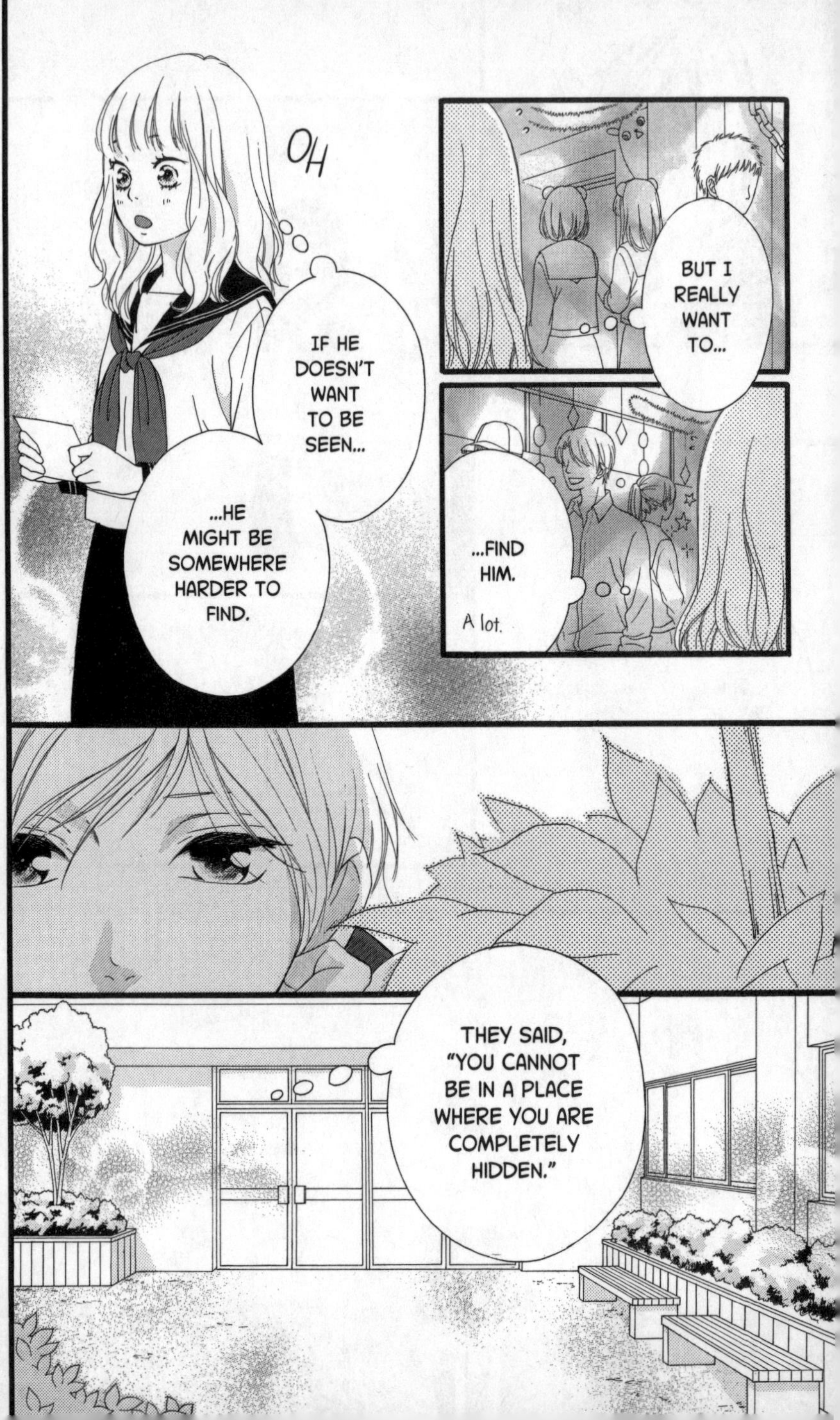
OH
IF HE DOESN'T WANT TO BE SEEN...
...HE MIGHT BE SOMEWHERE HARDER TO FIND.
BUT I REALLY WANT TO...
...FIND HIM.
A lot.
THEY SAID, "YOU CANNOT BE IN A PLACE WHERE YOU ARE COMPLETELY HIDDEN."

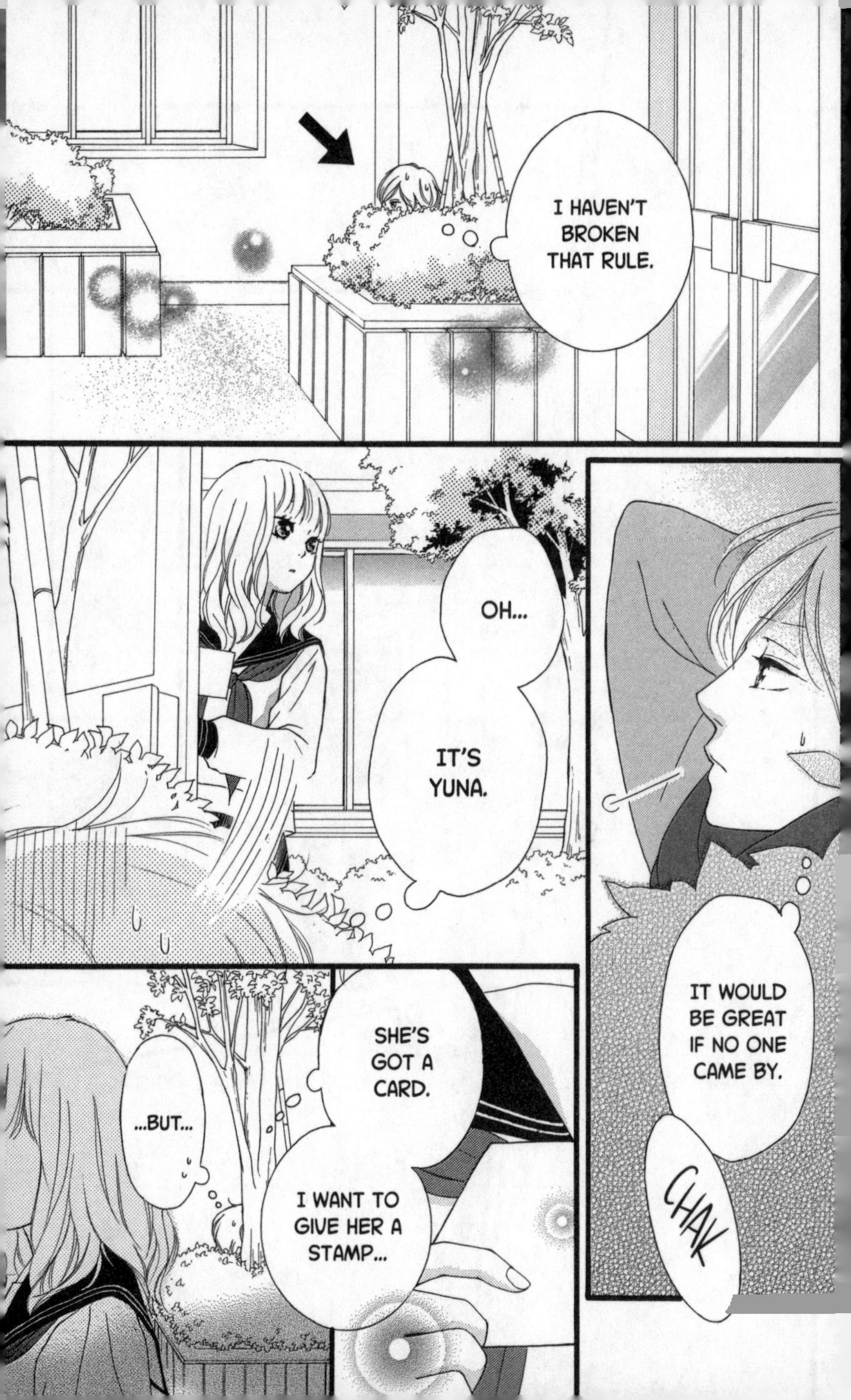
I HAVEN'T BROKEN THAT RULE.
IT WOULD BE GREAT IF NO ONE CAME BY.
CHAK
OH...
IT'S YUNA.
SHE'S GOT A CARD.
I WANT TO GIVE HER A STAMP...
...BUT...

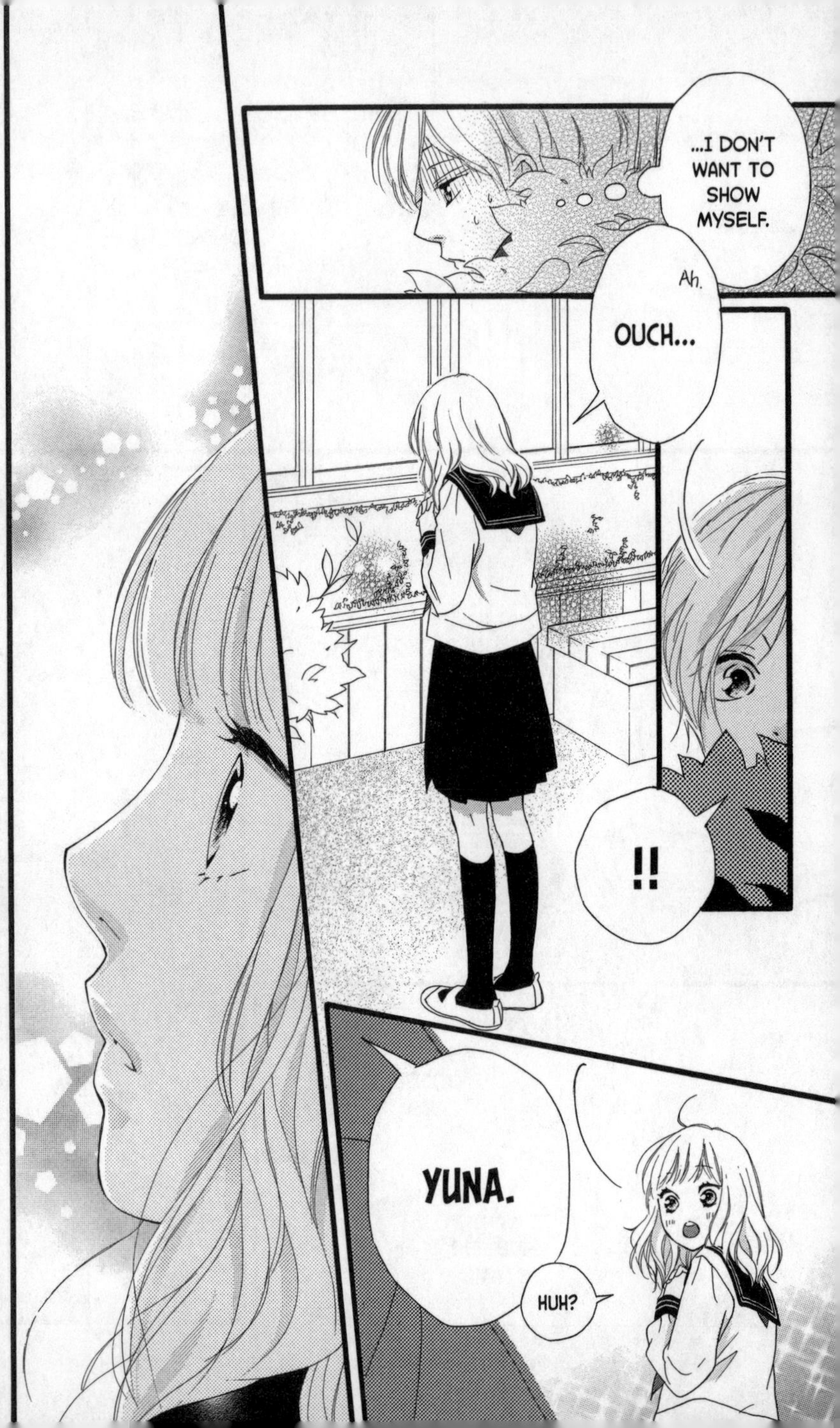
...I DON'T WANT TO SHOW MYSELF.
Ah. OUCH...
!!
YUNA.
HUH?

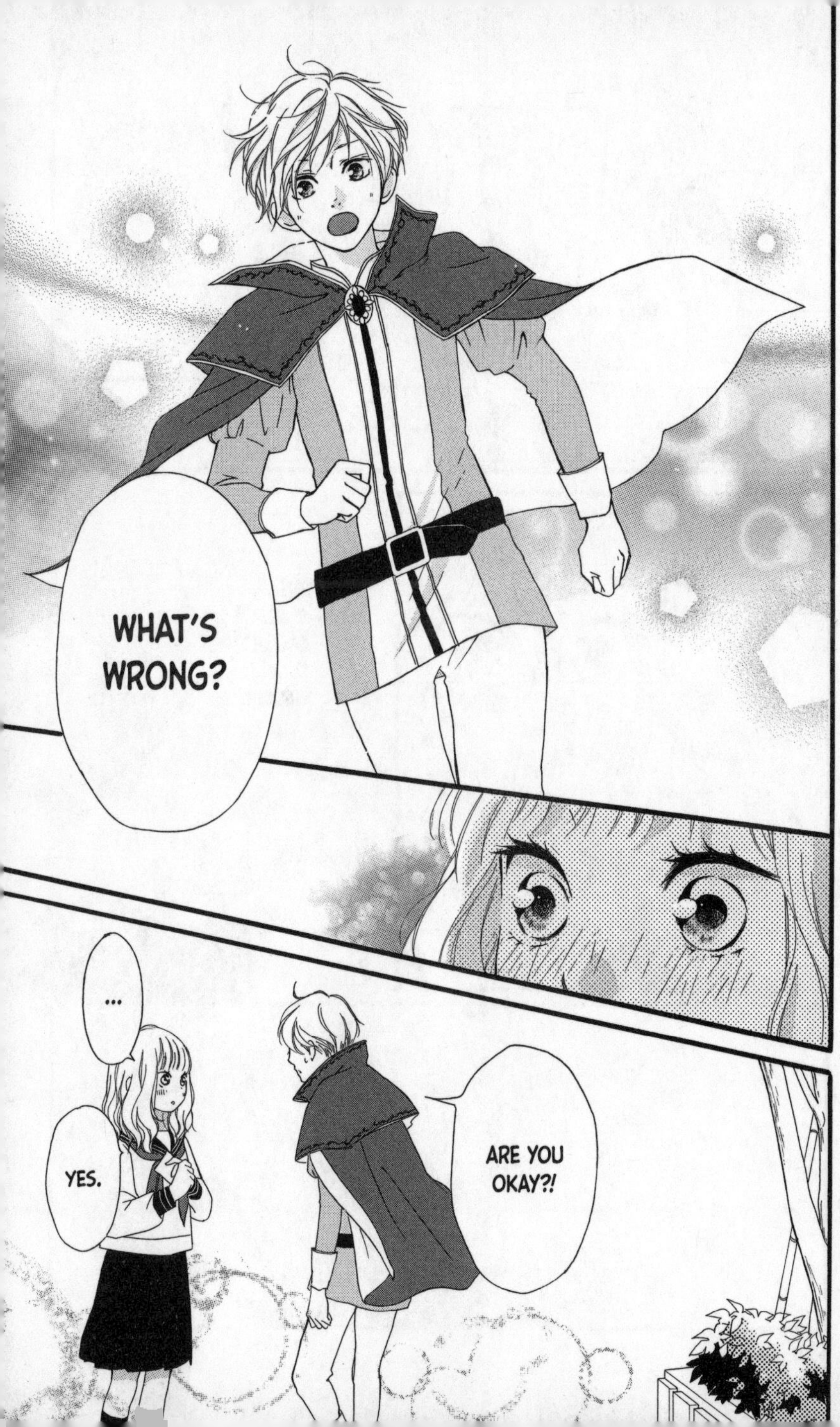
WHAT'S WRONG?
ARE YOU OKAY?!
...
YES.

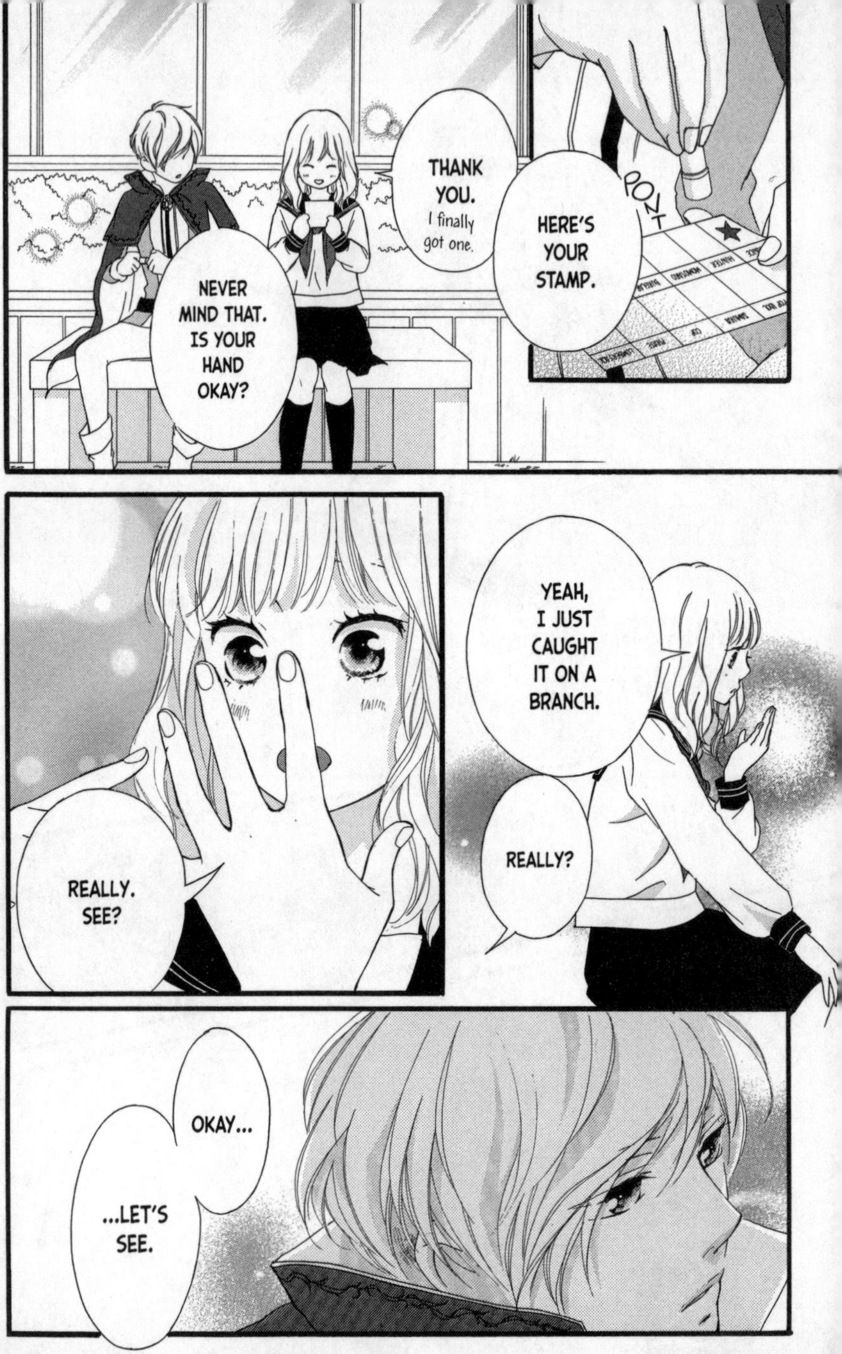
PONT
HERE'S YOUR STAMP.
THANK YOU. I finally got one.
NEVER MIND THAT. IS YOUR HAND OKAY?
YEAH, I JUST CAUGHT IT ON A BRANCH.
REALLY?
REALLY. SEE?
OKAY...
...LET'S SEE.

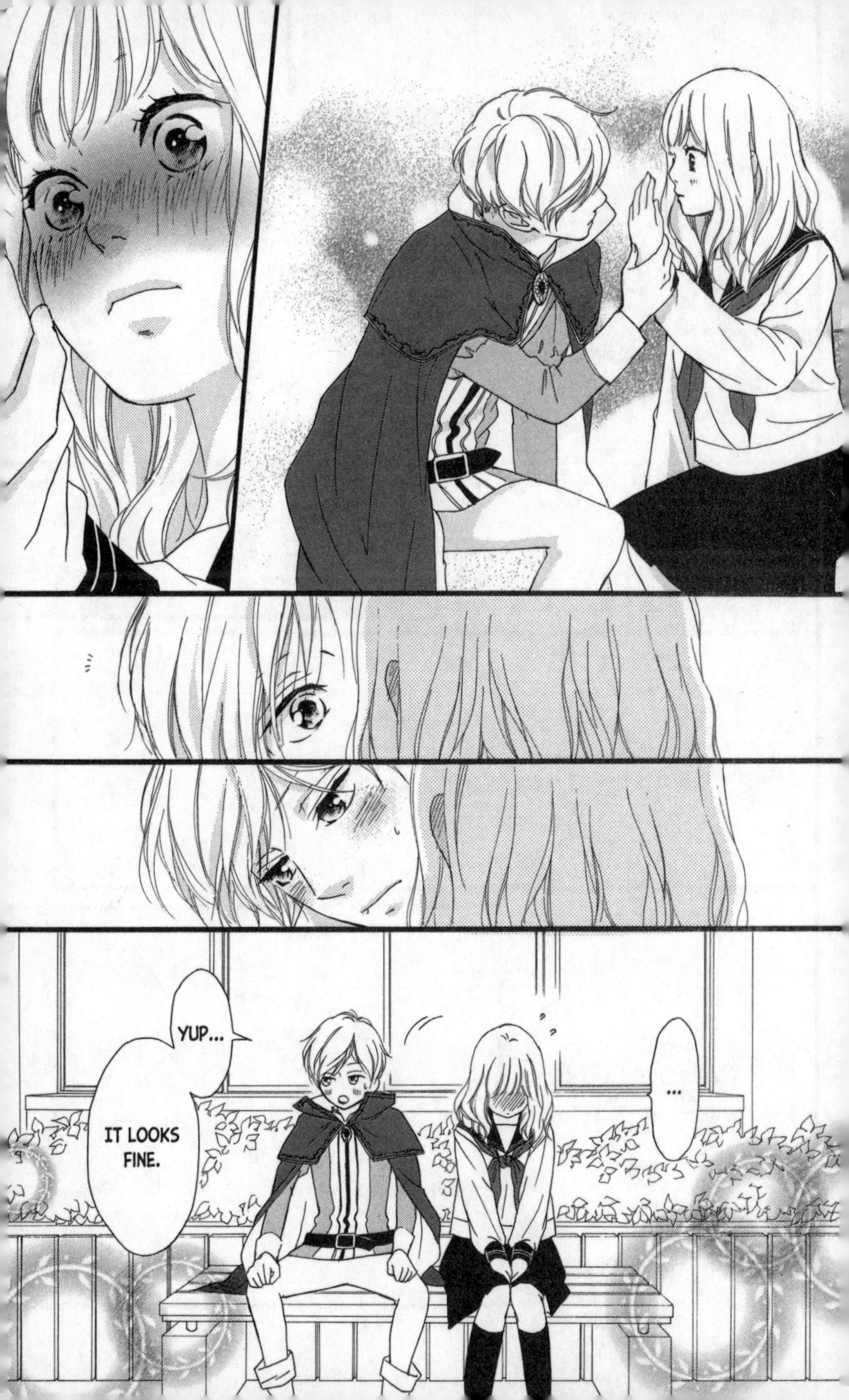
...
YUP...
IT LOOKS FINE.

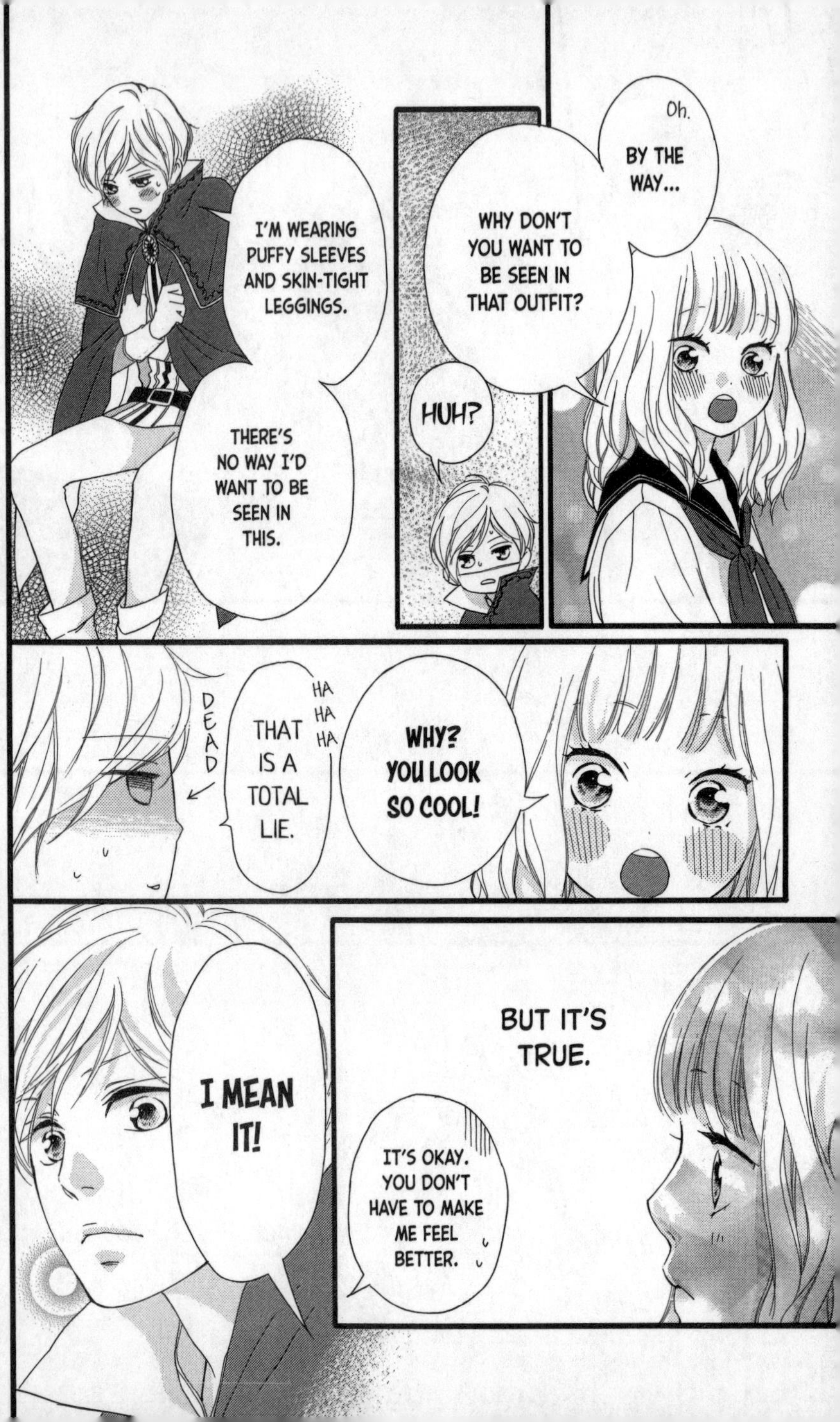
Oh.
BY THE WAY...
WHY DON'T YOU WANT TO BE SEEN IN THAT OUTFIT?
HUH?
I'M WEARING PUFFY SLEEVES AND SKIN-TIGHT LEGGINGS.
THERE'S NO WAY I'D WANT TO BE SEEN IN THIS.
WHY? YOU LOOK SO COOL!
HA HA HA
THAT IS A TOTAL LIE.
DEAD
BUT IT'S TRUE.
IT'S OKAY. YOU DON'T HAVE TO MAKE ME FEEL BETTER.
I MEAN IT!

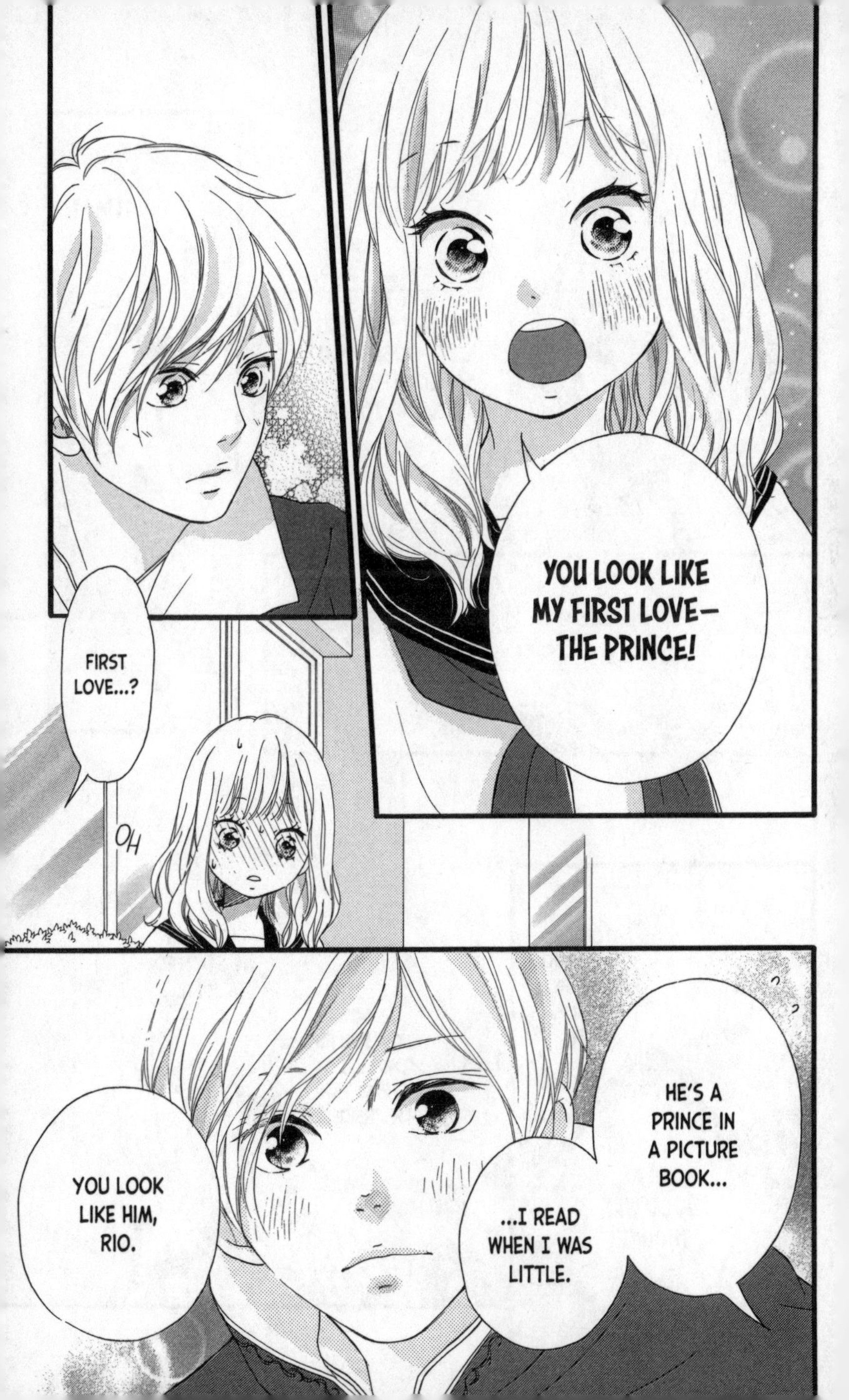
YOU LOOK LIKE MY FIRST LOVE— THE PRINCE!
FIRST LOVE...?
OH
HE'S A PRINCE IN A PICTURE BOOK...
...I READ WHEN I WAS LITTLE.
YOU LOOK LIKE HIM, RIO.

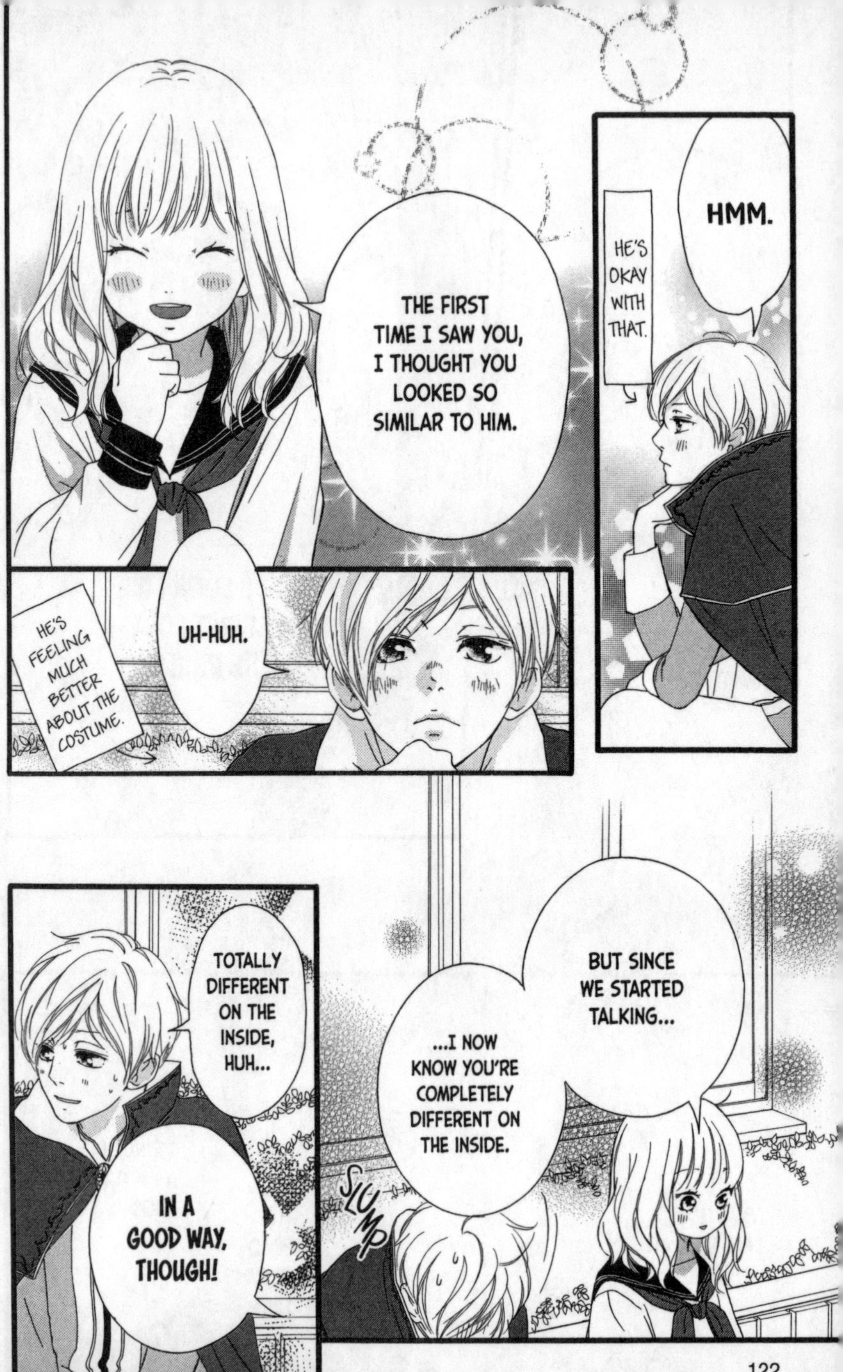
HMM.
HE'S OKAY WITH THAT.
THE FIRST TIME I SAW YOU, I THOUGHT YOU LOOKED SO SIMILAR TO HIM.
UH-HUH.
HE'S FEELING MUCH BETTER ABOUT THE COSTUME.
BUT SINCE WE STARTED TALKING...
...I NOW KNOW YOU'RE COMPLETELY DIFFERENT ON THE INSIDE.
SLUMP
TOTALLY DIFFERENT ON THE INSIDE, HUH...
IN A GOOD WAY, THOUGH!

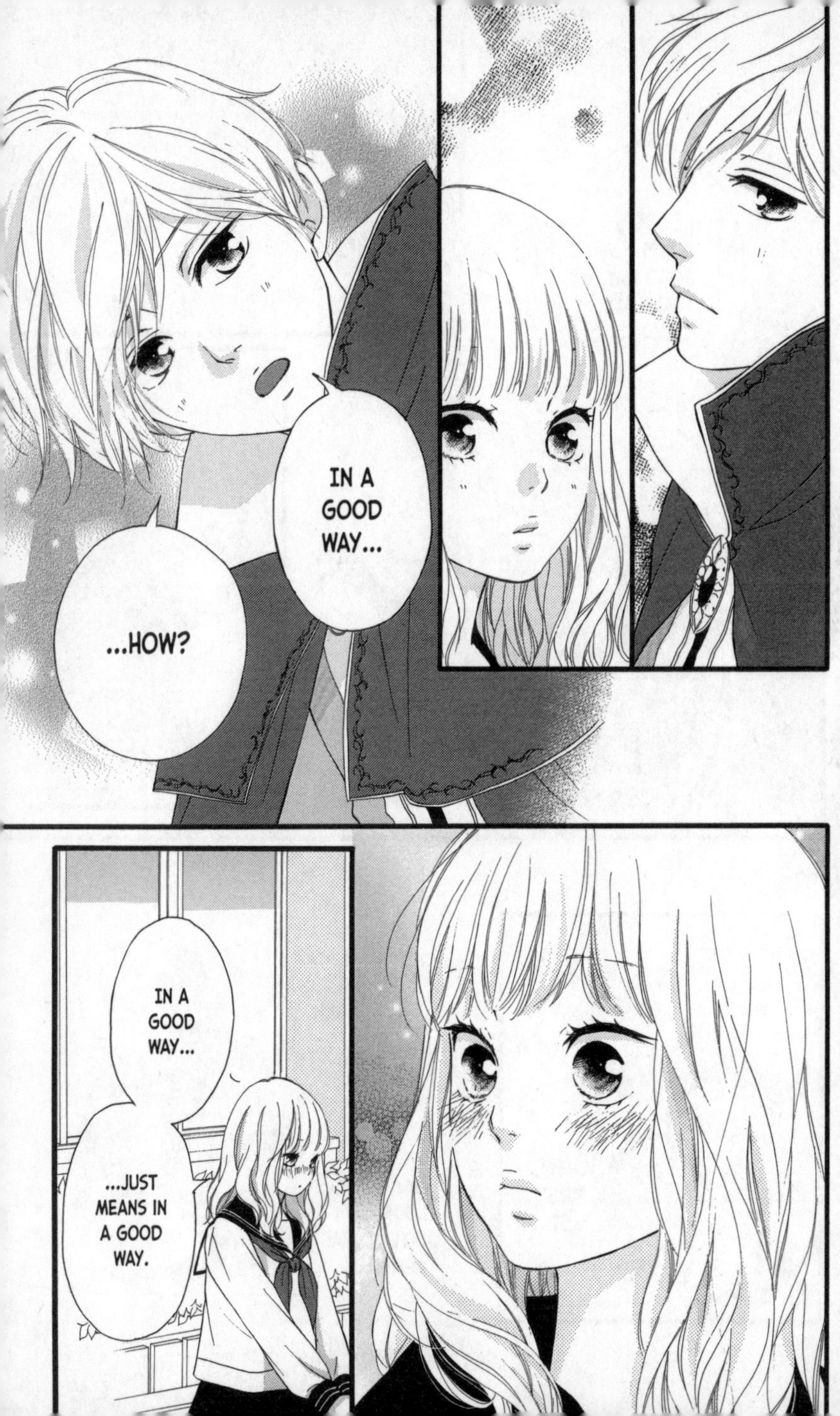
IN A GOOD WAY...
...HOW?
IN A GOOD WAY...
...JUST MEANS IN A GOOD WAY.

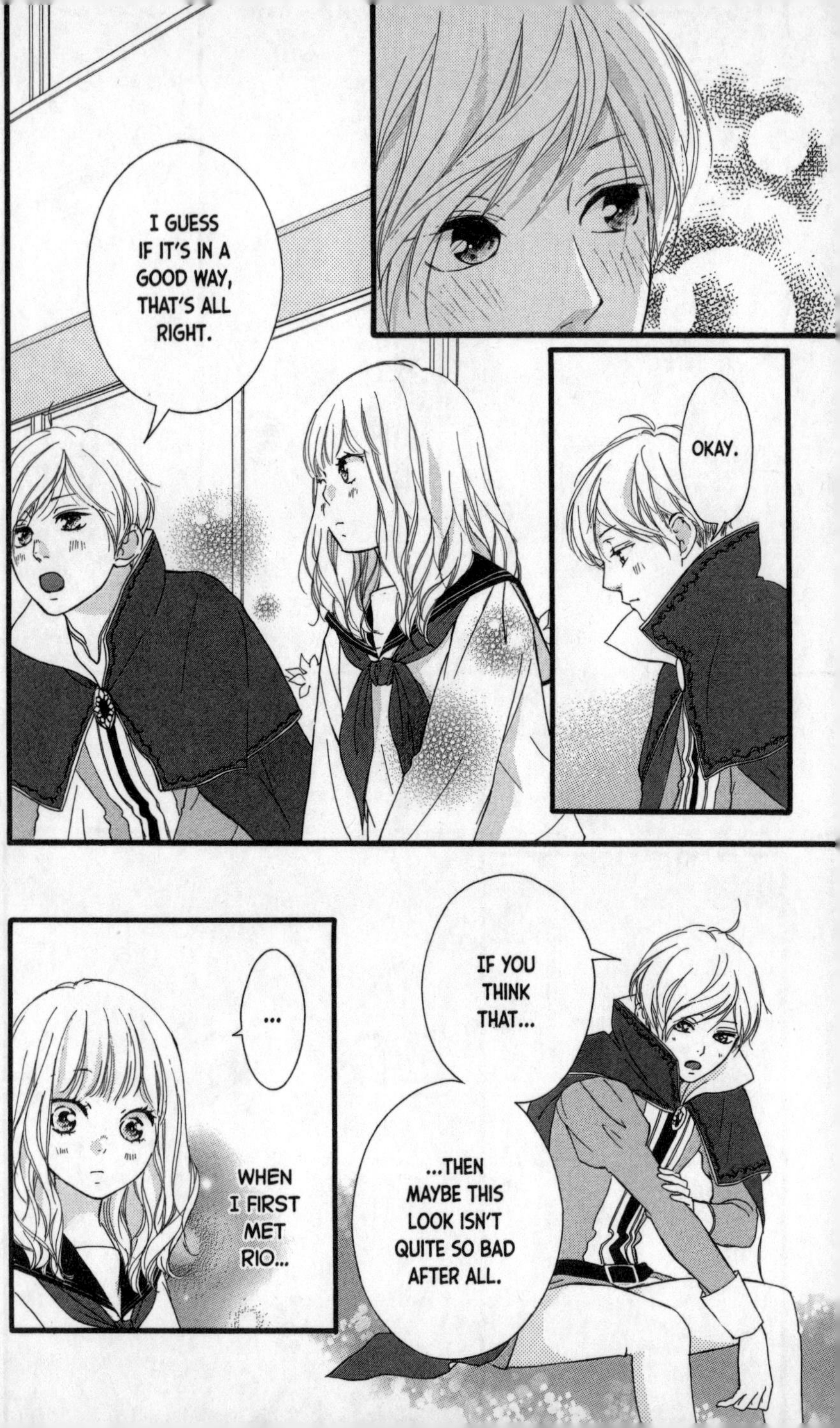
OKAY.
I GUESS IF IT'S IN A GOOD WAY, THAT'S ALL RIGHT.
IF YOU THINK THAT...
...THEN MAYBE THIS LOOK ISN'T QUITE SO BAD AFTER ALL.
...
WHEN I FIRST MET RIO...

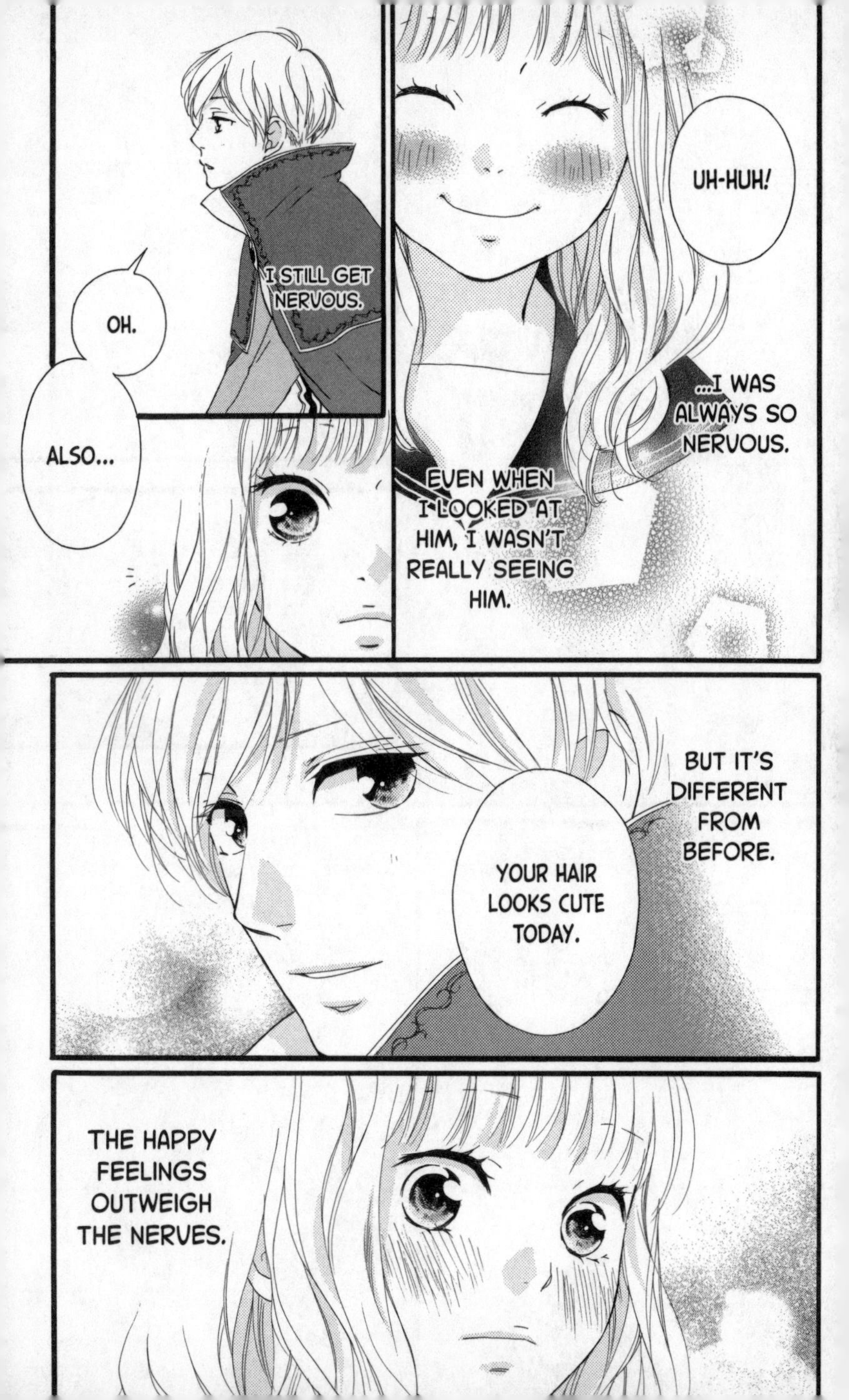
UH-HUH!
...I WAS ALWAYS SO NERVOUS.
EVEN WHEN I LOOKED AT HIM, I WASN'T REALLY SEEING HIM.
I STILL GET NERVOUS.
OH.
ALSO...
BUT IT'S DIFFERENT FROM BEFORE.
YOUR HAIR LOOKS CUTE TODAY.
THE HAPPY FEELINGS OUTWEIGH THE NERVES.

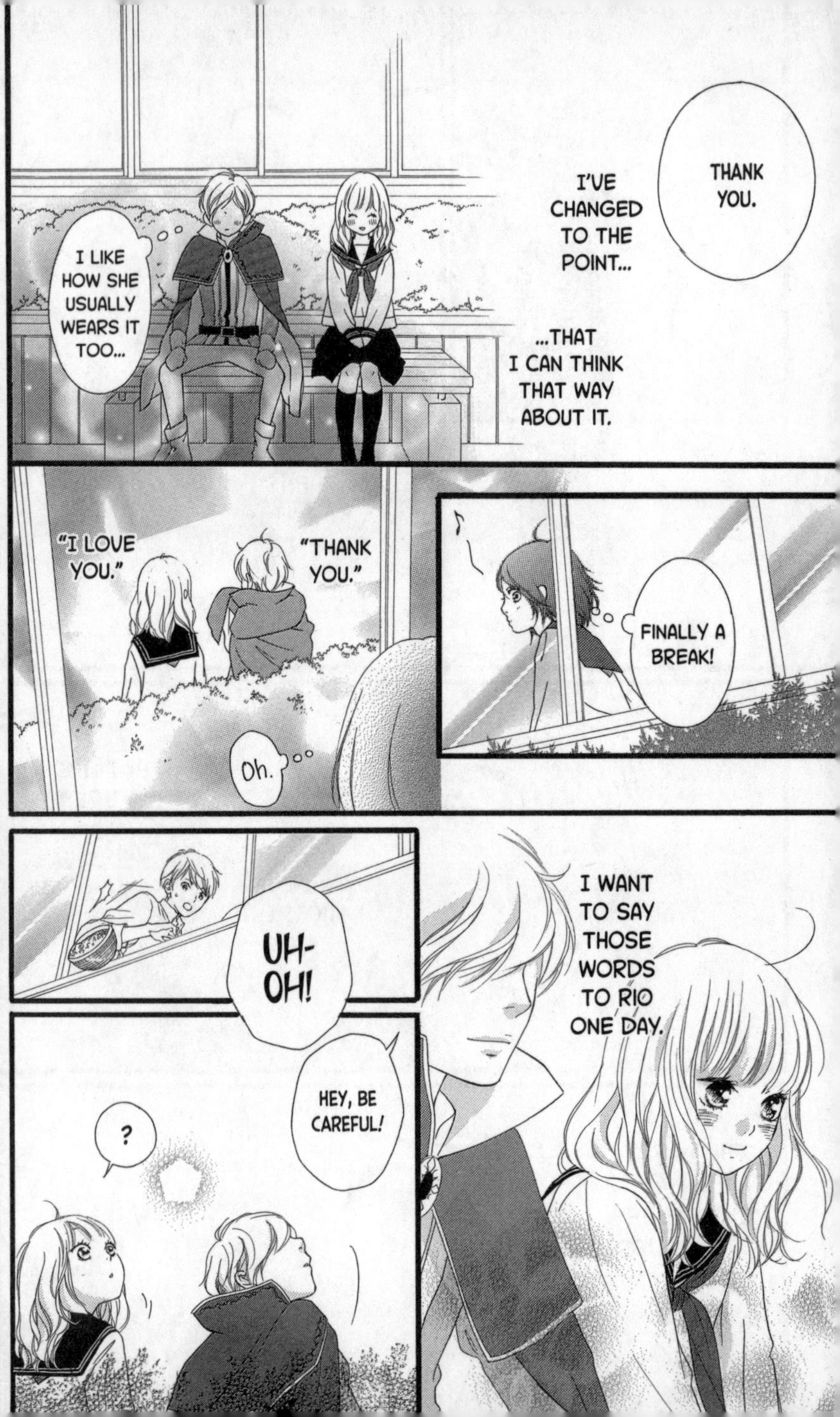
THANK YOU.
I'VE CHANGED TO THE POINT...
...THAT I CAN THINK THAT WAY ABOUT IT.
I LIKE HOW SHE USUALLY WEARS IT TOO...
FINALLY A BREAK!
"THANK YOU."
"I LOVE YOU."
Oh.
I WANT TO SAY THOSE WORDS TO RIO ONE DAY.
UH-OH!
HEY, BE CAREFUL!
?

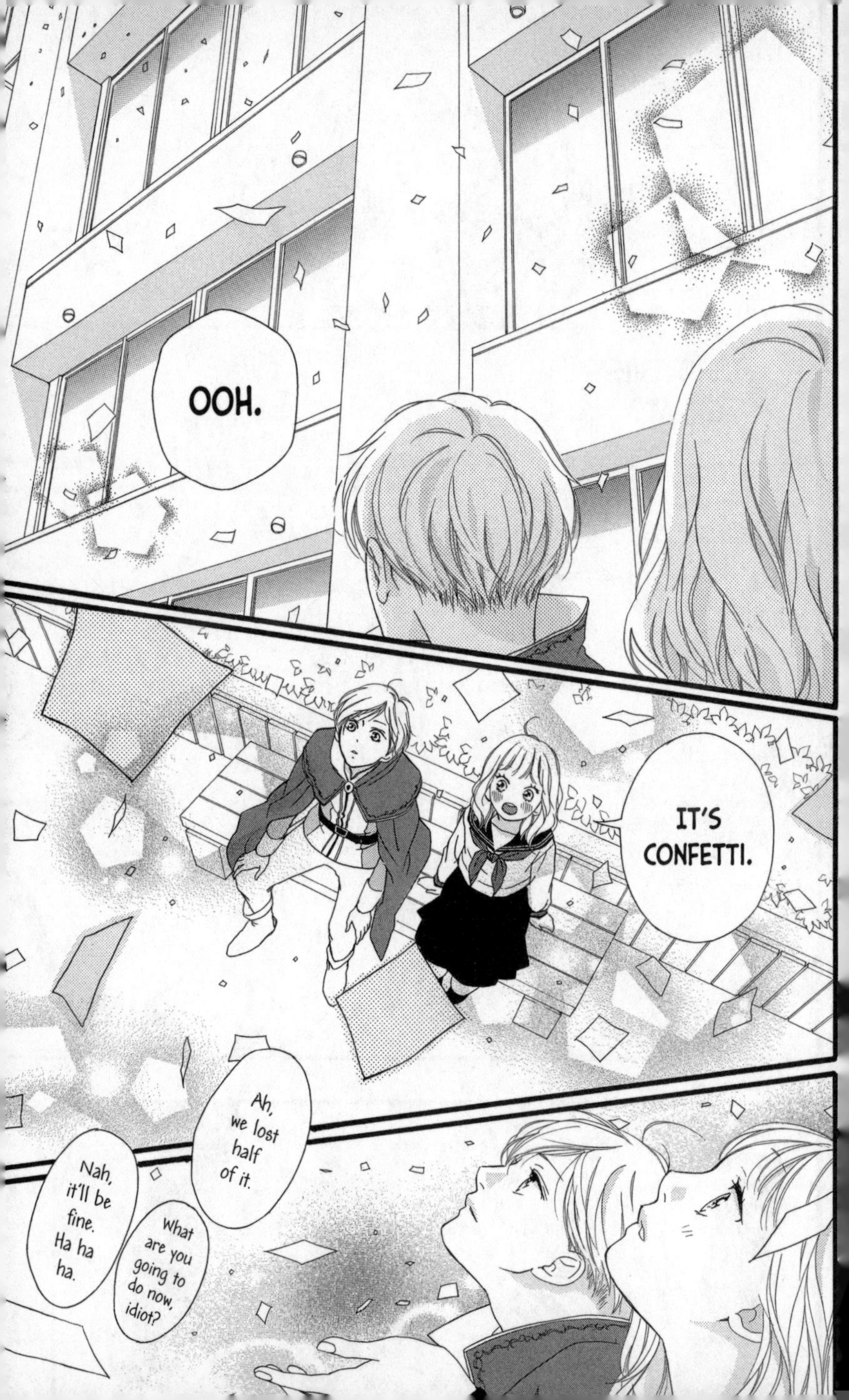
OOH.
IT'S CONFETTI.
Ah, we lost half of it.
What are you going to do now, idiot?
Nah, it'll be fine. Ha ha ha.

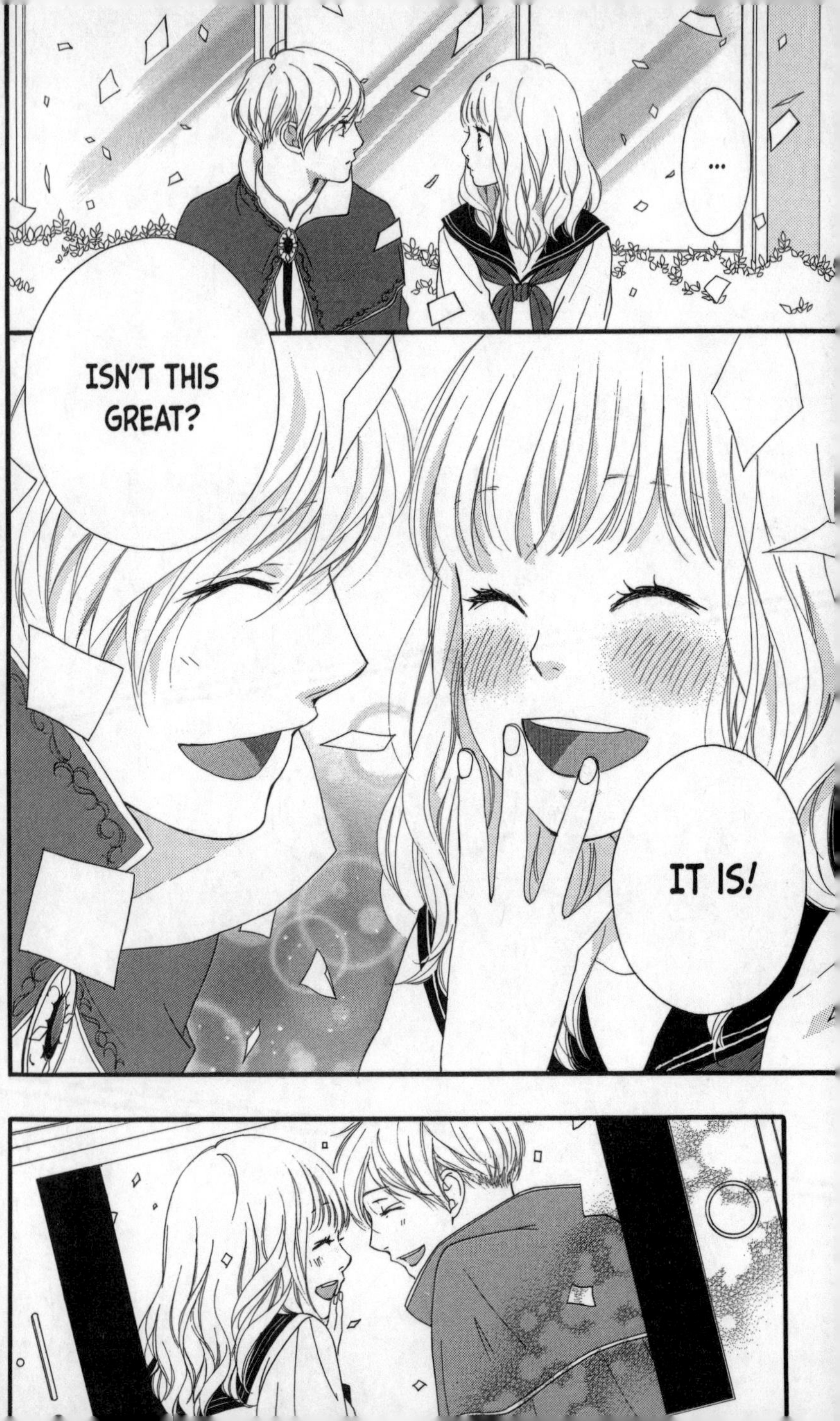
...
ISN'T THIS GREAT?
IT IS!

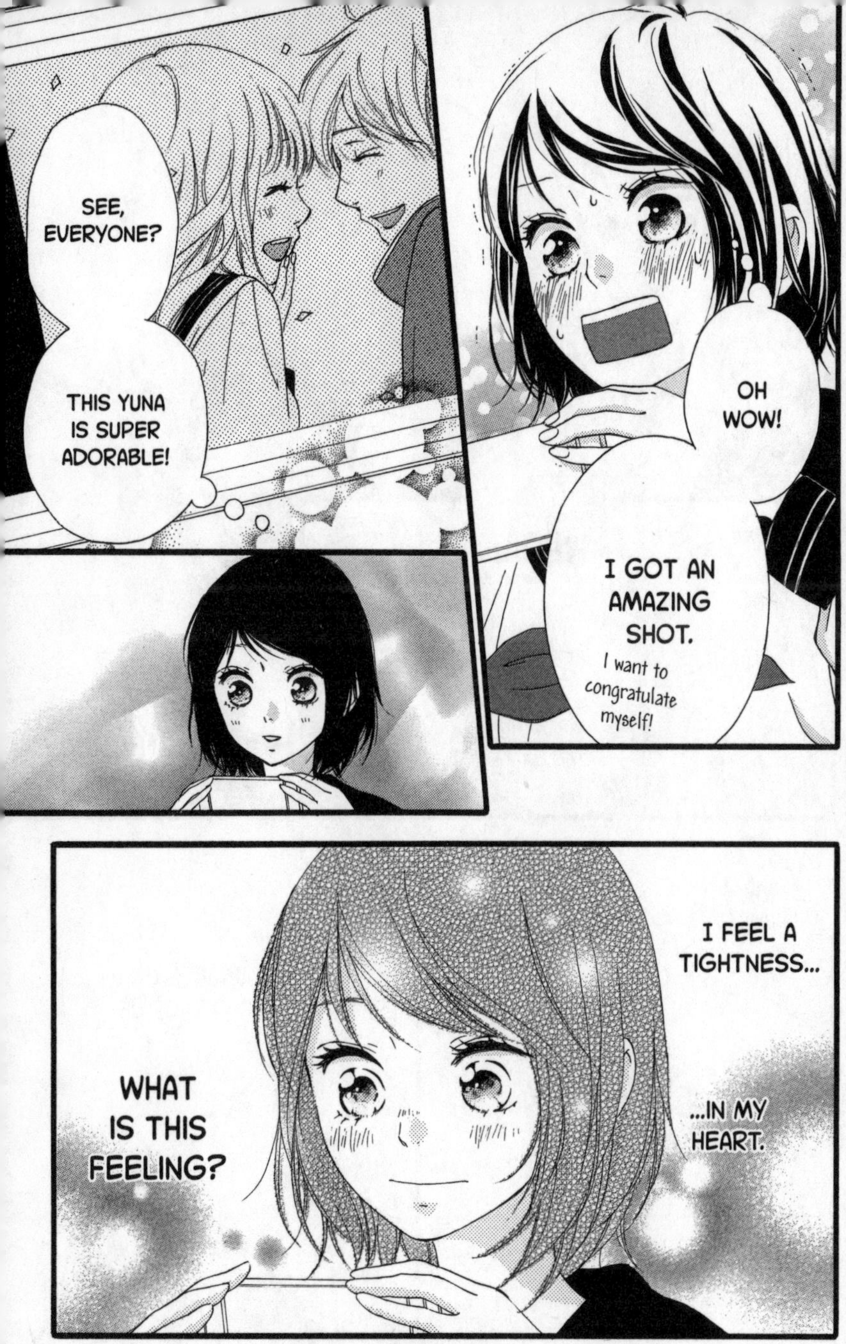
OH WOW!
I GOT AN AMAZING SHOT.
I want to congratulate myself!
SEE, EVERYONE?
THIS YUNA IS SUPER ADORABLE!
I FEEL A TIGHTNESS...
...IN MY HEART.
WHAT IS THIS FEELING?

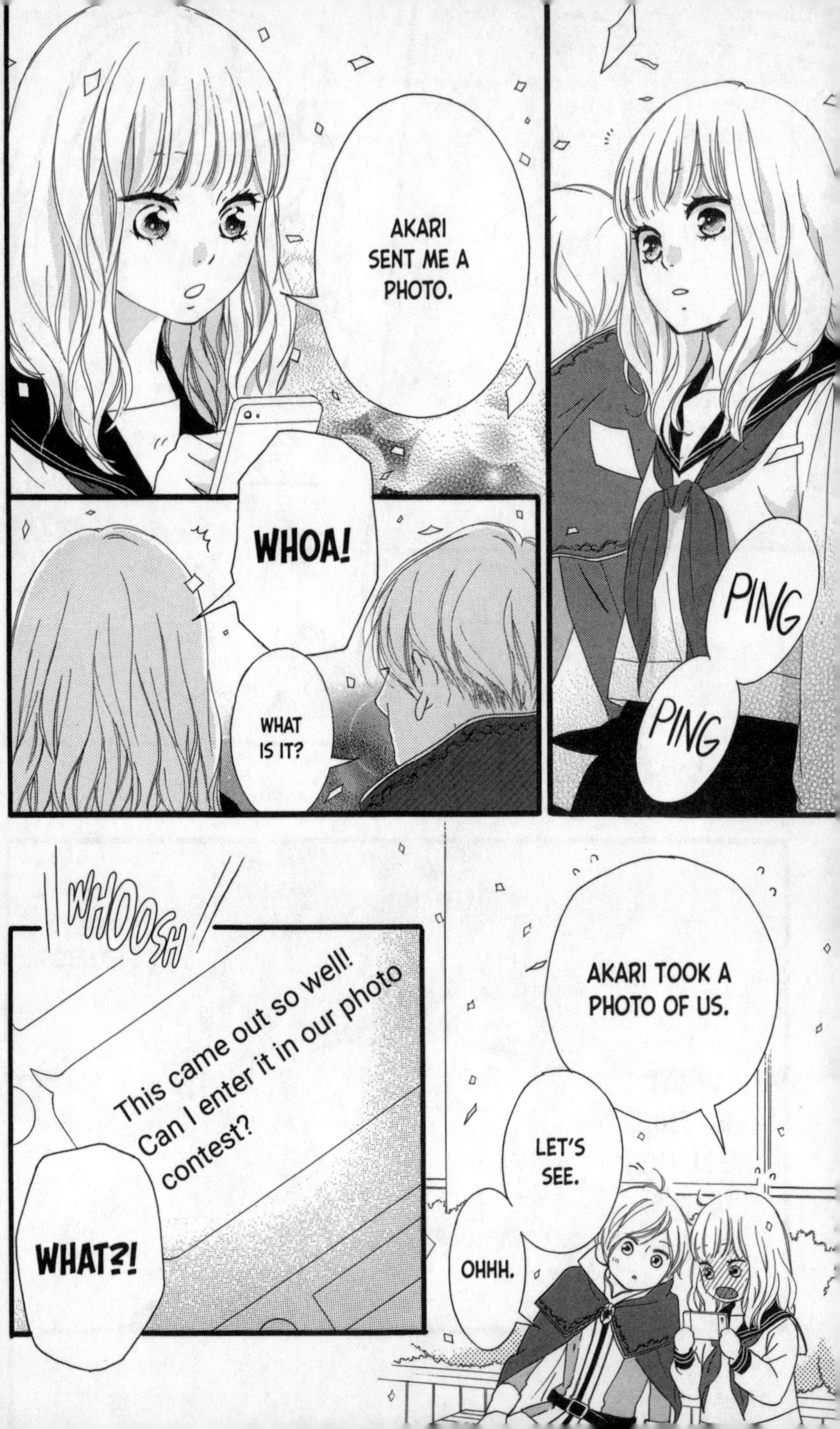
PING
PING
AKARI SENT ME A PHOTO.
WHOA!
WHAT IS IT?
AKARI TOOK A PHOTO OF US.
LET'S SEE.
OHHH.
WHOOSH
This came out so well! Can I enter it in our photo contest?
WHAT?!

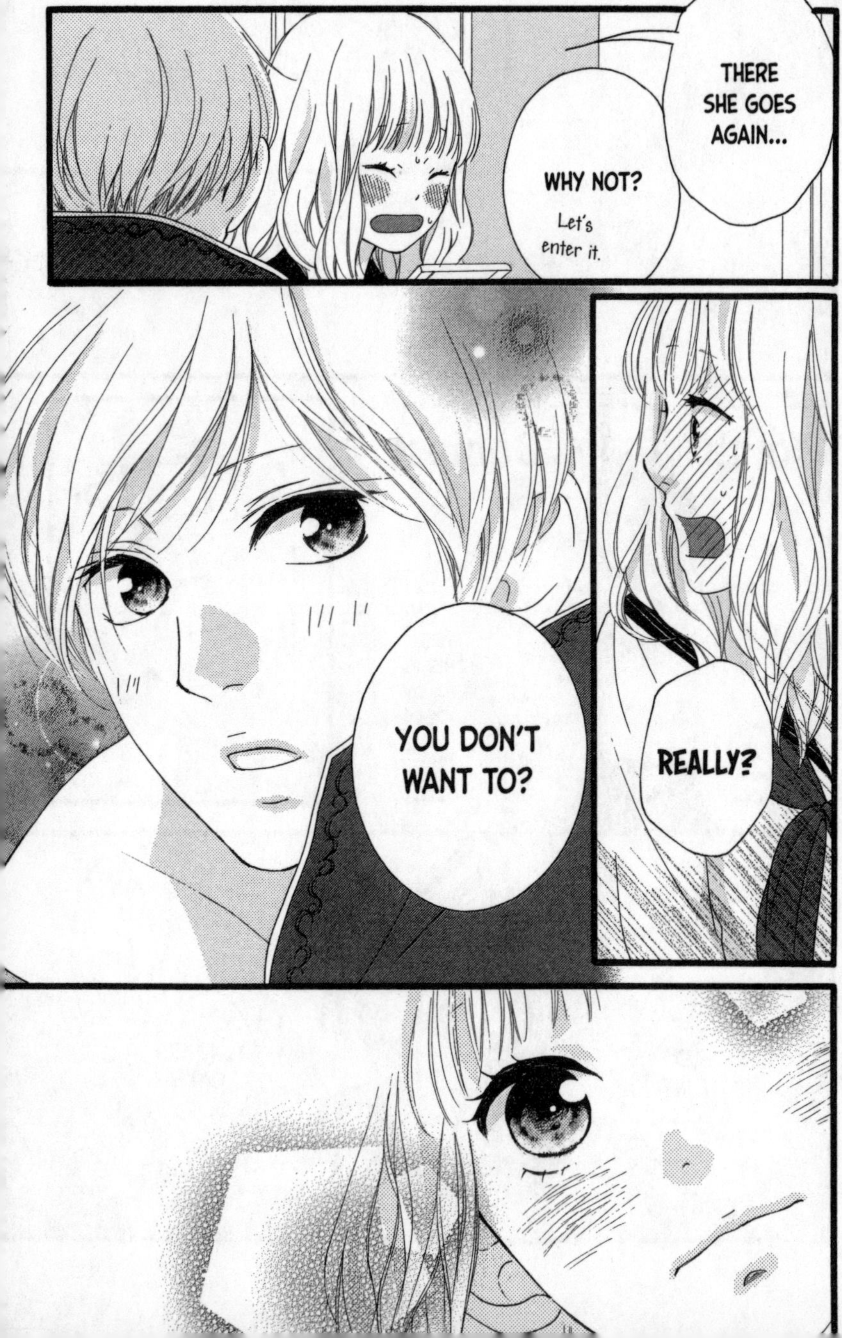
THERE SHE GOES AGAIN...
WHY NOT?
Let's enter it.
REALLY?
YOU DON'T WANT TO?

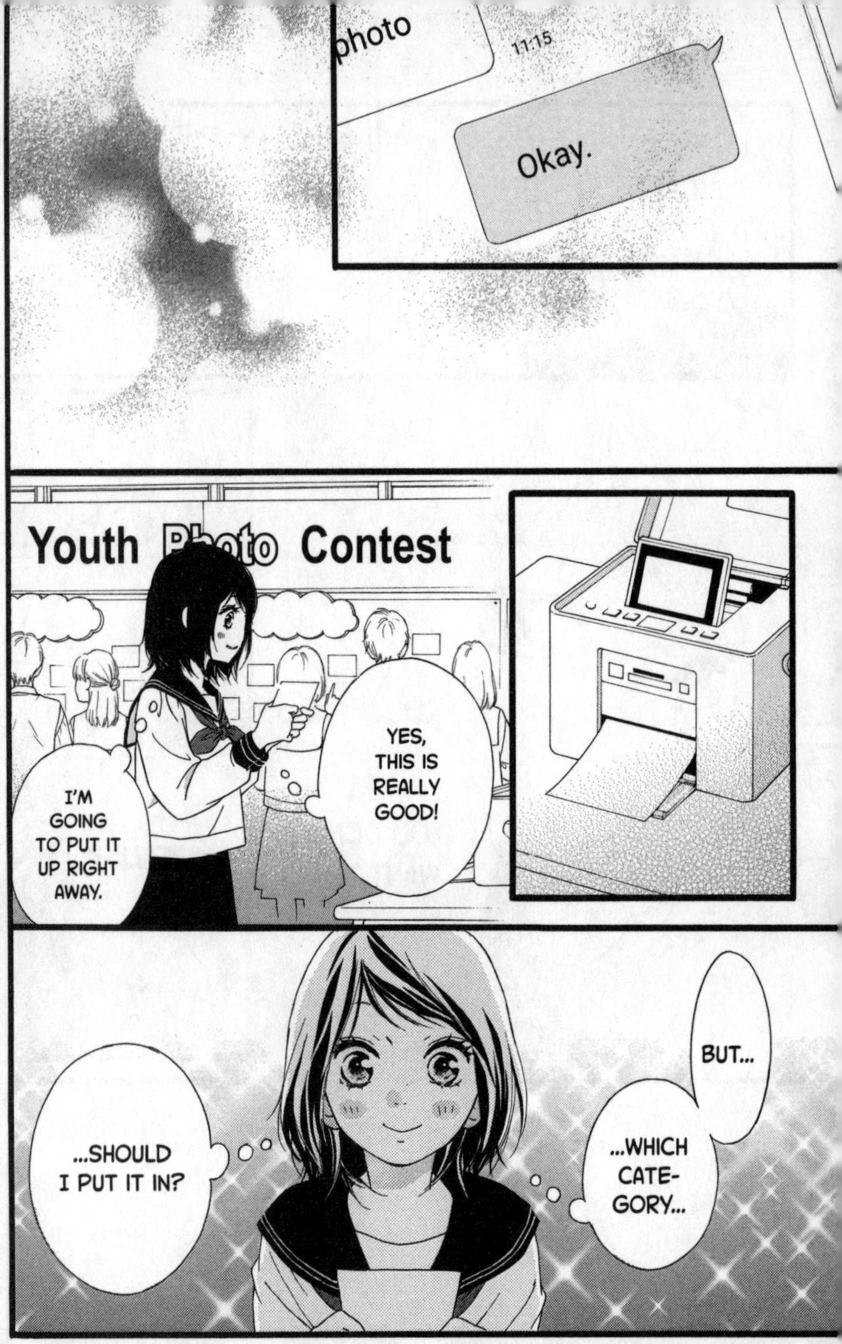
photo
11:15
Okay.
Youth Photo Contest
YES, THIS IS REALLY GOOD!
I'M GOING TO PUT IT UP RIGHT AWAY.
BUT...
...WHICH CATE-GORY...
...SHOULD I PUT IT IN?

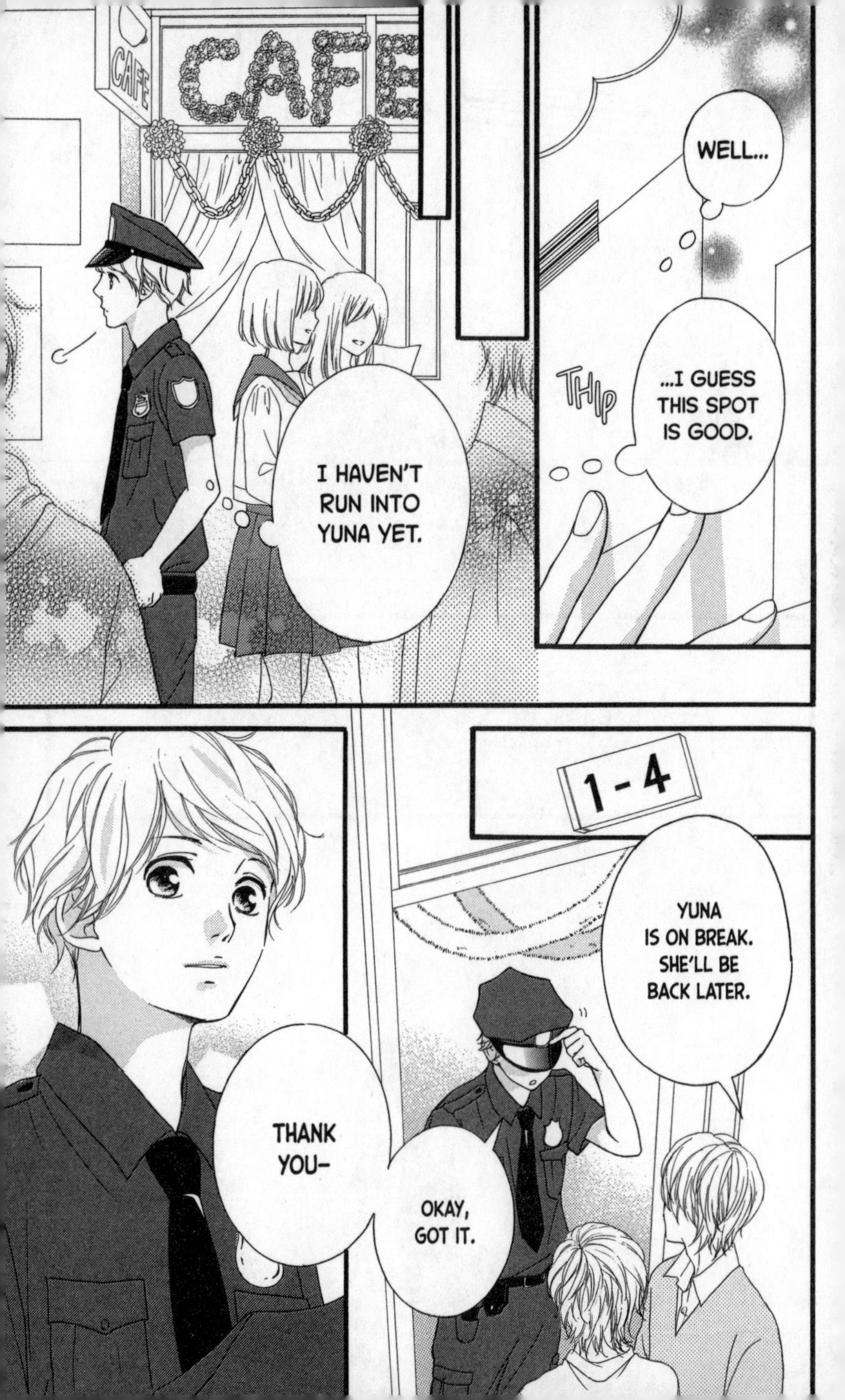
CAFE
CAFE
WELL...
THIP
...I GUESS THIS SPOT IS GOOD.
I HAVEN'T RUN INTO YUNA YET.
1-4
YUNA IS ON BREAK. SHE'LL BE BACK LATER.
THANK YOU-
OKAY, GOT IT.

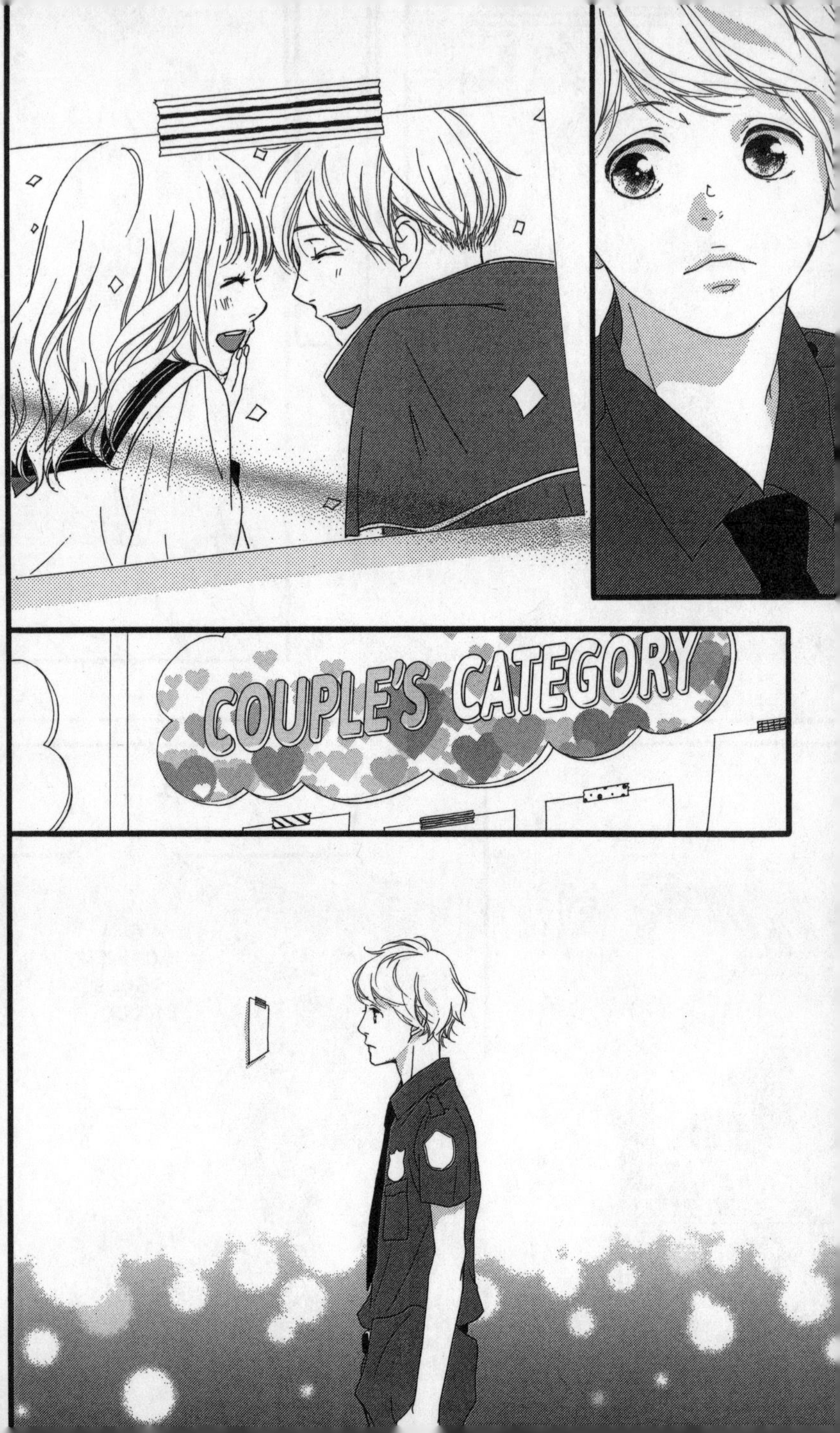
COUPLE'S CATEGORY

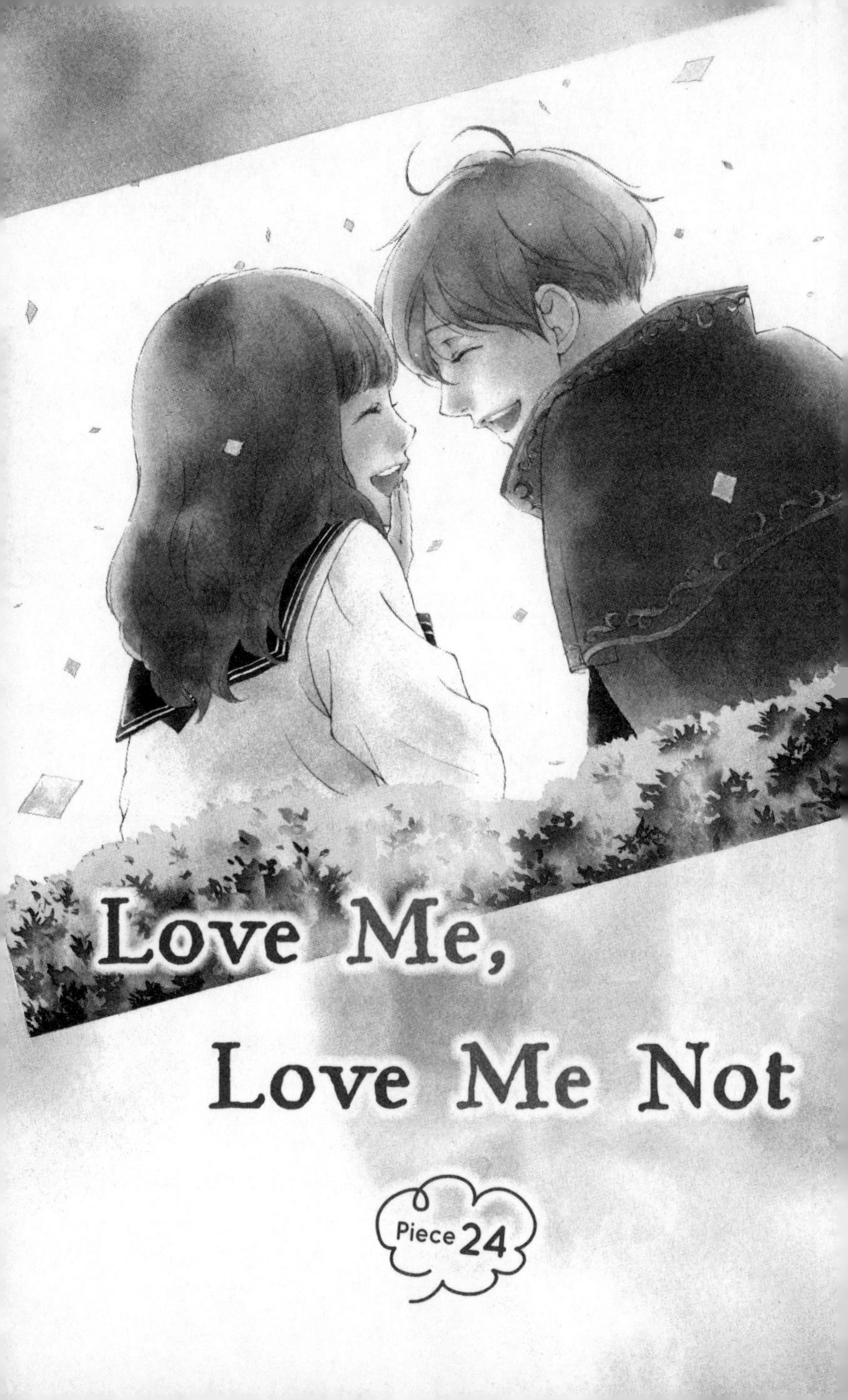
Love Me,
Love Me Not
Piece 24

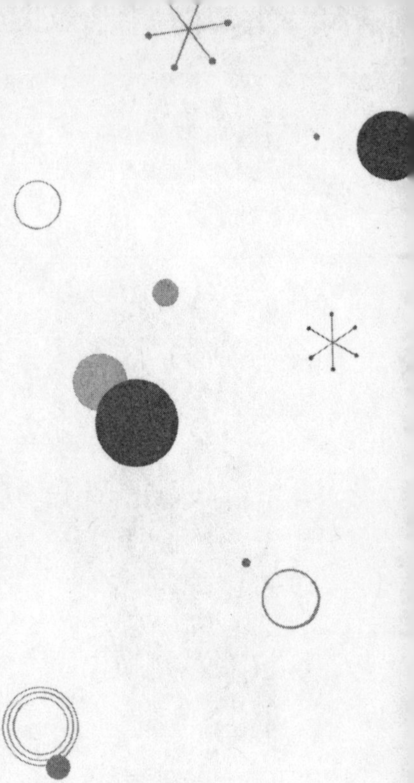

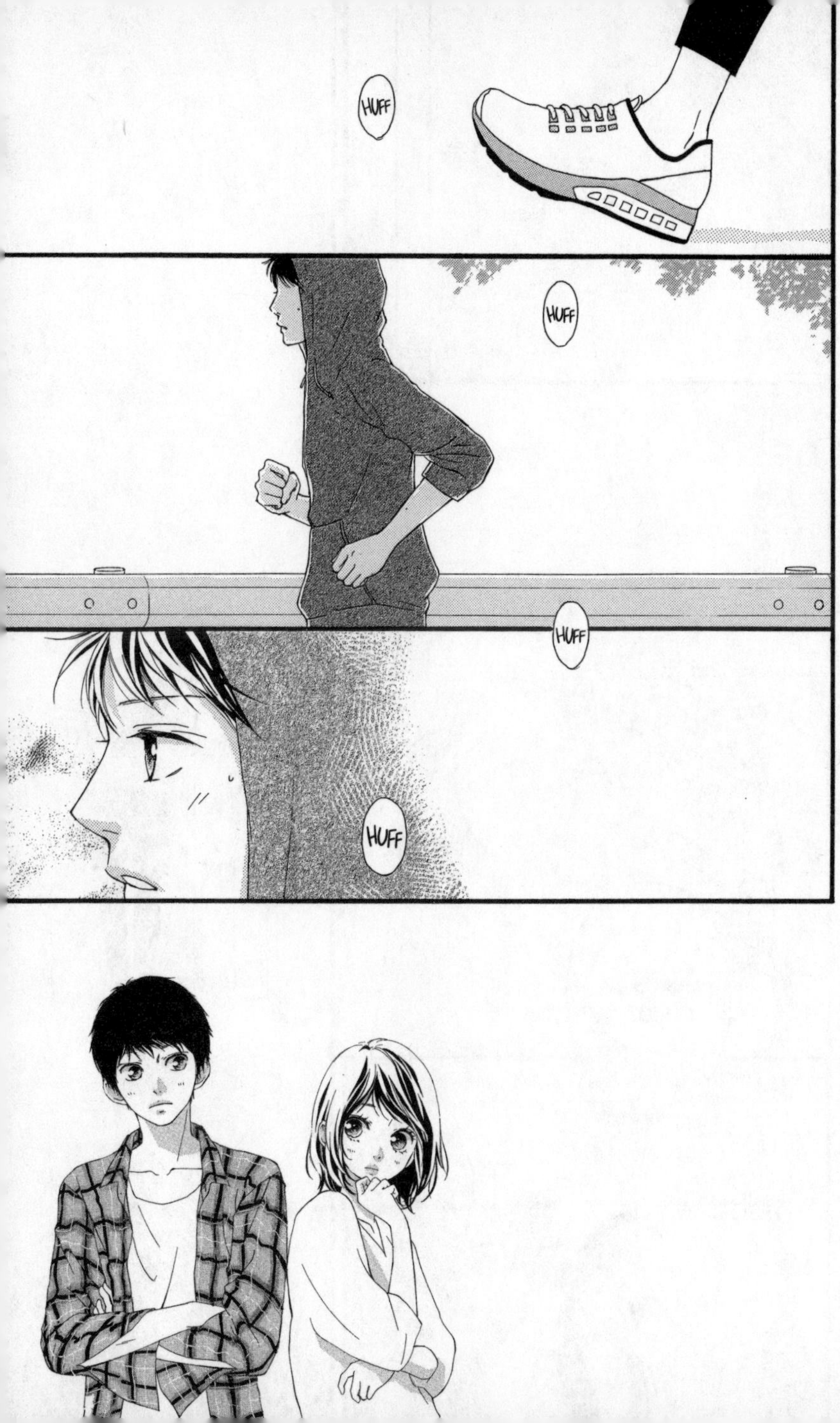
HUFF
HUFF
HUFF
HUFF

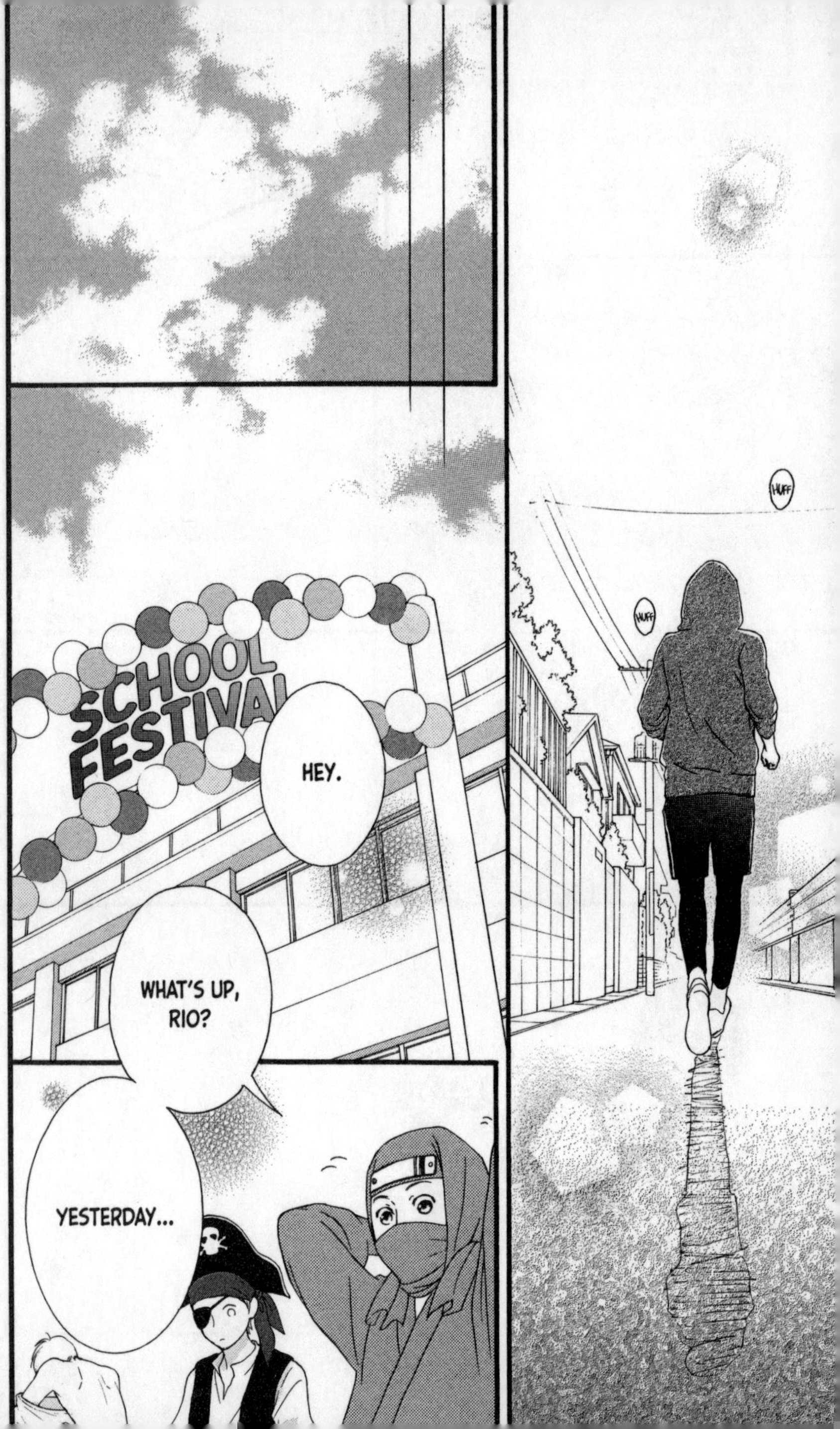
HUFF
HUFF
SCHOOL FESTIVA
HEY.
WHAT'S UP, RIO?
YESTERDAY...

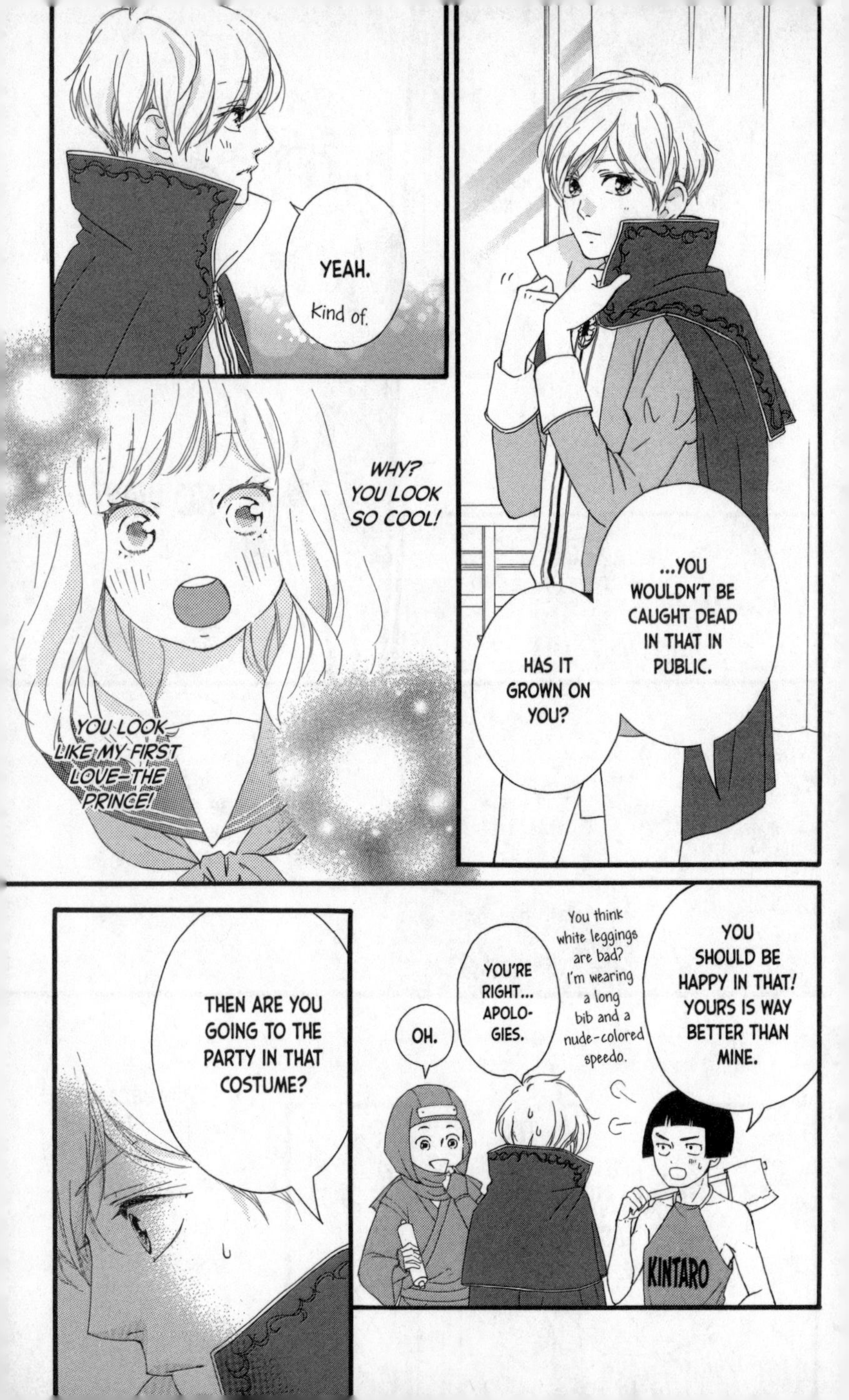
...YOU WOULDN'T BE CAUGHT DEAD IN THAT IN PUBLIC.
HAS IT GROWN ON YOU?
YEAH.
Kind of.
WHY? YOU LOOK SO COOL!
YOU LOOK LIKE MY FIRST LOVE—THE PRINCE!
YOU SHOULD BE HAPPY IN THAT! YOURS IS WAY BETTER THAN MINE.
You think white leggings are bad? I'm wearing a long bib and a nude-colored speedo.
YOU'RE RIGHT... APOLOGIES.
OH.
KINTARO
THEN ARE YOU GOING TO THE PARTY IN THAT COSTUME?

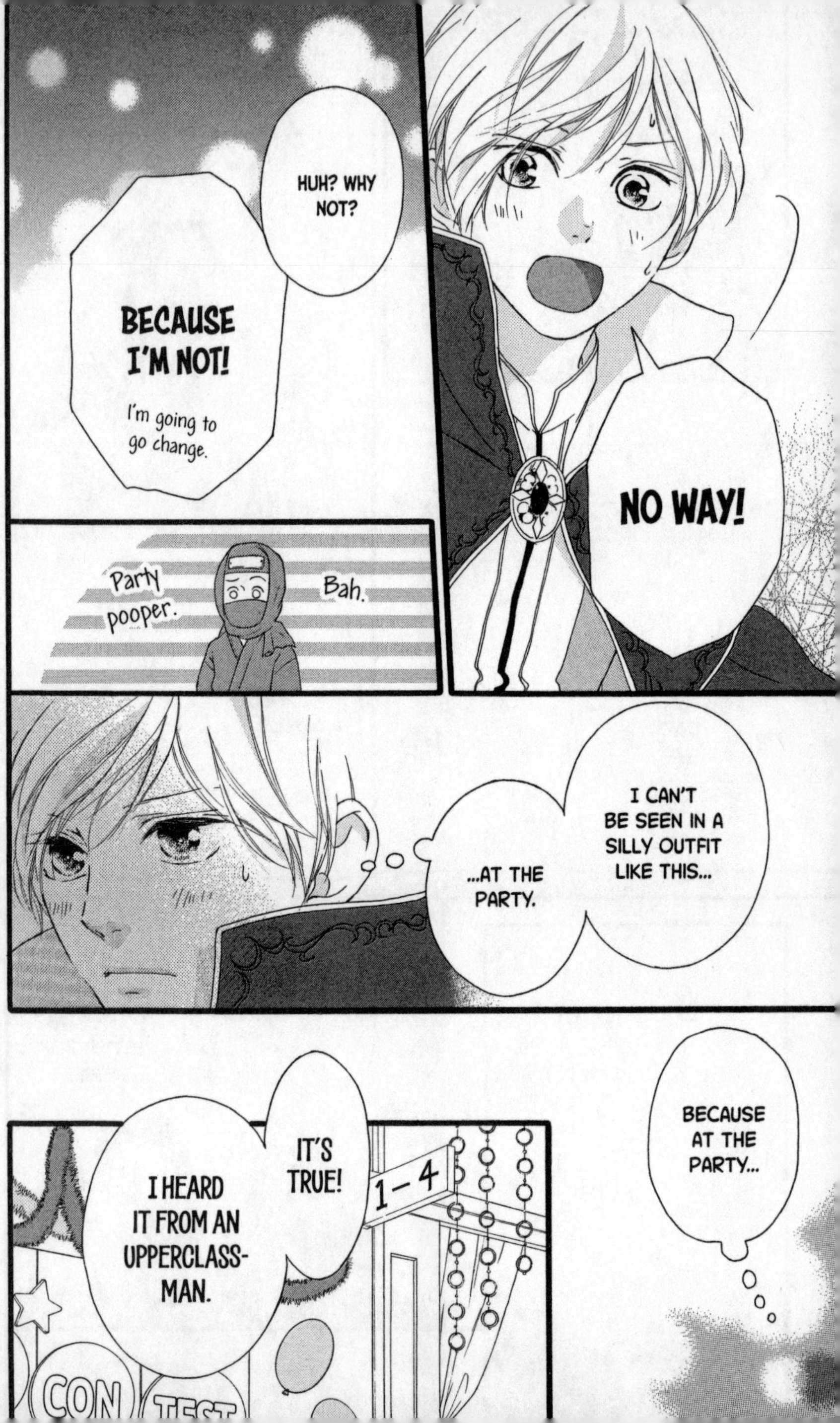
NO WAY!
HUH? WHY NOT?
BECAUSE I'M NOT!
I'm going to go change.
Bah.
Party pooper.
I CAN'T BE SEEN IN A SILLY OUTFIT LIKE THIS...
...AT THE PARTY.
BECAUSE AT THE PARTY...
IT'S TRUE!
1-4
I HEARD IT FROM AN UPPERCLASS-MAN.
CON

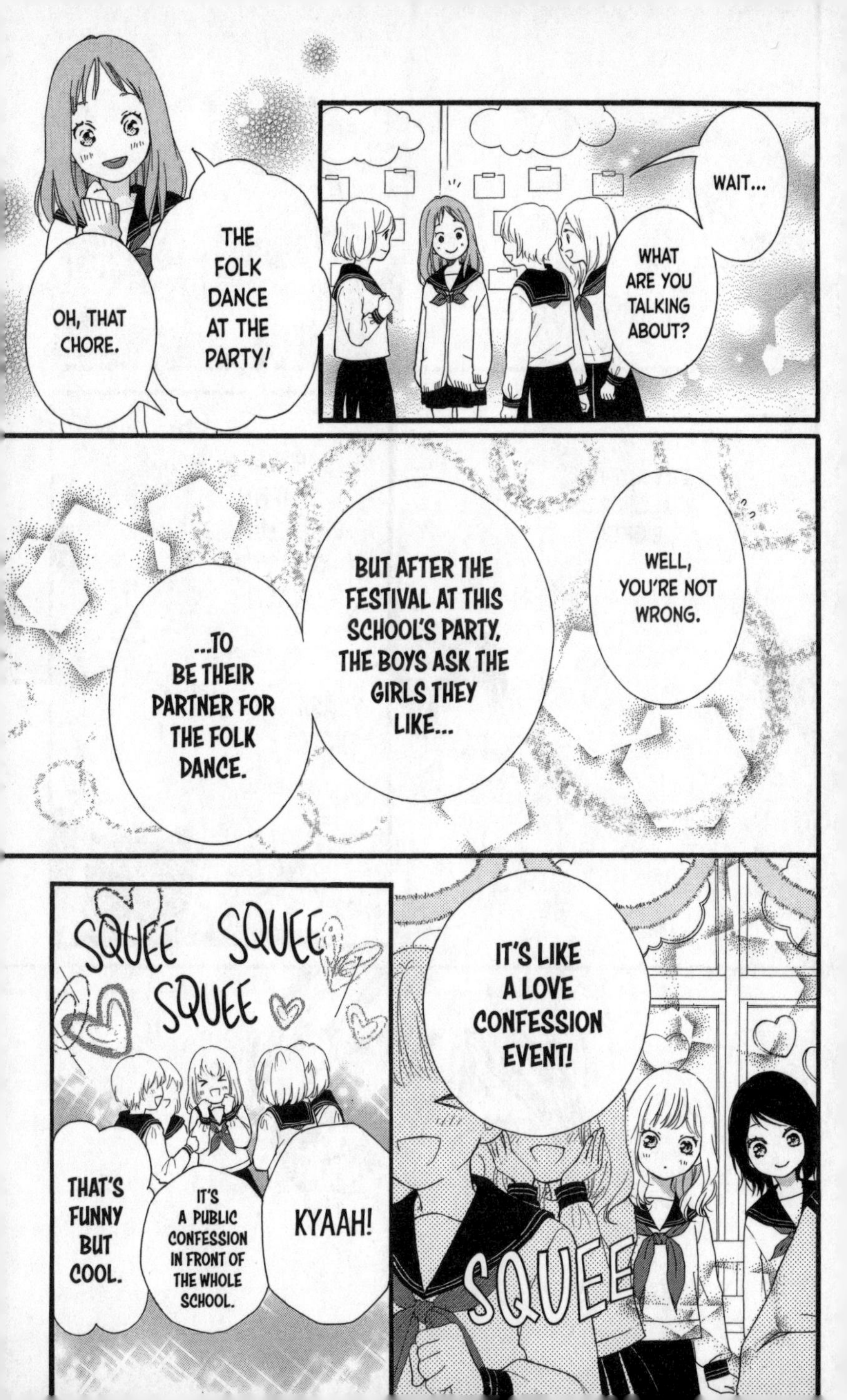
WAIT...
WHAT ARE YOU TALKING ABOUT?
THE FOLK DANCE AT THE PARTY!
OH, THAT CHORE.
WELL, YOU'RE NOT WRONG.
BUT AFTER THE FESTIVAL AT THIS SCHOOL'S PARTY, THE BOYS ASK THE GIRLS THEY LIKE...
...TO BE THEIR PARTNER FOR THE FOLK DANCE.
IT'S LIKE A LOVE CONFESSION EVENT!
SQUEE
SQUEE SQUEE
SQUEE
KYAAH!
IT'S A PUBLIC CONFESSION IN FRONT OF THE WHOLE SCHOOL.
THAT'S FUNNY BUT COOL.

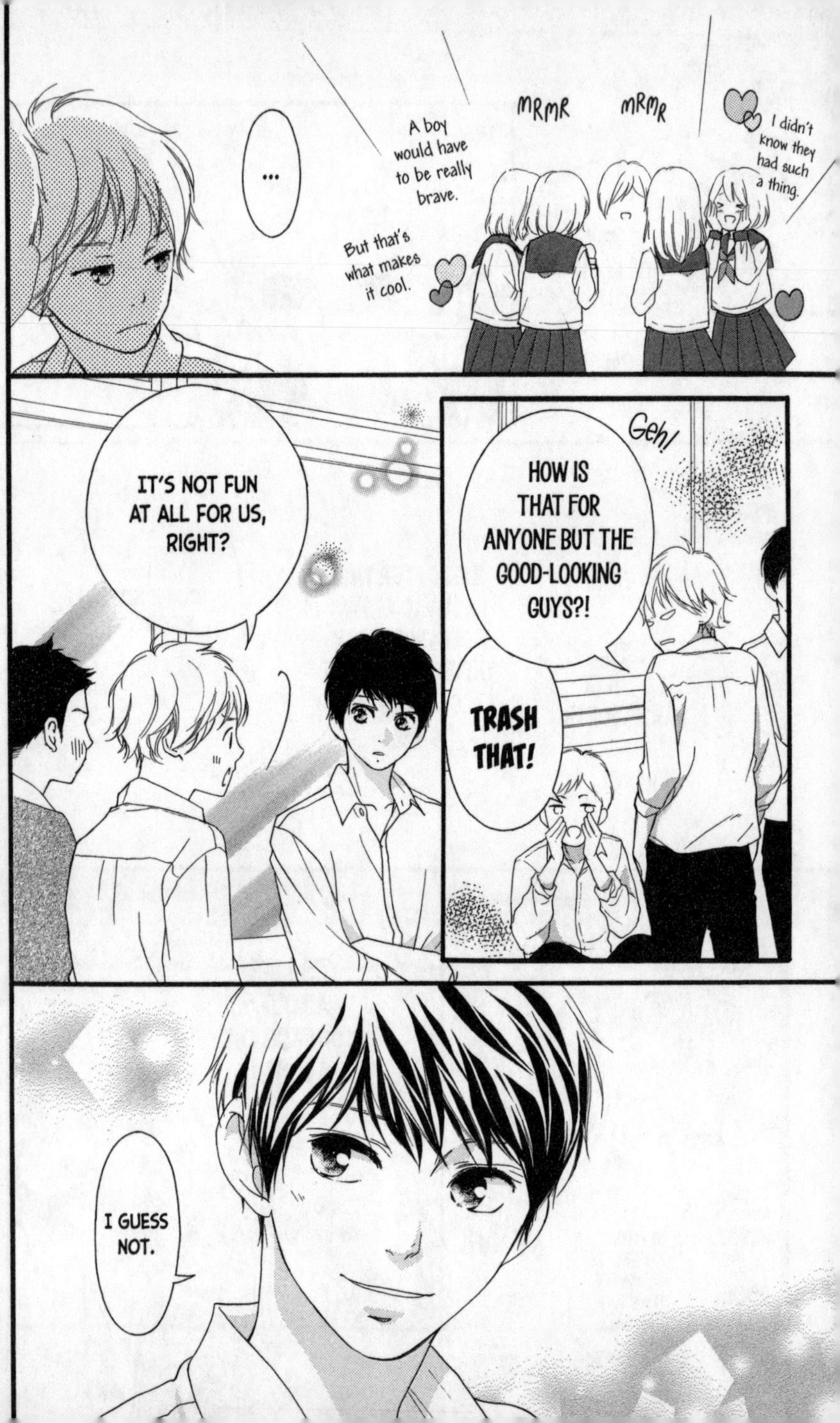
I didn't know they had such a thing.
MRMR
MRMR
A boy would have to be really brave.
But that's what makes it cool.
...
Geh!
HOW IS THAT FOR ANYONE BUT THE GOOD-LOOKING GUYS?!
TRASH THAT!
IT'S NOT FUN AT ALL FOR US, RIGHT?
I GUESS NOT.

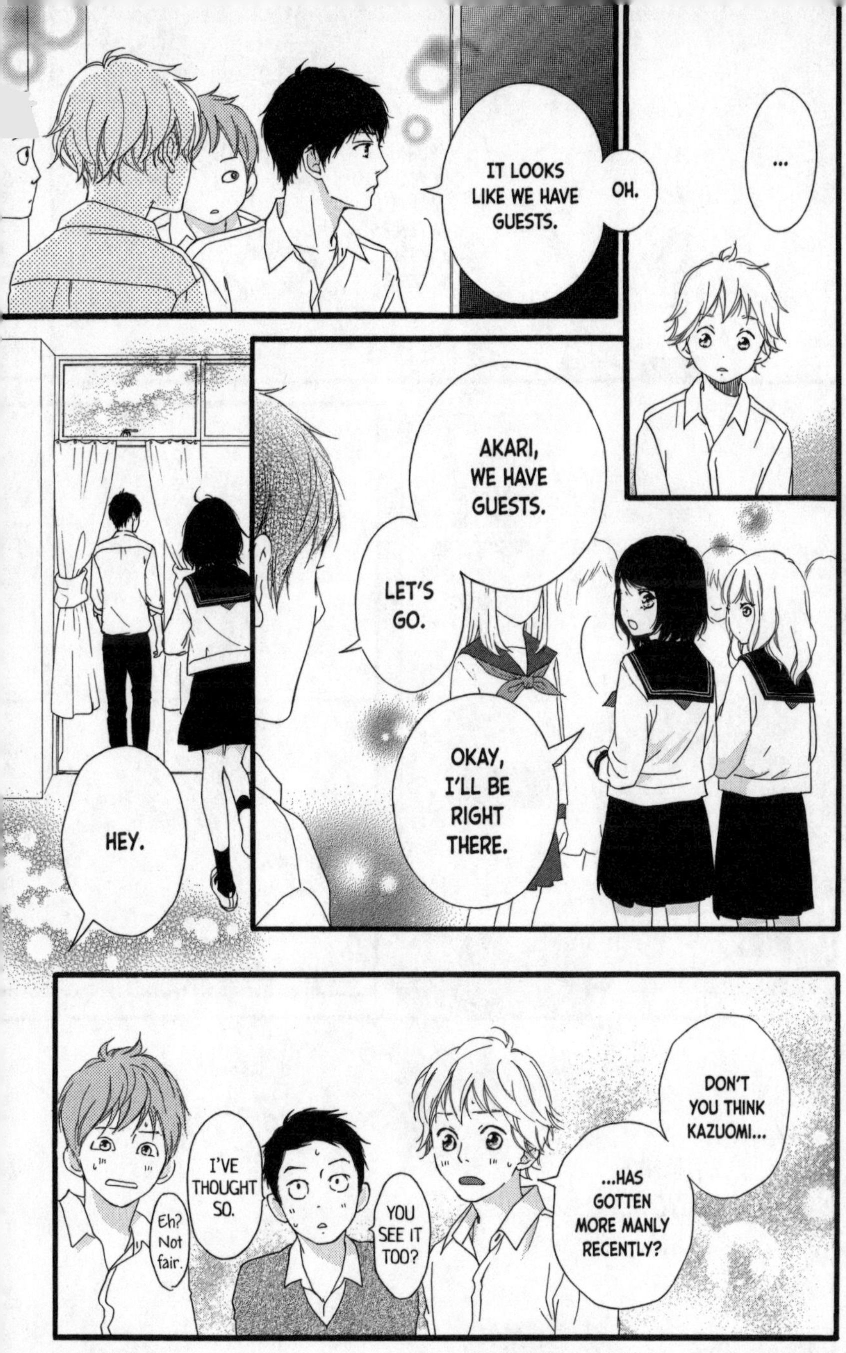
...
OH.
IT LOOKS LIKE WE HAVE GUESTS.
AKARI, WE HAVE GUESTS.
LET'S GO.
OKAY, I'LL BE RIGHT THERE.
HEY.
DON'T YOU THINK KAZUOMI...
...HAS GOTTEN MORE MANLY RECENTLY?
YOU SEE IT TOO?
I'VE THOUGHT SO.
Eh? Not fair.

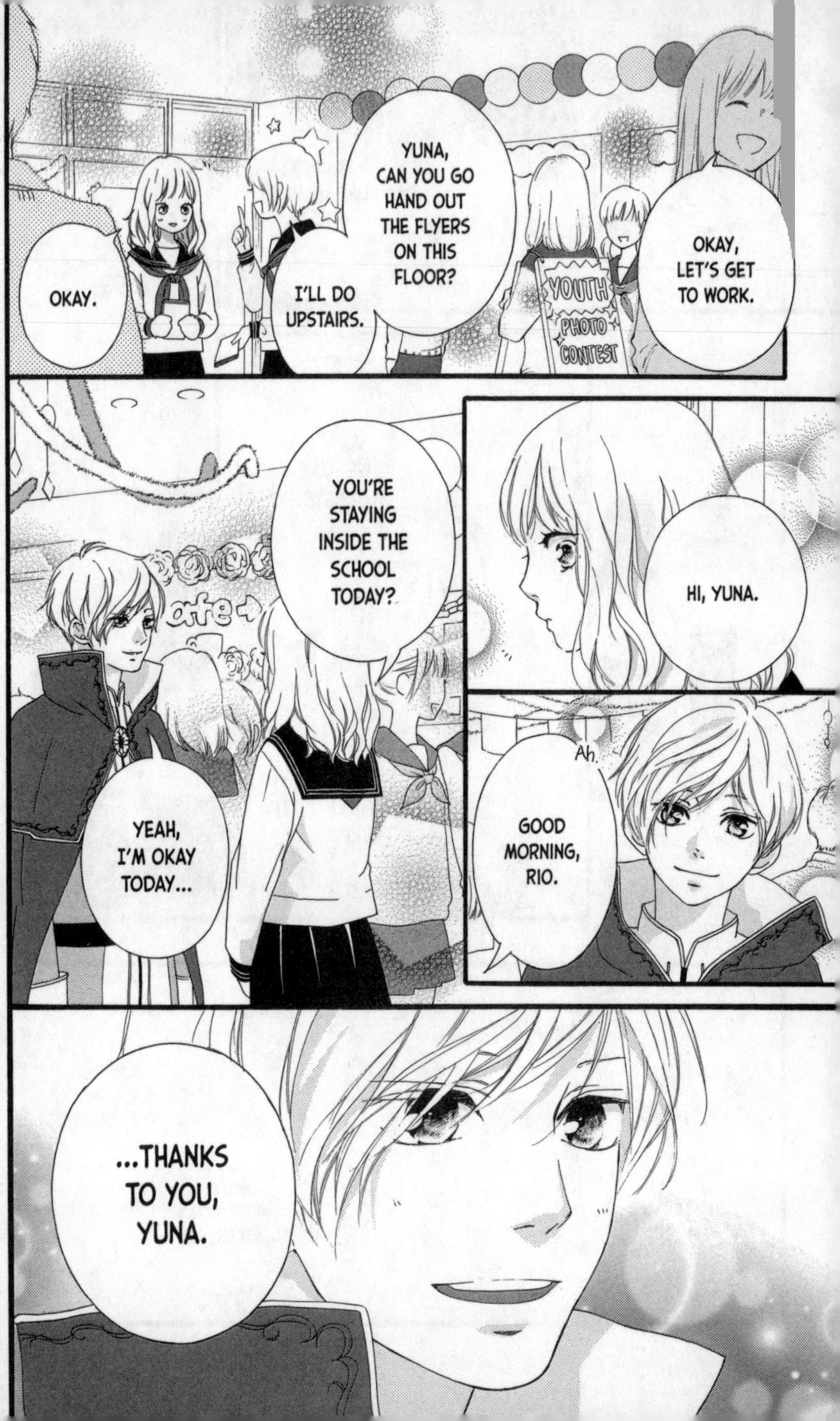
OKAY, LET'S GET TO WORK.
YOUTH PHOTO CONTEST
YUNA, CAN YOU GO HAND OUT THE FLYERS ON THIS FLOOR?
I'LL DO UPSTAIRS.
OKAY.
HI, YUNA.
Ah.
GOOD MORNING, RIO.
YOU'RE STAYING INSIDE THE SCHOOL TODAY?
YEAH, I'M OKAY TODAY...
...THANKS TO YOU, YUNA.

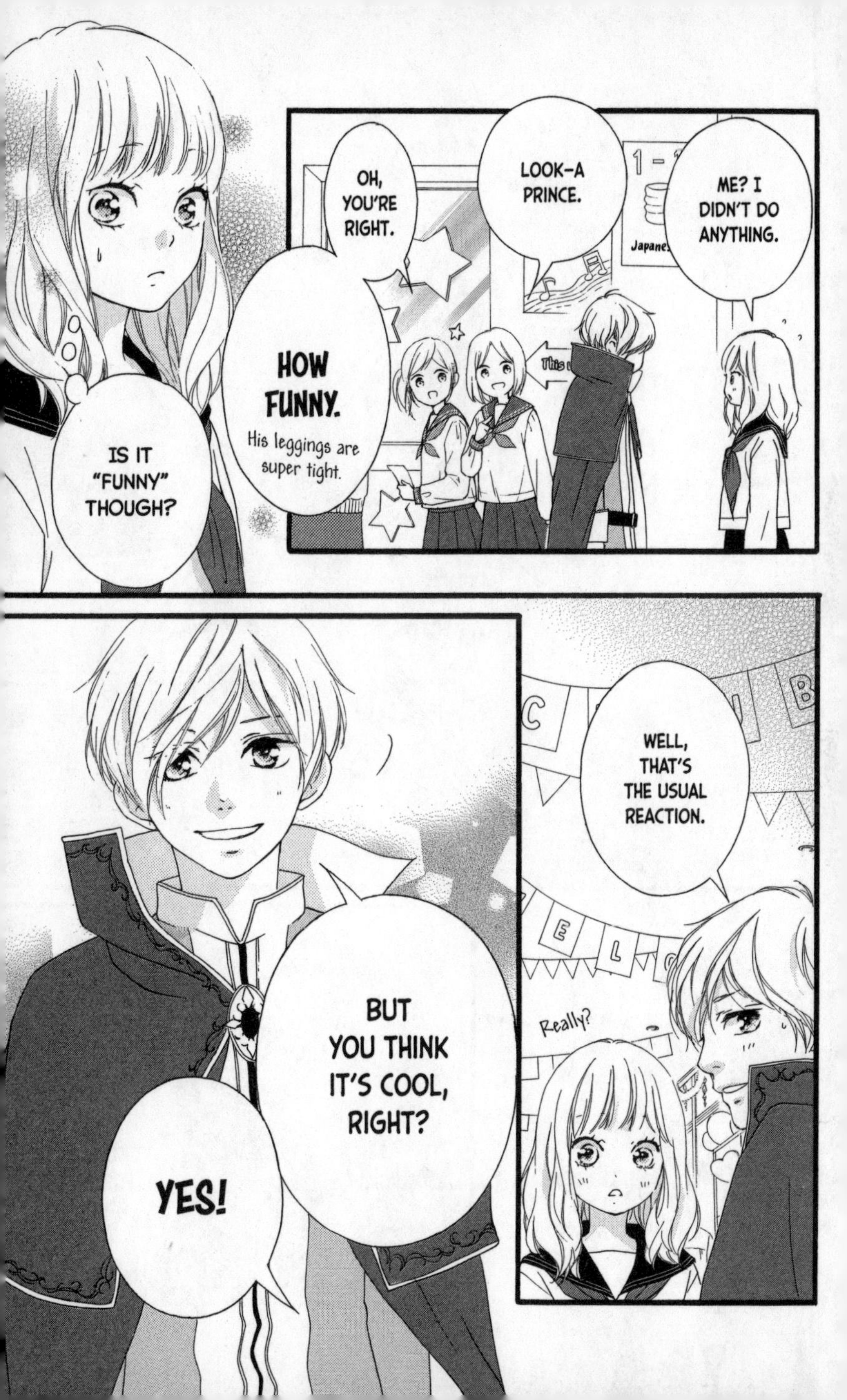
ME? I DIDN'T DO ANYTHING.
LOOK—A PRINCE.
OH, YOU'RE RIGHT.
HOW FUNNY.
His leggings are super tight.
IS IT "FUNNY" THOUGH?
WELL, THAT'S THE USUAL REACTION.
Really?
BUT YOU THINK IT'S COOL, RIGHT?
YES!

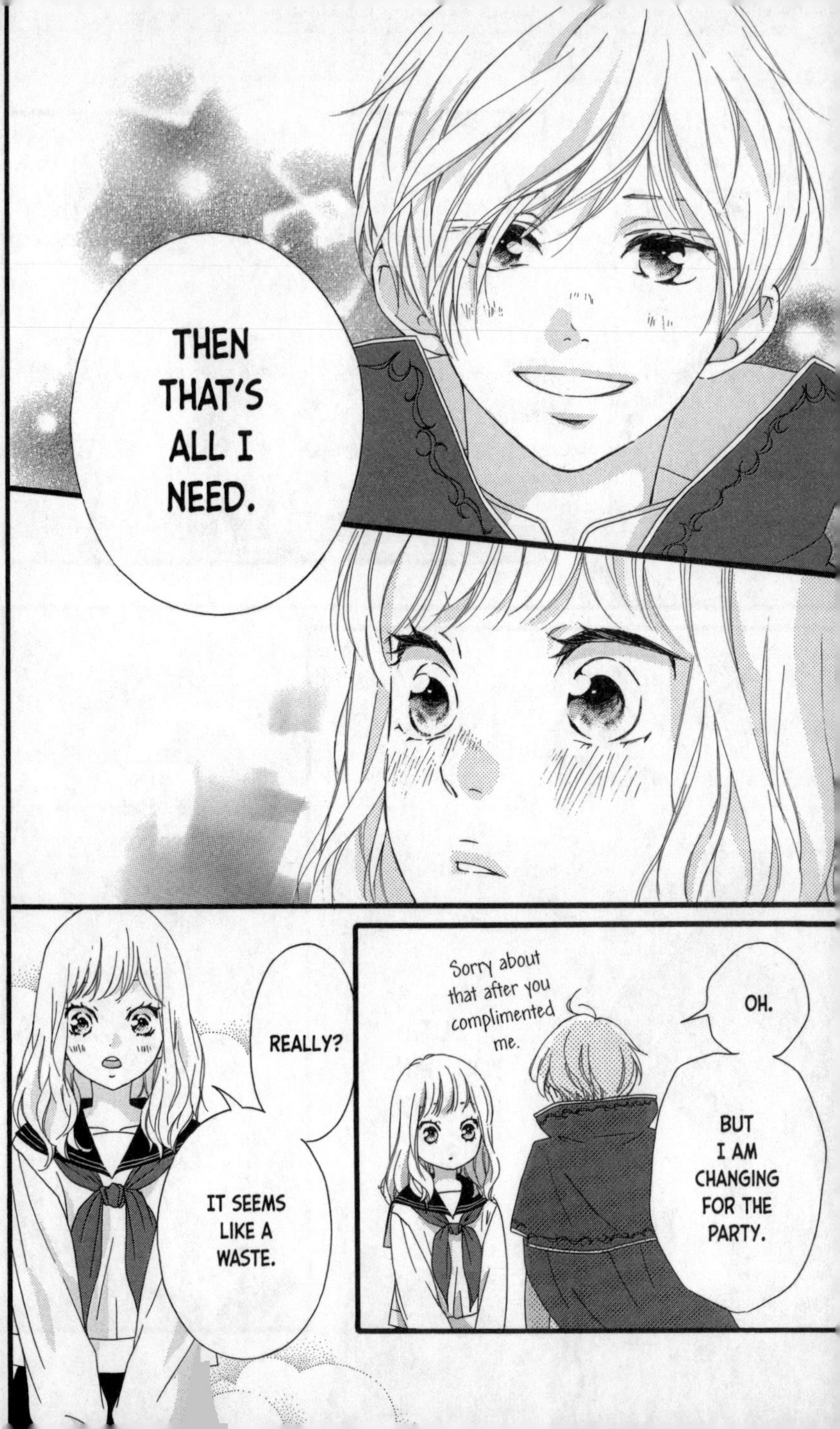
THEN THAT'S ALL I NEED.
OH.
Sorry about that after you complimented me.
BUT I AM CHANGING FOR THE PARTY.
REALLY?
IT SEEMS LIKE A WASTE.

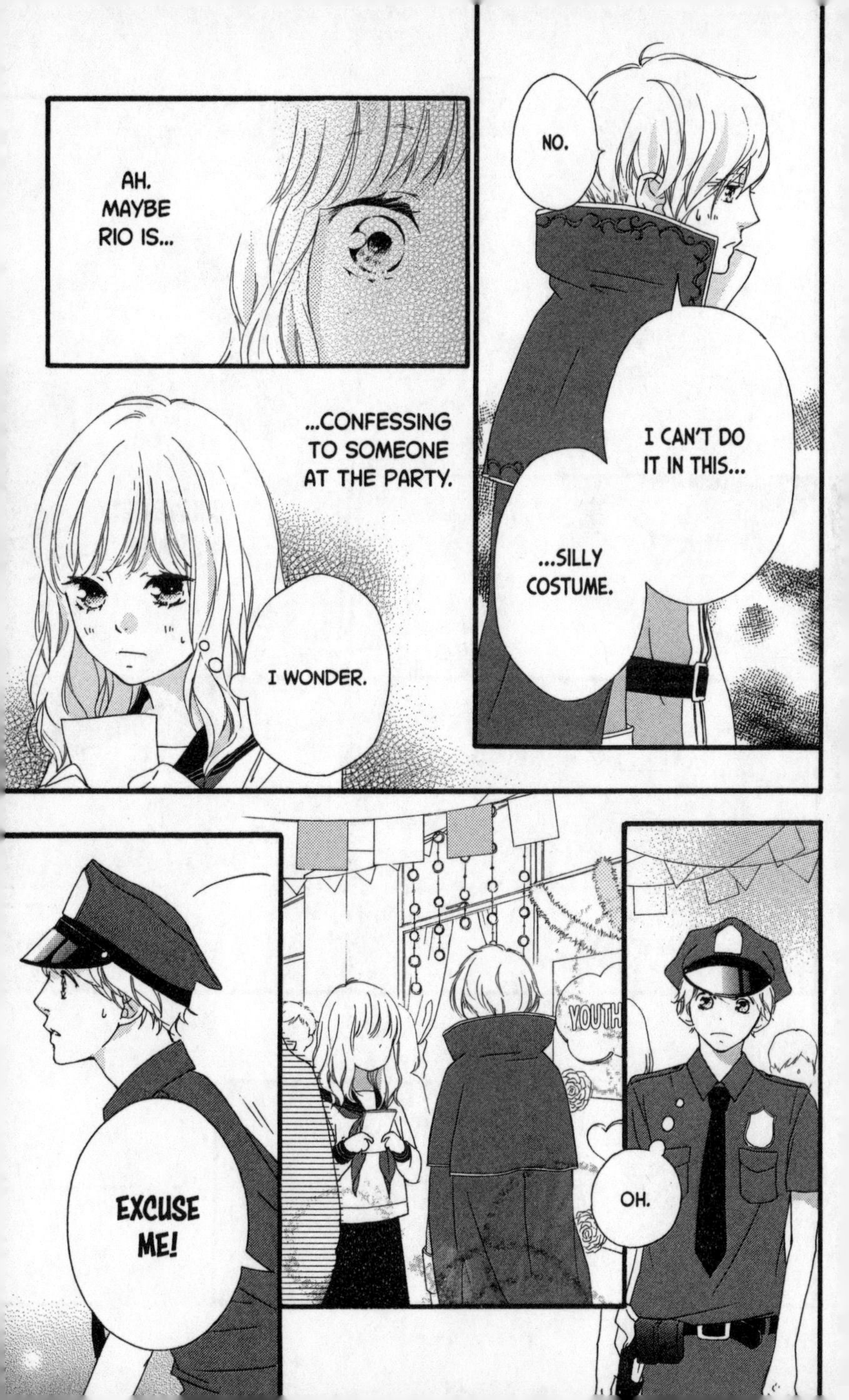
NO.
I CAN'T DO IT IN THIS...
...SILLY COSTUME.
AH. MAYBE RIO IS...
...CONFESSING TO SOMEONE AT THE PARTY.
I WONDER.
OH.
YOUTH
EXCUSE ME!

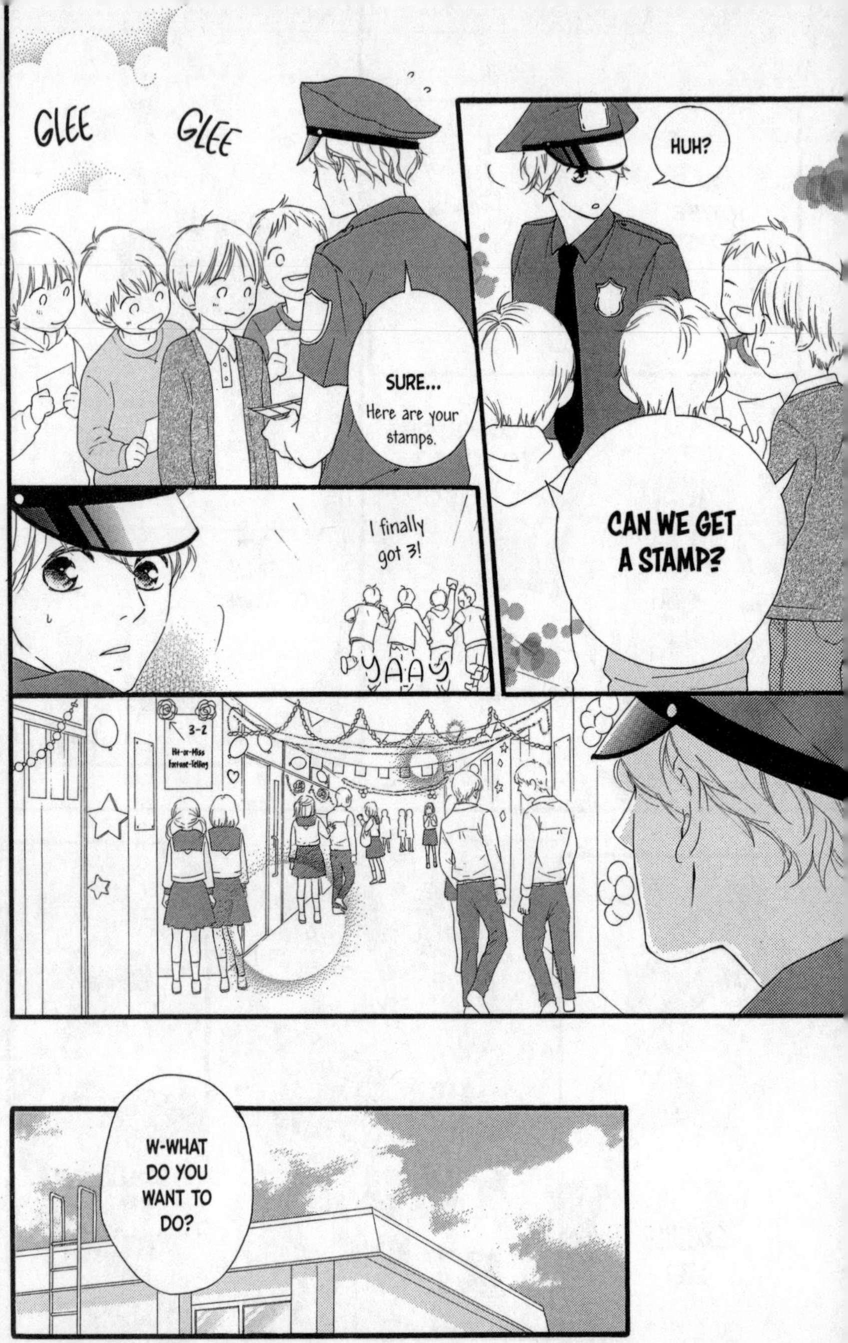
HUH?
CAN WE GET A STAMP?
GLEE
GLEE
SURE... Here are your stamps.
I finally got 3!
YAAY
3-2
Hit-or-Miss Fortune-Telling
W-WHAT DO YOU WANT TO DO?

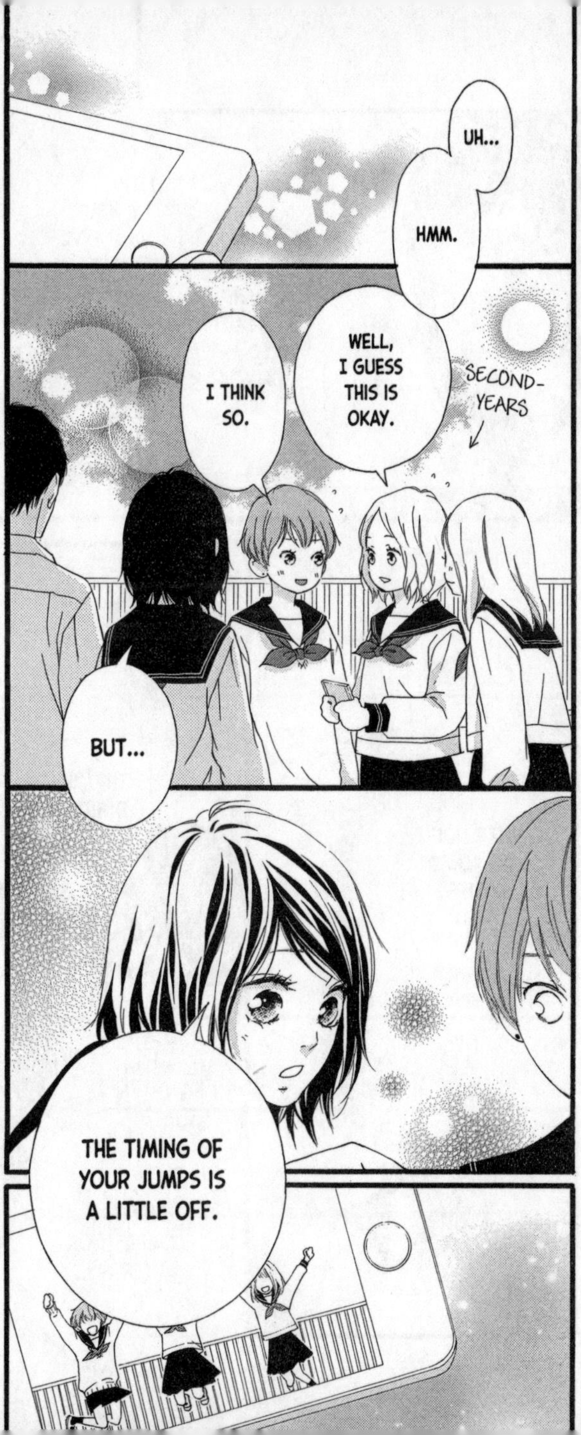
UH...
HMM.
SECOND-YEARS
WELL, I GUESS THIS IS OKAY.
I THINK SO.
BUT...
THE TIMING OF YOUR JUMPS IS A LITTLE OFF.

The other day I went with a couple of my assistants to Joypolis and nailed the VR experience. When we were there, they had a zombie-hunting game. (It's a different game now.) It was my first time doing VR, so I had no idea what to expect. The realism of it was mind-blowing. It can only be described as "wow"! It really feels like you are in a different world. We desperately fought off the never-ending flow of zombies, but midway through the game, a sudden bug in the system brought the game to a halt. We had to start over from the beginning. But thanks to that, it's like we had a practice round, so we were able to go up against the zombies much more calmly the second time. I do acknowledge that we were pretty chicken-hearted. Oh well. But it was so much fun!

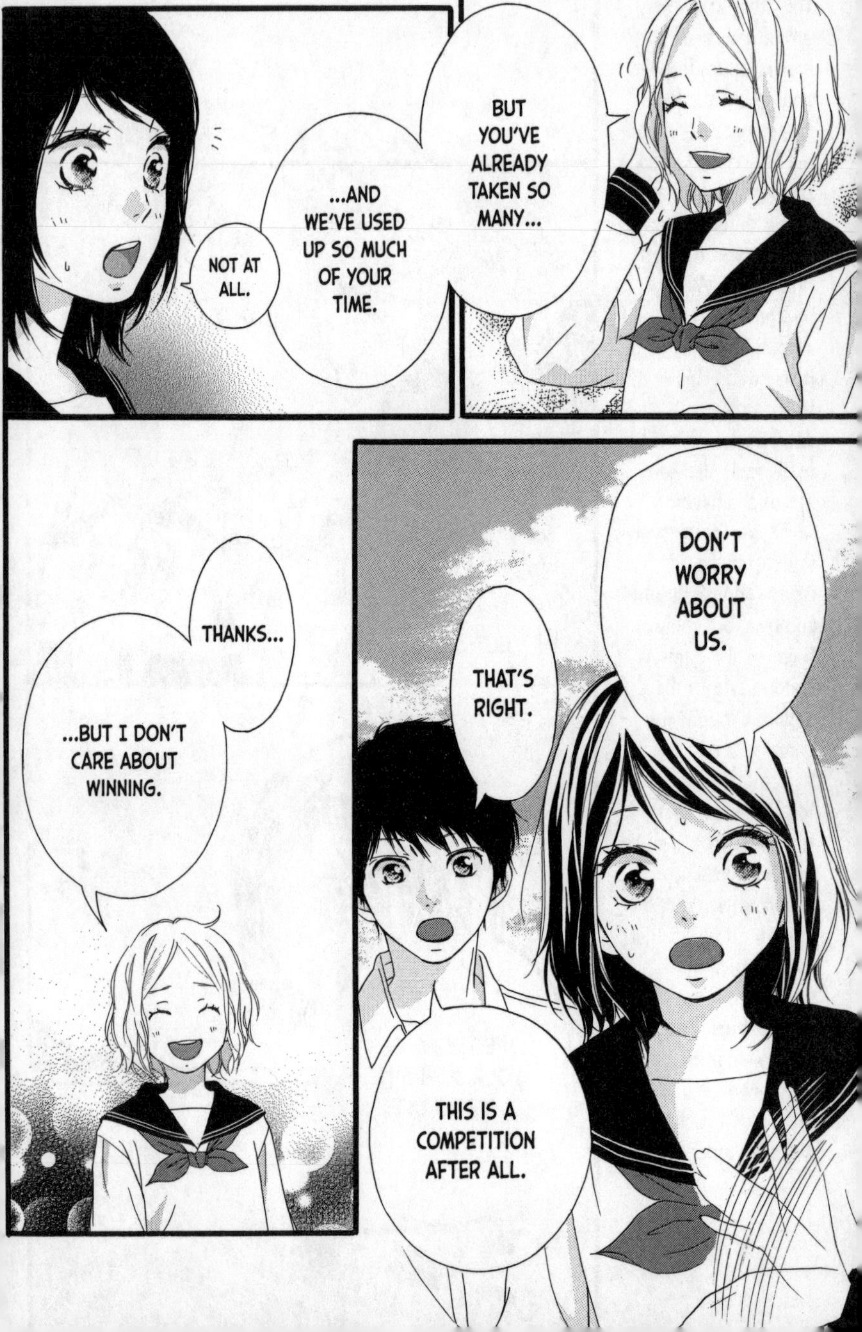
BUT YOU'VE ALREADY TAKEN SO MANY...
...AND WE'VE USED UP SO MUCH OF YOUR TIME.
NOT AT ALL.
DON'T WORRY ABOUT US.
THAT'S RIGHT.
THIS IS A COMPETITION AFTER ALL.
THANKS...
...BUT I DON'T CARE ABOUT WINNING.

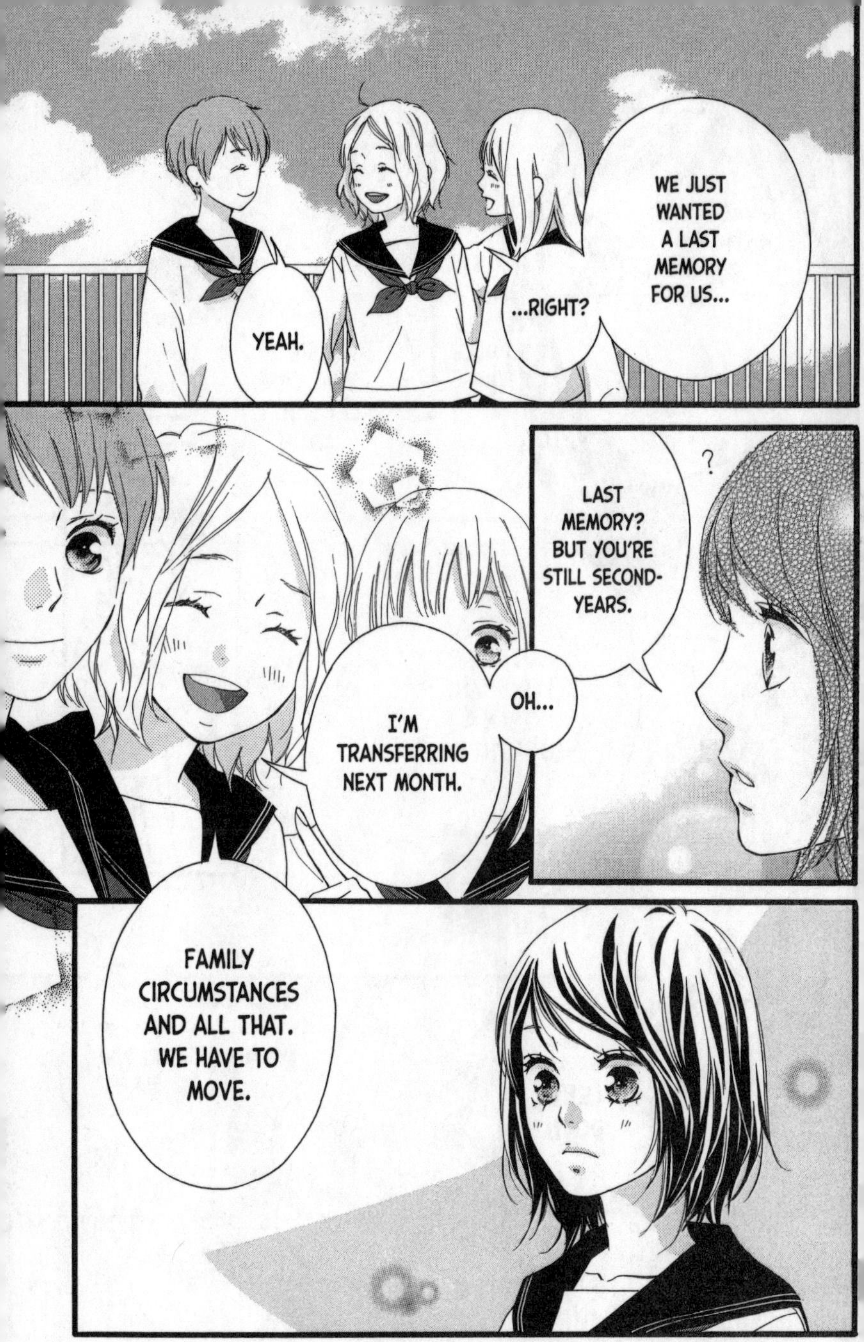
WE JUST WANTED A LAST MEMORY FOR US...
...RIGHT?
YEAH.
?
LAST MEMORY? BUT YOU'RE STILL SECOND-YEARS.
OH...
I'M TRANSFERRING NEXT MONTH.
FAMILY CIRCUMSTANCES AND ALL THAT. WE HAVE TO MOVE.

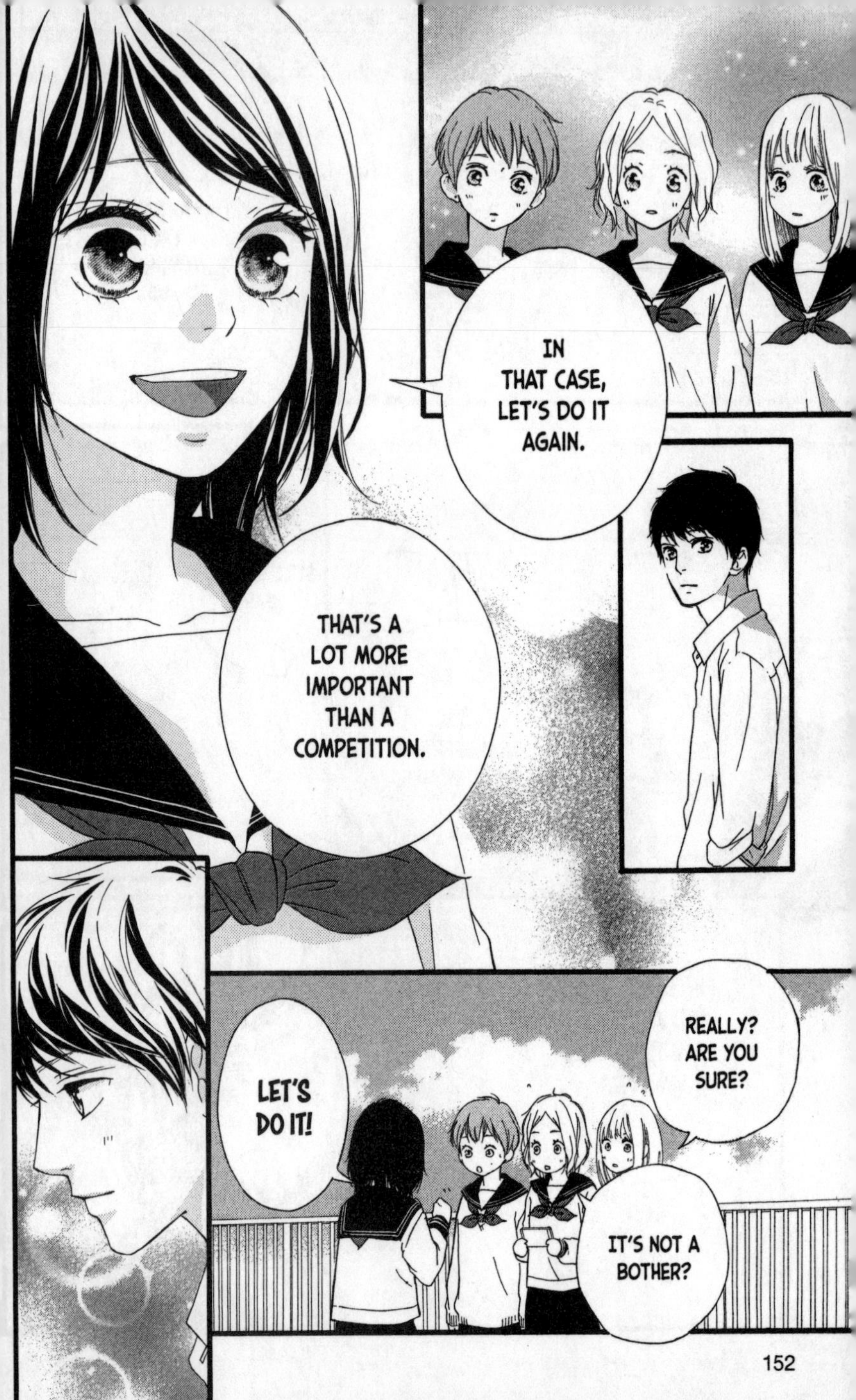
IN THAT CASE, LET'S DO IT AGAIN.
THAT'S A LOT MORE IMPORTANT THAN A COMPETITION.
REALLY? ARE YOU SURE?
IT'S NOT A BOTHER?
LET'S DO IT!

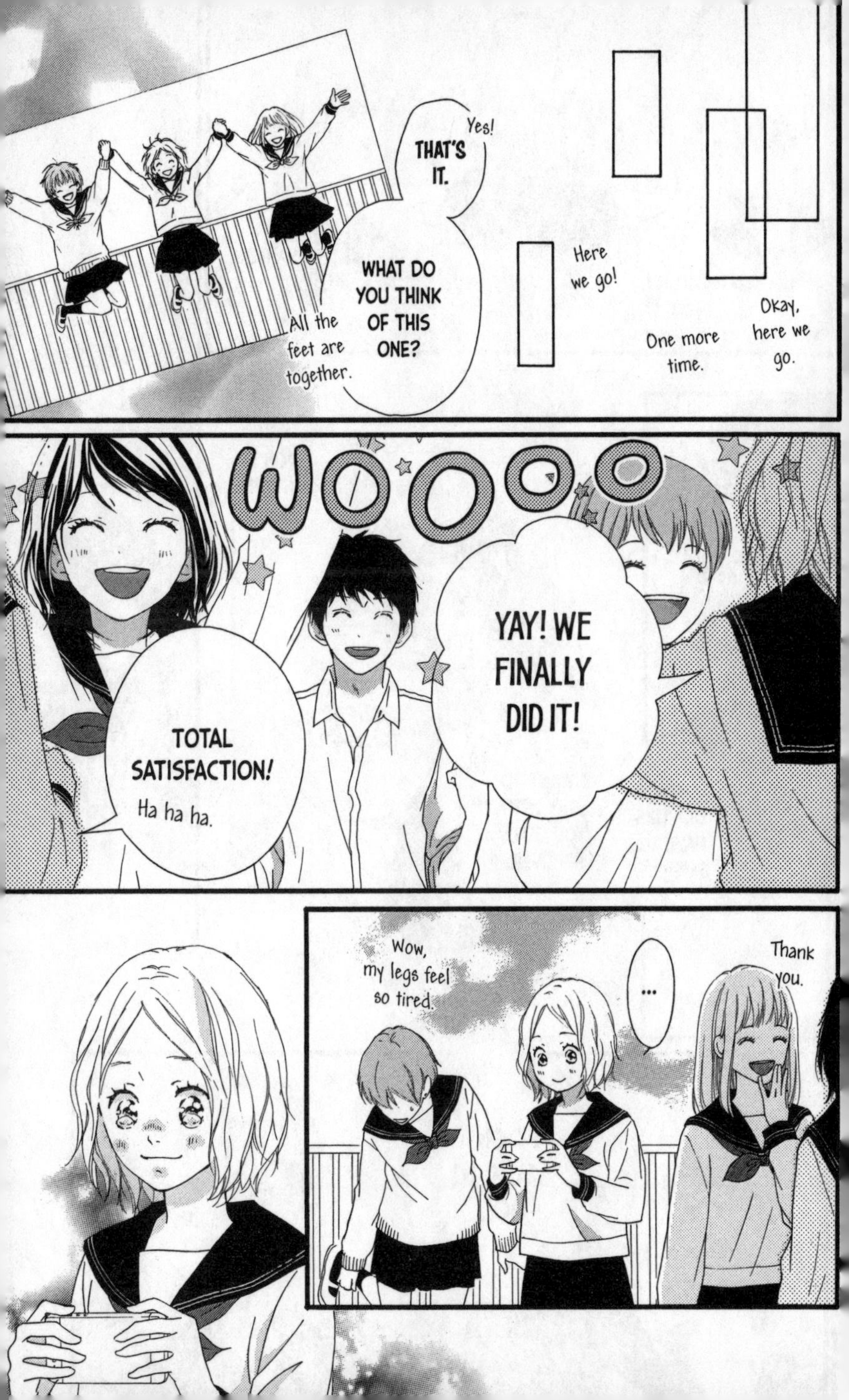
Okay, here we go.
One more time.
Here we go!
Yes!
THAT'S IT.
WHAT DO YOU THINK OF THIS ONE?
All the feet are together.
WOOOO
YAY! WE FINALLY DID IT!
TOTAL SATISFACTION!
Ha ha ha.
Thank you.
...
Wow, my legs feel so tired.

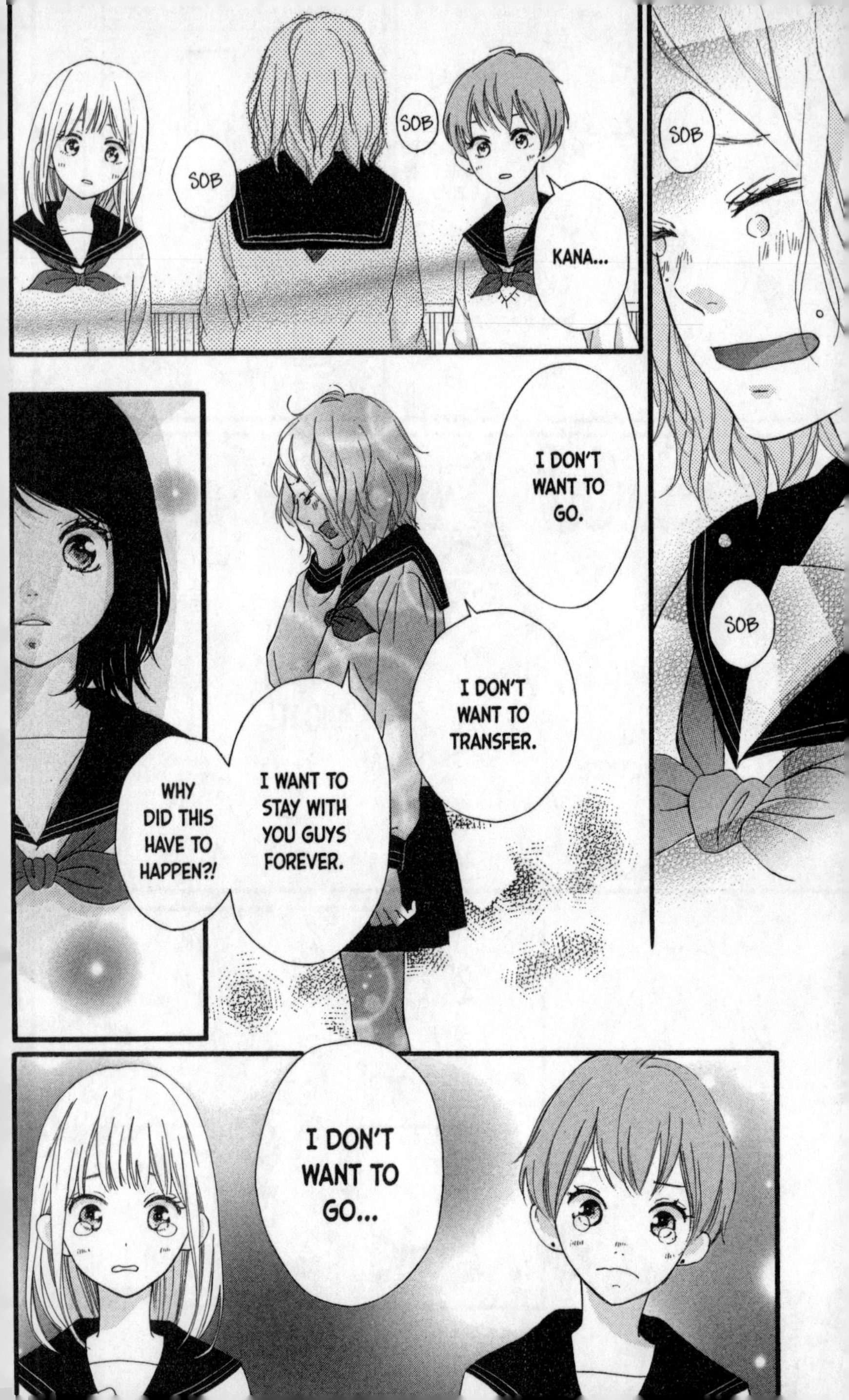
SOB
SOB
SOB
KANA...
SOB
I DON'T WANT TO GO.
I DON'T WANT TO TRANSFER.
I WANT TO STAY WITH YOU GUYS FOREVER.
WHY DID THIS HAVE TO HAPPEN?!
I DON'T WANT TO GO...

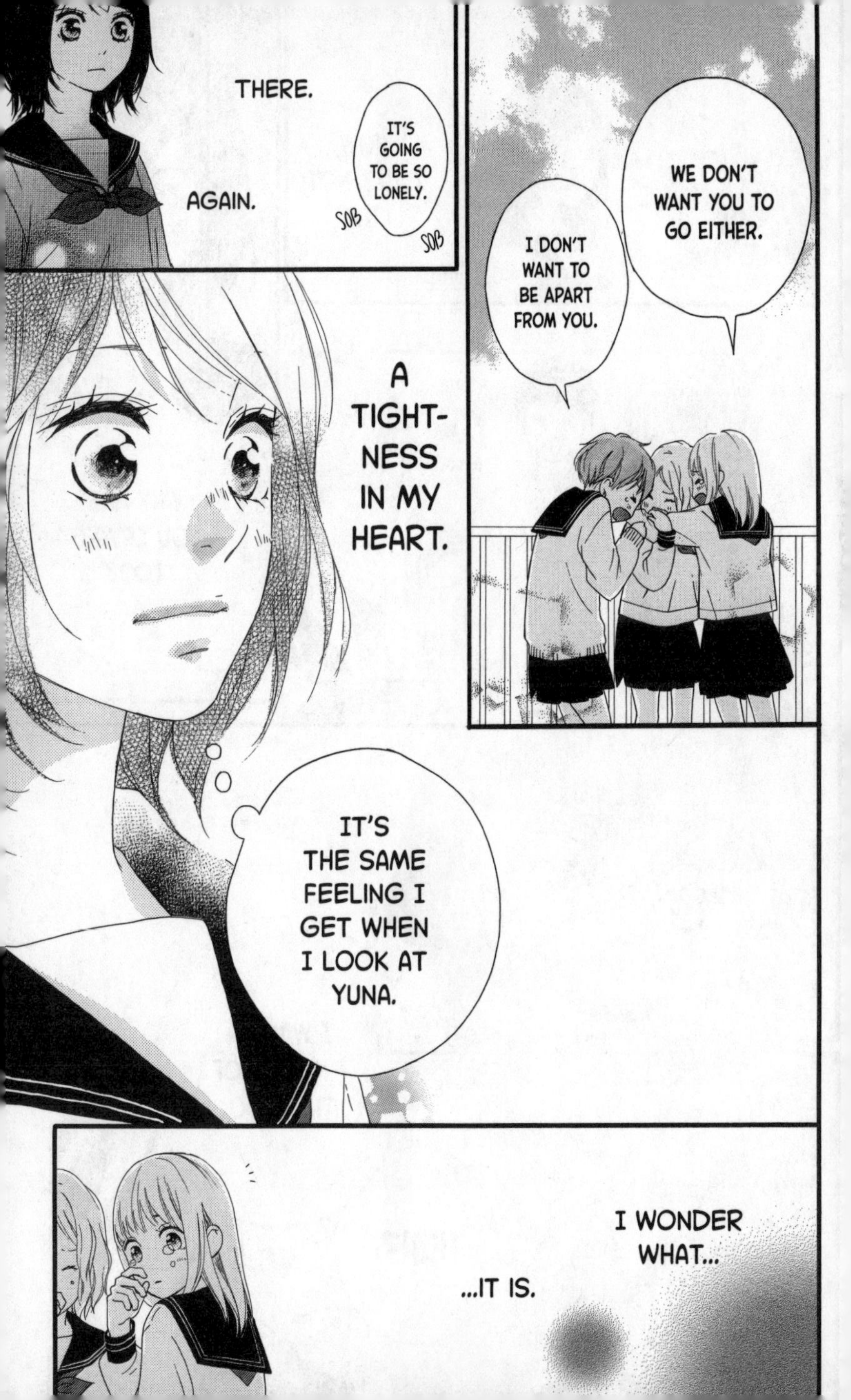
WE DON'T WANT YOU TO GO EITHER.
I DON'T WANT TO BE APART FROM YOU.
IT'S GOING TO BE SO LONELY.
SOB SOB
THERE.
AGAIN.
A TIGHT-NESS IN MY HEART.
IT'S THE SAME FEELING I GET WHEN I LOOK AT YUNA.
I WONDER WHAT...
...IT IS.

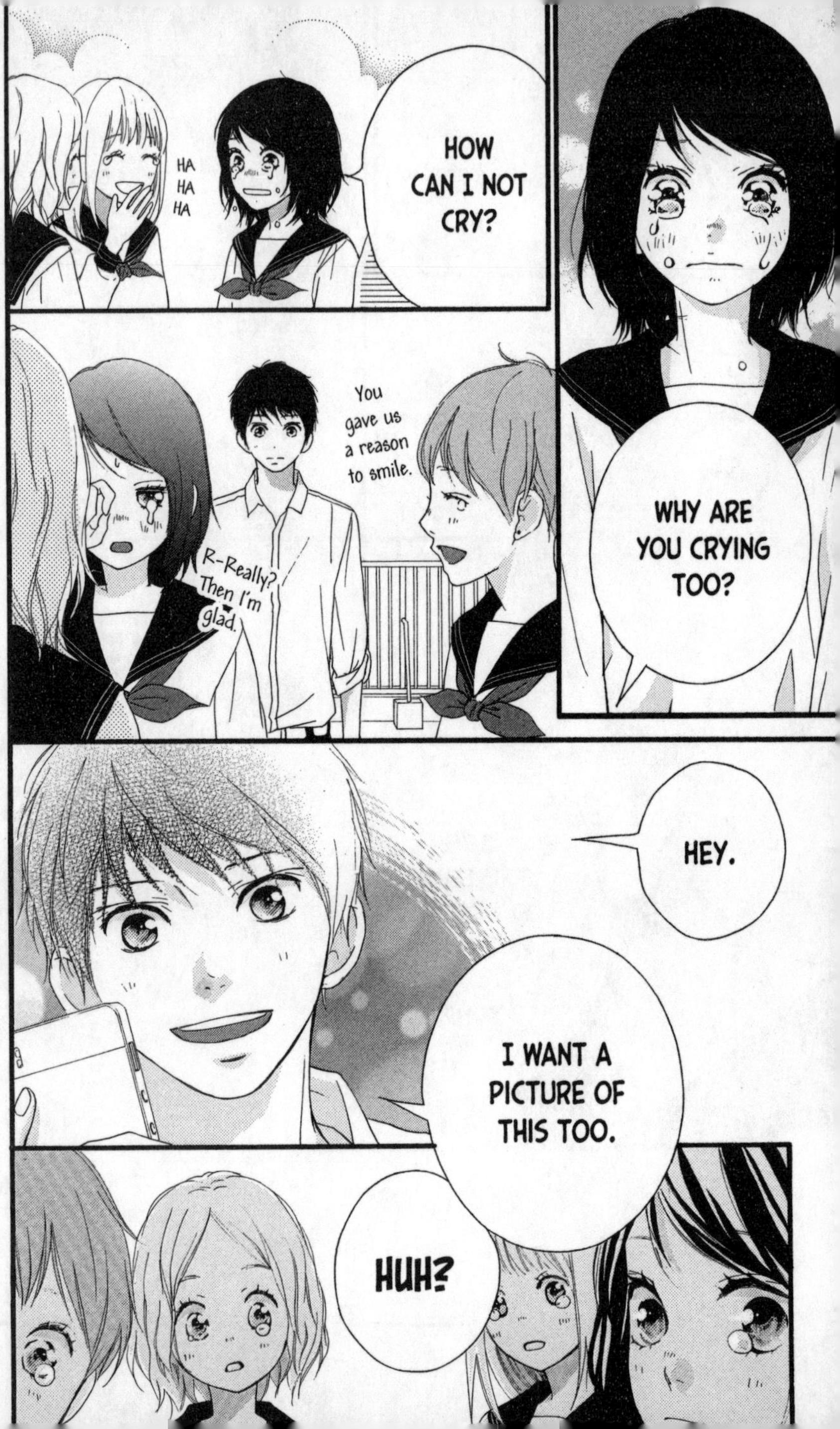
WHY ARE YOU CRYING TOO?
HOW CAN I NOT CRY?
HA HA HA
You gave us a reason to smile.
R-Really? Then I'm glad.
HEY.
I WANT A PICTURE OF THIS TOO.
HUH?

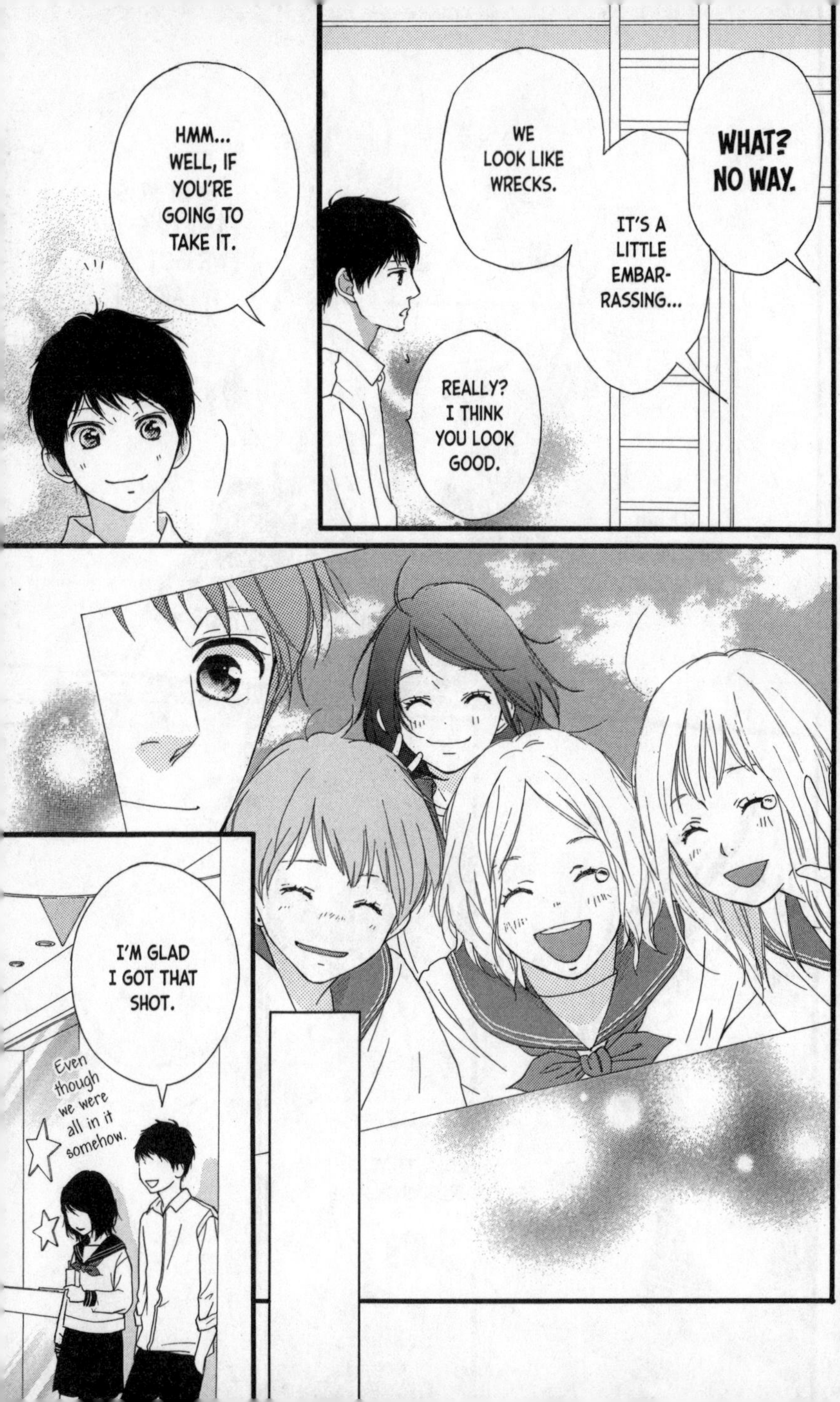
WHAT? NO WAY.
WE LOOK LIKE WRECKS.
IT'S A LITTLE EMBAR-RASSING...
REALLY? I THINK YOU LOOK GOOD.
HMM... WELL, IF YOU'RE GOING TO TAKE IT.
I'M GLAD I GOT THAT SHOT.
Even though we were all in it somehow.

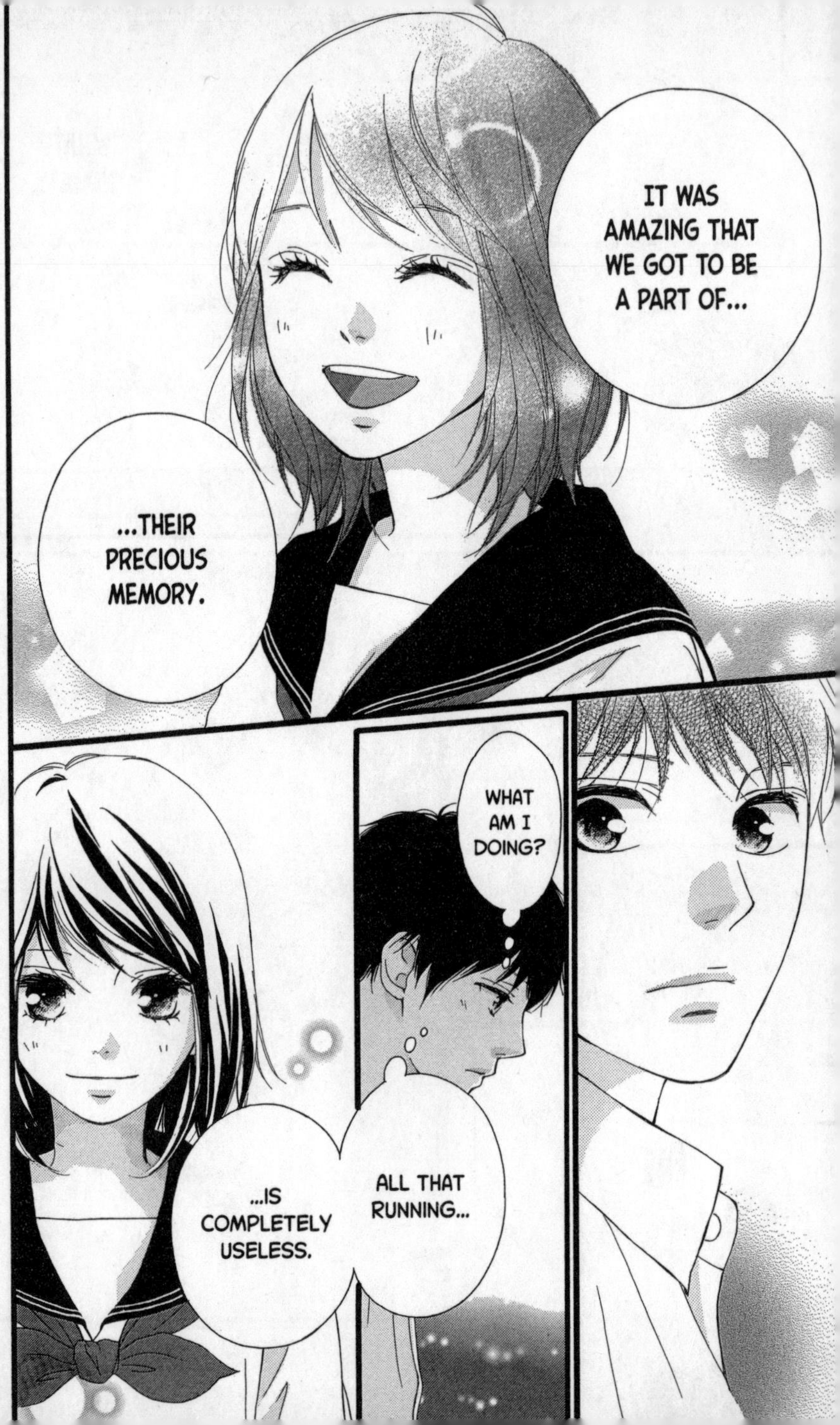
IT WAS AMAZING THAT WE GOT TO BE A PART OF...
...THEIR PRECIOUS MEMORY.
WHAT AM I DOING?
ALL THAT RUNNING...
...IS COMPLETELY USELESS.

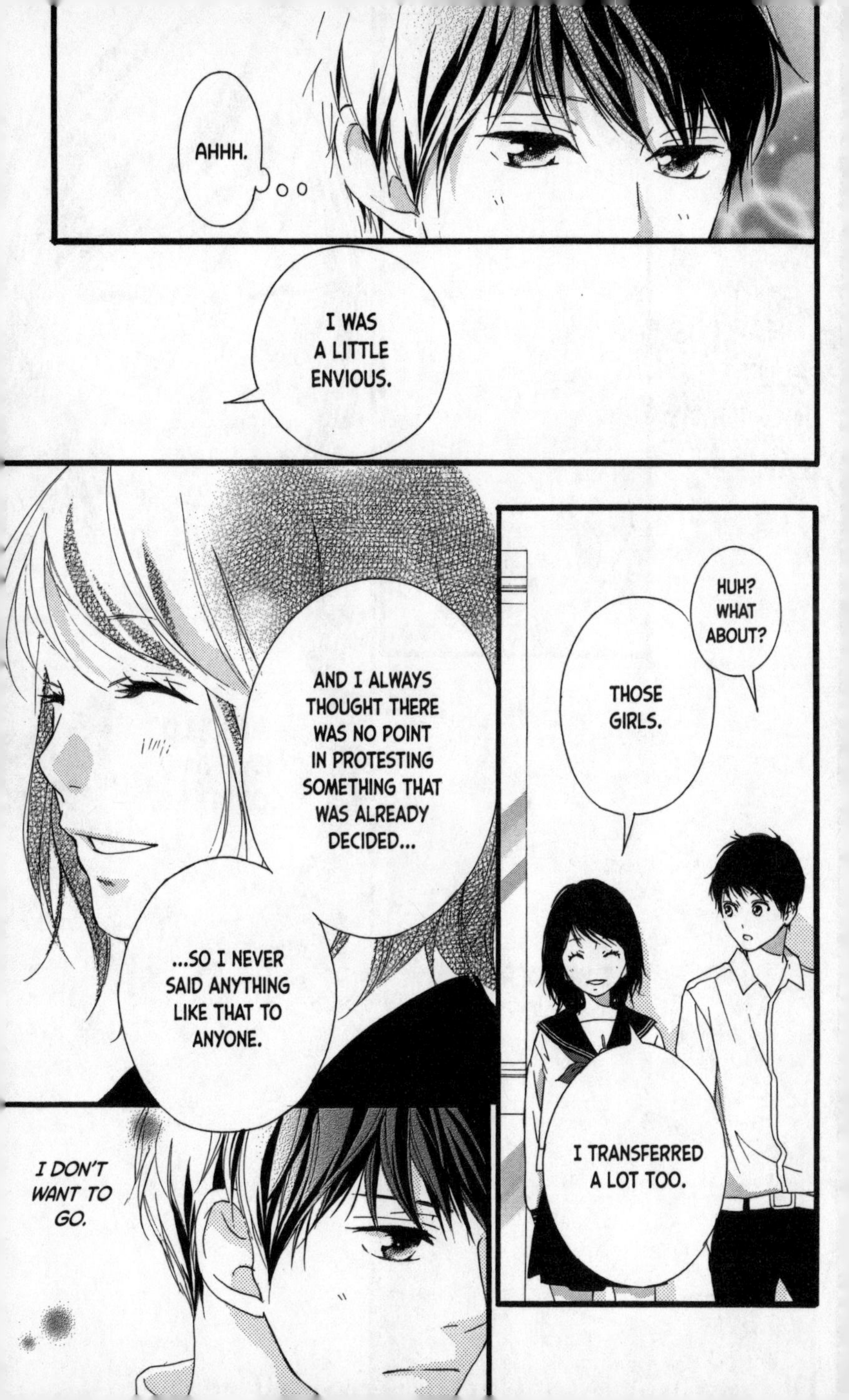
AHHH.
I WAS A LITTLE ENVIOUS.
HUH? WHAT ABOUT?
THOSE GIRLS.
I TRANSFERRED A LOT TOO.
AND I ALWAYS THOUGHT THERE WAS NO POINT IN PROTESTING SOMETHING THAT WAS ALREADY DECIDED...
...SO I NEVER SAID ANYTHING LIKE THAT TO ANYONE.
I DON'T WANT TO GO.

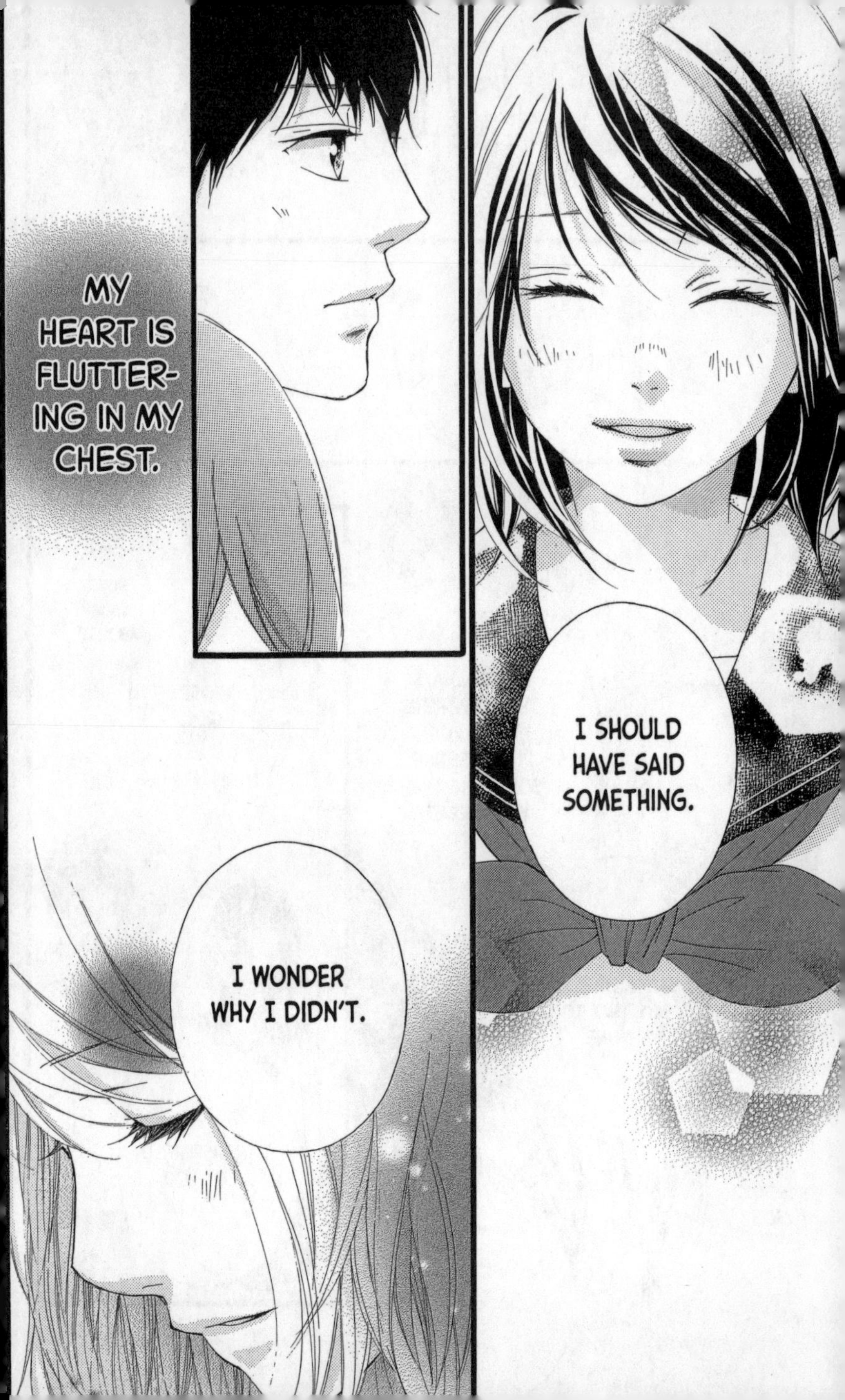
I SHOULD HAVE SAID SOMETHING.
MY HEART IS FLUTTER-ING IN MY CHEST.
I WONDER WHY I DIDN'T.

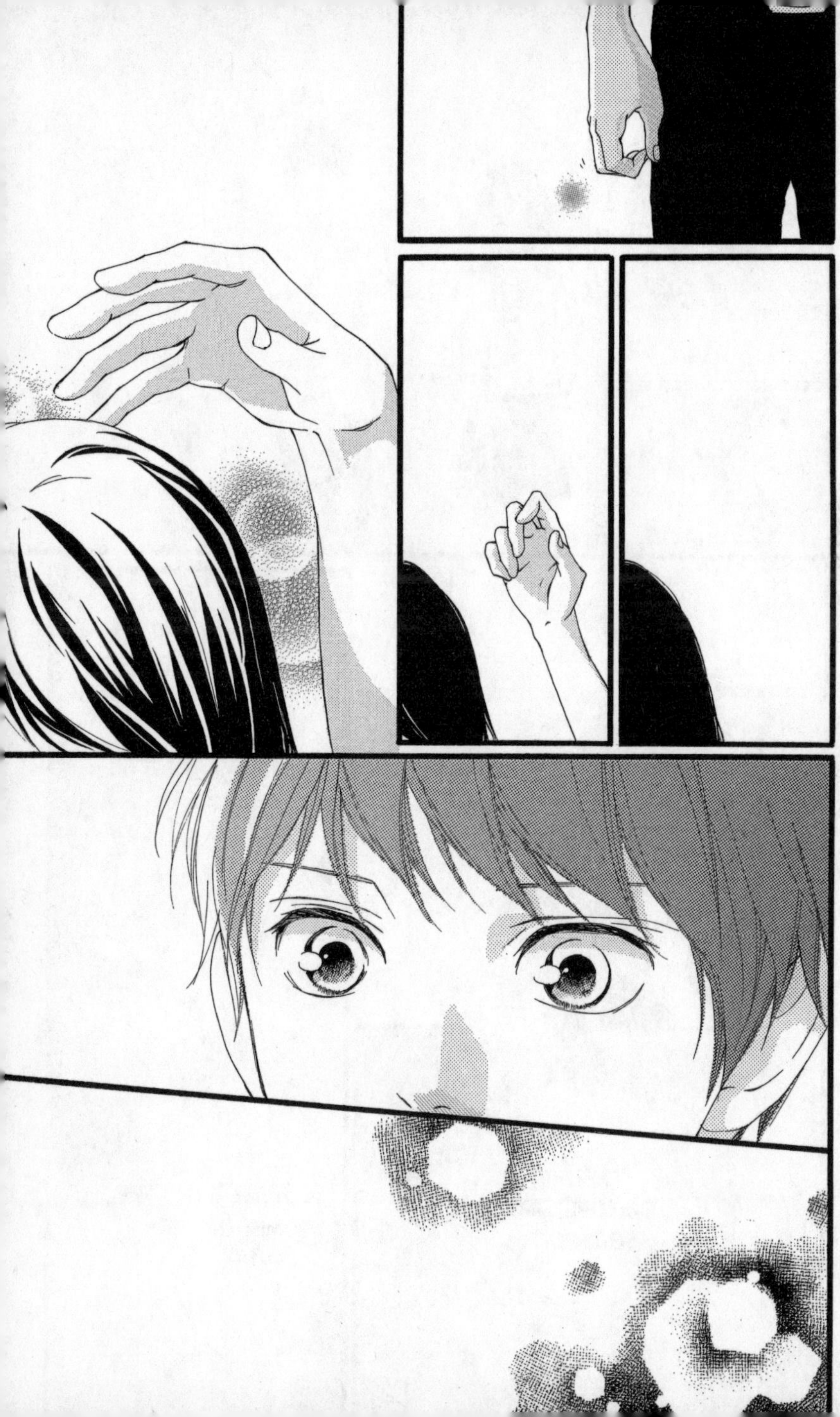

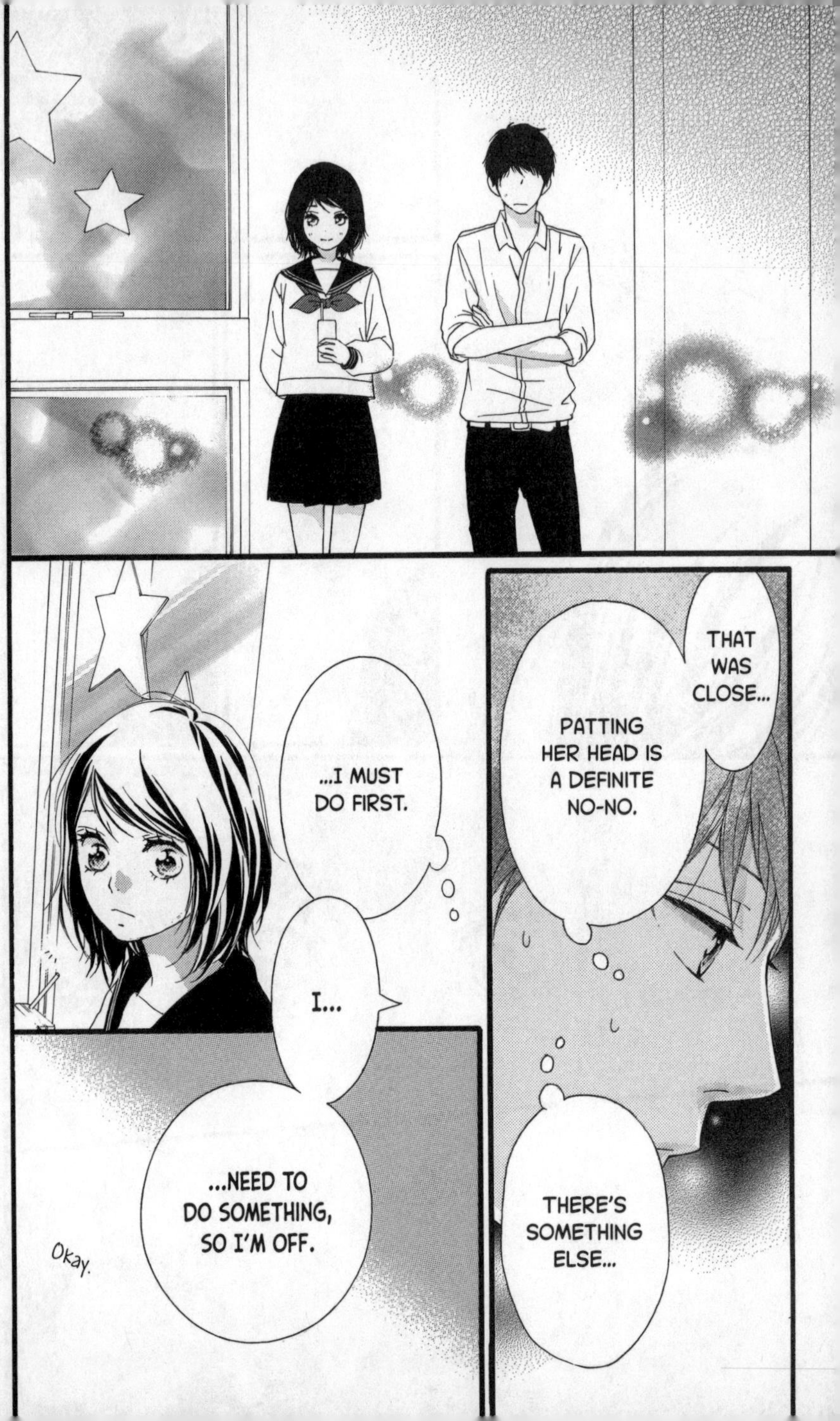
THAT WAS CLOSE...
PATTING HER HEAD IS A DEFINITE NO-NO.
THERE'S SOMETHING ELSE...
...I MUST DO FIRST.
I...
...NEED TO DO SOMETHING, SO I'M OFF.
Okay.

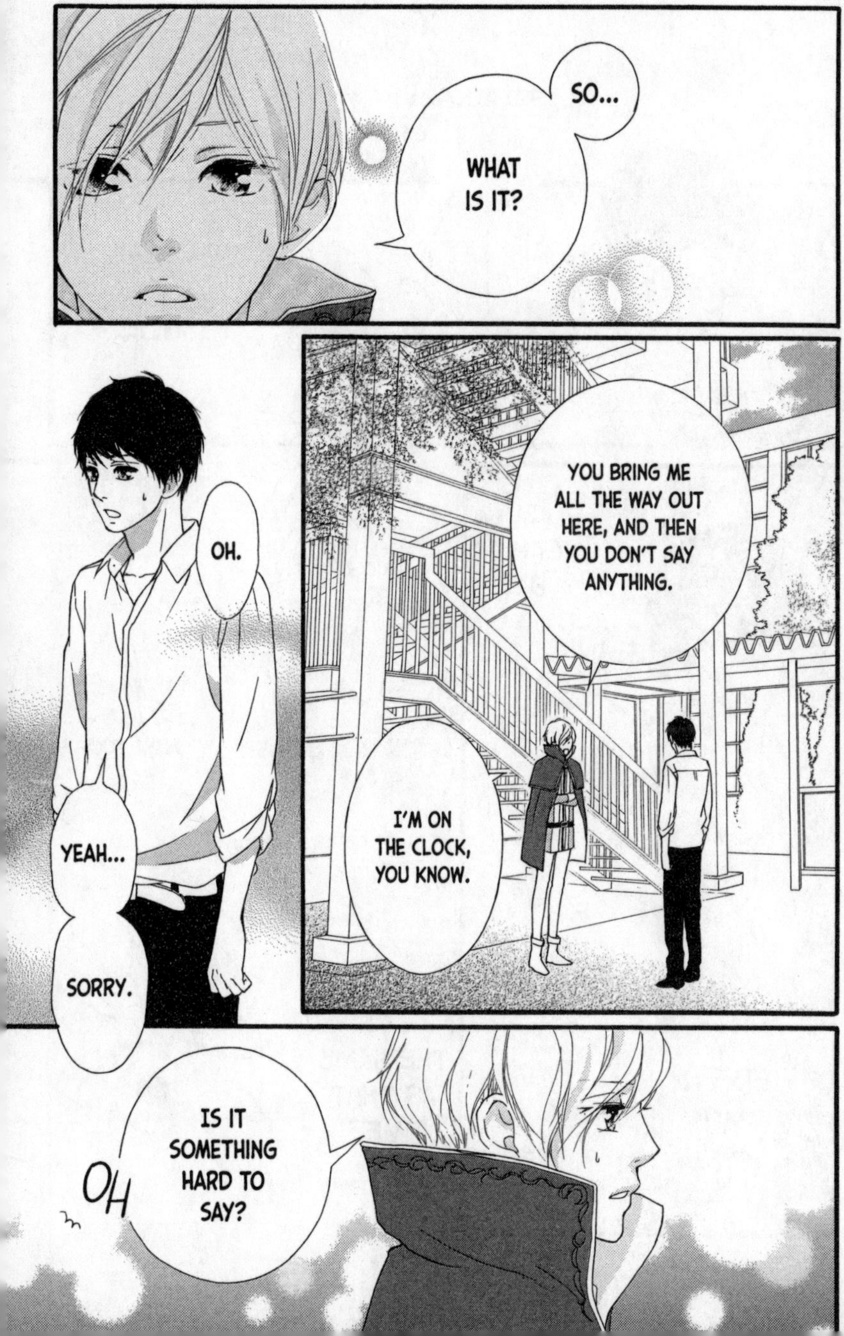
SO...
WHAT IS IT?
YOU BRING ME ALL THE WAY OUT HERE, AND THEN YOU DON'T SAY ANYTHING.
I'M ON THE CLOCK, YOU KNOW.
OH.
YEAH...
SORRY.
IS IT SOMETHING HARD TO SAY?
OH

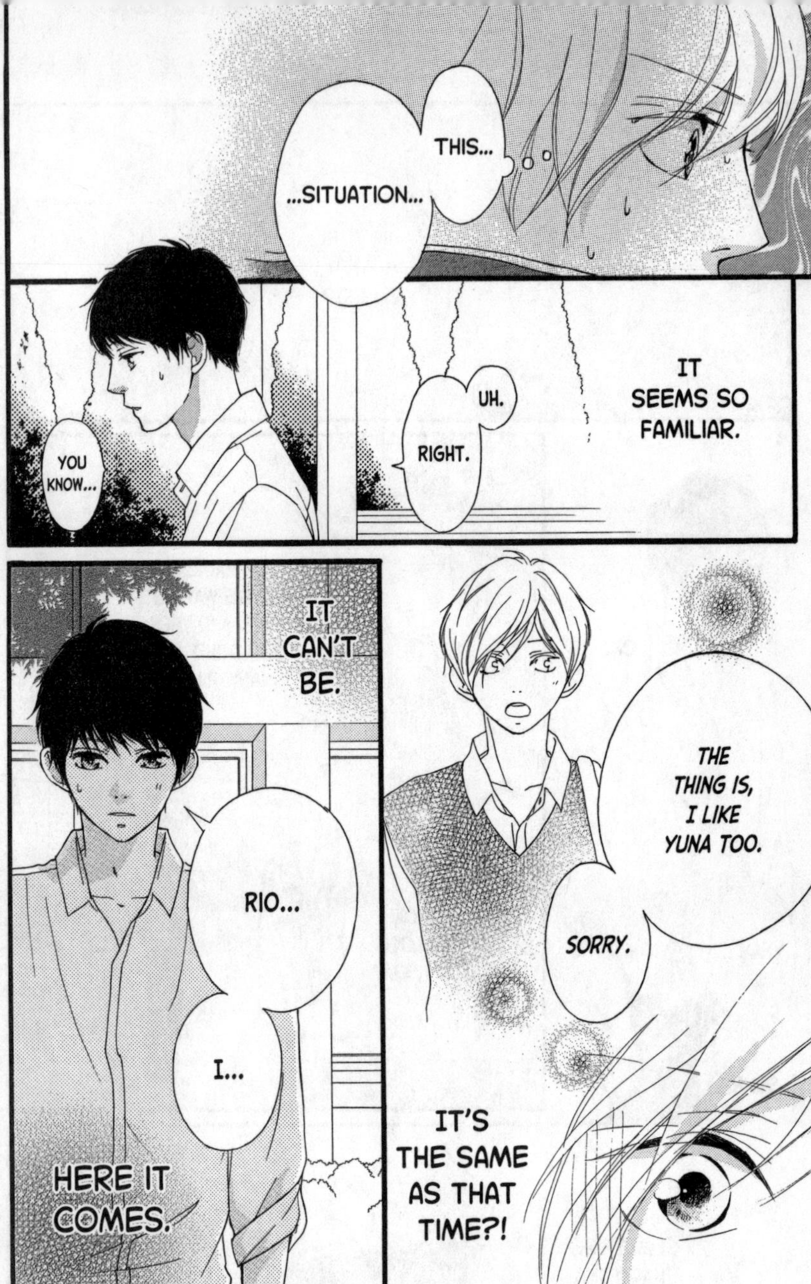
THIS...
...SITUATION...
IT SEEMS SO FAMILIAR.
UH.
RIGHT.
YOU KNOW...
THE THING IS, I LIKE YUNA TOO.
SORRY.
IT'S THE SAME AS THAT TIME?!
IT CAN'T BE.
RIO...
I...
HERE IT COMES.

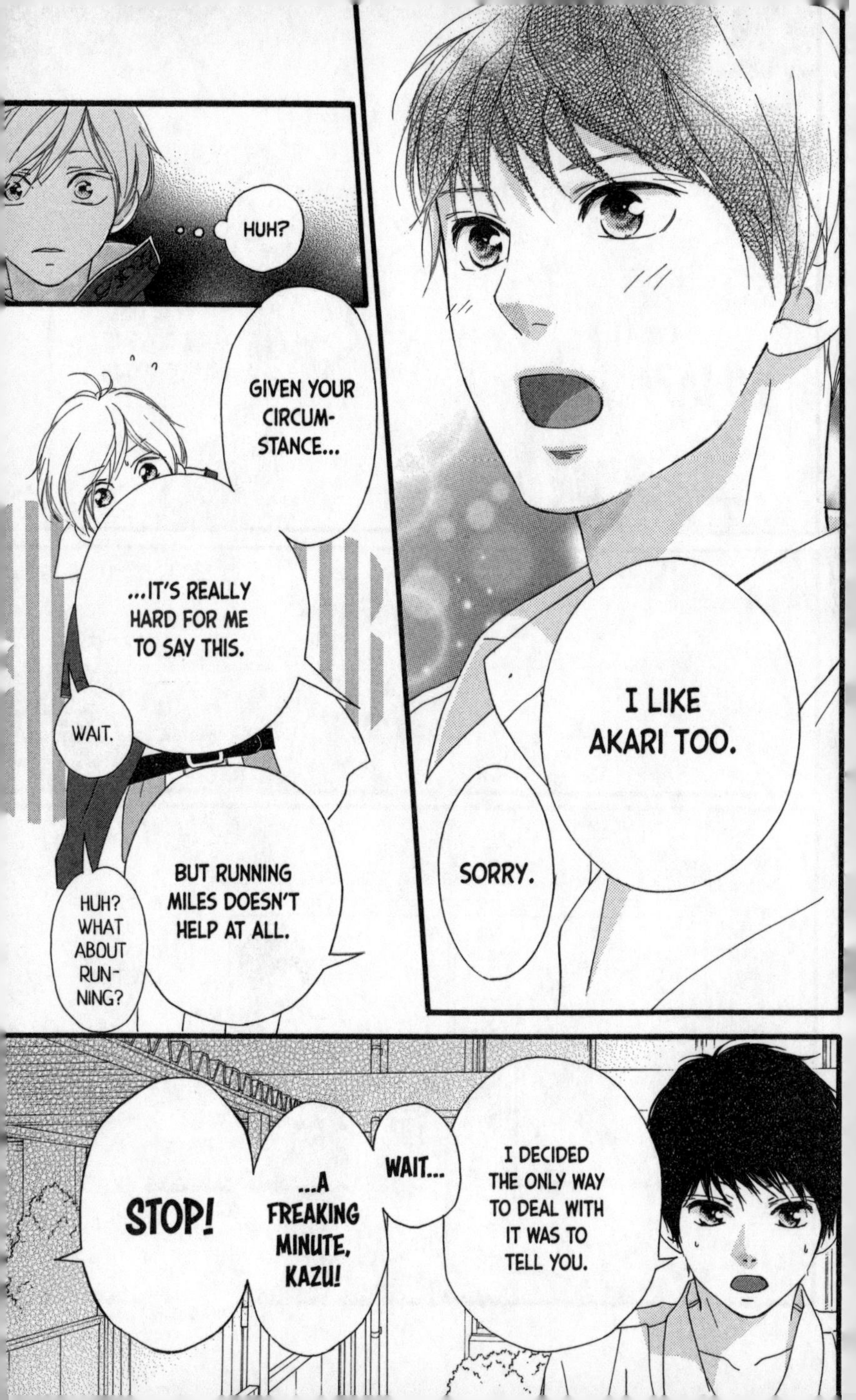
I LIKE AKARI TOO.
SORRY.
HUH?
GIVEN YOUR CIRCUM-STANCE...
...IT'S REALLY HARD FOR ME TO SAY THIS.
WAIT.
BUT RUNNING MILES DOESN'T HELP AT ALL.
HUH? WHAT ABOUT RUN-NING?
I DECIDED THE ONLY WAY TO DEAL WITH IT WAS TO TELL YOU.
WAIT...
...A FREAKING MINUTE, KAZU!
STOP!

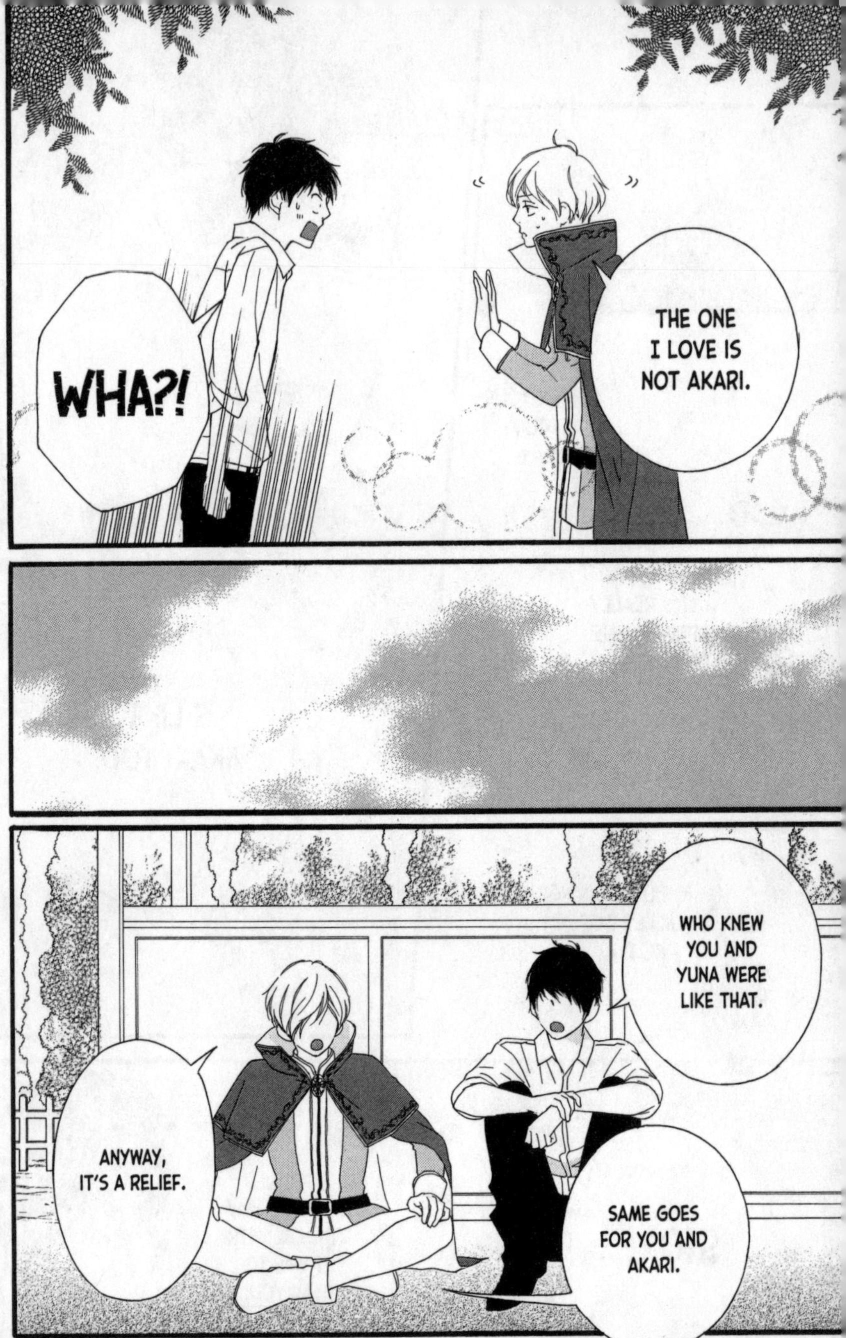
THE ONE I LOVE IS NOT AKARI.
WHA?!
WHO KNEW YOU AND YUNA WERE LIKE THAT.
SAME GOES FOR YOU AND AKARI.
ANYWAY, IT'S A RELIEF.

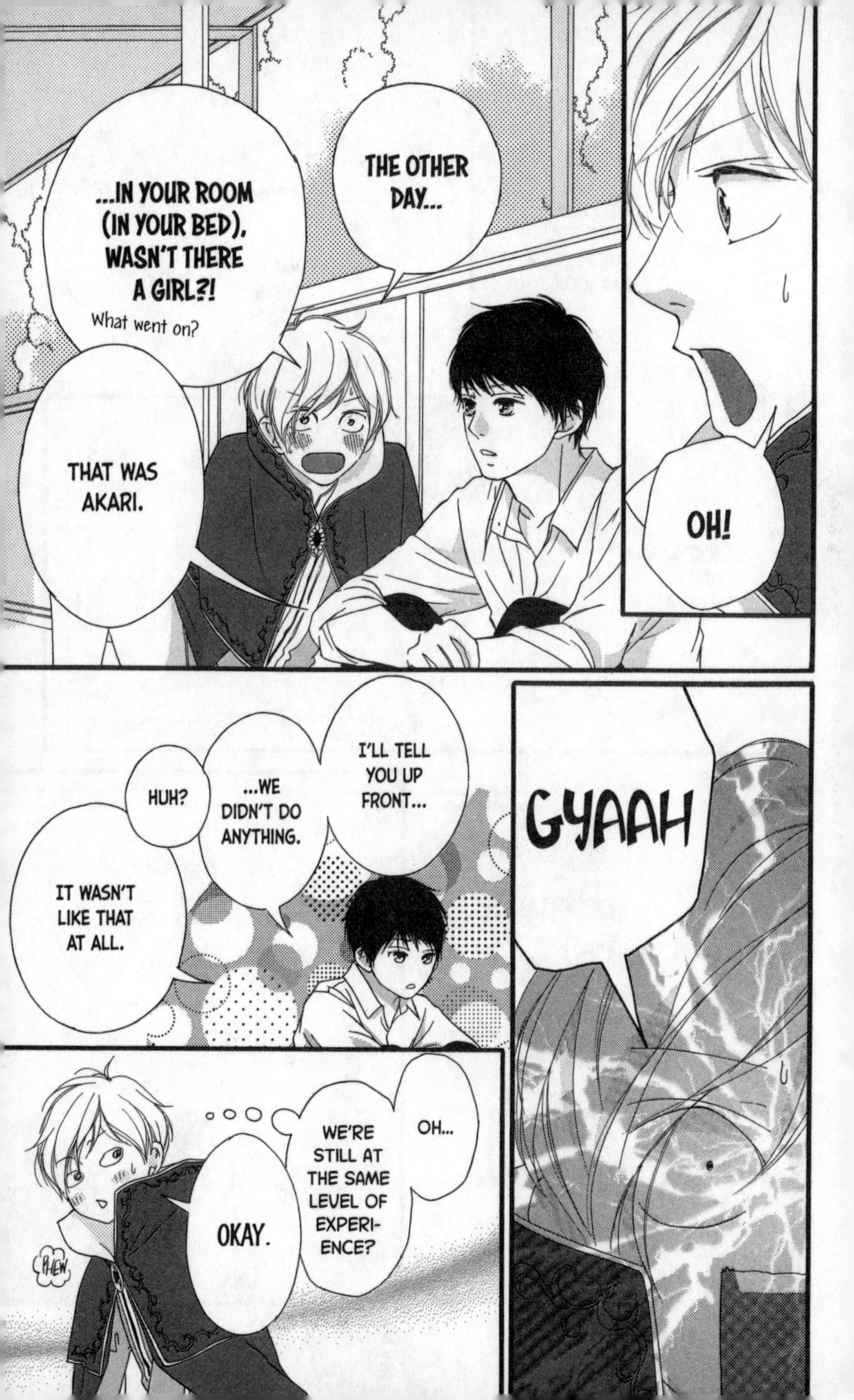
OH!
THE OTHER DAY...
...IN YOUR ROOM (IN YOUR BED), WASN'T THERE A GIRL?!
What went on?
THAT WAS AKARI.
GYAAH
I'LL TELL YOU UP FRONT...
...WE DIDN'T DO ANYTHING.
HUH?
IT WASN'T LIKE THAT AT ALL.
OH...
WE'RE STILL AT THE SAME LEVEL OF EXPERI-ENCE?
OKAY.
PHEW

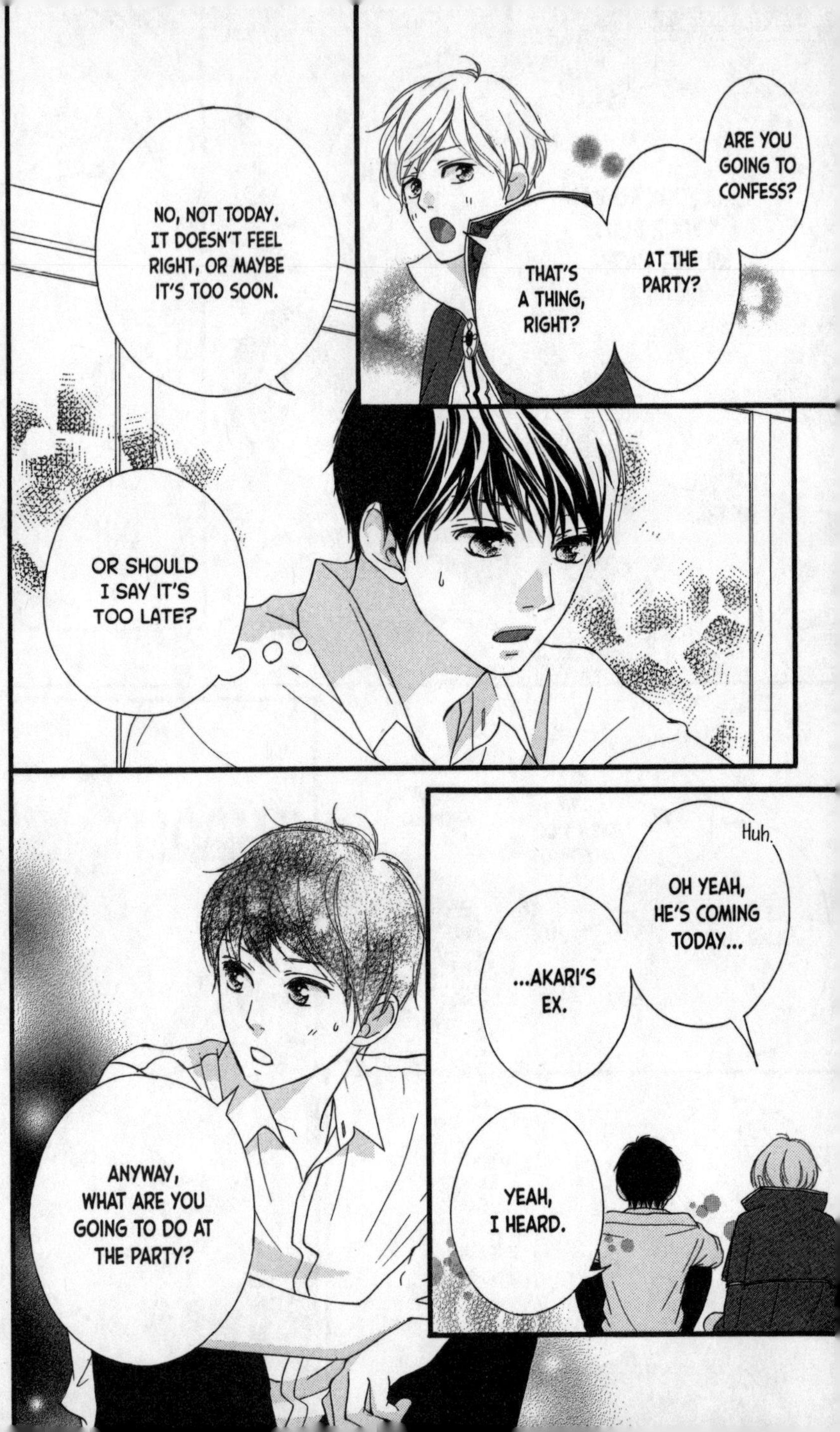
ARE YOU GOING TO CONFESS?
AT THE PARTY?
THAT'S A THING, RIGHT?
NO, NOT TODAY. IT DOESN'T FEEL RIGHT, OR MAYBE IT'S TOO SOON.
OR SHOULD I SAY IT'S TOO LATE?
Huh.
OH YEAH, HE'S COMING TODAY...
...AKARI'S EX.
YEAH, I HEARD.
ANYWAY, WHAT ARE YOU GOING TO DO AT THE PARTY?

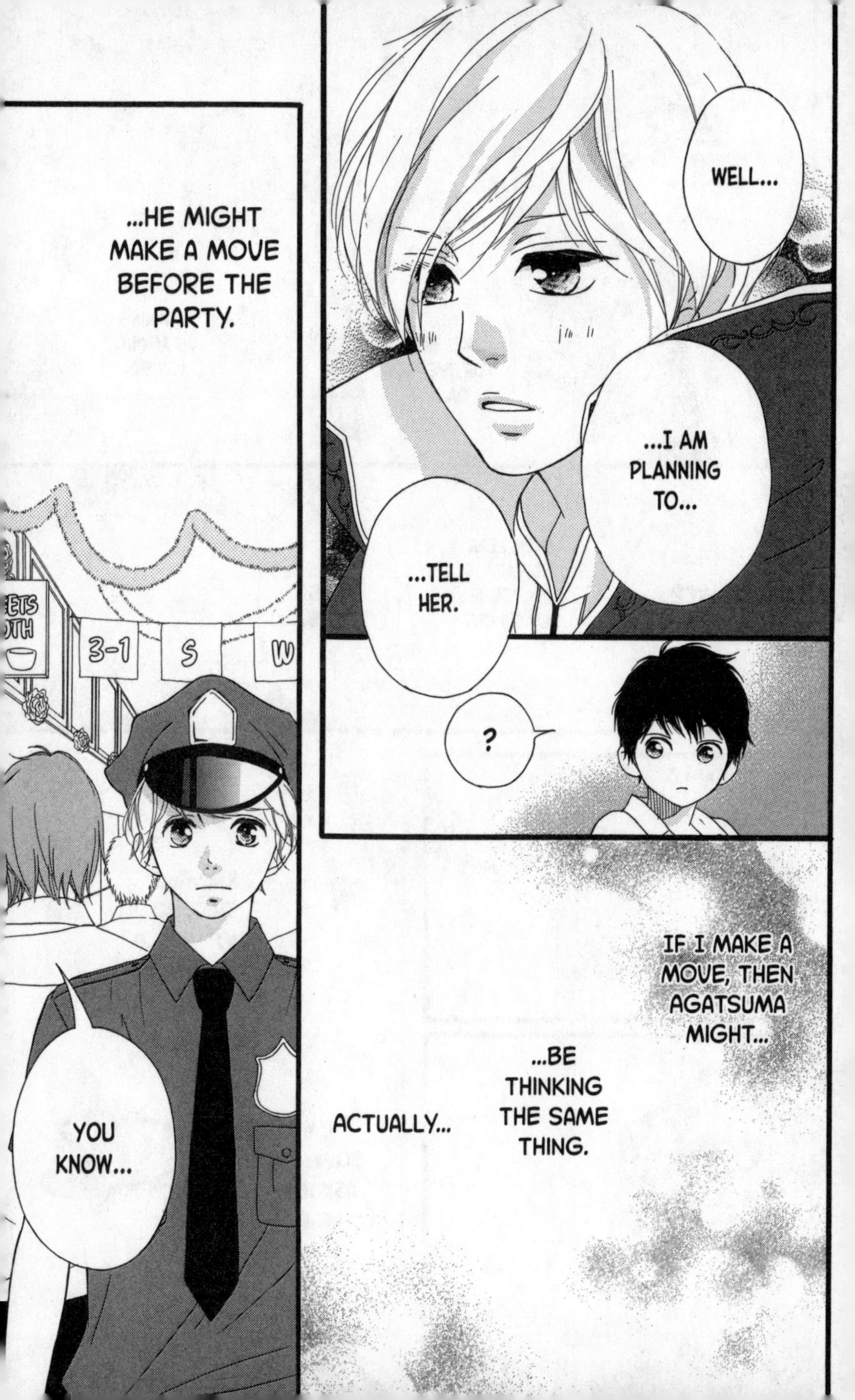
WELL...
...I AM PLANNING TO...
...TELL HER.
?
IF I MAKE A MOVE, THEN AGATSUMA MIGHT...
...BE THINKING THE SAME THING.
ACTUALLY...
...HE MIGHT MAKE A MOVE BEFORE THE PARTY.
3-1
YOU KNOW...

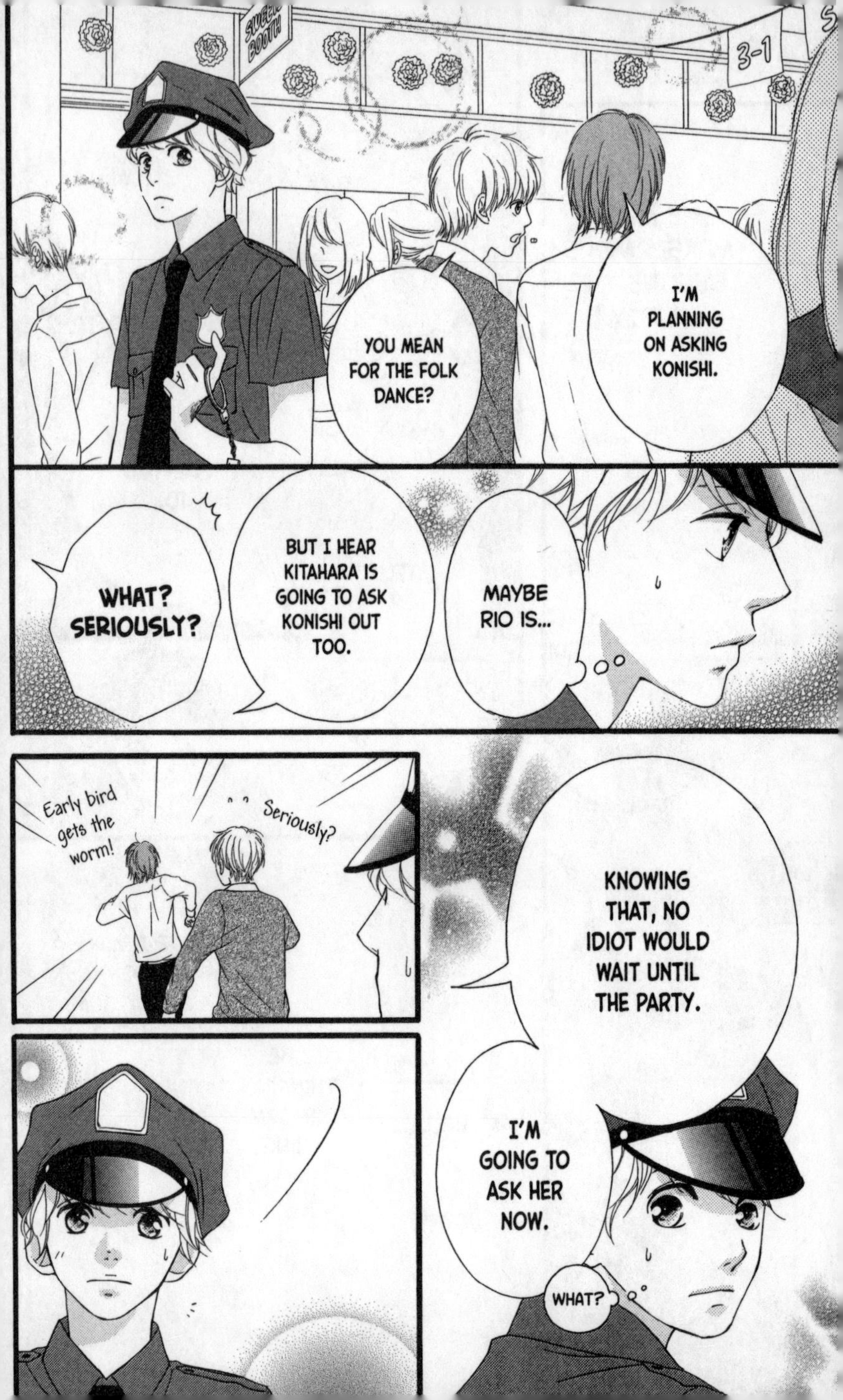
3-1
I'M PLANNING ON ASKING KONISHI.
YOU MEAN FOR THE FOLK DANCE?
MAYBE RIO IS...
BUT I HEAR KITAHARA IS GOING TO ASK KONISHI OUT TOO.
WHAT? SERIOUSLY?
KNOWING THAT, NO IDIOT WOULD WAIT UNTIL THE PARTY.
I'M GOING TO ASK HER NOW.
WHAT?
Seriously?
Early bird gets the worm!

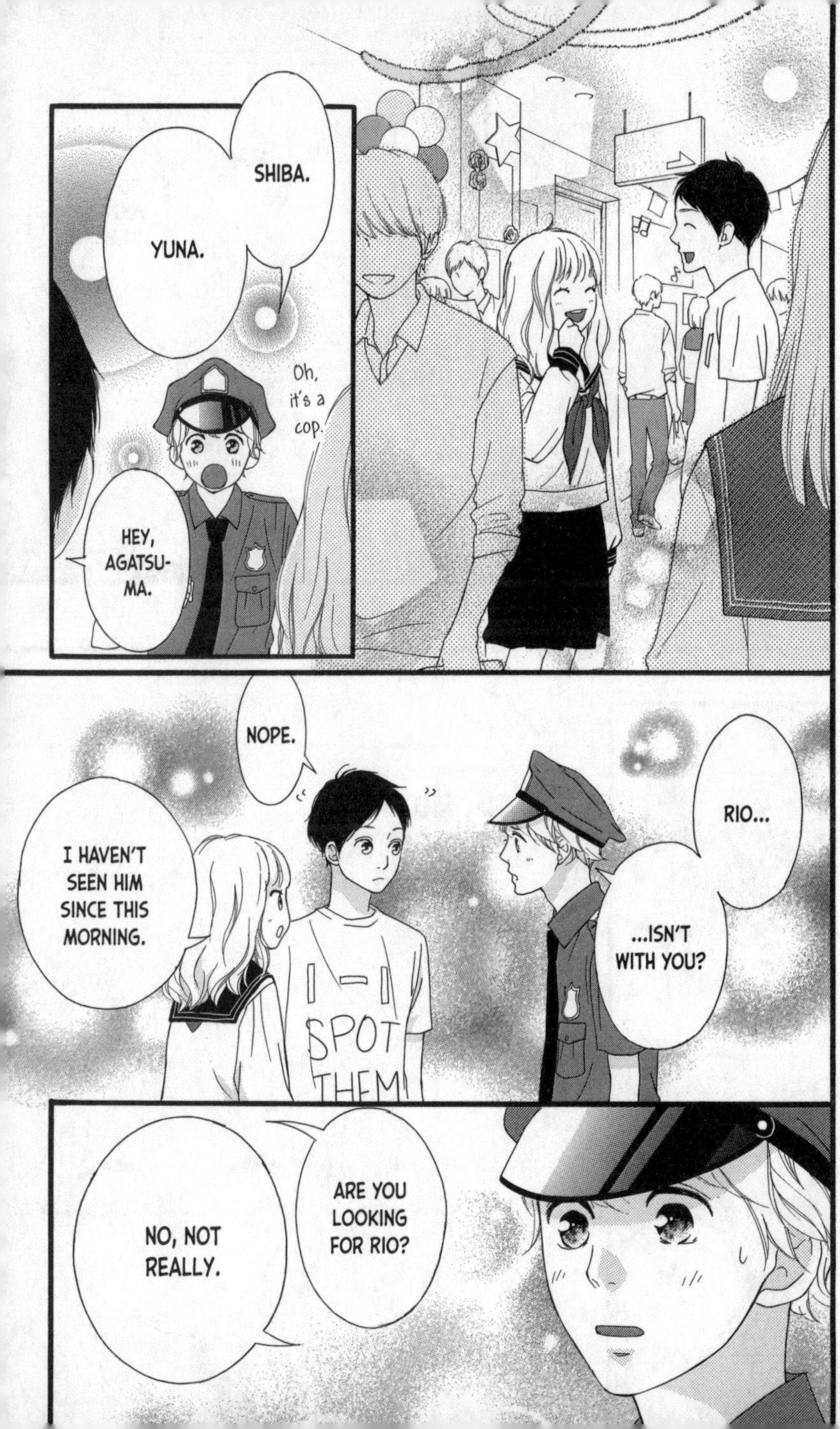
SHIBA.
YUNA.
Oh, it's a cop.
HEY, AGATSUMA.
RIO...
...ISN'T WITH YOU?
NOPE.
I HAVEN'T SEEN HIM SINCE THIS MORNING.
SPOT THEM
ARE YOU LOOKING FOR RIO?
NO, NOT REALLY.

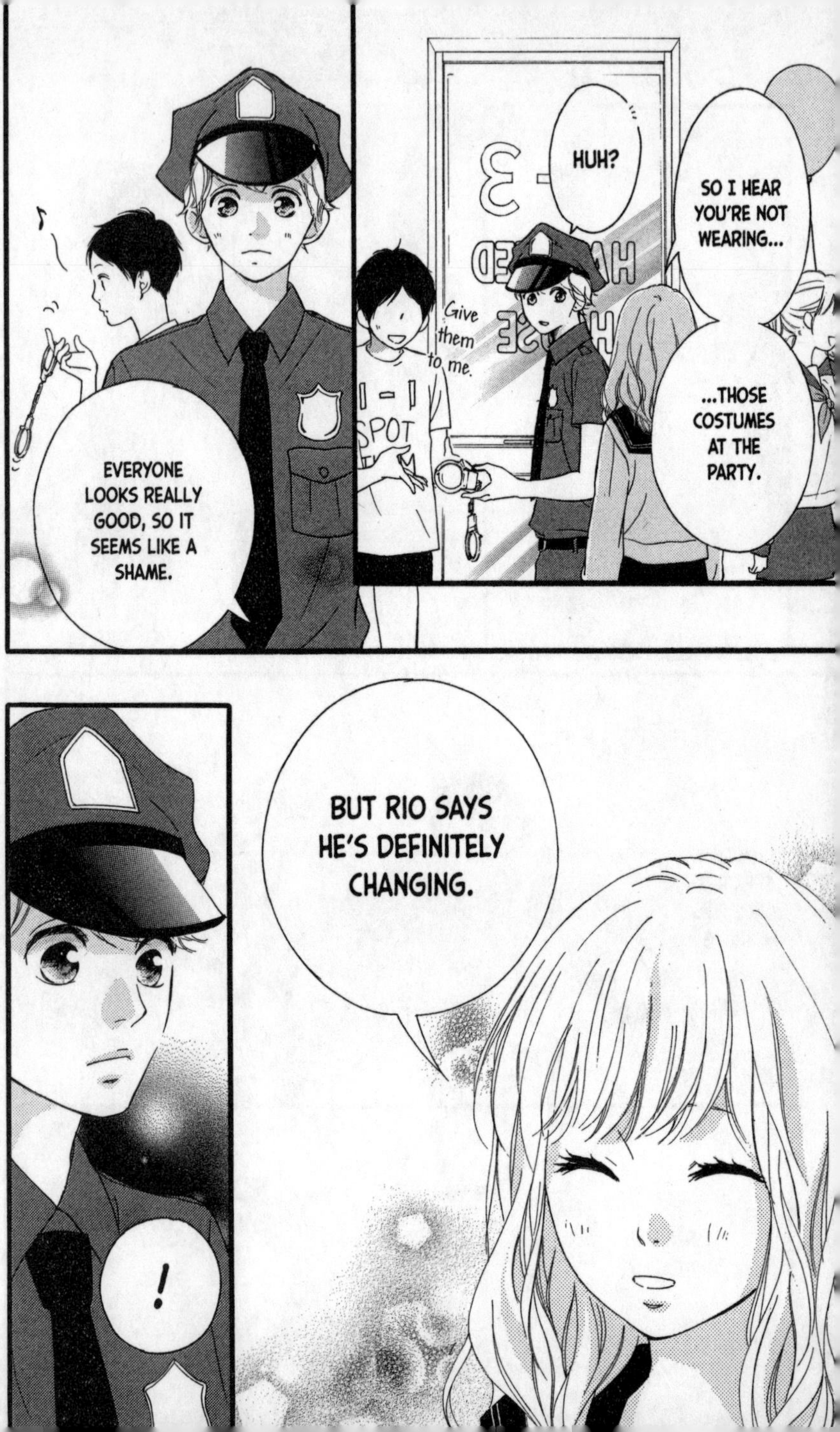
SO I HEAR YOU'RE NOT WEARING...
HUH?
...THOSE COSTUMES AT THE PARTY.
Give them to me.
EVERYONE LOOKS REALLY GOOD, SO IT SEEMS LIKE A SHAME.
BUT RIO SAYS HE'S DEFINITELY CHANGING.
!

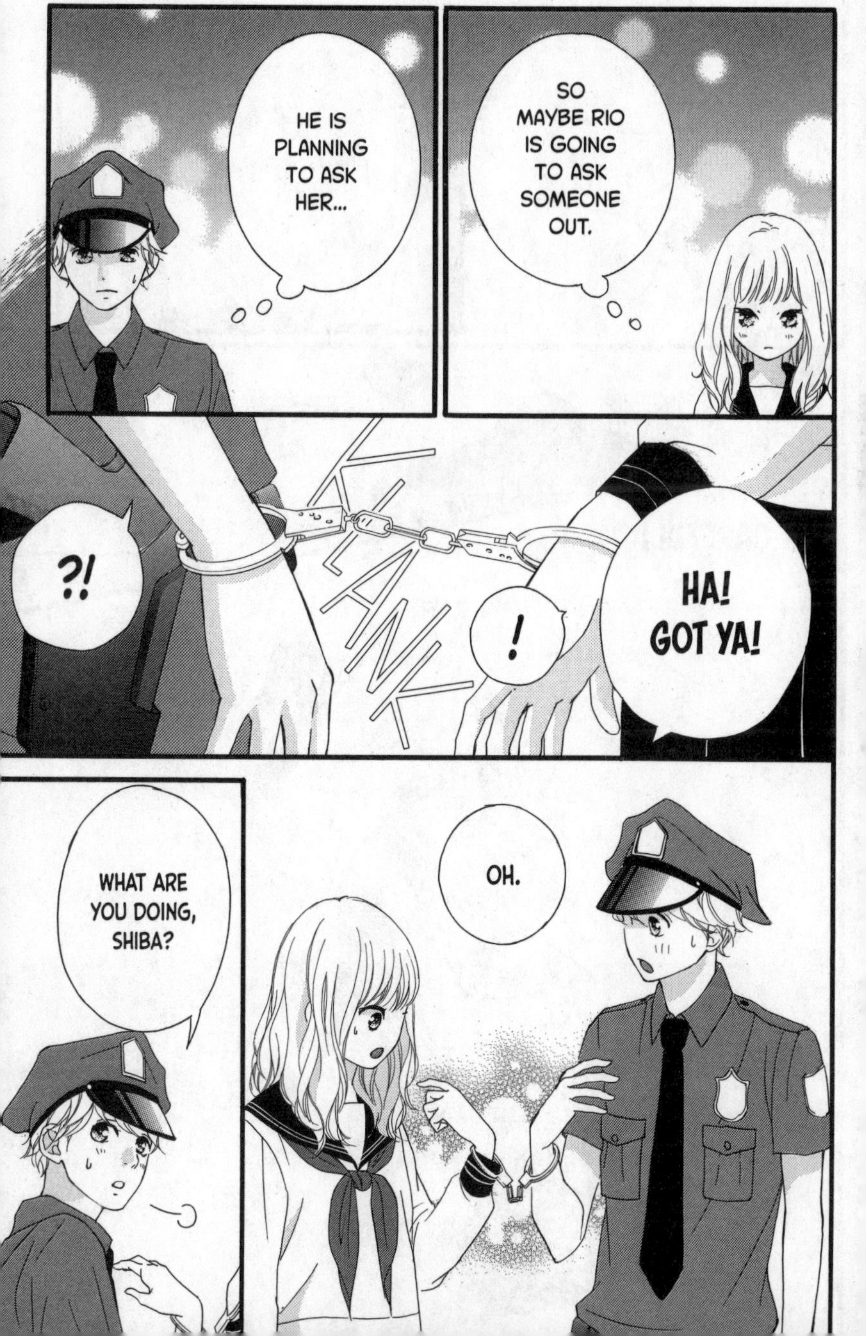
SO MAYBE RIO IS GOING TO ASK SOMEONE OUT.
HE IS PLANNING TO ASK HER...
HA! GOT YA!
KLANK
!
?!
OH.
WHAT ARE YOU DOING, SHIBA?

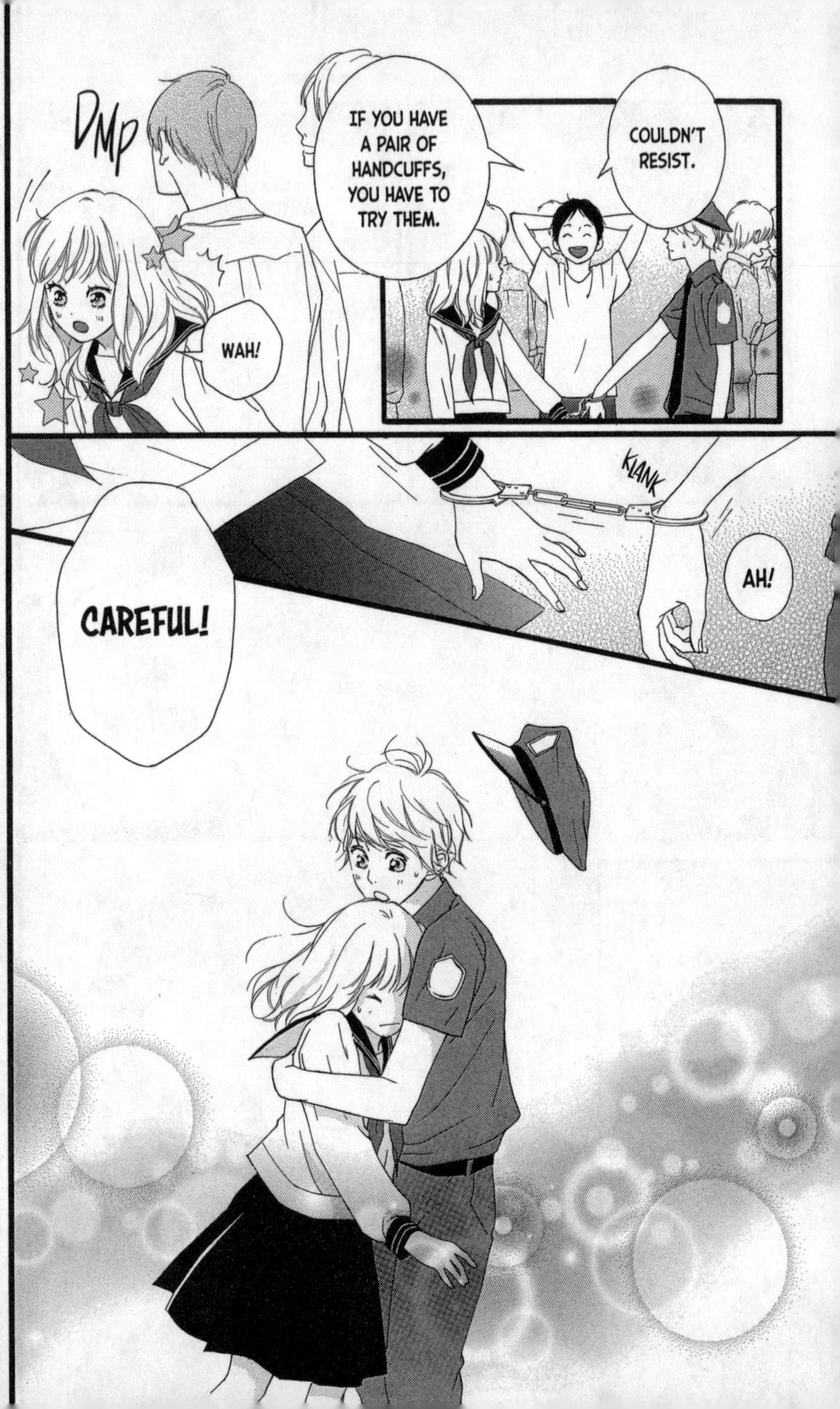
COULDN'T RESIST.
IF YOU HAVE A PAIR OF HANDCUFFS, YOU HAVE TO TRY THEM.
DMP
WAH!
KLANK
AH!
CAREFUL!

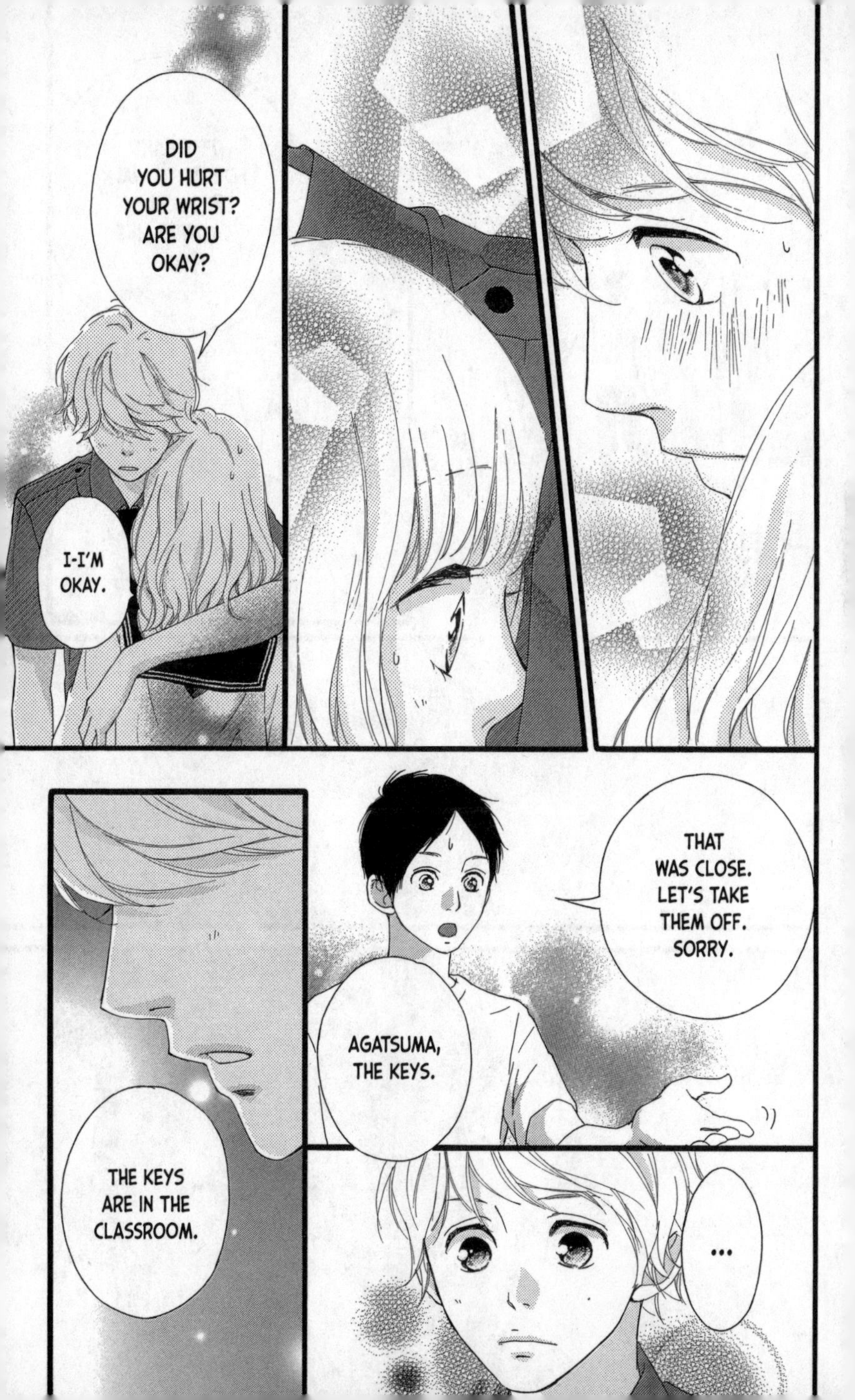
DID YOU HURT YOUR WRIST? ARE YOU OKAY?
I-I'M OKAY.
THAT WAS CLOSE. LET'S TAKE THEM OFF. SORRY.
AGATSUMA, THE KEYS.
...
THE KEYS ARE IN THE CLASSROOM.

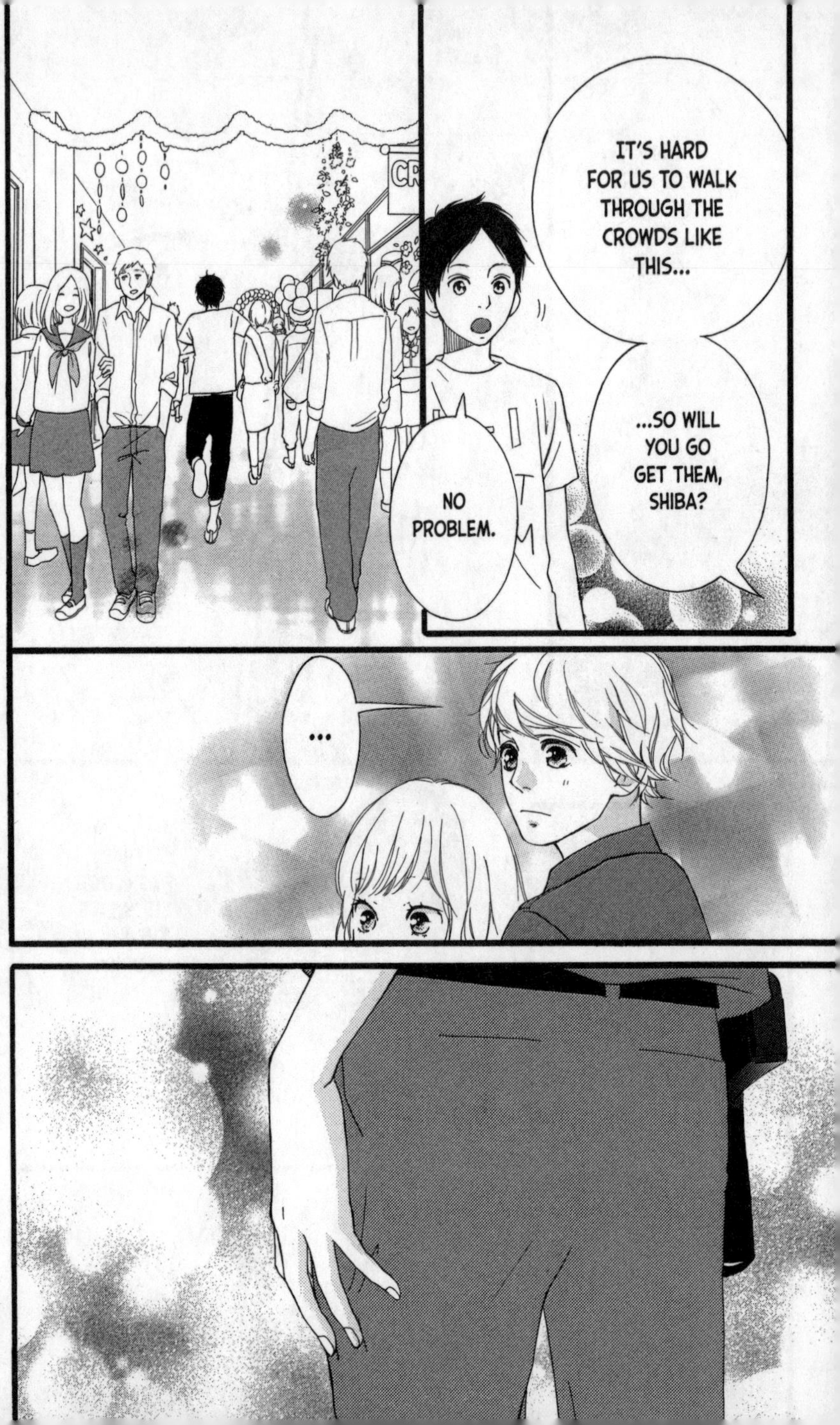
IT'S HARD FOR US TO WALK THROUGH THE CROWDS LIKE THIS...
...SO WILL YOU GO GET THEM, SHIBA?
NO PROBLEM.
...

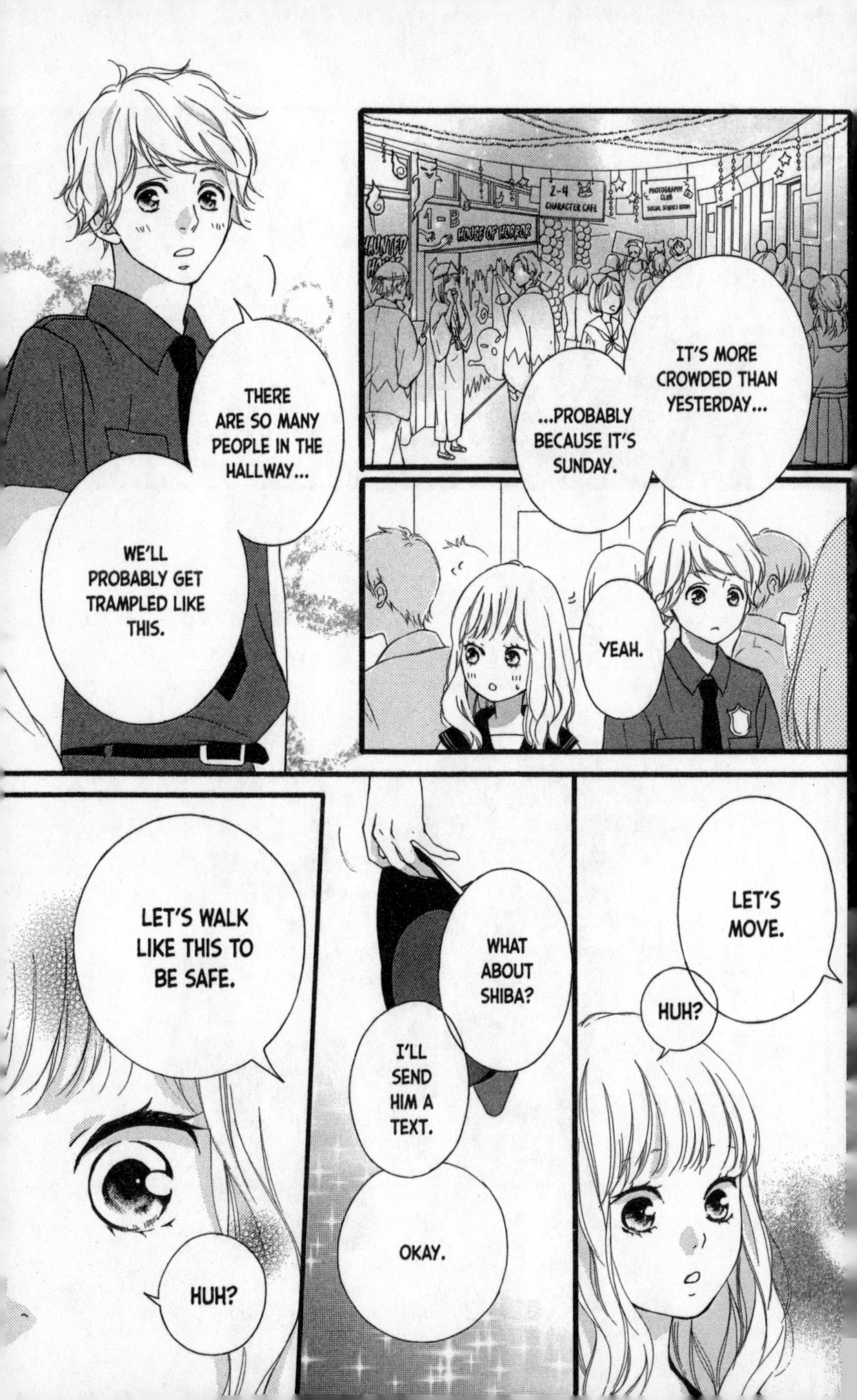
2-4 CHARACTER CAFE
PHOTOGRAPHY CLUB SOCIAL STUDIES ROOM
1-B HOUSE OF HORROR
IT'S MORE CROWDED THAN YESTERDAY...
...PROBABLY BECAUSE IT'S SUNDAY.
YEAH.
THERE ARE SO MANY PEOPLE IN THE HALLWAY...
WE'LL PROBABLY GET TRAMPLED LIKE THIS.
LET'S MOVE.
HUH?
WHAT ABOUT SHIBA?
I'LL SEND HIM A TEXT.
OKAY.
LET'S WALK LIKE THIS TO BE SAFE.
HUH?

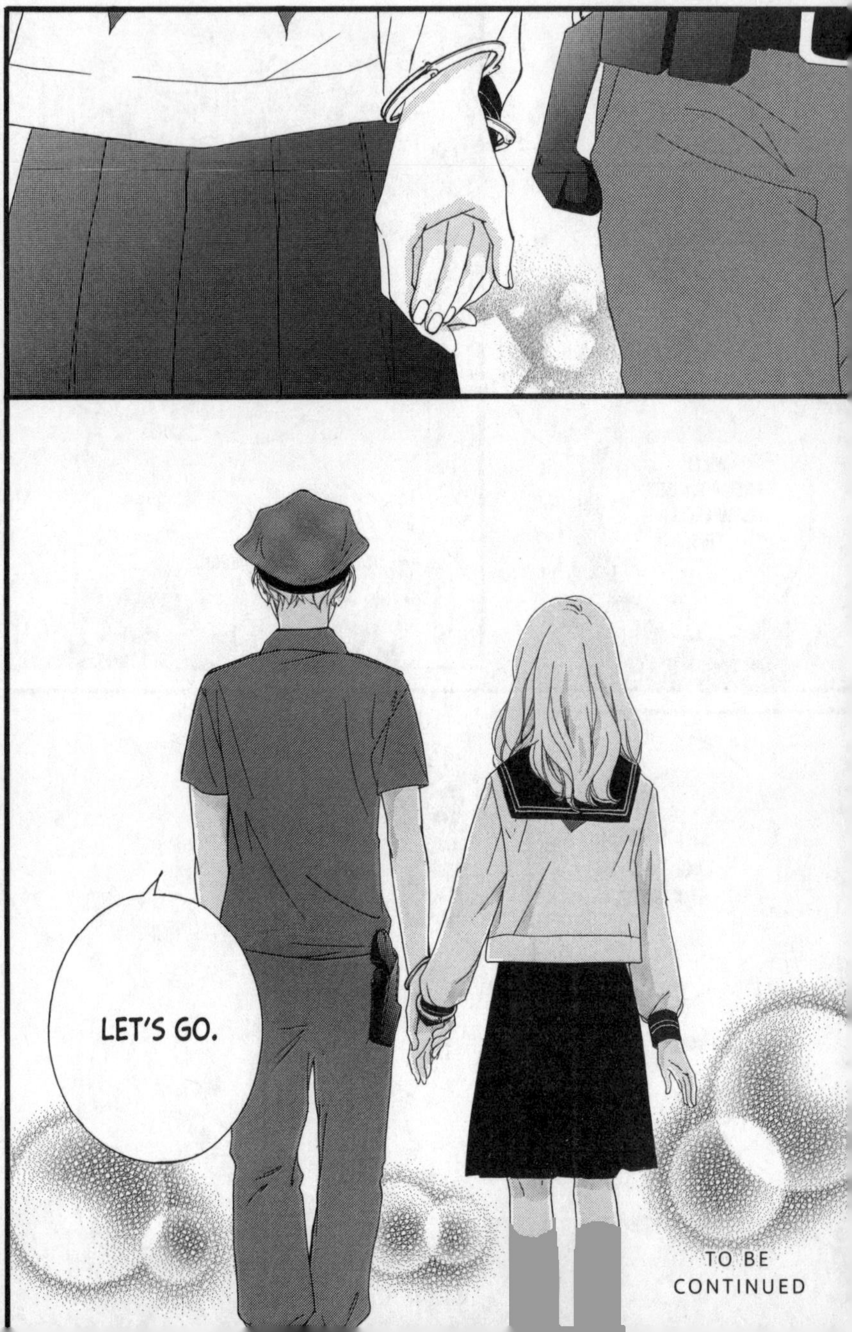
LET'S GO.
TO BE CONTINUED

AFTERWORD

Thank you for reading this to the end!

The school festival continues in the next volume.
I feel like something is about to happen. In comparison,
nothing ever happens to me, and I have a very peaceful
day-to-day life. Or so I thought... I recently got a new
contact person. It's been about ten years since the last
change. Thank you, I-sama, for taking care of me for all
these years. And to K-sama, I look forward to working
with you. I can be silly, but I will work very hard.
With change comes a new resolution to continue
working hard, so I hope you all will continue to support
me. Oh, and in the following pages, I've put in a bonus
manga called "The Sorrows of Young Ayumu Shiba."
Please have a read.

See you in the next volume!

Io Sakisaka

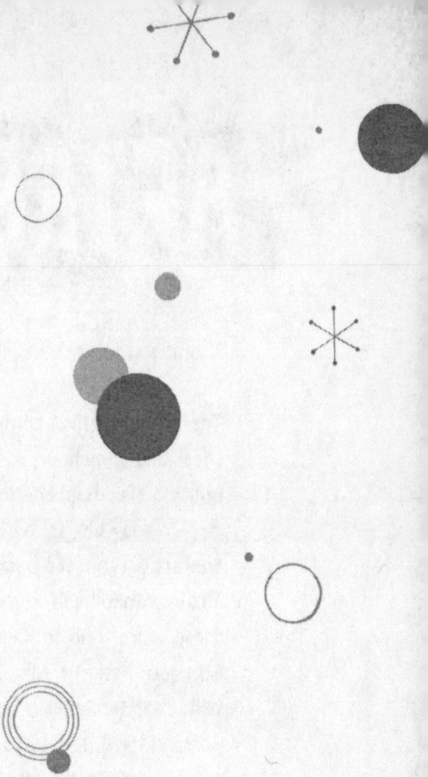

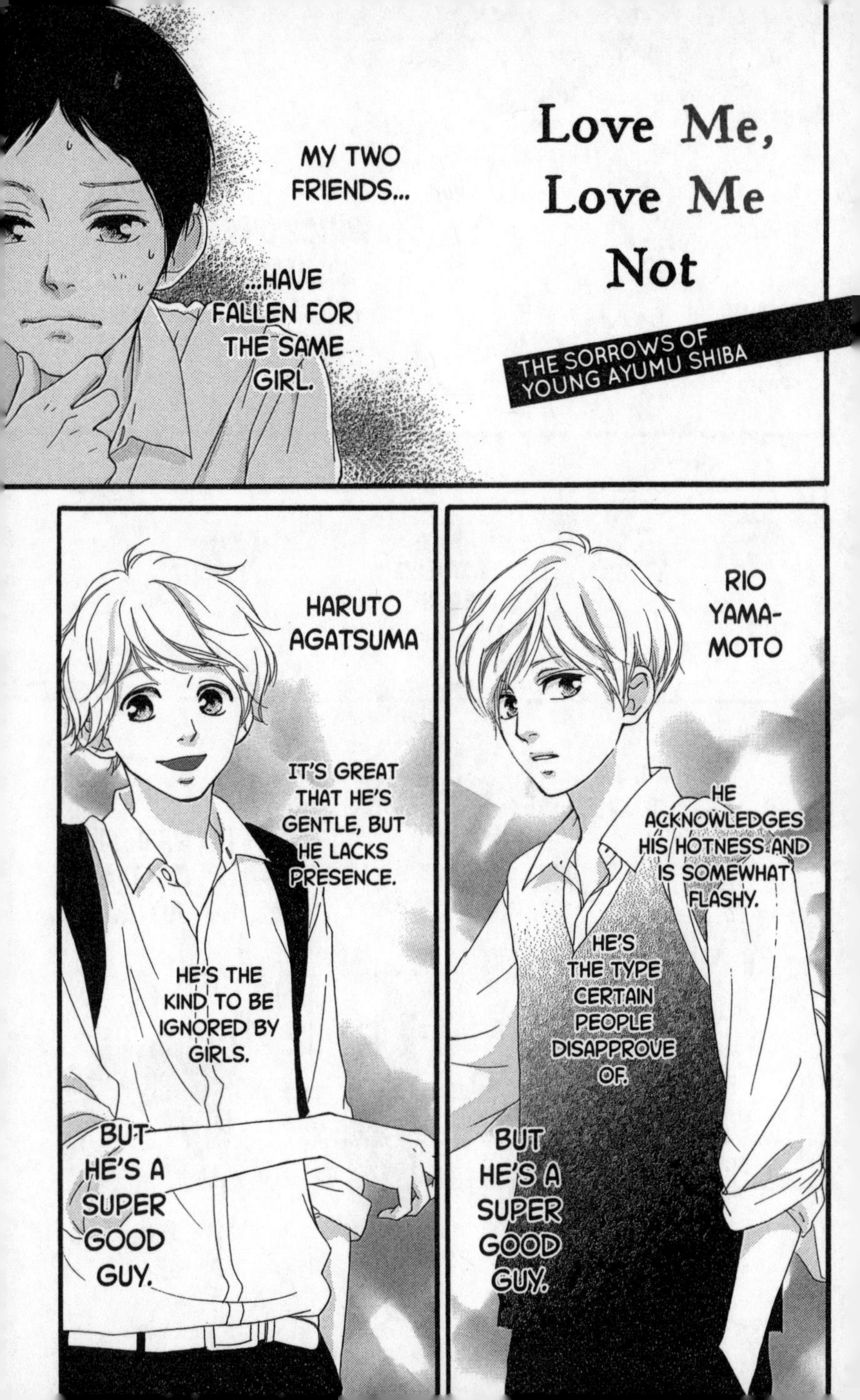
Love Me, Love Me Not
THE SORROWS OF YOUNG AYUMU SHIBA
MY TWO FRIENDS...
...HAVE FALLEN FOR THE SAME GIRL.
RIO YAMAMOTO
HE ACKNOWLEDGES HIS HOTNESS AND IS SOMEWHAT FLASHY.
HE'S THE TYPE CERTAIN PEOPLE DISAPPROVE OF.
BUT HE'S A SUPER GOOD GUY.
HARUTO AGATSUMA
IT'S GREAT THAT HE'S GENTLE, BUT HE LACKS PRESENCE.
HE'S THE KIND TO BE IGNORED BY GIRLS.
BUT HE'S A SUPER GOOD GUY.

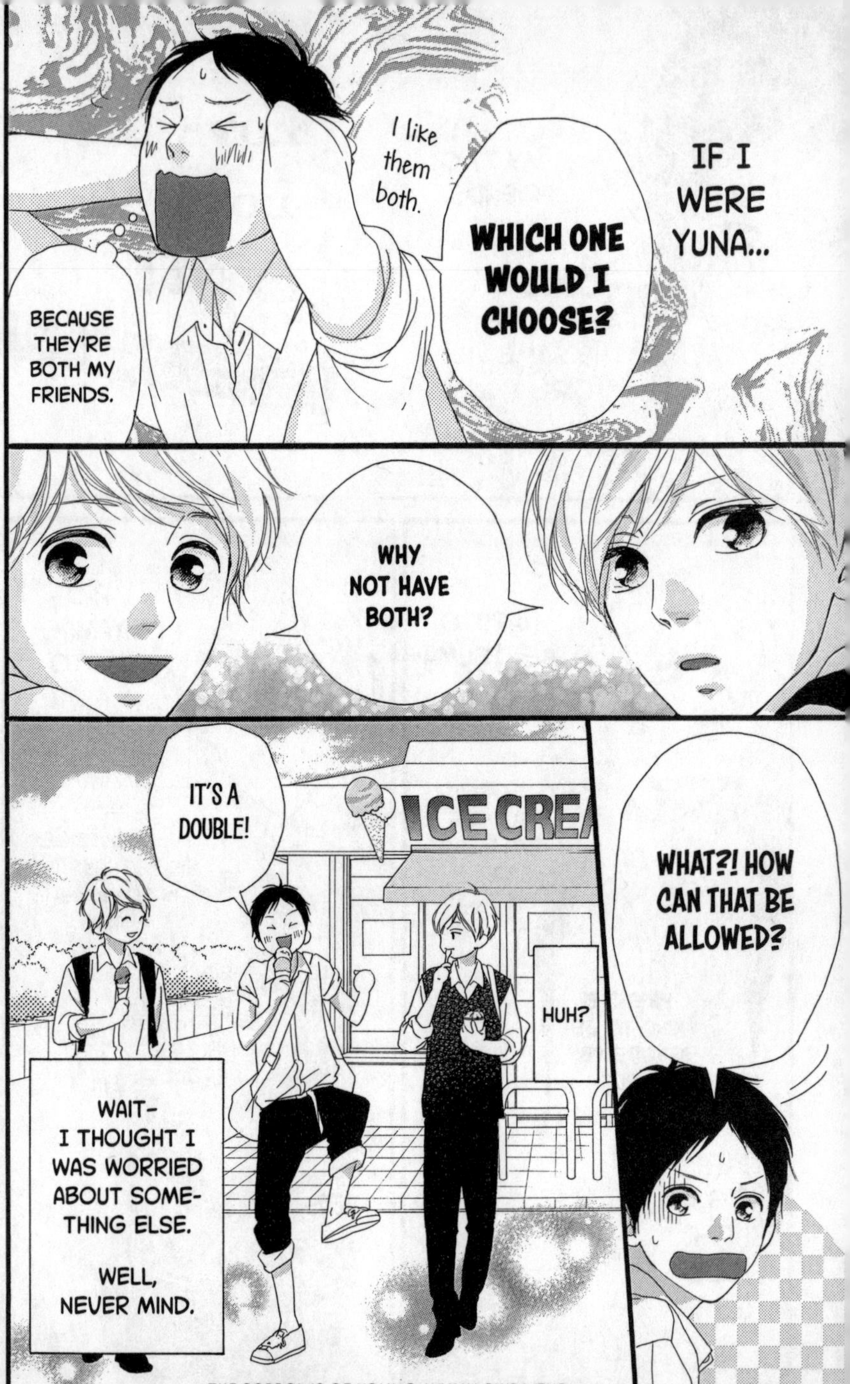
IF I WERE YUNA...
WHICH ONE WOULD I CHOOSE?
I like them both.
BECAUSE THEY'RE BOTH MY FRIENDS.
WHY NOT HAVE BOTH?
WHAT?! HOW CAN THAT BE ALLOWED?
ICE CREA
IT'S A DOUBLE!
HUH?
WAIT- I THOUGHT I WAS WORRIED ABOUT SOME-THING ELSE.
WELL, NEVER MIND.

THE SORROWS OF YOUNG AYUMU SHIBA/END

A while ago, the power button on my TV remote broke. All the other buttons on the remote are fine. It's a bit of a pain to have to get up to turn on the TV every time I want to watch something, but it feels like it would be more of a pain to go buy a new remote. So here we are.

Io Sakisaka

Born on June 8, Io Sakisaka made her debut as a manga creator with *Sakura, Chiru*. Her series *Strobe Edge* and *Ao Haru Ride* are published by VIZ Media's Shojo Beat imprint. *Ao Haru Ride* was adapted into an anime series in 2014, and *Love Me, Love Me Not* will be an animated feature film. In her spare time, Sakisaka likes to paint things and sleep.

Love Me, Love Me Not

Vol. 6

Shojo Beat Edition

STORY AND ART BY
Io Sakisaka

Adaptation/Nancy Thistlethwaite
Translation/JN Productions
Touch-Up Art & Lettering/Sara Linsley
Design/Yukiko Whitley
Editor/Nancy Thistlethwaite

First published in Japan in 2015 by SHUEISHA Inc., Tokyo.
English translation rights arranged by SHUEISHA Inc.

Printed in the U.S.A.

Published by VIZ Media, LLC
P.O. Box 77010
San Francisco, CA 94107

10 9 8 7 6 5 4 3 2 1
First printing, January 2021

ratings.viz.com RATED T TEEN

PARENTAL ADVISORY
LOVE ME, LOVE ME NOT is rated T for Teen and is recommended for ages 13 and up. This story centers around teenage relationships.

VIZ MEDIA
viz.com

Shojo Beat
shojobeat.com

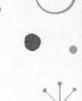

DAYTIME SHOOTING STAR

Story & Art by,
Mika Yamamori

Small town girl Suzume moves to Tokyo and finds her heart caught between two men!

After arriving in Tokyo to live with her uncle, Suzume collapses in a nearby park when she remembers once seeing a shooting star during the day. A handsome stranger brings her to her new home and tells her they'll meet again. Suzume starts her first day at her new high school sitting next to a boy who blushes furiously at her touch. And her homeroom teacher is none other than the handsome stranger!

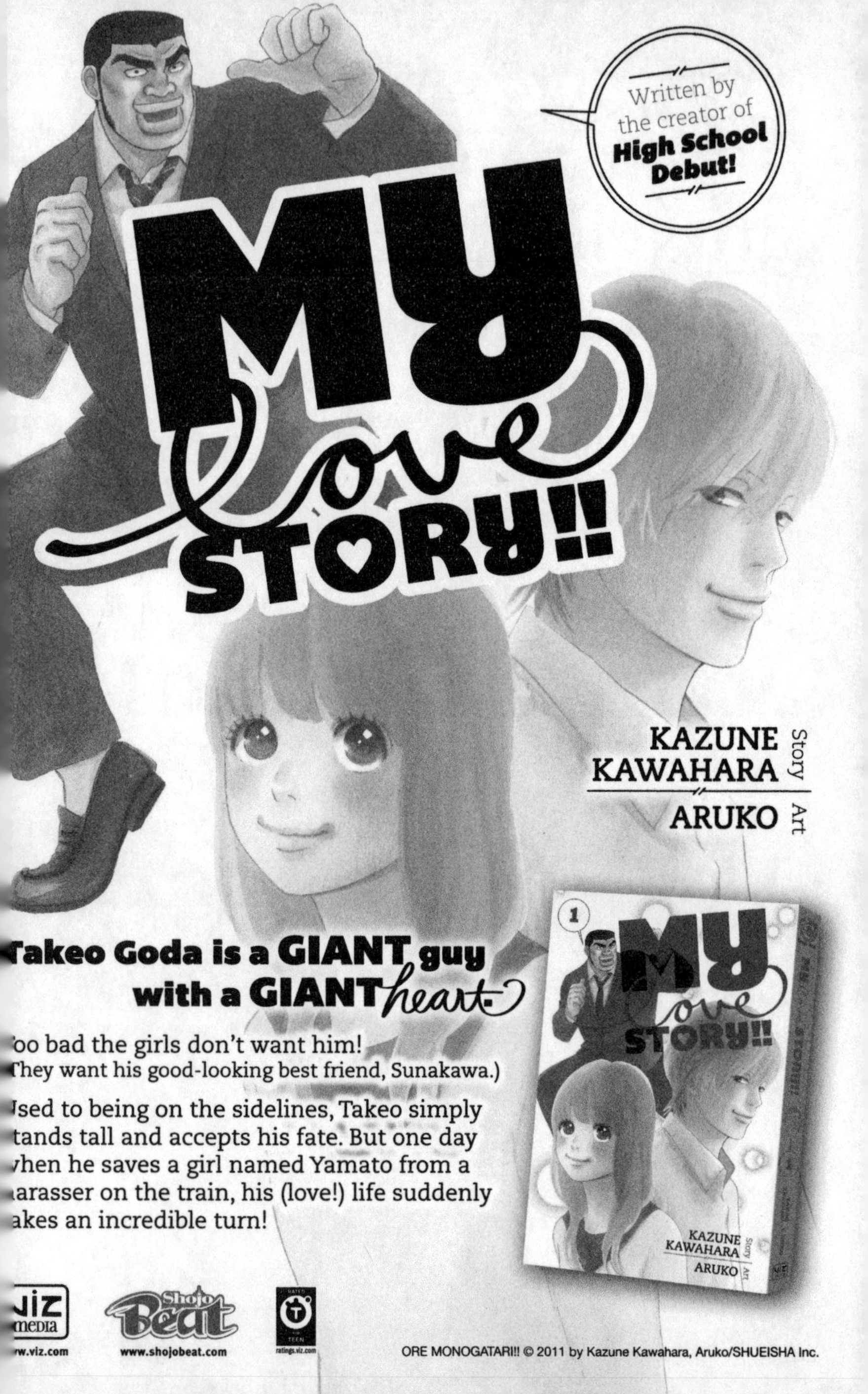
Written by the creator of High School Debut!
MY love STORY!!
KAZUNE KAWAHARA Story
ARUKO Art
Takeo Goda is a GIANT guy with a GIANT heart
Too bad the girls don't want him!
(They want his good-looking best friend, Sunakawa.)
Used to being on the sidelines, Takeo simply stands tall and accepts his fate. But one day when he saves a girl named Yamato from a harasser on the train, his (love!) life suddenly takes an incredible turn!
1
MY love STORY!!
KAZUNE KAWAHARA Story
ARUKO Art
VIZ MEDIA
Shojo Beat
RATED T TEEN
www.viz.com
www.shojobeat.com
ratings.viz.com
ORE MONOGATARI!! © 2011 by Kazune Kawahara, Aruko/SHUEISHA Inc.

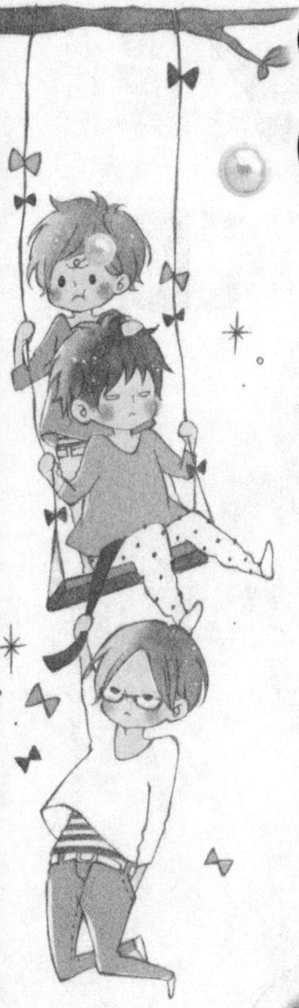

Honey So Sweet

Story and Art by Amu Meguro

Little did Nao Kogure realize back in middle school that when she left an umbrella and a box of bandages in the rain for injured delinquent Taiga Onise that she would meet him again in high school. Nao wants nothing to do with the gruff and frightening Taiga, but he suddenly presents her with a huge bouquet of flowers and asks her to date him—with marriage in mind! Is Taiga really so scary, or is he a sweetheart in disguise?

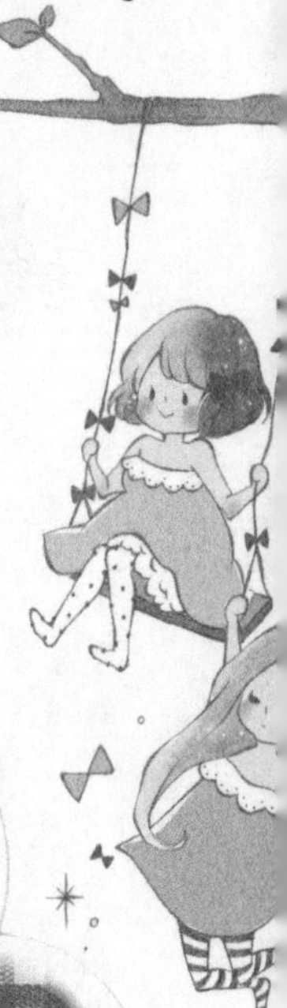

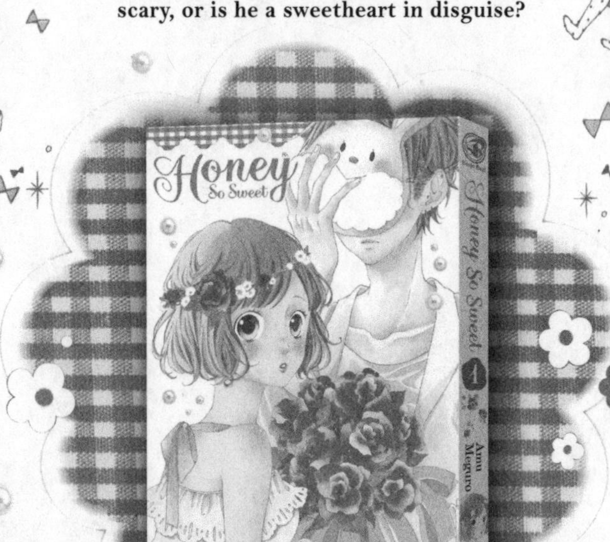
Honey So Sweet
Honey So Sweet 1
Amu Meguro
Story and Art by Amu Meguro 1

Shojo Beat

RATED T FOR TEEN ratings.viz.com

viz media
viz.com

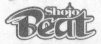

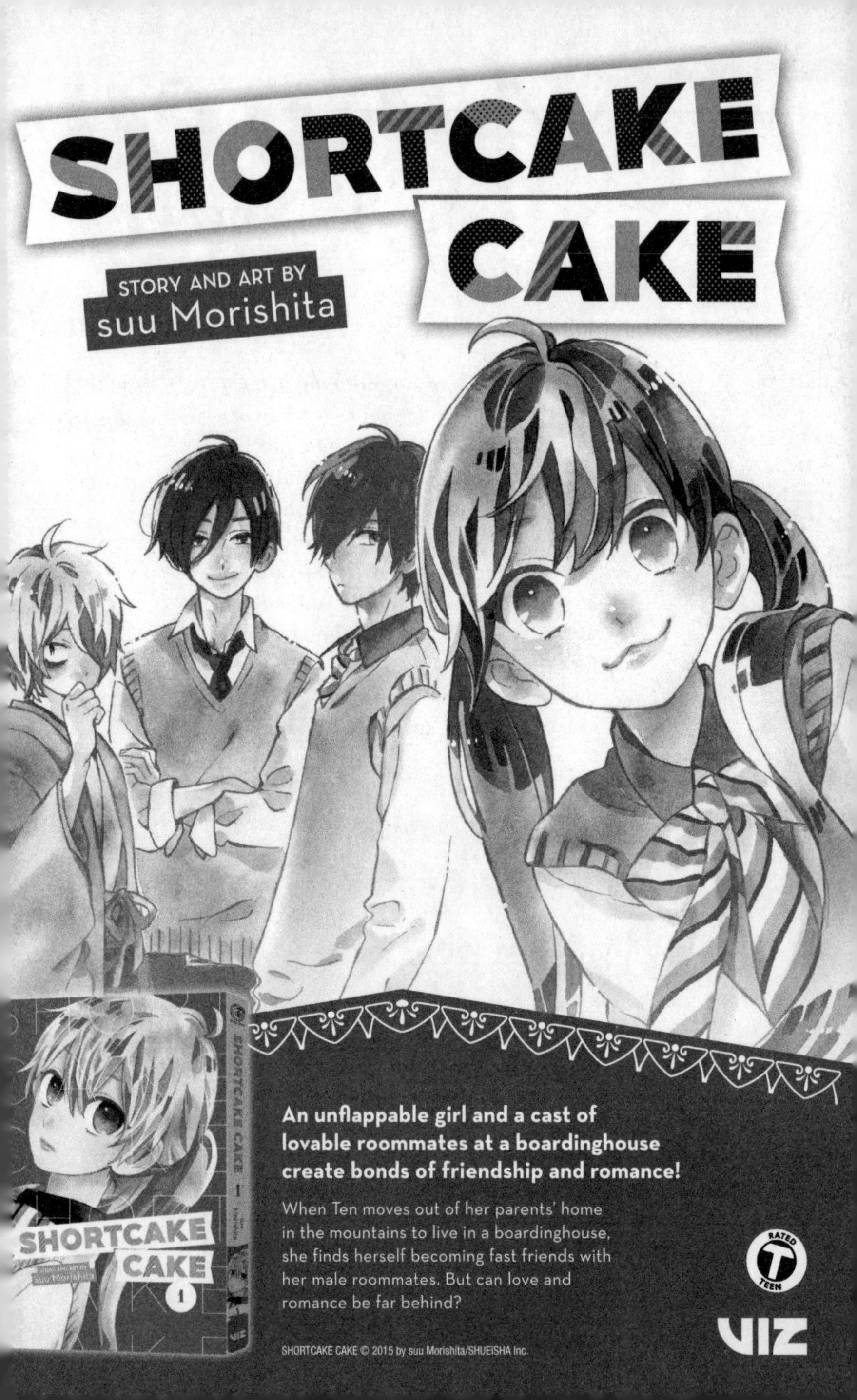
SHORTCAKE CAKE
STORY AND ART BY
suu Morishita
SHORTCAKE CAKE 1
An unflappable girl and a cast of lovable roommates at a boardinghouse create bonds of friendship and romance!
When Ten moves out of her parents' home in the mountains to live in a boardinghouse, she finds herself becoming fast friends with her male roommates. But can love and romance be far behind?
RATED T TEEN
VIZ
SHORTCAKE CAKE © 2015 by suu Morishita/SHUEISHA Inc.

Stop!

You may be reading the wrong way.

In keeping with the original Japanese comic format, this book reads from right to left—so action, sound effects and word balloons are completely reversed to preserve the orientation of the original artwork. Check out the diagram shown here to get the hang of things, and then turn to the other side of the book to get started!

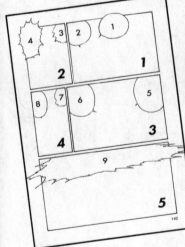